The Jewish Woman in Rabbinic Literature

A Psychosocial Perspective

The Jewish Woman in Rabbinic Literature

A Psychosocial Perspective

By

MENACHEM M. BRAYER

KTAV PUBLISHING HOUSE, INC.

HOBOKEN, NEW JERSEY

COPYRIGHT © 1986
MENACHEM M. BRAYER

Library of Congress Cataloging in Publication Data

Brayer, Menachem M.
    The Jewish woman in rabbinic literature. A psycho-
social perspective.

    Includes bibliographies and index.
    1. Women, Jewish—History. 2. Women in rabbinical
literature. 3. Women, Jewish—Psychology. I. Title.
HQ1172.B728   1986   305.4'862   85-8001
ISBN 0-88125-071-6
ISBN 0-88125-070-8 (pbk.)

MANUFACTURED IN THE UNITED STATES OF AMERICA

To Malka
My dear wife

A valiant woman is her husband's crown.
—Proverbs 12:4

אשת חיל עטרת בעלה

In Memoriam

Max Stern

*Benefactor and Pioneer
of Higher Jewish Education for Women*

Table of Contents

Preface

The case for the Jewish woman, based on our vast Hebraic literature, has never been tackled definitively.

A pity, this. The Jewish woman's niche in society was consistently misrepresented, her role misunderstood. She was depicted as enslaved, statusless, unimportant. This misapprehension was perpetrated by Jewish and non-Jewish historians, abetting and abetted by it.

The indifference by historians, psychologists, sociologists, and cultural exegetes of Jewish life throughout the ages to the enormous impact of the Jewish woman on society has resulted in the lamentable lacunae on the subject. The cause of this purblindness seems clear to me: most literary works and chronicles are the products of a man's pen—hence, the bias. The serious student of history, however, ought to be disinterested—hence, our own investigation. And if, as has been shown (Carlson and Carlson, 1960), the psychology of the woman is a neglected area of research in general, the psychology of the Jewish woman is, surely, terra nova!

Our study, therefore, will attempt—from a Jewish Anschauung—to shed light on the personality of our protagonist by divesting her of her stereotypic mold. Comparative contemporary social and psychological studies of the woman will intermingle with rabbinic ones in an endeavor to bring into sharper focus woman's status, social roles, behavior, and impact on Jewish life. In explicating the psychological makeup of the Jewish woman, we shall view her in historical perspective, drawing upon the Oriental, European, and modern American societies.

My aim in this work is to portray the dramatic qualities and the human side of the Daughter of Israel, as the prophets called her. Textbooks in Jewish history and psychology tend to give but meager if any attention at all to the Jewish woman and her rightful position in our society. Emphasis is rather on man and his creative role throughout history and, unlike R. Akiva, ignoring the woman behind his accomplishments. The study concludes with an analysis of the Jewish woman's condition today, which are bringing about an agonizing reappraisal of her worthiness as a person created in God's image.

Culling from a capacious traditional and secular literature, we hope to discern the total personality of the Jewish woman—*sui generis* and interacting—in society. To this end, however, we must not in the process demystify womanhood. To give the fair sex its fair due, by all means; to deny the feminine mystique, certainly not.

This book attempts to set forth the author's conviction that the Divine gift of the *Tzelem Elokim* (God's image) is endowed to the human being, man and woman alike. It carries with it the faith in the potential growth capacities of the individual in the everlasting relationship and dialogue between God and His human creatures.

When I started this book more than eighteen years ago, I underestimated the difficult task before me. Since no work existed that describes and integrates the findings on the personality of the Jewish woman, I had to undertake such an attempt myself with a deep sense of humility and trepidation. My aim was to enable both man and woman to share with me a global understanding and also gain a deeper appreciation of the feminine role in Jewish life throughout history. This herculean task came to fruition through the constant interpersonal contact I had throughout my many years of experience as an educator (of both sexes) as well as a practicing psychotherapist.

The author hopes that this work—a product of many years of labor—will assist not only the student of Jewish history and human behavior but also the interested reader who wishes to have a fuller and more traditional perception of the better half of humankind through the rabbinic spectrum.

Acknowledgments

In preparing this book, I have benefited from the efforts of my teachers, my many dear students, and much from my patients. "If I have seen further, it is by standing upon the shoulders of giants" (Sir Isaac Newton in a letter to Robert Hooke, February 5, 1675).

A special debt of gratitude is due to my revered father z.t.l., my foremost mentor and teacher, and to my beloved mother who nurtured me with love and inspiration, and whose criticisms and concerns have been pivotal in my maturation.

To my dear wife and children, Yigal, Nehama, and Nahum Dov, who were patient with me and were a continuous source of loving support and stimulation, I remain deeply grateful.

It is a pleasant duty to record my indebtedness to my very dear friends Dr. Norman Lamm, President of Yeshiva University, Dr. Marvin Weitz, Leonard Stern, Leon Charney Esq., Morris, Dena and Joseph Wosk and Rabbi N. Manuel z.l. for their warm support and encouragement.

I am thankful as well to my friends Drs. Herbert Dobrinsky, Charles Oler and Ralph Medjuck, Q. C. and to my friends of Halifax N.S. Dr. I. K. Lubetsky, H. Neuman, M. B. Feinberg, M. Forman, Dr. J. Greenblatt, E. Bowman, H. I. Jacobson, E. Whitzman, S. Goodman and E. Zebberman for their assistance.

Also, many thanks to Malca Nadbi and Rabbi Lyle Kamlet for their assistance and to Ktav Publishing House for their understanding and help in the editing of this book.

Finally, I should like to express my thanks to all my colleagues and friends who have helped me with this considerable task through their suggestions and encouragement.

If this study enriches the reader's understanding of the Jewish woman and helps contribute to the improvement of her self-understanding, our labors will have been well expended.

Introduction

All is credited to the woman.
—Gen. *Rabbah* 17:12

Every generation throughout Jewish history has included dynamic women of faith and action who grappled with important issues related to human rights and existence. They dared to act on their beliefs. The drama depicting the remarkable achievement of these daughters of the Jewish faith still remains unwritten. The dedicated Jewesses who struggled, fought, and lived to preserve the vibrancy of their living faith will always remain the ideal models to be credited with the genuine appreciation of and sense of commitment to the rich heritage which we all possess.

When the Torah wished to teach us a lesson in morality, it chose two women from amoral cultures: Tamar, the Canaanite daughter-in-law of Judah; and Suleika, the wife of the Egyptian Potiphar, the temptress of Joseph. The first represents righteousness and devotion; the second, pagan immorality. Both are prototypes of biblical didactics in moral behavior for future generations.

The biblical heroines Sarah, Rachel, Miriam, Deborah, Hulda, and Hannah were succeeded by similar fighters and martyrs for the Jewish faith, such as Judith, Hannah and her seven sons, and so many other heroines throughout Jewish history, all of whom brought honor and glory to the Jewish people.

Early Jewish history from the biblical period on assigned the Jewish woman the task of constructing and maintaining the Jewish home. The author of the Book of Proverbs exclaims in admiration: *Hakhmot nashim banta bayta.* "The wisdom of women built her house." (Prov. 14:1)

Woman, more than man, displays endurance in keeping the family going and managing all the work. Man, the age-old patriarch, has always alternately placed woman on a pedestal or under his subjugation.

Increasingly sharp criticism, based on sheer ignorance of Tradition,* has been levelled, asserting that the Jewish woman is relegated to an inferior status. Such opinions are uttered by scoffers of religion who seize upon selected talmudic dicta to support their contentions. It is time that an accurate exposition of the attitude of *halakhah* (Jewish Law) enlighten our contemporary Jewish assessment of the problem and dispel many of the misunderstandings relating to the position of woman and her rights of equality and emancipation. It will help liberate both sexes from their own sexual stereotypes and myths.

It took a thousand years to compose the Bible—the word of God to man; and it took another millennium to complete the unique commentary expounding on and elucidating the sacred text. Clarification was provided by the Talmud, which closed the gap between the biblical word and its application, extending and adapting its wisdom to later Jewish life. In so doing, an inexhaustible wellspring of rabbinic inspiration was provided for future generations; and, at the same time, the Torah became a practical code for the Jewish people.

The Talmud, which represents the Oral Law, was conceived as an extension of the Torah—the Written Law. This literature is a vast mine of knowledge, for it contains rich material in the areas of ethical and moral conduct, human relations, history, religious teachings, customs, folklore, and science.

Traditionally, then, Scripture found its supplement in the authoritative pronouncements of talmudic exegesis, both in its halakhic and in its aggadic aspects. By employing ingenious techniques and hermeneutics, the Talmud became the repository of Jewish doctrine and traditional *Anschauung*.

The talmudic, as well as midrashic, writings were the fruit of the academies in Palestine and Babylonia. They were compiled and developed from the completion of the biblical canon to the end of the fifth century C.E. Both the Babylonian and the Palestinian Talmud represent the *Torah she-be-al peh*, the traditionally transmitted and expounded Oral Law.

The Talmud was written not as an esoteric teaching for the chosen few but for the masses. Jewish education always stressed the teaching of the Talmud at a very early age, with increasingly higher levels of

---

*The term "Tradition" throughout this work is used in a rabbinic-legal sense, denoting the halakhic view, and not in the customary, conventional usage.

analytic study till old age. For generations the Talmud was diligently studied by the scholars both day and night, while laymen studied it only on the Sabbath.

The Bible never really stopped providing inspiration toward the divine goal of human perfection. Biblical Judaism coalesced into rabbinic Judaism with only changes in means and not ends.

What is pertinent today, however, is that the Talmud in its present form contains entire chapters devoted exclusively to scientific subjects, and that these subjects have been explored in an erudite manner by modern scholars who compared talmudic science with modern science. Talmudic psychology, a considerable part of which is devoted to woman, was the one scientific area that was either ignored or inadequately treated by modern writers.

One sphere remains entirely unknown to modern science, namely, the religiopsychological, especially that of the Jewish woman. It is the writer's intention to research this untrodden area. In our study, attention will be given to the total personality of the woman, including the behavioral, sensory, emotive, and cognitive features as depicted in biblical, talmudic, and later rabbinic sources.

This research encompasses the biblical, postbiblical, talmudic, midrashic, kabbalistic, and rabbinic sources. We will compare them with current psychological and sociological findings.

The author humbly recognizes the book's limitations: it does not try to do more than present the reader with basic source material and pertinent issues relating to the Jewish woman. True, we raise no issues that are entirely new. But, then, the subject iself is of perennial interest.

We attempted to add to the old questions particularly contemporary dimensions and tried the difficult task of giving a psychohistorical perspective to the Jewish woman, a most intricate and misunderstood subject which underwent the most radical social and historical modification.

Our task, therefore, is to offer the intelligent reader a comprehensive well to draw from for intellectual awareness and constructive balanced analysis.

1

Overview

The happiest women like the happiest nations
have no history."
—*George Elliot*

The Rabbis were keen observers of human behavior. No facet of human actions, however insignificant, escaped their attention. They might even have known more about science than what was recorded in the Talmud. We may assume that the compilers of this work did not intentionally care to set down findings in medical science, since medicine was not always directly relevant to religion. In matters concerning society, religion, and ethics the Rabbis astonish us with the power of their observations. They were, more than two millennia ago, aware of things upon which European scientists of the last century have only begun to shed light.

So, too, with the discipline of psychology. Between the second and fifth centuries the Rabbis of the Talmud and of the Midrash skillfully noted aspects of woman's behavior. If man knows not that there are differences between the psychological propensities of man from those of women, he cannot satisfy his obligations toward his wife nor toward his daughters or daughters-in-law. It is not enough to know that there are differences; he must know the details of the differences so that he can act upon them. These details must be known whether they be positive or negative.

Many of the observations have withstood the scrutiny of modern scientific knowledge, as will be shown throughout this study.

5

It is an accepted fact that customs and attitudes of people and nations have been evolving to accommodate various changing social condi-tions. The Rabbis recognized these changes in human behavior, espe-cially as reflected in the life-style of the woman. For example, in talmudic times it was within the boundaries of propriety for a woman to remove her ornaments in the street and show them to a friend, while five hundred years later the French Tosafists considered this unthink-able.

The Rabbis considered woman as belonging to a special class, one different from that of man: "What is right for women is not right for man, and what is right for man is not right for women. Women are a people for themselves."[1]

Whether the rabbinic view of woman was a direct result of her environment or whether the special treatment of the woman by Jewish Law was the result of the Jewish attitude toward her is not our primary concern. Though at times it may be necessary to cite Jewish Law to explain the status of woman, the main task of this work is to gather and elucidate material about the behavior of woman, material which runs the gamut of our literature.

However, let us bear in mind that both the Rabbis as observers, and the women who were being observed, were part of the Mideastern milieu, where customs and mores contributed a distinct psychology, different from our own. We must remember and understand the *zeit-geist*—and the indelible impressions it engendered upon the people— in the environment.

Throughout the ages woman has been almost as enigmatic as the "Mona Lisa." Even Solomon, the wisest of men, found woman unfath-omable, impenetrable. "One man among a thousand have I found; but a woman among all these have I not found" (Eccl. 7:28). Or in Shake-speare's words: "Who can read a woman?"

The woman has always been misunderstood. The Jewish woman in particular was even more a victim of historical misinterpretation and gross popular misconception. Even the Talmud—the infinite source of Jewish wisdom—was so often defamed by ignorance and malevolence.

Since the Rabbis lived in proximity to their wives, daughters, and mothers, it was not difficult for them to observe female actions and reactions to the variety of life situations. As we shall see later, the Rabbis who delved into the psychology of the woman apparently did not consider her mental and emotional makeup a sealed book.

The woman, with few exceptions, made no depositions; therefore, we must rely on observation as a method of psychology, a method much practiced by our Rabbis.

Woman's lot throughout history depended upon the customs and conditions that prevailed at various times. Among the early "shepherd tribes" the woman was not appreciated; she was merely bought or bartered away. Since she was considered merchandise, she was made attractive and accorded a modicum of education. Nevertheless, she was still the property of her husband, and after his death she became the property of his heir.

In time, her commercial value increased. She was considered a valuable farming tool and better care was taken of her. She began to appear in fine jewels and clothes, and greater attention was paid to her attractiveness and manners. Nevertheless, she was still obliged to look up to her husband, her superior. She had to revere him as a master.

In antiquity there was a striking disregard for the psychological nature of the woman and a lack of concern for the way in which she was treated. The primitive pagan woman was a victim of injustice and was considered an irrational psychological burden. She was like a slave, a domestic entity. Work, sex, and propagation were the sole reasons for her existence. The woman was a creature devoid of will or the power to choose.

Her self-image, too, was that of a slave. Woman's natural weakness led her to accept this badge of absolute self-abasement in silence. She submitted herself to drudgery, for which she was despised. When her usefulness ended, she was discarded, if despair did not drive her to suicide first.

Among the Hottentot, Indian, and Australian women, mothers killed their newborn girls to spare them a fate to which they themselves had been doomed. The woman was unclean, despised equally by men and the gods.

Among hunting tribes, the woman was the father's or husband's property, to be stolen, bartered, given away, hired out, or pledged.

On the other hand, we find that in China, India, Persia, and Arabia an attempt was made to compensate for bitter reality. The woman was idealized. She was lauded endlessly, her virtues extolled in prose and poetry. This only made the contrast sharper.

The Greeks and Romans, with their subdued manner and more refined tastes, were relatively kinder. They learned to see in woman more than mere chattel. Their higher sensitivity made their condescending view of woman-wife even crueler and more unjust than that of their savage, artless predecessors. To the cultivated Greek, the wife was merely the "spinner of wool" and the "preserver of grain." It was not the Greek woman's fate to be a partner in a god-pleasing communion between man and wife. Nor was the purpose of marriage to provide her, or for that matter him, with happiness and well-being. Her purpose in life was raising children for the state and toiling alongside the slaves, to enable her husband a life of enjoyment and refined intellectuality. A man's house was not his home. His wife was a prisoner in it. There she fulfilled for her turnkey her duties and obligations.

True, some women enjoyed full freedom and received great homage. These were the courtesans, though, not the wives. Philosophers and statesmen, the noblest of the nation, sat at their feet, and poets sang of their charms. Indeed her whole upbringing made this type of woman a most valued companion of man. The elite woman, contrasted with the married one, was duly satirized. When Theano, the scholarly wife of Pythagoras, was asked how she expected to become renowned, she answered in a Homeric vein, "weaving the loom and preparing the couch."

Though the Romans did not imprison their wives, they treated them as minors. They were the wards of father or husband. As a mother, the wife had no rights whatsoever. Nevertheless, to the Roman, woman did have some advantages. She participated in festivities and banquets and had some freedom of movement.

Calpurnius Piso Frugi, in his "Annals" (133 B.C.E.), laments the destruction of morals and decency. Wedlock, to the Roman, became a heavy burden. Eventually the Roman woman fell into the same deep depravity that had infected the Roman man. Thus, the basic pillars of family life were gradually destroyed.

The Christian view of woman was a harsh one. In Tertullian's words:

> O woman! Thou shouldst always wear mourning or rags, in order to show thy penitence, weeping and atoning for the crime of having corrupted humanity! Thou art the one who hast first tested the forbidden fruit, and transgressed the law of God; thou has seduced man, whom the devil himself did not dare to approach. For thy sake, O woman, Jesus had to die.[2]

The Roman Catholic legislation proclaimed: marriage is a union of man and wife, a mingling of their lives by human and Divine law. These words would seem to imply full and equal partnership, but this was not the case. Woman, in Catholic law, remained subservient in the home, having no legal rights over her children or property, a ward of her husband.

Let the wives be subject to their husbands in everything; for the husband is the head of the wife.

Let every man love his wife, but let the wife revere her husband.

I suffer not a woman to teach, nor to usurp authority over the husband, but to be silent.

For Adam was not deceived, but the woman being deceived, was in the transgression.

Man was not created for the woman, but the woman for the man.[3]

On the whole, in patristic literature marriage was considered a necessary evil.

Now let us turn to the Jewish view. The Bible tells us that both man and woman are alike, created in the image of God. The Hebrew word for man—ish—differs from the word for woman—ishah—only in the necessary feminine suffix -ah.

Speaking about "the regulations and rules for the position and treatment of woman" in the Bible and Talmud, Nahida Remy asks: "Have the ancient Jews been so much ahead of their time, or did modern legislators retrograde so far behind the ancient Jews?" Her answer is clear. "The special care and reverential regard for her [woman] are remarkable and fall nothing short of homage."[4]

The father had the right to promise his daughter in marriage, but the Mishnah and Talmud provide ample laws for her protection.* A bride had the right to choose the place where her first home would be. Refusal by the husband was grounds enough for divorce without any detrimental consequences to the wife, either morally or financially.[5]

The ketubbah,* the document that insures woman the protection of her rights, clearly enumerates the husband's obligations toward his wife, "work for thee, honor thee, support thee and provide for thee as is

---

* See Chapter 8.

the custom of Jewish husbands, according to the Laws of Moses and Israel."

The Jewish view of marriage is truly a positive one. The Jewish wife was free from slavery, submission, blind obedience. She was her husband's helpmate, her place at his side. Her counsel was sought; her honor and feelings were respected. The Talmud advises:

If thy wife is short, bend down to her to take counsel from her.

The husband shall beware of vexing his wife, for her tears easily flow.

Let a man be careful to honor his wife, for to her alone he owes the blessings of his house.[6]

The real appreciation of the woman's role and its importance may be summarized as follows:

It is the wife through whose efforts the blessings of the Lord come to the house. She teaches the children, encourages the husband to visit the house of God and the house of study. It is she who welcomes his coming home. She also fills the house with godliness and purity. On all her doing rests the blessing of the Lord.

On woman rested the responsibility of the sanctification and purity of family life, upon which rested the preservation of Jewish life. Recognition of this, the greatest of all responsibilities, brought with it the reward of the great dignity in the home. This serious responsibility was sternly protected. High standards of morality were exacted from the woman, breaches of which were severely punished.

The Talmud advocates a lofty standard in domestic life, in which husband and wife look upon each other as full or equal partners in life. It requires strict chastity on the part of both parties. Patriarchal civilization dedicated and even sanctified woman to chastity; likewise, rabbinic tradition never gave man sexual freedom outside the marital bond. Thus, equal demands were placed upon both sexes. While there was no legal laxity in Jewish tradition, other cultures permitted man sexual indulgence.

Unlike Catholic law, in Jewish Law the woman's property, which the husband was obliged to protect, remained her own. And even if the husband remarried after her death and had children with a second wife, the property of the first wife was inherited by her own children. Before any inheritance was settled among sons or other relatives, provision of the wife was seen to.

A daughter has precedence over inheritance settlements before sons and other relatives. If, however, a daughter cannot inherit, a compensation is provided for her dowry.*

2

Review of the Early Status of the Jewish Woman

There is a woman at the
beginning of all great things.

—*Lamartine*

Let us examine woman's position during biblical and postbiblical times. While some maintain that her position was never higher than that of the Oriental woman of the present era, others disagree. They picture the woman of the Bible or talmudic times as similar to the liberated woman of today.

Neither point of view is accurate. The fate of the Jewish woman was not that of the Oriental wife, who was entirely subservient to the will and whim of her husband. Neither was it that of the modern woman, who is given complete freedom to participate in all of man's affairs. Rather, between these two antipodes, a third stream emerges, and it provides us with an accurate picture of her position among the Jews. The woman enjoyed rights and liberties which did not inhibit her latent capabilities but rather allowed her the freedom to express herself.

The Israelite woman of the Bible was not subject to the whim of man but played an important role in her own right. This is clearly illustrated in the biblical verse: "In all that Sarah saith unto thee [Abraham], hearken unto her voice." (Gen. 21:12)

13

In the biblical verse "And Abram took Sarai his wife" (Gen. 12:5), the word "took" is interpreted by the *Zohar* to signify that he pleased her and persuaded her. "For a man is not permitted to take his wife with him to another country without her consent." The woman's will and consent were of paramount importance.[1]

THE SOCIAL POSITION AND STATUS OF WOMAN
IN THE BIBLE

The position of the woman is a yardstick by which the culture of a people may be measured. Nothing could be more significant than that the Hebrews called themselves the "daughters of Zion." Their relation to God was seen in the symbol of wedlock; God is the consort and Israel the wife of his youth, who proved faithless to her husband. He cannot send her away; an infinite love, forever renewed, draws the two together. It is in the spirit of the Bible that later teachers declare: "The women—they are the House of Jacob."[2]

The Bible is the oldest source of our knowledge of the Jewish woman. By the laws which regulate the life of the Jew, the Bible assigns to the Jewish woman her particular role. Though she is excluded from a variety of obligations, this exclusion defines her individuality.

CREATION

From the onset the Bible gives one of the oldest and finest expressions concerning the female sex. It declares that man and woman are of the same excellence and nobility; God created both man and woman in His own image; both are invested with the authority to subdue the earth and all its living creatures. In the story of creation we learn that man was created from the dust of the earth, woman from the rib of man. Hence, man's origin was considered more humble and inferior than that of woman. God created man before woman, but then you always make a rough draft before the final masterpiece.

One of the most piquant anecdotes in the Gemara concerns the daughter of Rabban Gamliel. A heretic, in speaking to her, accuses God of being a thief, for He stole a rib from Adam while he slept. Rabban Gamliel's daughter then cries out in mock alarm summoning a guard. When asked by the heretic why she is upset, she answers that thieves had broken in, taking her silver pitcher and leaving a gold one in its place. The heretic laughs, commenting that he would be delighted if such a thief were to rob him and leave him richer than before. She explains her parable by saying that Adam was also delighted when God removed a rib from him and replaced it with the more estimable woman.[3]

The relation which the sexes bear to each other could not have been more thoughtfully expressed than through Adam's exclamation: "This is now bone of my bones and flesh of my flesh." (Gen. 2:23) Neither sex is complete without the other. The mysterious attraction that draws the man to the woman, the woman to the man, was created by God. With the creation of woman begins social intercourse and love of one's fellowman. It has been remarked that man is the "weaker" sex, for it is he who stands in need of help, the strength of the woman being able to render it. Yet the paradox for woman is: "In pain thou shalt bring forth children; and thy desire shall be to thy husband and he shall rule over thee." (Gen. 3:16)

Man, by dint of his nature, is seen as the fighter for existence, the provider. Woman is seen as the giver of this existence, as "the mother of all life." (Gen. 3:20) Woman becomes the eternal renewer of mankind, the eternal mother, who gives birth to new life and shapes her relationship to man. Thus, man becomes the object of her yearning.

Woman needs man to help her carry out her destiny; man needs woman to fulfill his purpose in life. There is extreme dependence of man upon woman for her moral guidance and of woman upon man for his practical doing.

"And God created man in His own image, in the image of God created He him; male and female created He them. And God blessed them; and God said unto them: 'Be fruitful and multiply' . . ." (Gen. 1:27–28)

Since woman was created together with man in God's image, the Torah was given to both of them. Both alike are, in their spiritual nature, akin to God. The foundations of the Torah and most of its commandments are equally related to both man and woman. Just as their creation came about together, so is the Torah for both of them together.

Women are the beginning of the Torah, although they may not be Torah-educated. They are the prelude to the Torah, for they direct their children to the study of Torah.

And although their sexual differences point to their different roles, much of the destiny of both sexes is still identical. Even if man might have been traditionally considered master, he was never viewed as a creator. For man still needs encouragement, support and stimulus—toward perfection. This help man gets from woman—the source of rahamim (mercy), the heritage of our Father Abraham.

The human being was created for the higher purpose of worshiping

God. As the prophet exclaims: "For my glory I created him." (Is. 43:7) This concept of human spirituality gives purposeful meaning to our lives. By fulfilling the commandments of the Torah we direct our hearts to the Creator and exclaim in our daily prayer: "Blessed be our God who created us for His glory by separating us from the erring, giving us the Torah of truth, and thereby planting within us eternal life."[4]

The special charge of the Jewish woman, in addition to the *mitzvot* (commandments), is to uphold the Torah itself through her partnership with God in the creation of mankind and in the upbringing and the perpetuation of humanity. As an equal partner with man, woman represents the preparation to the Torah and its beginning.

Woman is the preliminary groundwork of the Torah, the very fabric of Jewish existence. She thus symbolizes the aspiration to perfection, the hope in mankind's creativity and perpetuity, and is the transmitter of values to each new generation.

Women's task was assigned to them at the Sinaitic revelation, when God addressed them first as the "House of Jacob" before addressing the men, or the "Children of Israel."[5] While the primary mission of men is to disseminate the content of Divine revelation, the women are to carry on the experience of that revelation.

It is not the quantity of *mitzvot* or the rituals performed that counts but rather the quality and the unyielding faith and inward devotion of the spiritual expression. In this respect, women are credited by Tradition to be more religiously sustaining in their inspiration and more worship-oriented than men. So we find stated in the Talmud: "The one who sacrifices much and the one who sacrifices little have the same merit, provided that the heart is directed to Heaven."[6]

THE BIBLICAL WORLD

Although it has been asserted that the biblical world was a man's world, this view may be contested. In the great moments of biblical Jewish history, the woman stood by the side of the man. In fact, because of the righteousness of the women came the redemption from Egypt. At the revelation at Sinai, the Torah was given to the women before it was given to the men. The prophetic spirit, *ruah ha-kodesh*, rests equally upon man and woman.[7] The woman in politics also figures prominently in the Bible: Miriam, the acknowledged leader of her people; Deborah, the judge; Jael, the praised heroine; Huldah, the prophetess; Hannah, the poetess; and Ataliah, the queen of the Judean Kingdom.

In the Bible, woman is portrayed with all her virtues and vices. Thus, we find Sarah eavesdropping curiously behind the door; we learn of the jealousy of Hannah and Peninah; and we read of the wanton women of Samaria.

Counter to these unfavorable characteristics we find the woman endowed with the fear of God, modesty, assertiveness, intelligence, a strong aesthetic sense, as a diligent, hospitable housekeeper, and as the wife who counsels her husband and educates her children.

The Talmud also pictures her existence as being different from that of the Oriental woman, who is isolated from the outer world. The woman of the Talmud is vitally related to and in contact with the world in which she lives. She is listened to by all members of society. She goes about unveiled, takes part with men at public affairs, and is far from being ignored. She participates in national festivals, enhancing the celebration with singing and dancing. Happiness and fulfillment of the Jewish nation came about through woman's participation: "Young men and maidens [rejoice in the dance], old and young together." (Ps. 148:12)

3

Biological and Cultural Differences

> The women's prerogative is more extended than
> that of men.
> —*Sifrei Pinehas* 27:4

Any extensive psychological study of womanhood and the woman's position in our society requires an appraisal of the fundamental biological differences between the two sexes as well as the relating of her character to social and cultural forces.

While woman shares many capacities and functions with man, the basic differences between the two sexes remain. An understanding of the psychology of the woman has only recently begun.

Before and during the middle of the nineteenth century, the woman's position was fairly stable and predictable. Her education was geared toward two main and interdependent goals: marriage and motherhood. Once married, the woman accepted her lot for better or for worse. If she remained a spinster, she was destined, in addition to her feelings of inferiority, to a life of frustration. Historically, woman's restlessness began to spread about a century ago.

We do not yet know the psychological effects and profound socioeconomic changes that will result from the feminine revolution for equality and emancipation. Its rumblings portend new opportunities in education, labor, and the professions. New freedoms are obtruding themselves upon the old order; and a new sense of identity is evolving,

19

which will change and affect it both personally and interpersonally. The woman's quondam role of mother and housewife only is being supplanted by a newer, more suitable one.

Any cogent psychological probe of the woman must consider her biological potentiality in a changing cultural matrix for a better understanding of concomitant changes in her personality. Cultural factors are known to contribute to sex differences in intellect, dependence, aggression, and emotionality.

Since the child in all societies is educated early on in the customs and mores of his milieu, much of the character formations or traits of the boy and the girl are directly affected by the distinct cultural attitudes of adults toward the male and female child. Man himself has not allowed enough respect for sexual, educational, religious, and social differences. When asked about femininity, Freud replied: "If you want to know more about femininity, enquire from your own experiences of life, or turn to the poets, or wait until science can give you deeper and more coherent information."[1]

Generally speaking, woman is more diminuitive and delicate than man, not having his muscular strength. Nowadays the anatomical differences in body structure between man and woman are fewer than in antiquity, man no longer being so strenuously engaged in labor as his male forebear. Still, according to Margaret Mead, these secondary sexual differences are not universally uniform. The only constant, universal exceptions in all races are childbearing and lactation—uniquely feminine traits.

Girls can be more verbally reasoned with than boys. They seem initially better equipped to appraise responses accurately and to respond verbally. Generally speaking, they appear to show more conformity, guilt, and resistance to temptation. Since they have fewer antisocial impulses to control, they are less tempted than males.

Women show greater light-headed emotionality, anxiety, and emotional instability, as shown by Oetzel (1966).

Girls show more interest in other people at an early age. (Goodenough, 1957) They tend to be more affectionate and manifest more pity for those who suffer. (D'Andrade, 1966)[2]

The reason for woman's light-headedness is that her work is spread out in many fields. Her duties are many and varied—ranging from housekeeping to taking care of her children and/or engaging in a career. Therefore, her peace of mind tends to be disturbed much more often than that of the man, whose work is mostly concentrated in a single area. The richness of a person's personality is determined by the measure of the range of experiences to which he has to adjust from birth to old age. Some people therefore find it easier to have an integrated view of life, life having interposed few demands upon them.

Neither sex is superior or inferior to the other. The difference relates to the different biological role each sex plays in life. Historically, woman has been placed in a secondary role in society. The dominant group has taken the right to offer her a status of separate-but-equal, reserving for man the power to give or to withhold. Woman was expected to remain eternally "feminine" to man's liking and not to compete with the masculine world. Somehow man took for himself what he considered his "natural" rights, while, for woman, he found a rationalization in the claim "Anatomy is Destiny."

Freud believed that women's weaker superego derived from the Oedipus Complex not having been resolved in the little girl, and that the pubescent girl had to accept her feminine passivity (because of the cultural change in her status of puberty); hence, the claim that women are traditionally motivated to search for esteem that comes from others' evaluations.

Freud's observations about the inferiority complex and other characteristics of woman being biologically determined were challenged by the neo-Freudian Clara Thompson, who explained female psychology in terms of the special influences on the woman of the Western world: her developmental restrictions, insincere sexual education, and socioeconomic dependency of the underprivileged sex.[3]

Freud and Hans Sachs have claimed that women often lack strong beliefs and a strong conscience. One must, however, admit that such lacunae are not universally true of women only. Erich Fromm points out that regardless of popular belief, women are more courageous, more realistic, and more concerned with the question of war and peace than men are. (Thompson, 1971)

The evidence warrants the conclusion that women show more superego in displaying less lawless behavior, more conformity, more upset after deviation, and a stronger moral code. (Schoeppe, 1953)

Nowadays, owing to changing social structures, the nature and role of the woman continue to take on new forms. Feminine role allocation will undergo more changes qualitatively and will continue to take on new forms. All biological findings indicate that woman's biology has unattested vigor and flexibility, that what we call femininity and masculinity is overwhelmingly determined by social and familial interactions.

Owing to man's long-entrenched cultural biases, the woman has long experienced unpleasantness, feelings of body shame, accentuated narcissism, loss of equality with boys, and a weaker superego than man. She was branded with having feelings of passivity and masochism. Such feminine characteristics—which Freud believed to be the result of her biological vicissitudes in a cultural setting producing dependency—became the patent traits with which woman was stigmatized by man. Woman was trained to fit a controlled sexual regimen, of being in greater need for love than man. She was discouraged in following intellectual, socioeconomic, and personal pursuits, the results of which must have contributed to her diminished sense of self, since her security and sense of approval remained dependent on stronger male figures.

Studies based on white middle-class Americans of all ages show that women, as compared with men, are more dependent, passive, and conforming. (Kagan, 1964; Tyler, 1965)[4]

Modern woman is now in a state of transition; she is beginning to emerge as a more independent person. Her basic nature, however, is still a mystery.

Recent psychological research on women indicates that states of passivity, dependency, and submissiveness, far from being goals, were traits that the woman was directed to develop and adopt. Until she can better develop her God-given creative resources, man stands indebted to her, guilty for not having encouraged her much earlier to tap and utilize her latent talents for her own growth and for that of humanity.

We define maturity as a state which integrates strength, responsibility, and love, or the ability to act and the capacity to care. Due to traditional sex-role education, men need to learn interpersonal skills, and women to balance their more pliant inclinations with a modicum of assertiveness.

Be that as it may, a complete description of woman's psychology must deal with her ability to love and need to be loved. We now turn to that subject.

4

On Love

I am my beloved's and my beloved is mine.
—*Song of Songs* 6:37

Of all the emotions man exhibits, love is unique. Love's universal ability to dominate all other passions distinguishes this phenomenon from all others. Other desires are directed toward the abstract, such as the love of knowledge, the love of power, and, chiefly, the love of God. However, in the special sphere of human love, the urgency is for man's sake: therefore, it is for him to seek his fulfillment in the immediate present and not in a sphere of the world beyond human understanding. As Max Brod asserts: "Human love is not directed toward the infinite. Rather, it is 'of this world.' "[1]

The universality of love, the most profound of emotions, makes it the most fascinating subject, creation's crowning good. Love is the most significant factor in both human and divine relations. In elaborating some of the views on this most difficult and least understood subject, it is not the author's intention to decide on the correct definition but, rather, to review the basic theories on love—both mystical and rational, sacred and profane—as they have transpired throughout history.

Although love's role differs in the life of men and women, it remains the supreme force for good or ill. Love has the ingredients of both the productive and the destructive; it is at once primitive and civilized, neurotic and normal. It appears in all literature, in the songs of the troubadours; it is the music of all nations, the inspiration of all arts, the language of life. From the ancient Sanskrit literature to the Chinese

23

songs of love, the love books of Ovid, and the vast erotic literature there exist more than two thousand treatises on love. And still many of us are ignorant of the importance of love and its vital impact upon our life.

Sexual morality in Western culture was based on the ascetic identification with self-defilement, which resulted in the obsessively misogynous denunciation by the early Church Fathers of sex as the essence of sin.[2] Thus an antithesis was created between flesh and spirit, which led to great tension concerning the role of love.

When studying the history of love in Western culture, we can see how love changed both in importance and in quality, how it was the molding influence of both family structure and woman's status, of philosophy and religion, as well as how it flourishes in the insecure climate of urban loneliness.

THE PSYCHOANALYTIC VIEW

Like an iceberg, only a small part of love is visible, and even the perceived part remains an enigma in all its aspects: from the religious to the ontological, the ethical and the social, the physical and the psychological. No satisfactory explanation has as yet been offered to identify the prime mover which sets off love's momentum. To Freud, it is the libido—or what Plato called the Eros—the quantitative biological expression for the energy of all those tendencies which motivates the human passion we call love. While assigning autonomous instinctual force to both love and aggression, Freud held that the sex drive of every child is first directed toward his parents but, because of the severe taboo, it is transmuted into acceptable forms; love is "aim-inhibited sexuality." Freud admitted at the end of his life that "we know very little about love." It was T. Reik, a Freudian disciple, who differentiated between love and sex, between a person who is sex-starved and one who is love-starved. While the peak of sex gratification is ecstasy, the peak of love is beatitude. The sex urge is originally objectless, while love is definitely an emotional relationship between a Me and a You. The riddle of love may be found in the diversities of the mutual discovery and exchange of the lovers' ego ideals.

Love is the categorical imperative of our culture, sanctioned by religion and tradition; it is considered the regulator of the interpersonal relations within the family.

In the emotional dialectic of marriage, mature love enables each partner to develop and grow, which leads to a further integrating of the personality and thus helps hold the marriage together with mutual respect and tenderness even after erotic passion recedes.

Karen Horney, a neo-Freudian, held that the neurotic use of love as a means of protection against anxiety is anything but favorable, since the very situation which creates the compulsive need precludes its gratification.[3]

Erich Fromm asserted that productive love alone permits freedom, that the strength of mature love derives from its allowing one to become parentlike (or God-like), giving without thought of return. Such love allows the most intense bond with humanity. Fromm held that the ability to love depends on one's capacity to emerge from narcissism. Love is the union of two lonelinesses. It depends on one's capacity to grow and to develop a productive orientation as one relates to the outside world and to oneself. The practice of the art of loving requires the practice of rational faith, the quality of certainty, firmness, and conviction, character traits that pervade the entire personality. He who loves with reservations, in the long run cheats both himself and the beloved.[4]

THE JEWISH VIEW

The Rabbis distinguished between two types of love: the "love which depends on something" (transient) and the "love which does not depend on something" (enduring).[5] The former was conceived as an evanescent relationship based on a physical cause, or physical attraction, which will pass away once the cause is gone. But that love which is not dependent on a physical cause, but is a love rooted in the spiritual and moral worth of the beloved person, will never pass away but will be as abiding as the firm values on which it is founded. As an example of the "love which depends on something" transient, the Mishnah mentions King David's son Amnon's infatuation with his half sister Tamar (2 Sam. 13), based on a mere sexual attraction, which, after being satisfied, turned into hate. Similarly, disappointed love makes us not only unhappy but cruel as well. Not so the "love which does not depend on something" transient, which is exemplified by the love of David and Jonathan. The latter, in his love for David, placed his own needs second to those of his friend. Jonathan was willing to face insult and to lose kingship in order that his loved one, David, could grow and unfold as his own individual self. (1 Sam. 20:4–30)

A close parallel to this rabbinic distinction between two types of love is Freud's concept of the duality of love. For him, love was a division of two distinct elements—sensuality and feelings of respect and affection. He later termed the distinction a contrast between "object-love" and "identification-love."[6]

Fromm's view was already expressed by hasidic thinkers, who saw in human love a mighty force, because it succeeds in imitating Divine love; even the poor replica has about it something of the greatness of the original.

The Zohar sees in the bond between male and female the secret of true faith.

R. Israel Baal Shem Tov (1700–1760), the founder of the hasidic movement, declared: "It behooves every man to reflect; whence is the source which evokes in me feelings of love, if not the love of God for his creation."[7]

R. Nahum of Czernobil (1730–1798), in his *Meor Enayim*, writes: "It is clear to us that human love is but an offshoot of the Divine love, for without Divine love, no love could be aroused within our heart."[8]

Love of God, too, springs from the need to overcome separateness and achieve union. When our Rabbis spoke of love, they consciously believed that they were helping man in an effort to achieve *imitatio Dei*, for love is the profound experience that comes to us from "on high," as Revelation. God is conceived as the Source of Love, and He reveals to us of Himself, enabling us to develop our capacity to love both the Creator and His creation, and this ability will bring us to deepen the awareness of the nature of God.

Social acceptance and favor are traditionally seen as a correlative to Divine acceptance. Said R. Hanina ben Dosa: "He who is pleasing to his fellowmen is also pleasing to God."[9] Kind and considerate conduct can be attained through our life together and can help each of us to find amiable pleasantness and human acceptance in our relationships. The designation *beriyot* (lit., creatures) embraces all of mankind, regardless of individual differences, which we must learn to tolerate. God created men and women for a general association. Even as all of us, being the creatures of God, enjoy the same relationship to Him, who is the sole Creator of all, and even as all of us are united through Him, so, despite our many differences, we should draw closer to one another and each of us try to see and accept the good in the other person. Indeed, *ruah ha-beriyot*—the spirit of mankind—is equal to *ruah Ha-Makom*—the spirit of God.

Religion is thus conceived as the "binding" process of man to his fellowman and of man to God. In hasidic ideology the mitzvah of ahavat Yisrael—love for the Jewish people—is equivalent to the mitzvah of ahavat Ha-Shem—love of God. Said the "Ohev Yisrael," R. Avraham Yehoshua Heschel of Apta (d. 1825); "Ahavat Yisrael and ahavat Ha-Shem are identical. The Anshei Knesset ha-Gedolah, when instituting our daily prayers, have preceded the declaration of the Shema by the benediction of 'ha-boher be-amo Yisrael be-ahavah'— 'who hast chosen your people Israel with love.' In Hebrew, both the word ehad, representing the One and Only God, and the word ahavah, love, have a numerical value of thirteen, symbolizing that both ahavat Yisrael and ahavat Ha-Shem are equal."[10]

Man has an inherent need to relate as a basis for any kind of sane living. In erotic love there exists a drive for union with another person. Brotherly love refers to all men, motherly love to the child, and erotic love is directed to one person, normally of the opposite sex, with whom union and oneness is sought. While motherly love begins with oneness and leads to separateness, erotic love, conversely, begins with separateness and ends in oneness. Thus states the Torah in its very beginning: "Therefore does a man leave his father and his mother, and does cleave unto his wife, and they become one flesh." (Gen. 2:24) This biblical ideal of the unique tie that binds man to his wife even closer than to his parents points to the monogamous marriage—a man cleaves to his wife, not to his wives—and to the sacredness of marriage relations, which goes back to the very birth of human society—to the initial intent of the Divine Creation.

The power of love can direct aggression to the service of human happiness. The same creative energies that generate human achievements in art and science motivate work and play, and animate our sex lives can, unmitigated by love, become a destructive force for the human race.

Man's conception of love differs from that of a woman because of the difference in their existential situations rather than as a result of the laws of nature. So it is, that a man in love possesses and integrates the beloved woman into his existence while she finds her destiny in abdication, yielding only when she believes she is deeply loved. The esteem and affection of the man eliminates any feeling of abasement by offering the woman an avenue toward transcendence of her essential dependence.

Woman's desire for perpetual love fulfillment is largely spiritual. Woman, in her desire for love, is, in fact, more spiritual than man in his.

for woman must be completely undivided: it must free his whole nature. A woman is far more grateful for the joys and blessings of love than a man. Since woman loves and serves love alone, this passion gradually comes to form the content of her life. A woman has a greater need for love than man—and, concomitantly, a greater need for security. Being loved is part of woman's natural life in the same way it is a part of man's. To make her personality attractive and seductive is imperative, we repeat, for purposes of security. In the past she could, perhaps, feel safe after she had married and then sometimes risk neglecting her charms; but today, with the present rise in divorce, the woman who depends on a man for her means of support and social position must continue to pay attention not only to her intellect but also to what may be called narcissistic pursuits, that is, personal enhancement and better appearance.

THE ABILITY TO LOVE

Love means different things to different people. Heretofore, the traditional American assumption has been that love should come before marriage and that a loving relationship be sought as the major goal of marriage. Marked changes in attitude have occurred within the last generation, which reflect shifts not only in the changing basis of family life but also in writings on the subject. Some have advanced the idea of the fulfillment of love as a human necessity, showing that love's impact on human affairs is a reality that all people have to come to terms with as a necessity for personal welfare and happiness. This need to express and receive love is recognized by our culture because of our better understanding of the role of love in our life. Love provides the protection, the strength, and the encouragement without which full growth is impossible.

We ought to differentiate here between immature and mature love. For not every person is capable of experiencing mature love and building a meaningful man-woman relationship. Not a few of us lack the essential experiences which are conducive to the capacity to love, and therefore relatively few people find mature, stable love relationships. For all our modern scientific sophistication, our thinking with respect to the nature of love is confused and is more characteristic of the primitive mind with its reliance on magic than it is of the civilized mind.

According to Lord Byron, love is "a sort of hostile transaction very necessary to keep the world going." To love is more than to like. Zick Rubin's study (1973) shows that love is different from liking and consists of three components: attachment, caring, and intimacy.[11]

Attachment is the need to have contact and to be fulfilled with the other person. It is the passionate desire that Greeks call eros. Caring is the concern, the wish to give, fulfill, and satisfy the other party. The Greeks called it agape. According to Rubin, eros and agape represent the reciprocity of the love relationship. Intimacy is the mutual understanding in the union—the exclusive bond between two people. These three elements are missing in the process of liking. While related to loving, liking consists of positive evaluations, respect, and perceived similarity. While the elements of fantasy and conflicting emotions are present in love, they are not found in friendship.

ON THE VARIOUS TYPES OF LOVE

We know that different aspects of love affect different areas of the marriage. One ought to compare the three Greek words eros, philos, and agape, which are often translated by the one English word "love."

Eros, having specific reference to desire, the sexual drive, is confined by Tradition only to the marriage bond and is affected by the sensitivities of the people involved.

Philos, which primarily connotes friendship and affection, is the basis for the decision to carry out the marriage.

Agape, or affection, often called "Divine love," is related to an intellectual process that transcends emotional and physical needs and fixes rather upon the welfare and dignity of its object.

Fortunate is the man who is loved by a woman, but the one to be envied is he who loves, however little he gets in return. Love is the most complete and noblest relationship. Love puts the welfare and happiness of the other person before one's own. Its true relationship includes respect, admiration, friendship, and intimacy, all fused into one deep and indivisible emotion with its own grace and charisma.

Quite different from love is infatuation, the first exciting flush of love which requires two conditions: idealization and the location of a person as a focus of attention. Reality is disregarded or distorted and is considered an antidote for infatuation.

Infatuation can appear at any age; it is usually temporary and, therefore, can create problems. Infatuation is a feeling that can be an enjoyable part of early courtship and may develop into mature love or lasting friendship that rests on the mutual satisfaction of numerous needs. While love makes the lover a servant to his feelings and his idealizations, infatuation is primarily devotion to ego enhancement.

ROMANTIC LOVE

In romantic love one finds the earmarks of democratic action, namely, that nothing should stand in the way of love, neither social, economic, educational, nor other differences. The basic component of romantic love has, from the twelfth century, been the denial of sexual expression, with consequent sublimation and spiritualization. Unlike other societies, where techniques to control love were developed, Western culture is practically the only one that emphasizes falling in love as a basis for marriage.

However cynical and paradoxical our times may seem to us, most people in Western society still regard romantic love seriously, value it highly, and feel cheated if they do not experience it. In most societies of the past, romantic love was viewed as somewhere between a form of extramarital recreation, portrayed in plays and stories, and a dangerous psychological disturbance.

Love of the romantic-myth variety has an irrational, ecstatic, and mercurial quality. Today it is being popularized by the motion-picture industry and other mass media. In reality, human love is a multifaceted subjective experience that varies markedly with age and other characteristics of the subject as well as type of object and situation. Critics of romantic love claim that an emphasis on such love encourages instability in marriage. Compatible backgrounds promote the success of the relationship.

The romantics held that jealousy is the inevitable shadow cast by the perfect contours of real love. While it is difficult to define jealousy by its feeling, which may oscillate between fear, sorrow, and shame to anger, suspicion, and humiliation, it can be defined by its function. Jealousy is that undesirable egoistic side of the system of love which has as its special end the possession of the loved object. In the words of Goethe: "Jealousy is a divination of affinity with still another." A Russian proverb proclaims: "Jealousy and Love are sisters." Passion is unique. While originally the word meant suffering and the endurance of pain when associated with love, it conveys the notion of emotional storm and excess.

Different from passion (love suffered), which springs from *eros*, romance passes away, by definition, depending upon the quality of the obstacles left to be overcome. Although very rarely consummated in normal happiness, romance presents every possibility of expiring. It always challenges the stability of marriage and the foundation of family life. And although popularized, romance is more a way of feeling love than of acting it, for love action springs from *agape*. Passion prefers torment to happiness, it thrives on obstacles; but while it exalts, it also depresses its victims. When love is really integrated, it brings forward tenderness, gratitude, and a mutual respect that supercedes receiving passion.

The romantic myth rose from the courtly love patterns called *l'amour courtois*, or Frauendienst, developed by the privileged aristocracy and glorified by the troubadours in song. Romantic love has traditionally been considered an uncontrollable emotion that happens at first sight. It runs counter to the reality of social stratification and the desires of the group that its members marry among its own members. Therefore we find romantic love often occurring unexpectedly and without foresight. The salient components of romantic love are fatalism—the notion that some couples are meant for each other; idealization—the intense, uncritical overevaluation of the loved one; and sexlessness—self-mastery to maintain the ethereal quality of the knight's love. It is unfortunate that this mythical romantic love, which originated as an exclusive feature of the medieval courtly life, should now be prominent in the sex-obsessed Western culture and is surely devastating in its effects.

A more enriched relationship, quite antithetical to romantic love, is mature love, or the realistic heterosexual affectional bonds. Here, instead of being idealized, the mate is accepted with all faults and virtues. Here differences in personality are maximized between the two partners as sources of enrichment of the relationship rather than as limitations of it. To love is to admire with the heart; to admire is to love with the mind.

A distinction must be made between measures of *liking*, reflecting how we see individuals on task-oriented activities, and those of *loving*, where our feelings of attachment, caring, and intimacy are involved.

One must also differentiate between *falling* in love, which may be relatively easy, and *remaining* in love, which involves the ability to build and maintain a stable relationship. Contrary to popular stereotypes, men may fall in love more easily than women. Women may also fall out of love more easily than men. To make a love relationship successful, a sensitivity to the dynamics of the relationship is required, as well as the crystallization of the real image of the partner. Theodore

Reik[12] believes that all love arising out of a basic dissatisfaction with oneself results in the creation of an ego-ideal or perfectionism in all qualities deemed important. This in turn results in expectations and demands made on a person to measure up to these perfections. In short, Reik claims, love in its essential nature is an emotional reaction-formation to envy, possessiveness, and hostility.

While we may not agree with Reik's theory, it is important to consider the kinds of needs people have and the quality of the relationship which emerges, whether they be mature or immature needs. These in turn are determined by the degree to which the needs involved are conducive to the intellectual and emotional development of the partners and how realistic they are. Physical love is an ephemeral spark designed to kindle in human hearts the flame of a more lasting love. It is the outer court of the temple.

Confusion and ignorance regarding the nature of love causes many people to get a distorted perception of this most profound of emotional feelings. The emotionally immature and unstable are preoccupied with the self and with their own problems. Consequently, their ability to relate interpersonally in a meaningful way is blocked and made markedly difficult, if not impossible.

Not so in mature love, where we are moved toward a capacity for good will, to grant the other person full right and affirmation to his unique humanity. The capacity to love another maturely develops out of specific types of human values and relationships which are recognized as operating within society. This capacity is rooted in a wide variety of personal and social influences that begin at birth and continue in the family and in its social involvements. The development of the individual's capacity to love maturely operates in the following periods: childhood, and preadolescence adolescence.

Love's ingredients are togetherness, reciprocal responsiveness, and sensitivity and understanding for the partner's needs that contribute to the intellectual and emotional growth of the partners; and the partners must be rooted in reality. As such, mature and healthy love is viewed as an integration of personalities, which results from the continuous process of adjustment and readjustment of the personalities involved.

When we take sex either as a justification or as a signal of love, we can be led into the same needs, expectations, and demands that infatuation makes us liable to. Sexual fidelity has been and still continues to be an important constituent of love even in our age of changing morality. We covet sexual exclusiveness in love more than emotional or intellectual exclusiveness. Just as we need the other person to keep us from being lonely, we also want commitment and devotion for the future, a sort of permanent guarantee that love won't end. It is not so much that "love" loses its meaning; our problems with love are with our expectations. Our concern is not so much what to call love but rather how to achieve it, and with learning honestly how to be in love.

Out of the many shades of meaning of love, each of us has his own personal meaning. We all need affection and companionship. Emotional immaturity is a barrier to intimate connections and to the acceptance of the emotional offerings of others.

A relationship in which one person "needs" more than the other, or in which both people are taking and neither is giving, is apt to be poor in intimate contacts. As we move towards others we develop a range of expressive emotions. Such intimate connections can occur only if one person does not stand in a superior position to another, or when the couple has the ability and volition to transcend or disregard differences or position. Intimate contact is viable only if people do not adhere rigidly to their social role or psychological inequalities.

Besides attention and commitment, an intimate relationship requires self-respect and self-knowledge, mutual respect, and open communication actively displayed. Given the fact that intimacy inevitably brings conflict, one can work to allow conflict to enrich rather than damage the relationship through concern for the nurturance, growth, and welfare of one's self and the self of another, as well as the growth of self and other through the relationship.

In the words of Kahlil Gibran in The Prophet:

> Love gives naught but itself and takes
> naught but from itself.
> Love possesses not nor would it be
> possessed;
> For love is sufficient unto love.

LOVE IN THE BIBLE AND IN RABBINIC LITERATURE

Judaism places great importance on love. It asks an important question regarding the concept of Love. Does love necessarily remain unfulfilled, or can it be compatible with worldly and spiritual fulfillment? The Jewish view is that Love is a "this worldly miracle," not only a spiritual relationship, but one which finds its fulfillment in the erotic relation between man and woman. The biblical poem, Song of Songs, is a bridge toward understanding this concept. Allegorically, we may see the "Song" as an interpretation of the spiritual relationship that exists between a man and a woman. Judaic love is founded upon this poem's *leitmotif.* The Song of Songs best testifies to the concept of "this-worldly miracle," which is essentially the miracle of Love. This love does not ignore physical enjoyment but rather experiences the pleasure of physical passion, and at the same time it is enjoyed as something eternal—something seriously weighty—as the flame of God, mystically viewed as the love of God to the Knesset Israel.[13] Thus we can readily see that the Judaic concept of love with its major tenets of both worldly and spiritual fulfillment has not been altered for more than two thousand years.

A Jew was exhorted to marry and to love his wife. The Rabbis believed that no marriage can thrive when devoid of love, since they assumed that all people love their wives. "Whoever marries a woman with whom is incompatible violates five commandments of the Torah."[14]

A primary principle of the Bible is the scriptural doctrine of the love of God, love for God, and love for one's fellow man. These last two commandments are so related that the latter springs from, or is conditioned by, the first. Love for our fellowmen (Deut. 10:19) emanates from our love for God, which itself has its source in the knowledge we have of the love which God has for us (Mal. 1:2) and as revealed in His words and acts to men. (Deut. 7:8) The love of man in the Bible springs from a heart renewed and possessed with love of God, expressing man's essential worth and dignity. It is the kind of love in which the egoistic impulse is conquered; it originates from a heart with a genuine disposition, sincere and unbegrudging. To claim to love God when love for one's fellowman is absent is vain and fallacious.

Biblically, love is that principle which leads one moral being to long and delight in another, resulting in a fellowship in which both partners coalesce in the joy of giving.

In the Prophets, the love of God derives from His relationship with Israel as an emerging nation. Its proof is found in the Lord's Divine acts toward the people of Israel and His special covenant with them. (Hos. 11:1; Is. 63:9; Ezek. 16:7-14, 60-61)

God's multiphasic manifestations of love and superabounding grace are expressed in a variety of Hebrew terms to denote the all-embracing Divine Love both in its theological and in its ethical attributes, such as *hesed*—mercy or loving-kindness; *hain*—grace; *tov* or *tuv*—goodness;

tzedek—righteousness; emet—truth; kadosh—holy; ne'eman —faith-ful; rahum—merciful; and so on. He shows His Divine character through the mercy kept for thousands of generations toward those who love Him. (Exod. 20:5-6) God's ways are proclaimed to us in the thirteen characteristic qualities of the Divine Nature—His attributes of Mercy (yod gimel mekheelin derahmein) revealed unto Moses: "The Lord, The Lord God, compassionate and gracious, long-suffering, and abundant in goodness and truth; keeping mercy unto the thousandth generation, forgiving iniquity and transgression and sin. . ." (Exod. 34:6-7) These attributes of Divine Mercy are the dominant refrain in all our prayers of repentance. Throughout the Bible the preeminent religious message is that of God's revelation of His gracious purposes in history and His acts for human salvation. (Ps. 103:6-7)

The primary duty of a person, according to the Bible, is to love God with all his mind, heart, soul, and strength. (Deut. 6:5) This requirement is based in part on the natural relation of man to God as His dependent creation. (Deut. 8:17-18; Is. 1:3, Ps. 95:6-7; 100:3) Such love requires intelligence and true knowledge (yedeeah) and is not a self-contained experience. Its aim is universally humane; it overflows and extends in love to others; it abounds and encompasses all creatures and all creation. It is the love of patience and kindness, of humility and hope, of modesty and suffering, of faith and truth; it is the love of belief. It excludes envy; it shuns wrong and affirms good. This kind of love represents the comprehensive, all-powerful motive of the Mosaic law and the teaching of our practical religion.

A primary character of active love is that of giving, which includes aliveness, attainment of self-respect, as well as the elements of care, responsibility, respect, and knowledge. These ideas were long ago expressed in Kabbalah, where command of love is based on the concept of imitatio Dei, to influence and to give "for the sake of giving."[15] Giving for the sake of receiving is not love. Included as acts of giving are such commandments as teaching, the imparting of knowledge, making the bride and groom joyous at their wedding, and the spreading of one's gladness and joy to others. In marriage, this concept is symbolized by the need for the groom to give an object of value to the bride. The commandments of giving charity and gifts to the poor are further examples of preparations leading to the true fulfillment of loving one's neighbor.[16]

Under the commandment of "love thy neighbor" the Jew is required to be alert to the needs of his friend. This requirement becomes evident from the biblical affirmation in response to Cain's question: "Am I my brother's keeper? (Gen. 4:9) One must show readiness to fulfill every vital need of one's friend, whether monetary or spiritual. If one sees his friend following the wrong path, one must try to correct him. "All love that is without correction," says R. Yossi Bar Hanina, "is not love,"[17] for it shows lack of concern for the friend's spiritual needs. The same conditions exist in marital love. Included in a marriage are the obligations upon the man to fulfill his wife's needs for food, clothing, and marital relations.[18] If one is not prepared to care for and respond to the needs of another—one cannot love.

Judaism also demands mutual respect by the partners. Many laws and customs are based on the consideration of *kavod ha-beriot*, respect for people. All the precepts relating to the ordering of our social life were presented to us under the Divine Seal, "I am the Lord," thereby eliminating any motive for practicing them for selfish gain.[19] As stated previously, love that is for the sake of receiving is, in Judaism, not considered love.

Mosaic law commands us to love the stranger. This is bound up with the historical fact that "you [Israelites] were strangers in the land of Egypt." (Lev. 19:34) The command to love is dependent on the ability to identify. The necessity for such knowledge can symbolically be seen in marriage, as expressed in the biblical root *yadoa*, to know and to love.(Gen. 4:1) The notion of love as the seat of knowledge was expressed by the Ramban in the kabbalistic work entitled *Iggeret Ha-Kodesh*.[20] One must have respect for one's wife, who is not merely an object for one's gratification but an individual in her own rights. This may be the intent of the Bible twice telling the story of creation of woman—the first, when man and woman are created together, to stress the unity of their bond; the second, when woman is created separately, to stress that each must nevertheless, be respected as an individual. (Gen. 1:27; 2:21–22)

Indeed, marriage during the biblical, and even talmudic times, was not denied the romantic touch, so beautifully described in the early Oriental literature. One can fully understand why talmudic and mid-rashic works, dedicated solely to law and exegesis, do not abound in such romantic descriptions, considering the laconic style of the Sages and their deep sense of modesty, restraint, and reservation in matters of domestic and intimate privacy. Nonetheless, throughout the vast laby-rinth of legal casuistics and argumentation, one is able to cull apho-risms in the realm of romance, love, and sexuality reflecting the knowledge of the Sages based on observation and pragmatic findings in their own life and milieus.

The Torah informs us of the fact that "Jacob loved Rachel; and he said: 'I will serve you seven years for Rachel, your younger daughter' . . . and Jacob served seven years for Rachel; and they seemed unto him but a few days for the love he had to her." (Gen. 29:18, 20) To the Greeks and Romans, this would have seemed preposterous and ridiculous. The mere fact that the biblical text, which is so laconic in many instances of laws and commandments, which are only hinted at, depicts in such uncharacteristic detail this pastoral and tender idyllic love between the two young Israelite shepherds is surely an indication of an early Hebrew concept, if not a universal ideal—that love ought to be considered a prime prerequisite for marriage. (The numerous metaphors illustrating the parallel of God's love to Israel, with that of the bridegroom to his bride, are well known, while talmudic and midrashic lore adheres to the same analogy.)[21]

The northern French exegete R. Joseph Bekhor Shor (1085), commenting on the above text, asks: "Shouldn't seven years appear as seventy to the lover who is eagerly waiting for his beloved?" How, then, could it seem to Jacob "but a few days?" Bekhor Shor explains that Jacob's love for Rachel was so great, and her worth so priceless, that it appeared to him that her father, Laban, was giving her away for a song, since such a worthy and beautiful wife was being given to him for such little time and labor.[22]

An interesting comment is offered by R. Levi Itzhak of Berditchev on the biblical passage: "And Jacob kissed Rachel . . . and Rachel was beautiful and of good appearance, and Jacob loved Rachel." (Gen. 29:11;17–18) On the surface, it is surprising that Jacob our father, the chosen one of the forefathers, should be influenced by beauty. For the attribute of the righteous lies in the reverse: "False is the charm and beauty is vanity." (Prov. 31:30) But the answer is as follows: It is known that our forefather Jacob used to serve God with the attribute of Glory. Everything he had in him was a glorious spark; even though the vessel was material, he lifted up the glorious spark to the Origin above and served God with it. Because of this, it is said "And Jacob kissed Rachel . . . and Rachel was beautiful.[23]

Only in egocentric love, in which man's intentions are only for hedonistic pleasure, does man yearn for the swift passage of time. Every day is like a year in his eyes. Jacob's love was a deeply spiritual experience, without any one-sided ulterior motives. This type of love is not related to elements of time, and so seven years are considered like a few fleeting days.[24]

The essential feature of love can be seen in the longing, the desire of the lover and his beloved to be together. This sense of togetherness, shared by both parties, involves not only intoxication of the heart but humility and care, and perhaps most significant, understanding. Agnon, too, states: "In understanding with their hearts, lovers return to each other, and thus are healed of their longing . . . in this world."[25]

Hasidic teaching points to two kinds of love. The first is love of oneself. The love of one's reflection in the beloved returns to the self and there is a sweeping desire to be close to the beloved, and seeing him or her is cause for rejoicing. This anticipation causes frustration and impatience; the nearness of the beloved and even the anticipation of being close do not make these wane. Therefore it was said concerning Jacob: "And Jacob worked for Rachel seven years and they were in his eyes like a few days in his love for her." (Gen. 29:20) Jacob loved Rachel and not himself. He was anticipating her with a peaceful soul; even when he was far from her, he was always engrossed in his love for her, and so time flew. The second kind of love, the biblical command for brotherly love, "And thou shalt love thy neighbor as thyself" (Lev. 19:18), is described by R. Akiva as being the *klal gadol ba-Torah*, the fundamental rule in the Torah. R. Akiva continues to say that the rest of the Torah, the remaining commandments, are only preparation for this one commandment.

R. Akiva's essential rule of this law of love is derived by Ben Azzai, his contemporary, from another biblical verse: "This is the book of the generations of Man. In the day that God created man, in the likeness of God made He him." (Gen. 5:1)[26] The cardinal point relates to the concept of humanity, the brotherhood of man. All people are created in the Divine Image, and only the belief in one God can lead to the affirmation of human love and the unity of mankind.

The stress Judaism places on love is to overcome separateness. In Kabbalah, man is described as possessing the *ratzon le-kabel*, the desire to receive, while God is described as the possessing *ratzon le-hashpia*, the desire to influence, to give. Man is thereby as separated from God as is one end of infinity from the other. The purpose of love is to change man into a *ratzon le-hashpia*, to bridge the gap and, finally, to reach unity with God, thereby overcoming this cosmic separateness. Love asks for faith, and faith for firmness. But love demands only love.

Love is an act of will, a decision to make a commitment. And although love needs no teaching, in the words of Fromm love is an art that must be learned. It requires practice. One does not just "fall into" love but must work at it; one must decide to make the mastery of the art of love his ultimate concern. In short, "To love somebody is not just a strong feeling—it is a decision, it is a judgment, it is a promise."[27] Love as a biblical commandment implies that it is an act of will, not chance. The additional commandment to love, and to have compassion for even one's enemy (Exod. 23:4–5), is proof that Judaism does not relegate love to the sphere of mere emotion. Even in marriage, Judaism adds to the emotional aspect, reason and judgment being necessary requirements for marital love. The ketubbah, the Jewish marriage document, which reads like a business contract, further supports this idea. It comes not to lower and debase emotional feelings but, rather, to raise the love, to add to it the quality of reason and judgment required in accepting obligations.

The ability to love is acquired by degree; it is a relative process without absolute standards. The complexity of a loving nature precludes generalizations. Experience and understanding, however, can help one to sense the types of lovable people who are capable of loving.

There is no love without bodily desire. There is no veneration and adoration of a being of the opposite sex which is entirely devoid of sexual components. A happy marriage is built on spirit, mind, and body.

Marriage can increase a person's ability to love and be loved, provided the personality was not badly damaged by a traumatic childhood. The knowledge of being loved increases one's feelings of security and one can thus give more of one's self in many different ways. A good marriage, therefore, can provide the proper ground, sanctioned both socially and religiously, to help develop the cycle of loving and being loved.

Brotherly love is based upon the experience of human unity. First, as implied in the commandment of "love thy neighbor as thyself" (Lev. 19:18), is the sense of equality. Second, remembering that all the commandments are merely a preparation for the one commandment of "love thy neighbor," is the demand for kavod ha-beriot, respect for others, which is the basis for love.[28] The biblical injunction "Thou shalt not avenge nor retain any grudge against the children of thy people" (Lev. 19:18) is cogently described by the Rabbis as the need to view all men as being one body composed of many limbs.[29]

The classic dictum by Hillel (end of 1st c. B.C.E.), the famous Tannaitic

Rabbi, stands out as a guiding beacon in human relations. "Do not do unto thy fellow what you would not have him do unto you."[30] Hillel's exhortation requests us to be loving and kind unto our fellow creatures and thus fulfill the word of God. The biblical statement regarding man and wife as becoming "one flesh" (Gen. 2:24) and the concept of "all Israel being bound up one to the other"[31] are further contentions that the experience of oneness is basic for true love, but Judaism also requires the need for self-respect as a basis for love. The biblical condemnation of suicide demonstrates strongly the need for self-respect.[32] Most striking, however, is the statement by Hillel, "If I am not for myself, who is for me; if I care only for myself, what am I?"[33] This points to the rabbinic requirement of a feeling of self-worth and self-reliance in order to enhance the good in others.

We therefore maintain that it is impossible to love someone else unless you show concern for yourself first. A normal degree of acceptable narcissism is required before one can manifest altruistic concern. Selfishness and self-love, far from being identical, are actually opposite. The selfish person is incapable of loving himself much, his own self-image being poor and unproductive. The Torah does not ask that you love anyone *more* than yourself but just *as much* as yourself—*kamokha*. And so, Hillel says, "Love your fellow creatures, for all mankind without distinction are the creatures of God.[34]

Therefore, Hillel paraphrased the biblical precept into "Whatever is hateful unto thee do it not to thy fellow." This rule he declared to be the whole Law, the remainder being but a commentary on this fundamental principle of the Torah. The prophets' sublime conception of universal morality is but an extension of the Torah's "Golden Rule," encompassing the unity and brotherhood of mankind.

The affirmation of this noble gift of God's love is a recurrent theme throughout the Bible where man-woman love is often used by the authors of the Scriptures to symbolize the *amor intellectualis Dei*—the rational love for God suffused with emotional adoration.

Among the rules of equity and human welfare, love is paramount. The Torah regulates our behavior and our humane intentions in our interpersonal relations. "And thou shalt do that which is right and good in the sight of the Lord . . ." (Deut. 6:18), meaning, you should act in such a way in which you feel that God, who is love Himself and calls you to love, would recognize it as good and as right in relation to your fellowman.

The Sages urge us not to be inflexible in the pursuits of our rights when dealing with others but equitable and correct. One ought to show readiness to renounce one's rights for the benefit of others as long as no personal loss is incurred. Only when through selfless devotion one actively contributes to the establishment of the happiness of his fellowmen does one truly become human in the image of God.[35]

Stendhal considers love "the miracle of civilization. There is nothing but a physical love of the coarsest kind among savages or barbarous peoples. Modesty gives love the food of imagination and therefore gives it life".[36]

The eyes of love look through the spectacles of beauty so that they can see only beauty, and overlook anything that is not beautiful. This self-persuasion involves autosuggestion. It puts out of sight, and enables one to overlook, insults and wrongs. Love means the ability to accept the faults of the beloved. One who sees defects in the love object and cannot overlook them does not really love.

It is good to love and to be loved but not in a possessive fashion. Tolerance of each other's shortcomings is part of love. In the words of Solomon, the biblical counselor, "Hatred stirs up strife, but love covers all transgressions" (Prov. 10:12) where the lover overlooks his beloved's faults through understanding forgiveness.

What then is love? The inclining and joining of two hearts together, writes R. Yedaiah Ha-Penini. In supplying emotional support reciprocally, the loving partners still preserve their individuality and independence. Better not to agree with your wife and love her than to agree with her and not love her. "Enjoy life with the wife you love, all the fleeting days of your life." (Eccles. 9:9)

Love is the most successful human attempt to escape loneliness. Without love, life would merely be something to be endured, not lived. Love is universal. It cuts across races, classes, creeds, color, and age. As a procreative energy, love is God's creation and gift to humanity and is guided by Him for the purposes of human welfare. Life would lose much richness, if not its savor, if humans could not experience this most sublime of emotions. "True love is the ripe fruit of a lifetime," says J. Lamartine.

The sense of spirituality, of mystical sanctity expressed in true love, as depicted in the Bible, was expounded in the hasidic literature. There are two kinds of love, says R. Israel Baal Shem Tov: love between man and his woman, which is of an intimate kind, for it is not becoming for a man to kiss his wife in the street but in privacy; and love between a brother and a sister, or a mother and her son, which is of an overt kind.[37]

The beginning of love between a man and his woman is confidential and private; while the love between a brother and sister is in the open.

This was also the simile of the poet in the Song of Songs:

> Oh that you were like a brother to me,
> that nursed at my mother's breast!
> If I met you outside, I would kiss you,
> and no one would scorn me. [8:1]

Rabbinic tradition attributes to King Solomon the authorship of the Song of Songs. He was inspired to compose it on the day when he had completed the building of the Holy Temple in Jerusalem. R. Akiva even went as far as to attribute the greatness of the day to its Song rather than to the Temple. "For all the biblical songs are holy, the Song of Songs is holy of holiest." Tradition has therefore interpreted the Song of Songs as the most sacred metaphor containing the reciprocal love and praise between God and Israel.[38]

The most difficult of all Torah commandments is the constant infinite love of God expressed in the *Shema,* recited twice daily by the Jew: "*Ve-ahavta et Ha-Shem Elokekha*"—"You are to love the Lord, your G-d." (Deut. 6:5) This love is not a compulsory command, for how can love be commanded? This love of G-d is the expression of the ever-present consciousness of God a Jew feels every moment of his life. It manifests the Jewish recognition of the Divine manifestation in all of man's endeavors, in his own existence as part of the universal design, as the crown of creation. It is love in its supreme form. The study of Torah and observance of the commandments are the ring of betrothal through which God sanctified Israel and obligated Himself to feed them and to sustain them.

The Hafetz Hayim in eulogizing his departed son told the following inspiring story. During the terrible pogroms of the barbarous Bogdan Chmelnitzky and his Cossack hordes in the Ukraine, a Jewish boy was murdered. He was the only child of his widowed mother. The poor bereft woman knelt over her child's dead body, looked up to Heaven, and exclaimed: "Master of the universe, until now half of my love was offered to you and half went to my son. Now that my son is dead, I offer *all* my love to you."

In genuine love, the lover abandons all thoughts of personal gain. True love is selfless. Without love there is neither faith nor hope. Love, and nothing else, is able to animate us to the full. The soul is not where it lives but where it loves.

God, who is the Source of Love, endowed the human being with this most sublime of emotions, which the mortal can fully give back to his Maker by sublimating his pleasures and passions into devotional service to God.

Such is the spiritual quality of the love expressed in the Song of Songs. Not to know love is not to live. Live to love and you will love to live. The lesson one can derive from love is to love better. The more you bring to love the more love brings to you. It is far more important, and there is more pleasure, in loving than in being loved.

> Set me as a seal upon your heart,
> As a seal upon thine arm;
> For love is strong as death,
> Jealousy is cruel as the grave;
> The flashes thereof are flashes of fire;
> A very flame of the Lord.
>
> [Song of Songs 8:6]

In these magic words depicting the heavenly love of the Jerusalem maiden to her beloved, she longs for his constant nearness. Loving with reservation is deceptive in the long run to both lover and beloved. Like the seal worn by the Oriental woman over her heart (or by the man upon his arm), she declares her eternal love, irresistible as death, which none can overcome (in European poetry, too, death is always linked to love). "And because of that love, seal me upon your heart and arm manifesting your love in deed, so that you do not forget me." (Rashi) For such love is supernatural, a magnificent flame.

> Many waters cannot quench love,
> Neither can the floods drown it;
> If a man would offer all the substance of his
>   home in exchange for love,
> He would be utterly condemned.
>
> [Song of Songs 8:7]

Nothing can destroy true love in its hearty spontaneity and abundance. Young love is mutually nurtured from the mind and from the heart, from the soul and from the spirit. Paradoxically, as a physical phenomenon, love is much more strongly excited by spiritual associations of the sexes, by expressions of emotions, thoughts, and words rather than by physical associations. It is all-embracing and is therefore all-demanding.

There were always love marriages in Israel based solely on the decision of the young pair, even if not always with the blessing of the parents. A youth need not obey his parents if they urge him to marry another girl, richer than the one he loves.[39] We know of young Jewish girls in biblical and postbiblical times, who, unlike their Near Eastern neighbors, were not always confined to the house, worked in the fields and vineyards, attended the cattle, worked outside as shepherdesses, and even had conversations with men within the accepted moral codes of their environment.

We can see that loving and being loved coexist harmoniously. For "When a man is intimate with his wife, the longing of the eternal hills wafts about them." What does this mean? It means that when a man loves a woman so that she is always with him, the commandment of human love is fulfilled. Martin Buber makes the same point when he writes: "The You of her eyes allows him to gaze into a ray of the eternal You."[40]

Harmony in marriage is a Divine reward. "He who loves his wife very dearly" (literally, as his own body), of him Scripture says: "And thou shalt know that thy tent is in peace." (Job 5:24)[41]

So important is love for woman in her marriage that "a woman prefers poverty with the love of her husband to riches without it."[42]

According to Freud, a woman submerges her total personality when in love, wishes to integrate completely with the love object, even at the expense of self-denial and ego dissolution.

Man does not find true fulfillment except in his love for his wife, when his emotional ties and love for his parents are transferred to her.[43]

Says R. Eliezer Papo: How good for a man to have a devoted friend. Someone with whom to take counsel and not rely on his own understanding, but he must be a faithful friend unto him and there is no one more faithful to a man than his wife. Therefore, it is said, "if your wife is 'short' bend down and speak to her," and he should be advised by her—a proper suggestion according to the Torah, to justice and fine logic.[44]

Such a concept was inconceivable to the Graeco-Roman culture. Through one of his fictitious characters, in his essay on love, Plutarch asserts that true love is impossible between man and woman. Greeks and Germans, who ascribed prophetical wisdom to women, reserved their love for their own sex.

Love, regardless of how ethereal it may appear, is so intimately related to all of life that it cannot be considered meaningfully as an abstraction. While sex and love are not identical, they are forever intertwined and understandable only when so related. "The blessing of the Lord is found only where there is a happy communion of man and woman."[45]

Sex is so inextricably related to the whole human psyche that it cannot be understood in isolation from the evolving human individual but only in the fullest interaction between two self-extending partners.

Saadiah Gaon (882-942) counsels husband and wife to be affectionate and love each other "for the sake of the maintenance of the world, as Scripture says: 'A lovely hind and a graceful doe, let her breasts satisfy thee at all times; with her love be thou ravished always.' " (Prov. 5:19) A husband should express "his desire for his wife in accordance with the dictates of reason and religion and to the extent required in order to bind them closely together."[46] Delicacy is to love what grace is to beauty. "Speak low," says Shakespeare, "if you speak love."

There is far more to the sexual experience than the gratification of a passing appetite or the pursuit of a casual pleasure. It is an expression of a deeper relationship that unites two people at every level of their existence. It involves commitment to each other in body, mind, and soul.

In his book *Vikuah al Ha-Ahavah* (*Dialoghi d'Amore*, a philosophic work dealing with the love of God), Yehudah, (Leone Ebreo) the physician, the son of Don Itzhak Abravanel (1460–1521), writes as follows:

It is obvious that the love of a husband and wife is pleasant; but it must be bound up with good too; which is the reason why a reciprocal love does survive the enjoyment of its delights, and, not only persists, but grows continually, through its participation in the good. Moreover, the good and pleasurable elements in married love are supplemented by that of advantage; for each of the spouses is ever deriving benefit from the other, which greatly contributes to the fostering of their love. Thus married love, being pleasurable essentially, is preserved by its connections with both advantage and good.[47]

Love is not a simple emotion but a complex of many emotions. Love is often compared with water: dammed up and unused it becomes stagnant; only when it flows is it fresh. So one partner not only meets one's self-regarding needs but also in depending on the other allows one's self to the other.

The act of loving is unconsciously motivated by the need to be loved—a predominant need in all human beings. In the instinct of love, which is innate in us, we really express man's *joie de vivre*—the underlying motive in all interpersonal expression of affection. Love is not just an external accompaniment but the very essence out of which life is fashioned.

Love is practical in allowing for each partner's deficiencies. Love is blind to defects, claims the Talmud.[48] Mature love acknowledges the right to individuality. Immature love is a neurotic form of dependency on each other. Some men expect to get from their wives in their adult life what they got from their mother as infants. These are the "eternal sucklings," as Stekel coined them, who expect in their adult infantilism to receive love instead of giving it maturely.

Giving is more joyous than receiving, not because it is a deprivation, but because in the act of giving lies the expression of one's aliveness.

Since the human being is born with the capacity to love, he must learn to cultivate this human flower and help it develop healthily. One must actually experience and feel love in order to understand it. One must experience it before one is able to perceive it in others. It must be felt and fully expressed, not just verbally, but by one's behavior, actions, and emotional relatedness to the other. Although love may be fully expressed even in complete silence, or in the dark, or merely by eyeing other one, "love at a distance, however, is only a fantasy, not a real experience. The desire for love becomes a passionate love only when it is sensually realized."[49]

From a psychoanalytic view, it is the father image woman seeks in her beloved, namely, the man in her father rather than the paternal element; thus she is reconstructing under the guise of adulthood an earlier situation as a little girl, without necessarily seeking a wishful reincarnation.

"Only in love can woman harmoniously reconcile her eroticism and her narcissism . . . these sentiments are opposed in such a manner that it is very difficult for a woman to adapt herself to her sexual destiny."[50] Love entails ignoring and forgoing oneself in favor of the love object, as illustrated by the talmudic maxim: "When our love [between me and my wife] was strong we both used to sleep together on the width of the sword; now that our love is not strong, a bed of sixty cubits does not suffice us."[51]

Once one develops the capacity to love, to share, and, above all, to give of oneself, love becomes unselfish and mature, embracing good-will, humane concern for the other, self-abnegation, and an offering of oneself on the altar of love. It is no longer self-protection of the grown-up child in us, motivated by selfishness and fear, but rather a total manifestation of altruistic concern and immersion with the other, of mutual contentment, vitality, and security in each other. Indeed, the final goal of human love, as in religion, is the living identification and cleavage with the loved one.[52]

Love is a product of the effort toward togetherness; it is not an accident, but comes through the mastery of one's desire, the acceptance of the sacredness of the partner's right to differ, and the mutual molding through respect and concern by means of the dialogue experience. It is, as such, an adventure in giving to each other, as the Mishnah clearly states: "If love depends on some selfish end, when the end fails, love fails; but if it does not depend on a selfish end, it will never end."[53] Kabbalah holds that in love is found the secret of Divine Unity,[54] for since Divinity Itself is the source of love, love is the best avenue to reach God.

It is noteworthy to point out that the verb *yadoa*—to know—in biblical Hebrew is used both in relation of man to God in the sense of a most intimate relationship and special selection (Amos 3:2, Ps. 1:6) and as the explanation for man's intimate love and union with woman. "And Adam knew Eve his wife." (Gen. 4:1) In this sense human love takes on spiritual meaning. As Buber explains:

One cannot divide one's life between an actual relation to God and an inactual relation (I-It) to the world. The encounter with God does not come to man in order that he may prove its meaning in action in the world. Action in the world is demonstrated by human love, the sphere between human beings.[55]

One rediscovers oneself and gains insight through genuine love, founded on mutual recognition. It is a transformation, rebirth, and revelation all at once. Traditional Judaism never conceived any other male-female relationship than through the institution of marriage based on love and companionship. "Man should love his wife as himself, and to honor her more than himself, and to show compassion to her, and to protect her as one would protect one of his limbs."[56]

Traditionally, a man's chief love was always given to his first wife. "Said R. Yochanan: When a man's first wife dies during his lifetime, it is as though the Temple had been destroyed in his lifetime. When a man's wife dies in his lifetime, the world becomes dark for him." The same holds true for the woman.[57]

One's first love was considered irreplaceable. "Everything can be replaced except the woman of your youth." Indeed, man finds contentment only with his first wife.[58]

The memory of one's first love persists even after another source of marital comfort takes its place. Should a man re-marry, he remembers the deeds of his first wife. Freud's contention is that the husband is, so to speak, never more than a substitute for the woman's first, beloved man, not that man himself. The reverse is just as true.

A touching example of the devotion and perseverance of a woman in love is illustrated in the following narrative about a wife who became the prototype of the famous wives of Weinsberg. The husband, though attached to her, had to divorce her according to the tradition of that time, which provided for divorce after ten years of childlessness. Before they separated, the husband, to prove his kind feelings toward his wife, allowed her to take along whatever she cherished most in the house. She took nothing, but while her husband was fast asleep, she had him carried on the couch on which he rested, into her parental home. He was so touched by her attachment that he did not divorce her and afterward they were blessed with children.[59]

Love remains the most enigmatic of life experiences.[60] For thousands of years, poetry and music have extolled it in all tongues, yet its essence remains undefinable.

5

Marriage and Matrimony

It is impossible for man [to live] without woman,
and it is impossible for woman [to live] without
man, and it is impossible for both [to live] without
the Divine Presence.

—*Yer. Berakhot* 9:1, 12

Marriage is a special association between two persons whose relationship is highly personalized, deeply significant, and profoundly influential upon the personality of each of them. Judaism assigns to marriage so high a value that it gives husband and wife a special status. They are members of a unique association, regardless of their individual natures.

Marriage is universal and is one of the oldest institutions of civilization. The peoples of antiquity had many customs, ceremonies, and special laws connected with this institution. Marriage assured protection of the family even in primitive life.

In both Israel and Mesopotamia, marriage had to be contracted formally. A written contract is mentioned in the Apocryphal story of Tobit (7:13). Marriage was well-established among the Jews in the Graeco-Roman era, although it is difficult to know its provenance. The custom existed in very early times in Mesopotamia, and the Code of Hammurabi declares that a marriage concluded without a formal contract is invalid.

49

There still exist several marriage contracts originating from the Jewish colony at Elephantine (5th c. B.C.E.). The Elephantine marriage contracts contain the formula pronounced at marriage made out in the name of the husband: "She is my wife and I am her husband from this day forever."[1] The woman herself made no declaration. In the Apocrypha, Sarah's father Reuel says to Tobit: "Henceforth, thou art her brother and she is thy sister." (Tobit 7:12 and 8:7)

The talmudic Sages were unusually perceptive of human behavior in general, but in the realm of marriage and family they show extraordinary insight. The family in general, and marriage and divorce laws in particular, were human psychological necessities. They took into account the emotional and psychological needs of the woman. The security, the conflicts, family rivalries, anxiety, the importance of the individual's adaptation to social realities, were all squared with the structure and framework of *halakhah*. The mental health of the woman was paramount in the *halakhah*. This can easily be seen in case after case discussed by the Gaonim in their responsa and in later rabbinic literature. This approach was not restricted to one local community but was universally applied.

Jewish tradition believes that "the union of man and woman is from God."[2] "Forty days prior to the conception of the infant, a heavenly voice proclaims, 'the daughter of so and so [is to be married] to so and so.' "[3]

Not only is the marriage Divine handiwork, for "to effect union between man and woman is as difficult as the dividing of the Red Sea,"[4] but the bride also is *Heaven-sent*—an idea that is enshrined in the wedding benediction: "Blessed art Thou, O Lord our God King of the universe, who hast made man in Thine image, after Thy likeness, and hast prepared unto him out of his very self a perpetual companion."

A Roman lady asked a Rabbi, "In how many days did the Holy One, blessed be He, create the universe?" "In six days," he answered. "What has He been doing since then up to the present?"—"He has been arranging marriages." "Is that His occupation? I, too, could do it. I possess many male and female slaves, and in a very short while I can pair them together." He said to her, "If it is a simple thing in your eyes, it is as difficult to the Holy One, Blessed be He, as dividing the Red Sea." He then took his departure. What did she do? She summoned a thousand male slaves and a thousand female slaves, set them in rows, and announced who should marry whom. In a single night, she arranged marriages for them all. The next day they appeared before her, one with a cracked forehead, another with an eye knocked out, and another with a broken leg. She asked them, "What is the matter with you?" One female said, "I don't want him." Another male said, "I don't want her." She forthwith sent for the Rabbi and said to him, "There is no God like your God and your Torah is true; what you told me is quite correct."[5]

Nevertheless, "man has free will in the choice of a proper wife," claims R. Judah Ha-Hasid, as suggested by the talmudic counsel offered on the subject.[6]

According to Mencken, "Marriage is the woman's proper sphere, her Divinely ordered place, her natural end. It is what she is born for, what she is trained for, what she is exhibited for."[7]

In Judaism, marriage is a primary religious duty. It is considered as important as the studying of the Torah, and one is even permitted to sell a Torah scroll, in order to marry off a daughter.[8]

The first biblical commandment, that "a man leave his father and his mother and cleave unto his wife, and they become one flesh," (Gen. 2:24) is interpreted by Rashi as being "the words of the Holy Spirit," meaning that this verse was not spoken by Adam but was the inspired comment of Moses, in order to instill the Jewish ideal of marriage as a unique tie that binds a man to his wife even closer than to his parents."[9] It is man whom Scripture enjoins to cleave to his wife, and not the woman, physically the weaker, who is to cleave to her husband. This shows that man's nature requires for its physical, spiritual, and social completion a wife—man's better self.

The biblical, as well as the talmudic and rabbinic, ideal of marriage is monogamy. This is derived from the biblical exegesis "a man shall cleave 'to his wife,' not to his wives."[10] Of all the Rabbis mentioned in Talmud (about 2800 in number), there is only one who is recorded as having had two wives.

Although the Pentateuch did not originally prohibit polygamy in early Jewish history, monogamy was still the ideal. This is reflected in the prophetic comparison of symbolically equating God's relation to Israel to that of a marriage—the classic ode dedicated to the industrious woman in Proverbs 31—and the admonition of the last prophet, Malachi, against bigamy, God being an ever-present witness of the marriage contract. (Mal. 2:14)

"If it had been fitting for Adam to have been given ten wives, the Lord would have given them to him. Yet, he gave him but one."[11]

The patriarch Abraham had, at first, only one wife, Sarah, and only because she was barren did he take, at Sarah's behest, her handmaid Hagar. (Gen. 16:1–2) This was the custom of the patriarchal period. According to Hammurabi, the husband may not take a second wife unless the first is barren, and he forfeited the right altogether if the wife herself gave him a slave as a concubine. The husband may himself take a concubine even if his wife has borne him children, but she never shares the same rights as the wife, and he may not take a second concubine unless the first one is barren.[12]

In the above instances there exists a state of monogamy, for there is never more than one lawfully wedded wife. These customs, though, were not always adhered to. Jacob married the two sisters Leah and Rachel, and their maids Bileah and Zilpah (Gen. 29:15–30; 30:1–9), while Esau had three wives of equal rank. (Gen. 26:34; 28:9; 36:1–5)

Isha was a general term used for wife and concubine. If the first wife had borne him no children, it devolved upon the husband to marry a second wife or take a concubine. In a polygamous family, laws were instituted to protect and equally provide both for the wives and their children without partiality.[13]

In Israel, under the judges and the monarchy, the old restrictions fell into desuetude. Gideon had "many wives" and at least one concubine. (Judg. 8:30–31) The kings were allowed eighteen, with the exception of King Solomon, who kept a larger harem.

It is noteworthy that the books of Samuel and Kings, which cover the entire period of the monarchy, as well as the Wisdom Books, record only a single case of bigamy among commoners (that of Samuel's father, at the very beginning of the period).[14]

Historically, monogamy was the general practice among Jews during the Second Commonwealth, and definitely was the practice of the Rabbis (the Tannaim, Amoraim, and Gaonim) during the talmudic and post-talmudic times, especially in the Ashkenazic communities.

In the year 1000, the Synod of Rabbenu Gershom Ben Judah of Mayence issued the prohibition on polygamy for the Ashkenazic communities, which is still in force today. This is the current law in the State of Israel, where it includes the Sephardic Jews as well.

To the Jews, marriage is both a social and religious institution, which serves a dual function:

1. That of building a home and family (Gen. 1:28) after the severance

from the parental umbilical cord, with the expected child as a sacred and central theme. Judaism saw in a prolific marriage, enriched with children, the perfect human creation, in the image of God, to build His-our world for posterity.[15]

2. That of developing companionship, by perceiving the woman as an *aizer kenegdo*, a life partner and helpmate of man in all his endeavors, in order "to become one" and to develop their personalities to the maximum of human fulfillment.

The Torah acknowledges the vital need for physical, emotional, and social companionship, whereby a person can find full psychophysical satisfaction and purpose in life and thereby function interpersonally as a partner with the Creator in bringing forth life and continuing creation. Such a relationship can exist only within the confines of a self-imposed marriage discipline, voluntarily and maturely accepted by mutual consent and respect—a human dialogue in mature understanding.[16]

The sociopsychological processes of marriage promoted by Judaism in the dynamics of achieving marital unity comprise integration, identification, differentiation, emulation, idealization, enhancement, and interhabituation, which help create a calm, even-functioning unity of thought and action in the long road of family adjustment.

THE FAMILY

The family occupies the primordial and central place in Judaism. Jewish tradition, beginning with the Bible, always emphasized the basic values in the formation of the Jewish family, stressing the character traits of those members of the family whose personality was imbued with the noble values of purity, sanctity, and stability.

The family is a kaleidoscopic projection of the varied aspects of the larger Jewish family in its historical setting, and its national, cultural, and ethicoreligious reactions to the legalistic discipline imposed upon the family by the Divine Law. Thus, the purity and stability of the Jewish family acted as a safeguard against sexual immorality. They enhanced woman's position to the status of matron of the house. Though different in her activities from man, the woman was equal to him as far as the community welfare and filial respect were concerned—as a "Divine blessing" to man.

In the intimate encounter between man and woman it is only under the cloak of marriage that there can be true reverence for the mystery, dignity, and sacredness of life.

The Jewish family life was imbued with sincerity, fidelity, and purity, both literally and figuratively. Premarital chastity is an old but still valid element of the Jewish ideal of marriage, whereby a new and lasting relationship is to be built on the foundation of a tabula rasa, both sexually and emotionally, for a spiritual communion of body and soul and for the integrity of the family unit. In this sense the greatest institution of life was solemnized "according to the Law of Moses and Israel," in the name of the Lord, and has served to determine and preserve the values of the Jewish society as a primary socializing agency.

The Jewish family was always viewed as a very stable group. The early patriarchal pattern of life in the agricultural, rural family, was always depicted as incomplete and unwholesome without the "help-mate"—the God-given woman. Kabbalah calls the unmarried man *palgo gufo* (half a body), for "Man is not even called 'man' till united with woman."[17]

Traditionally, the very first of the 613 commandments given to the Jews is "Be fruitful and multiply" (Gen. 1:28)—the first Divine blessing bestowed upon mankind by God. The family is the vehicle through which this command is accomplished. The sacredness and centrality of the child in Judaism rests upon this first commandment to build a family. The roles of reproduction and of socializing the child in the ways of society are basic familial functions, the latter entrusted to the woman according to Jewish Law.[18]

Today's American family has undergone transition and has experienced the loss of many traditional functions. As shown by Parsons and Bales, only two basic duties prevail: "First, the primary socialization of children so that they can truly become members of the society into which they have been born; second, the stabilization of the adult personalities of the population of society."[19]

In contrast to the Greek's attitude toward woman, the Jew regarded the Jewish woman as the ruler of the household, the dominant, central figure of influence and love. A wife is not a man's shadow or subordinate but his other self, similar and equal, his "helper," in a sense in which no other creature on earth can be. Woman was not formed from the dust of the earth but from man's own body. We have here a wonderfully conceived allegory designed to set forth the moral and social relation of the sexes. From this stems woman's dependence upon man and the close relationship between the two.

The woman was formed out of the man's rib; hence it is the wife's duty to be near and ready to be a "help" to her husband; it is the husband's duty to cherish and defend his wife always, as part of his own self, since "a wife is like a man's own being."[20]

It is neither sovereignty nor unmitigated imperiousness for the husband that Judaism requires; neither a relationship of master-slave, nor of subjugator and subjugated. Woman is an equal, to be treated with love, care, respect, and devotion by the man, which are to be continuously manifested throughout marriage. Numerous dicta and teachings advocating such a positive relationship to one's wife reflect the Rabbis' appreciation for the esteem and worthiness of the woman.

The Rabbis require the Jewish husband to eat and drink less than his means allow, clothe himself in accordance with his means, and honor his wife and children above his means. He is requested to economize but to buy her nice clothes, jewels, perfumes, and other cosmetics to please her, and also to attempt to placate his wife in order to maintain shalom bayit—marital harmony. R. Helbo said: "Be careful about the honor of your wife, for blessing enters the house only because of the wife. Honor your wife, that you may become enriched."[21]

R. Hanilay said: "A man who has no wife lives without good, without peace. Of him who loves his wife as himself and honors her more than himself, and brings up his sons and daughters rightly, and marries them early, Scripture says: 'Thou knowest that thy tent is in peace.' " (Job 5:24)[22]

Since God created man and woman "in His image," both are spiritually akin to God. They are alike in terms of the reverence and respect due them by their children.[23]

A prime link in the Jewish chain of Tradition, the family unit is not merely a social creation for the circumscription of sex and for the provision of an orderly method of procreation. It is the result of a Divine command, and, therefore, sanctified.

The harmony of man and woman in the marital bond is but a reflection of the unity of God, who planned this very unity of nature.[24]

Marriage is called "the building of joy" in the Talmud and is therefore accompanied by ceremonial festivity. Marriage, from a Jewish perspective, was never just a civil contract but, rather, a Divine institution where reverence, true dignity, and mutual rights and obligations were elevated above the arbitrary will of the two partners.

Whereas in a civil contract these rights and obligations evolve from an agreement by the parties, in a Jewish marriage these are determined and imposed by religious morality and the civil law. This represents a high duty and conscience, the continuation of the Divine process of creativity.

Love, family, and the mating instinct are outstanding features of marriage. Sex and the manifestations of the sex instinct are the pillars upon which marriage was established. Marital happiness depends to a large degree upon sexual adjustment, which, in turn, is related to sexual responsiveness.[25]

A marriage divested of its spiritual aspect is beneath human dignity, and without its physical dimension, beyond human purpose and power. If either side is lacking or inadequate, the marriage bond is in peril.

Tradition claims that among those "banned by heaven is a Jew who has no wife and he who has a wife but [wants] no children."[26]

Halakhah considers the sexual drive of the partners a natural part of life. It therefore channeled this craving, allowing the libidinal drive to find full expression in a disciplined order, the Jewish *regimen sanitatis*, thereby enhancing the *homo orgiasticus* and elevating him to a sublime state of *homo spiritualis*. Judaism called for the *sanctification of life:* so that one can become a "partner with God in the creation of the universe," in the process of *imitatio Dei.*[27]

Marriage thus became a self-imposed duty, a religious obligation in the process of God—man partnership. By building a home, sharing love, rearing children in a familial atmosphere of affection and respect, man contributes to the welfare of humanity and society.

Marrying a woman from among one's kith and kin was an ancient and highly desirable custom, which was adhered to for generations and still exists.

Ample evidence in the book of Genesis indicates that, among the patriarchs, marriage between uncle and niece, between nephew and aunt, and especially between cousins was frequently entered into and preferred to marriage with women outside the family. It would seem that cousinly marriages may have been preferred because of the desire to preserve property within the family.

Under Mosaic Law, marriage between certain relatives was prohibited under severe penalty. Although reasons are not given in every case, the tenor leads us to believe that the prohibitions were moral rather than biological. The source of the prohibitions may be the woman in her three roles of mother, sister, daughter. One may not marry a woman with whom one has had a relationship that is incompatible with marital union and is classified as incestuous—*arayot.* (Lev. 18:20)[28]

Great emphasis is placed on the sexual purity of men and women, and this pertains to the period before and after marriage. Premarital sex was never sanctioned in Judaism: "An unmarried man who has sexual relations with an unmarried woman with no matrimonial intention renders her thereby a harlot." Instead, the Rabbis insisted on early well-planned marriages; they discouraged any disparity in age; they approved sexual needs only within the framework of marriage.[29]

From biblical times, a Jew, in selecting a bride, was exhorted to consider carefully not only the bride's personal qualities, such as intelligence, character, and personality traits, but also such factors as her family provenance, status and position, hereditary traits, mental and physical health, upbringing, and education.

"A man should try to marry a woman of a good family, who enjoys an honorable and unblemished reputation. He must not think of the woman's beauty only, but of the quality of her acts. A woman's supreme beauty is not in her face, but in her fair and just deeds."[30] That is why the wise men have repeatedly warned against marrying a woman solely for her beauty. "Many a wealthy home has been ruined by folly, while a good and intelligent woman, though poor, enriches a house."[31] In the words of Joseph ibn Kaspi (1297–1340): "When you are twenty years of age build thy house, marry a wife of good family, beautiful in form and character. Pay no regard to money, for true wealth consists of a sufficiency of bread to eat and raiment to wear."[32]

The high regard in Judaism for the family is well known, and this also asserts the religious truth that a proper marriage is based on the harmony of souls and character, both mentally and emotionally, as expressed in both halakhah and aggadah.

Marriage, then, is more than a physical, natural, or socially legal union. It is a sacred relationship between husband and wife sanctioned by God Himself. This is evident in the Hebrew concept of kiddushin, the term for marriage, denoting a sacred union or a hallowed state of dedication and matrimonial living, sanctifying and preserving that which had been made in His image.[33] The sacredness of marital togetherness harks back to the very birth of Judaic society, being part of the design of Creation.

When R. Akiva referred to the command "Thou shalt love thy neighbor as thyself," he declared that it was a fundamental principle of the Torah. He proclaimed universal love not merely as the ideal advocated in the Torah but as the only true standard of human relationships. Two corollaries of this rule require one to "Let your fellowman's honor be as dear to you as your own" and to "Let the property of your fellowman be as dear to you as your own."[34] How much more so does the precept of human love find its fulfillment in the natural union between man and woman—the most comprehensive emotional and moral principle with the direct involvement of the Divine. "If man and woman," claims R. Akiva, "have merit, the *Shekhinah* is between them; if they do not have merit—fire consumes them." (Rashi explains that God has divided his name *Yod-Hei*, by placing the letter *yod* in the middle of the word *ish* (man) and the letter *hei* at the end of the word *isha* (woman); if discord separates the couple, the Lord removes His name from them, which changes the words into *eish ve-eish*—meaning destructive fire).[35]

After God created man, He did not comment, as He did with His other acts of creation, that the creation was *ki tov*—good. Perfection of man, as implied, is not possible within him alone but rather in conjunction with his wife. Only then is the word *tov* (good) to be applied: when both man and wife complement each other's functions.

R. S. R. Hirsch offers an interesting interpretation of the expression *aizer ke-negdo*. *Aizer* means to help, as well as to restrict and limit (*atzor*). Hence the purpose of the woman is to help her husband by relieving him of some of his obligations, thereby enabling him to concentrate his time and efforts on Torah. This help is neither jointly with nor against him—but opposite and parallel to him on a footing of equal independence, functioning in areas that are uniquely hers.

In the same vein, R. Aha notes: "If a man marries a godly wife, it is as though he had fulfilled the whole Torah from beginning to end."[36] We thus see how a compatible match of two loving partners in the spirit of the Torah brings with it the grace of Heaven and the spiritual fulfillment of the Law.

Special importance was placed on proper mating and compatibility, for there were also cases of ill-mating. "In Palestine they used to ask a man when married: 'Findeth or find?' (*matza* or *motze*). *Findeth*, because it is written, 'whoso findeth a wife, findeth a great good' (Prov. 18:22); *find*, because it is written, 'And I find more bitter than death the woman.' " (Eccles. 7:26)[37]

The most important consideration in the *shiddukh* (matchmaking) was the "crown of Torah" worn by the bridegroom—as suggested: "A man should sell everything that he has in order to marry the daughter of a scholar [*talmid hakham*], and his daughter to a scholar." Marrying an ignoramus (*am ha-aretz*) was considered a shameful calamity[38].

Compatibility in terms of unfit family provenance was a strong consideration in marriage counseling of the youth. Rabbah bar Bar Hanah said: "He who takes a wife who is not fitting for him, the Writ stigmatizes him as though he had ploughed the whole world and sown it with salt" (being ashamed of the unseemly marriage, one will try to conceal it) . . . "He who marries a wife who is not fit for him, Elijah binds him and the Holy One, Blessed be He, flagellates him."[39]

Although rank and family status were stressed, one was discouraged from marrying a wife of superior rank, for a man should rather "go down one step [in the scale of rank] in choosing a wife"[40] (Rashi: lest she shouldn't accept you and dominate you).

Tradition declares: "There are four motives in choosing a bride: Some marry for physical pleasure; some for social prestige; some for material advantage; and some marry for the glory of Heaven [rearing a family]—only the latter will find satisfaction." And "whoever marries a woman for the name of Heaven, the text ascribes to him as though he had begotten her: and "his children will redeem Israel."[41]

Marriage is certainly in harmony with reason, if the desire for physical union is not engendered solely by bodily beauty but also by the desire to beget children and bring them up wisely.[42]

The child represents the link between man and wife, a living witness to their love, a symbol of rejuvenation, and the immortality of the human race.

Judaism has always aimed at the propagation of healthy children, and various laws pertaining to the eugenic side of the family include preventive devices to ensure a more robust, healthy-minded, and physically sound community.

Hereditary traits were very important to the Rabbis. One was warned against marrying a person of ill-repute or who suffered from mental illness, epilepsy, leprosy, or other deficiencies, for eugenic reasons.[43]

For the same reason, R. Eliezer ben Pedat recommends that one "marry into a good family to insure good offspring." "A girl of good stock, though poor and an orphan, is worthy to marry a king."[44]

The Bible gives no specific information about nubility. (Gen. 29:26) It seems certain that girls, as well as boys, were married very young. Therefore it is quite understandable that the parents made all the decisions in the arrangement of a marriage; the girl's consent, however, was required. With the exercise parental authority, the feelings of the young couple were always considered.[45]

In discussing the marrying age, the Talmud considered both human nature—the sexual urge—and the groom's life commitment to the study of Torah.

Celibacy was uncommon and strongly condemned in Judaism. "When a bachelor attains the age of twenty and is still unmarried, he incurs God's displeasure, for all his days are spent in sinful thoughts." It is, therefore, to avoid such Divine discontent that one is advised, ideally, to marry at eighteen.[46] That early marriages were in vogue in the Middle East we know from parallel Oriental sources of the neighboring countries around Israel. This custom is still maintained by the Sephardic communities today.

A story is told of Rav Hisda, who said: "The reason that I am superior to my colleagues is that I married at sixteen (so that my mind was not filled with impure thoughts)." In fact, early age was actually advised by Raba, who said to R. Nathan Bar Ammi: "Whilst your hand is yet upon your son's neck (while you have influence on him) marry him off, viz., between sixteen and twenty-two. Others state, between eighteen and twenty-four."[47]

Another rationale for marrying young was to enable the couple to teach their grandchildren Torah. "You shall make them known to your children and children's children; we must marry early that we may teach our children's children."[48]

The custom of early marriages was also motivated by economic reasons. As long as the Jews were farmers, and needed people to till the soil, an early marriage brought a greater number of children into the family, who when grown, are available to work the land. Practical considerations rather than religious requirements, therefore, led to this custom of child marriages.

Postponement of marriage was permitted to students of the Law, who consecrated their life to the study of Torah, so that they might fully concentrate on their learning, free of marital worries.

A case like that of Ben Azzai, who never married because of his total dedication to Torah, was unique indeed.[49]

The wives of the scholars were credited with the merit of their husband's learning of Torah and were awarded a share in it. "There are the wives of the scholars (*talmidei hakhamim*) who chase the sleep from their eyes (sitting up all night and waiting for their husbands' return from the *Bet Hamidrash*) in this world and achieve thereby the life of the world to come."[50]

Nevertheless, the above pronouncements as to the duty and age of marriage did not always regulate practice. Maimonides counsels that one ought to prepare himself, both intellectually and materially, before he entertains the responsibility of marriage. "The Torah taught us proper conduct: (Deut. 20:5–7) first a man should build a home, plant a vine-yard [prepare himself professionally], and afterwards should he marry."

"It is the way of men of wisdom that one first acquires an occupation giving him a livelihood, and secures living quarters, and only then takes a wife; but an immature person begins by marrying a wife; then, if he is able, he acquires a house, and only in his later years, he looks for an occupation, or else lives on charity."[51]

Parents were obligated to marry off both their sons and their daughters in accordance with Ben Sirah's advice: "Marry your daughter and sorrow will depart from your house, but bestow her upon a man of understanding."[52] Parents were advised to consider the compatibility of the prospective groom in terms of his age and his status. "The Lord will not pardon him who marries his daughter to an old man, or takes an elderly wife for his minor son."[53] Similarly, a father was exhorted not to let his daughter grow old in his house but to find her a husband as soon as she is ready for marriage. "Your daughter has matured—marry her off" because "it is fobidden to leave her unmarried after she has matured." The Sages considered marrying a girl (ketanah) before she attains the childbearing age as sinful.[54]

Furthermore, one could avail himself of the services of the match-maker (shadkhan) or a shaliah as a matrimonial agent. Matchmaking was practiced among many peoples and has had a venerable history among Jews, especially in the Middle Ages and in shtetl life, up to modern mechanized forms of computerized pairing. It also served a useful social pupose and was popular in talmudic times and thereafter. The status of the shadkhan as a professional was acknowledged by the takanot of the community, which also specified the exact remuneration for his services.[55]

It is from the attitude of modesty that the institution of shadkhanut developed during the Middle Ages, to facilitate the process of marriage through an intermediary who brings the bridegroom and bride together and helps negotiate the agreement to be incorporated in the betrothal contract—the tenayim.

The issue of modesty, or tzeniut, is possibly one of the reasons why the Bible entrusted the father with the right to betroth and marry off his minor daughter; hence the father, not the girl, is the contracting party. If a minor, after her father's death, has been given in marriage by her mother or brother(s), for the sake of placing her under a reliable and often loving husband, she has the right to repudiate this contract before two witnesses and be freed without a bill of divorce (*get*). Thus the Law gave full free choice to a girl when reaching her majority (at the age of twelve years and one day) to chose her own life partner, to protest and to annul a marriage contracted during her minority without her true consent. This annulment of marriage is called *mi'un*.

Since, originally, daughters were given into marriage by fathers almost before the girls attained their maturity, and without the full, conscious consent of the bride, and without the bridegroom's having seen his chosen, Rab (3rd. c.) "forbade the solemnization of a marriage which had not been preceded by a courtship, and enjoined fathers not to marry their daughters without the consent of the latter. A woman is permitted to marry her chosen partner over her father's protest."[56]

The full, conscious agreement of the young couple was mandatory. (Gen. 24:58) Deeds of betrothal and marriage may not be written except with consent of both parties. The Rabbis deduce from the biblical text on the betrothal of Rivkah to Itzhak that a woman cannot legally be given away in marriage without her consent. A father is obligated to wait until she comes of age and says: "This is the man of my choice."[57]

The custom of betrothal existed in early Israel. The verb *aras*, meaning engagement or betrothal, occurs eleven times in the Bible.

Legal texts show that engagement was a recognized custom with juridical consequences, similar to the state of marriage.[58]

In postbiblical times, betrothal *in absentia* of the parties became valid only when a couple had previously met. For a man may not betroth a woman before he sees her, lest he later find in her a blemish and then she will repel him, whereas the All-Merciful said: "But thou shalt love thy neighbour as thyself." (Lev. 19:18)[59]

Identification and recognition of the bride was, as noted, a prerequisite to betrothal. In this respect, it is recorded: "A scholar (*talmid hakham*) who desires to betroth a woman, should take with him a layman (*am ha-aretz*) who is accustomed to look at women and knows about them), for a scholar is not in the habit of taking note of a woman's appearance."[60] (Rashi)

From Glückel of Hameln's diary (1645–1724) we get a picture of how parents used to match their children and plan their wedding. Milk and honey were served to the bride and groom at the betrothal meal at the groom's home, based on the verse in Song of Songs (4:11): "Honey and milk are under your tongue."

Explanations are in order while we consider the institutions of betrothal—erusin and marriage—nissuin, or kenissah (home taking), during the Second Commonwealth, since these concepts were quite different in ancient times.

1. Erusin, or the betrothal ceremony, comprises kiddushin (consecration) and was considered a formal act by which the woman became legally the man's wife, except in regard to sexual intercourse and some pecuniary modifications.

2. Nissuin, or kenissah, was the actual marriage or home taking, when the husband took (lakah, or nassa) his bride, through physical union at the nuptial celebration, and brought her from her father's home into his own home. It is this act that marked off the nissuin, or marriage proper, from the erusin or betrothal. This was preceded by the bride's receiving the ketubbah, or the marriage contract, from the bridegroom. Hence we discern, during talmudic times, two separate stages, though very closely allied, preceding married life: (1) erusin and (2) nissuin, or the kenissah. In posttalmudic times the almost universally accepted custom was to combine the erusin and the kiddushin under the huppah at the nissuin—the wedding ceremony.

Kiddushin is a sacred spiritual trust entered into between the bride and groom to be united in conjugal happiness and love in the spiritual holiness of their new home, the mikdash meat—or the sanctuary of love.

Just as the unmarried woman of the Bible and in the Orient was under the authority of her father, so the married woman was under the authority of her husband. A wife was listed among her man's or baal's possessions.[61] The custom of buying off the bride from her father involved the mohar—the traditionally required payment—in addition to the mattan—the voluntary gifts presented to the bride at betrothal. (Gen. 34:12) Originally, mohar and mattan were both paid in cash yet were clearly distinct from each other: Mohar was given to the father, a legal and compulsory remuneration, expressing the financial side of marriage, while mattan was the gift given to the bride, a voluntary and social act, symbolizing, perhaps, the romantic element of the union.[62]

In early biblical times a man could substitute service for the payment of the mohar, as Jacob did for both his marriages, to Leah and Rachel; or by accomplishing an appointed task, as David did for Michal, and Othniel for Caleb's daughter.

This money, or its equivalent, given to the bride's family, obviously gave the Israelite marriage the appearance of a purchase. *Mohar,* though, far from a price paid for the woman, was a compensation given to the family. The husband acquires a right over his wife, but the woman herself is not bought or sold.

A man was expected to request the hand of his bride from her father. Indigent men, in later times, were frequently forced into bachelorhood and celibacy because of poverty when the payments by the adolescent bridegroom to the bride's father were impossible. Hence many of the young men were barred from marrying. To remove this barrier to marriage, Shimon ben Shatah (1st C. B.C.E.) instituted a reform by substituting the customary purchase price of the cash *mohar* with a nominal marriage token—the *perutah* plus a note of indebtedness for the rest, to be paid only if the marriage is dissolved through death or divorce. Such an arrangement came into effect only with the woman's acceptance.

With this enactment, the *mohar* was transformed into a divorce price instead of a marriage price. (In order "that he may not be able to divorce her at his whim.")[63] Another reason for the payment of the *mohar* at the dissolution of the marriage was *mishum hina*—to offer the woman some financial position to enable her to remarry (R. Hananel), or to make the hazards of marriage less poignant to the woman (Rashi). The *kesef kiddushin*—or the coin of the value of at least a *perutah* given to the bride at betrothal—was later substituted by the ring, or *tabaat kiddushin*—which, historically, is the symbolical cash *mohar.*[64]

This provision, though, did not always resolve the problem, because of the precarious economic situation of the period. This instability led to the custom of having the bride help support her husband, if he was a worker or artisan, or reverse the role of provider and sole supporter of her Torah-learning husband, as in the case of R. Akiva, and Ben Azzai.[65] This way of life is still prevalent in Orthodox American and Israeli societies, where the young husband spends his time learning at the *Kollel,* while his young wife is at work.

On the other hand, when the husband simply indulged in idleness at the expense of his wife's labor, he was strongly reproached, as Ben Sirah remarks: "When a woman maintains her husband he is an object of anger, of reproach and of shame." (Ben Sirah 25:22)

Another compromise to overcome the economic hardships affecting the marriage institution was the adoption of the custom of taking the husband into the bride's parental home for at least a year, instead of requiring him to provide her with a new home, which he could not afford. This arrangement later evolved into the institution called *kest*, known so well during the *shtetl* period in Eastern Europe.

The period of betrothal lasted for twelve months. "A virgin is given 12 months . . . to prepare her marriage outfit."[66] During this time she lived with her father, but she was considered legally married although she was not allowed to dwell with her husband until she was taken from her father's home, after the wedding, to her husband's. Infidelity on her part at this time was considered adultery. If the betrothal was broken, she could not go free without the bill of divorce, and if the husband died during the *erusin* period, she fell subject to laws of levirate, i.e., betrothed to the oldest brother of the deceased.

The levirate marriage, an ancient custom, was already practiced in various forms by other primitive societies and is found in the Hittite laws, among the Hurrites of Nuzu, Ugaritic literature,[67] and ancient Indo-Europeans, Indians, Persians, Greeks and Romans, but is not mentioned in the Hammurabi code. It was the technical name (*levir* in Latin is a husband's brother) for the marriage with the widow of a childless brother (*yibum*). The widow is called *yebamah*, her brother-in-law *yabam*. The purpose of this marriage was to obviate what was regarded as calamitous: the family line becoming extinct, a man's name perishing, and his property going to others. By having the surviving brother of the childless deceased, or any agnate—even the father or a remote kinsman—marry the widow (*yebamah*), an heir of this levirate marriage was deemed the son, not of the natural father, but of the deceased brother, to whose inheritance he succeeded.

The biblical source for the levirate institution is Deuteronomy 25:5–10, and this institution survived among Jews to postexilic times.[68] The Bible allows the *yabam* to refuse to take her to wife, an act considered disgraceful in ancient times. The *yabam* then has to submit to the ceremony of untying (*halitzah*). This ritual consists of the removal of the *yabam*'s shoe by the childless widow in front of the *Bet Din*. The *yebamah* rebukes him and says: "So shall it be done to the man who does not build up his brother's house." (Deut. 25:5-9) *Halitzah* frees the *yebamah* to remarry outside her husband's family, while the surviving brother, who was slated to marry her, could evade the duty of such a union. In his default, however, he suffered public disgrace.

Theoretically, *yibum* is still presumed to be obligatory—for a variety of reasons—already from the Amoraic period and even after the formal excommunication of all polygamists by Rabbenu Gershom in the year 1000. But, practically, levirate marriage was inadvisable, and *halitzah* became the accepted practice among the great majority of observing Jews.[69]

In ancient times, dowry was considered to be the daughter's share inherited from her father. Sons succeeded their fathers; daughters left him. Upon leaving her father, the daughter received her share of the inheritance in lieu of succession, as a parting gift—[called in early Hebrew, *shiluhin*], already mentioned in the Bible (Gen. 24:59; 29:24, 29; 1 Kings 9:16) and by Philo. Dowry was also considered in postbiblical times a parental obligation that helped to enhance the girl's chances for marrying. The talmudic term *nedunyah*, or *nadan* (from the Assyrian *nudnu* meaning "dowry"), referred to a bride's outfit and household equipment given by her father.[70] The board and maintenance, or *kest*, was sometimes included in the *nedunyah*, to enable the young groom to continue his talmudic studies at the Yeshiva.

In Hebrew terminology, dowry is called *nikhsei tzon-barzel* (iron flock)—in Roman law, *pecus ferreum*—meaning iron security, *nedunyah*, or *shum*; while the private possessions of the bride are termed *nikhsei melog*, *parapherna*, or *usufruct*. The *nedunyah*, which is entered into the marriage deed, the *ketubbah*, is conveyed under terms of tenancy to the groom; the *nikhsei melog* is given to the bride and does not figure in the *ketubbah*.

From the *melog*, the husband had only the usufruct without any rights to the capital, or any privileges without the wife's free consent. She could freely and independently dispose of her own property *melog* which she received as a wedding gift or any other private property she may have had prior to her betrothal, after betrothal, or after marriage. A restriction was introduced at the end of the Second Commonwealth, whereby "the property acquired by the wife after nuptials, if she sold it, the husband can claim back from the purchaser."[71]

The property given to the daughter by her father varied with the financial means of the family. It may be noted that a Jewish woman, Ernestine Rose, initiated a petition to the New York legislature in 1837 to give married women property rights and appeared before that body to fight for the passage of a liberalizing statute. In contrast with the enfranchized citizen of our day, a married woman, then, both in the United States and in the rest of the world, had little independent standing in the law. Her property, earnings, and children belonged to her husband. This fight continued for years until Mrs. Rose finally succeeded in inducing the legislature of New York to enact a law that conceded the married woman legal rights to her own property.[72]

One of the oldest institutions of great socioreligious merit, particularly after the Bar Kokhba period, was the charitable provision for needy brides which came from the community fund named *Hakhnasat Kallah*. Throughout the Middle Ages and till our day, there was hardly a Jewish community without such a charity provision for the bride; indeed, "To walk humbly with thy God" (Mic. 6:8) refers to dowering a bride for her wedding. Moreover, the dowry of an orphan bride was the responsibility of the community, which used to tax its Jewish members for this highly worthy cause.

The communal legislation of Hamburg and Altona, in 1726, adopted regulations to enable an indigent father to secure a dowry for his daughter. Help for needy young women to obtain a dowry was arranged by public collections, which held the *mitzvah* on the same level with that of redeeming captives.[73]

A marriage ceremony was conducted by R. Moshe Isserles of Cracow (1525–1572) (the RaMa—codifer and foremost commentator of the *Shulhan Arukh*) against the written traditional prohibition of having a wedding ceremony performed on the Sabbath. The bridegroom refused to go to the prepared *huppah* until given, in advance, the full dowry. As the Sabbath drew near, the rabbi finally convinced him to spare his bride, a poor Jewish orphan, the shame and public insult, since she had no dowry; and to enter the *huppah* immediately.

In validating the case, R. Moshe Isserles quotes Rabbenu Yaakov Tam in his responsum, and R. Moshe of Coucy (SeMaG),

> that in times of great emergency, marriage is permitted on Sabbath. There can be no greater emergency than this case in which a grown orphan girl was being put to shame. It would be a lifelong disgrace for her, enough to set her apart from all other girls. Great, indeed, is the commandment to be considerate of the honor of human beings (*Ber.* 19b) . . . The rabbinical prohibitory decrees were not meant to apply in times of emergency, and on this we stand. . . .[74]

The marriage contract, *ketubbah*, written in Hebrew and Aramaic, contains the obligations between husband and wife. It refers also to the settlement and provision for the widow, called *mezonot*, and for the payment of alimony to the divorced wife as agreed to and fixed before marriage. This is in addition to the voluntary allocation by the man of the *tosefet*—the supplementary divorce settlement—and to the return of the *nedunyah*—the dowry which the wife had brought to marriage.

Thus the *ketubbah* consists of three parts: *yikar ketubbah*, *tosefet*, and *nedunyah*. The *ketubbah* was instituted as a safeguard for the woman against hasty divorce.

The minimum settlement for a virgin was 200 zuz, and for a remarrying widow, 100 zuz. This may have originated from the biblical custom of the bridegroom paying the bride's father the "marriage indemnity for virgins." (Exod. 22:16)

The lack of a *ketubbah* at the marriage ceremony invalidates the sexual union thereafter. The *ketubbah* is given by the bridegroom to the bride at the wedding. It must be permanently kept by the bride, and, if lost, a drawing up of another such contract, signed by two witnesses, called *ketubbah deirchasei* (a lost marriage deed), is required.[75]

The *ketubbah*, then, is a legal protection for the bride, to whom the bridegroom, among other obligations, pledges:

> ... Be my wife according to the law of Moses and Israel, and I will work for you and maintain you in accordance with the custom of the Jewish husbands, who toil for their wives, honor, maintain and support them in integrity.[76]

The development of a meaningful man-woman relationship is intimately related to the patterns of courting and/or dating which people pursue. Dating was not always important since, in the past, young people began their relationship by courting rather than dating. Where marriages are agreed upon by the persons directly involved, rather than by their families (as in the Orient), the society must make some provision for premarital association and for mate selection.

Courting, which was expected to result in marriage, was under the rigorous control of the family, neighborhood, and tradition. In biblical times the harvest season was the time earmarked for the young men to choose their maidens in the vineyards, as when the Benjaminites captured the dancing daughters of Shiloh. (Judg. 21:23) We find patriarchs and leaders such as Jacob, Moses, David, and others courting their beloved ones.

In seeking out a mate, social aggressiveness is required to initiate such an encounter. In civilized societies it is a man who aggressively seeks out the woman and not vice versa. It was always the custom for the man to court the woman. The only instance in the Bible of a woman taking the initiative is that of Mikhal, King Saul's daughter who fell in love with David. (1 Sam. 18:20) The Talmud rationalized the male initiative in saying: "Normally, a man seeks after a wife, and it is not the way of a woman to seek out a husband; whoever loses an article goes out in search for it. The man must ask the woman to be his wife, and not the reverse, because it is the man who sustained the loss of his rib, and so he sallies forth to make good his loss again."[77]

During the Second Commonwealth, we are told of a specific courting season, and of marriage proposals twice a year, when, through public dances, Jewish maidens had the opportunity of being freely sought by their suitors and, in kind, of freely giving themselves in marriage, on the Fifteenth of Av and the Day of Atonement. These days were considered holidays. The Mishnah claims:

> There never were in Israel greater days of joy than the Fifteenth of Av and Yom Kippur [at the conclusion of the fast and promise of Divine forgiveness]. On these days the daughters of Jerusalem used to walk out in white garments, which they borrowed in order not to put to shame anyone who had none. The daughters of Jerusalem came out and danced in the vineyards exclaiming at the same time, "young man, lift up thine eyes and see what thou choosest for thyself." The beautiful among them called out, "set thine eyes on beauty for the quality most to be prized in woman is beauty"; those of them who came of noble families called out, "Do not set thine eyes on beauty but set thine eyes on [good] family." For "Grace is deceitful, and beauty is vain; but a woman that feareth the Lord, she shall be praised." (Prov. 31:30) "Look for [a good] family, for woman has been created to bring up a family." The homely ones among them called out, "Carry off your purchase in the name of Heaven, only on one condition—that you adorn us with jewels of gold."[78]

Virginity was highly esteemed throughout history, especially in the Orient, and certainly by the Jewish people. Since Jewish Law required chastity of both sexes, early marriages were encouraged. A bride was expected to enter her canopy as a virgin. This rule applied not only to the priestly caste but to all people alike. Biblical regulations on this subject reflect a highly moral attitude toward the marriage institution, which should, after all, be founded on trust and fidelity; evidence of such breach of confidence on the part of the bride was considered an offense against the honor of the family and the national conscience. "She did not merely degrade herself, but every virgin in Israel," states the Midrash.[79]

An example of virtuous virginity is illustrated by R. Yohanan, who once overheard a virgin who prostrated herself and prayed: "Lord of the Universe, You created Paradise and *Gehinnom*. You created righteous men [Rashi: to inherit Paradise] and wicked men [Rashi: to inherit *Gehinnom*]; may it be Thy will that men should not go astray because of me.[80]

Chastity in man was also considered a virtue. "R. Zutra Bar Tobiah said in Rab's name: What is meant by the verse, 'We whose sons are as plants grown up in their youth; whose daughters are as corner pillars carved after the fashion of the Temple.'?" (Ps. 144:12) "We whose sons are as plants" alludes to the young men of Israel who have not experienced the taste of sin; "whose daughters are as cornerpillars," to the virgins of Israel, who reserve themselves for their husbands."[81]

The Midrash finds a symbolism with the zodiac order of Virgo, the sign of the month of Elul (following Leo, the sign of Av), reflecting that "man rejoices in a virgin."[82]

A virgin maiden was given twelve months to prepare her trousseau, while the bridegroom was allowed three days to prepare the wedding feast (Sunday, Monday, and Tuesday), for "Wednesday is the customary wedding day for virgins." These festivities were to continue for "the seven festive days" following the marriage of a virgin, three days for a widow, and only one day when the marriage is between a widower and a widow.[83]

The wedding of a virgin was always an occasion for lavish festivity; people gathered from all around to partake in the traditional commandment of *simhat hatan ve-kallah*. Usually, a virgin's wedding was celebrated with more pomp and fanfare than that of a widow; thus "a virgin's wedding is talked about." It is interesting to note that at a virgin's wedding the guests were served at the conclusion of the dinner—*canabis*, to relax one's mental state.[84]

Since marriage was considered the keystone of genuine morality, the highest ideal uniting two souls in holy communion, the marriage ceremony was celebrated in accordance with traditional customs; the sense of joy and merriment dovetailed the exalted spirit of sanctity and togetherness. This ceremony, named *kiddushin*, was also called *hilloola*, or "song of exultant praise."

Attending upon a bride was considered one of the acts through which a man imitates God's ways, as R. Yehudah bar Il'ai said, "For God Himself engaged in attending the needs of Eve and even served as the best man at her wedding to Adam, as stated, 'And He brought her unto the man.' "[85]

So important was the union of man and woman in Jewish Law that a girl's betrothal could even be arranged for on the Sabbath.[86] Jews were traditionally exhorted to participate and "to give joy to the bridegroom and the bride."[87]

The spindle was considered a "symbol of womanhood." Spinning was considered an art and an act of valor. (Prov. 31:19) At the birth of a daughter a father would bless her: "May it be Thy will, Eternal God, that I rear my daughter to sew, knit, spin, and perform pious deeds." Nowadays it is proper to wish a daughter the same blessing one wishes a son: "le-Torah, le-huppah, u-le-maasim tovim"—to be reared in the spirit of Torah, for marriage, and for good deeds."[88]

On the Sabbath preceding the wedding the spinholts festivity was held. Dating back to talmudic times, it referred to the bride-to-be, who was to spin yarn skillfully and thus announce her forthcoming wedding. It also officially assigned the exact date of the huppah in accordance with the community's schedule. On the spinholts Sabbath the bride and groom would each celebrate in their own home, serving the guests sweets and drinks for the toasts and le-hayim wishes. The bride, dressed in her rokel—gown—was entertained on Sabbath afternoon by her unmarried girlfriends and relatives singing love songs and was later accompanied to the tantz-hoyz, or dance hall. These customs, already recorded by R. Yaakov Molin (d. 1427, Worms), continued in Germany well into the eighteenth century.[89]

On the wedding day the virgin bride was carried through the city in full dress upon a handsome palanquin, a curtained litter made out of golden embroidered garments. It was borne on the shoulders of men of the highest social position.[90] It was a religious duty to join the procession and contribute to its gaiety. This old biblical custom was mentioned several times by Jeremiah: "The voice of myrth and the voice of gladness—the voice of the bridegroom and the voice of the bride." (7:34; 16:9; 25:10) So important, in fact, was this commandment that even the study of the Torah was to be interrupted by the Rabbis and their disciples, who were encouraged to add their numbers and join the festivity.

R. Yehudah bar Il'ai sat teaching his disciples; a bride passed by. "What was that?" he asked them. "A bride passing by," they replied. "My sons," he said to them, "get up and attend upon the bride. For thus we find concerning the Holy One, blessed be He, that He attended upon a bride," as it is said, "And the Lord God built the rib" (Gen. 2:22) If He attended upon a bride, how much more so we![91]

Much praise was lavished upon the Jewish bride in song and dance to endear her to her bridegroom. According to R. Yonathan, it was even "allowed to look intently at the face of the bride all seven days [of the wedding week] in order to make her more beloved to her husband" (as he sees that all admire her beauty). In this respect, our Rabbis taught: "How does one dance [recite or sing] before the bride? Bet Shammai say: 'The bride as she is' [one does not exaggerate in praising the bride]. And Bet Hillel say: 'Beautiful and graceful bride' [Every bride should be praised as beautiful]."

Out of the many bridal songs in early Palestine only one small stanza is known to us (in addition to Psalm 45 and Song of Songs), which reads: "No paint, no powder and no waving of the hair and still a sweet gazelle-eyed girl . . ." Several stories are related in the Talmud, where Rabbis used to joyfully entertain the bride to make her merry. "R. Yehudah bar Il'ai used to hold a myrtle and dance in front of her saying: 'Beautiful and amiable bride;' " R. Shmuel bar Rab Itzhak used to dance while juggling with three myrtles; R. Aha went as far as to dance with her while carrying her on his shoulder, though he was exceptional for his holiness. From these early traditional dances later originated the Hasidic *mitzvah tanzel*, where the Rabbis and other men dance with the bride individually, each holding onto a corner of a kerchief. Even Agrippas, the Jewish king, foregoing his own honor, is said to have paid homage to a bride, explaining that, while he wears the crown every day, the bride wears her crown only on her wedding day.[92]

Traditionally, men and women always danced separately. Only relatives (such as father and daughter, and brother and sister) were the exceptions.[93]

To allay the anger of the evil spirits as well as warding off any threats of death the *todtentanz*, or the Dance of Death (already recorded in the fourteenth century), was introduced at a wedding ceremony, accompanying the mournful melody of a dirge and concluded by a joyous dance.

Such a popular *dance macabre*, already mentioned by Glückel of Hameln and which probably stems from the fourteenth-century Black Death, continued for centuries throughout European lands and was meant to symbolize man's victory over the fear of death.

The groom would bestow special gifts on the bride. During the Crusades in Germany the groom would present the bride with a new belt, while later in the seventeenth and eighteenth centuries, *sivlonot*, or special gifts, were exchanged by both groom and bride through the Rabbi of the community at a special festivity.[94] A seventeenth-century custom in the German province of Hesse (and most probably in other cities) required of the groom to buy new pairs of shoes for his bride and her female relatives for the wedding ceremony.

THE WEDDING CEREMONY

In talmudic times and later, the bride would wear a wreath of myrtle—*henuma*—during her *huppah*. In later times the veil over her face was referred to as *henuma* also.[95]

The colorful adornments of the bride stem from biblical times. It is recorded that "a bride is to be adorned and enter her canopy with twenty-four adornments. She is to be perfumed and anointed and bejeweled. "The Lord Himself performed this task for the first bride in the Garden of Eden."[96]

The bride's face covered with a veil (an ancient custom still practiced today, especially in Eastern etiquette) was traditionally reminiscent of Rebekah's, since she, according to Genesis 24:65, "took her veil and covered herself" when she first encountered Isaac. Virgin brides walked (and still do) to their wedding canopy with their head veiled and with their hair loose. In posttalmudic times it was customary for her to cut her hair off after the marriage has been consummated.[97]

Often the groom put his cloak or his *talit* (an early tradition of the biblical times: Ruth 3:9) over the bride's head, and following the ceremony the groom would place his doublet, girdle, and cap into his wife's bosom.[98] This transfer may have also symbolized shared possession. This eventually evolved into the custom of *badekhen*, where the groom, followed by the Rabbis, covers the bride's face with her veil before going to the *huppah*, a tradition still observed among Orthodox Jews.

In biblical times the bridal pair wore crowns of roses and myrtles and olive branches, intertwined with saltstones and pyrites, among threads of gold and crimson, which were often the handiwork of the rabbinic students. Already Isaiah speaks of the "bridegroom who decketh himself with a garland, and as a bride adorneth herself with her jewels." (Is. 61:10) The bridal garland, originally made of gold with a golden city design on it, was discontinued as a sign of religious and national mourning during the war against Titus (70 C.E.) and replaced with a fine woolen cap, just as the bridegroom's gold-embroidered silks were replaced during the Vespasian war with wreaths of myrtle entwined with papyrus linen.[99]

The bridal procession, a biblical custom, was originally the actual transference of the bride to her husband's home, and the *huppah* or canopy, under which Jewish weddings are still celebrated, was, in ancient times, either the canopied litter occupied by the bride during the procession or the actual apartment to which the married couple retired after the wedding.

Tradition records that when a boy was born a cedar was planted; at the birth of a girl, an acacia. The trees, though, were felled before the wedding to provide the wood for the bridal canopy or litter.[100]

Wine was channeled through pipes before the bridegroom and the bride, and roasted ears of corn and nuts were thrown in front of them as a symbol of prosperity, the latter custom still followed in many lands in various forms. Similarly, a rooster and a hen were brought forth before the newlyweds to symbolize fertility.[101]

The wedding ring is not mentioned in the Talmud. It was introduced into the wedding ceremony during the seventh century and was used in Palestine somewhat earlier than in Babylon. The ring came to displace the old gift of money (or the equivalent of money) with an article which, itself, symbolically represented the yet older acquisition of a bride by direct purchase. The wedding ring was not necessarily made of gold; it could even be made of baser metal, as long as the bride was—*a priori*—informed both of the *kiddushin* representation of the ring and of its real value. For this reason, the wedding ring must not have any jewels, since a specialist would be required to appraise the true value of the jewel.[102]

Exemptions and privileges were granted by the Rabbis to the young couple—whose sins were forgiven on their wedding day.[103]

These immunities were based on the biblical consideration that "When a man has taken a bride, he shall not go out with the army or be assigned to it for any purpose; he shall be exempt one year for the sake of his household, to give happiness to the woman he has married." (Deut. 24:5) For the same reason, the groom was exempt from all public duties and responsibilities. The bridegroom was also excused during the wedding period from the ritual of reading the *Shema* (which requires mental concentration of which he was not capable, worrying as he was about his nuptial obligations; and/or of dwelling in a small and crowded *sukkah* during the wedding meal for the entire seven wedding days.[104] A woman is considered a bride for thirty days after her wedding. "A groom may not enter the bridal chamber till the bride gives him permission."[105] "A bride is allowed to wear her jewelry during the "thirty days" of mourning [after her parent], and certainly after the thirty days in order that she should not become repulsive to her husband."[106] She was freed from the strict regulation requiring immersion in the *mikvah* the first day after the wedding, lest it spoil her makeup. A bride is permitted to wash her face on *Yom Kippur* because she has to preserve her beauty and endear herself to her husband. She was exempted as well from other required rituals. The bride and bridegroom were considered like a queen and king, who do not set out without an escort, and were therefore given special guards before the wedding.[107]

A bride had the right to choose Israel as her domicile where her home was to be. Refusal by the husband was enough grounds for divorce, with no detrimental consequences to the wife, either morally or financially.[108]

PSYCHOLOGICAL ASPECTS OF WOMAN'S ROLE AND POSITION IN MARRIAGE

It was duly noted by the Rabbis that woman's strongest desire was to have a husband. Marriage, they claim, is so meaningful to the woman that she derives pleasure from the mere engagement even though she knows that it is nothing more than a formal prelude to a probable marriage. (They observe, though, that the importance of marriage is equally great for man and woman).[109]

While the man, in selecting a wife, will scrupulously consider even the slightest physical blemish of the woman, she, in her willingness to marry, is not always that particular about choosing a husband who is entirely without physical defects. Still, there is a limit to woman's willingness to compromise her aesthetic judgment: if the defect is very conspicuous, or amounts to a deformity, she will not be willing to marry him.[110]

Although woman is exceedingly eager to marry, she is not willing to debase herself by accepting betrothal money, if the amount is not in keeping with dignity. Neither will she consent to marry if she cannot have legal assurances that, should her husband die, she will be given preference over the debtors and relatives in the settlement of his estate.[111]

There is a fourfold reason behind this desire to marry; in addition to her longing for motherhood, the woman wants companionship and love; she wants a protector who will care for her and carry the yoke of married life; and she is eager to gratify her sexual longing.

Researchers have found that the main satisfactions for wives in marriages were (1) companionship in doing things together with the husband; (2) the chance to have children; (3) the husband's understanding of her problems and feelings; and (4) the husband's expression of love and affection.[112]

Companionship and understanding for the partner's needs were accepted motives in Jewish tradition, indeed encouraged by the Sages. As an example, one can cite a twentieth-century rabbinic authority of Jerusalem, R. Yosef Hayim Sonenfeld. He shunned idle conversation but wished to dispel any loneliness in his wife. He therefore conceived of the idea of arranging to study with her every day from the *Shulhan Arukh Orah Hayim*.[113]

When the woman cannot find a husband who fulfills all these requirements, she may still be happy to marry one who serves only as a protector and enables her to escape the problem of singlehood.

Before the consummation of her marriage, a woman is called (in Hebrew) "the daughter of so and so." After conjugality, she is called *ishah* (woman), says the *Zohar*. Or in a modern rendition: "A woman burns and yearns for marriage because marriage not only means sex, it means social status, entry into the adult world . . ."[114]

She is proud of having a husband and "Even if her husband be as small as an ant, it places her among the women of nobility," or, "Even though he be a carder, she will call him out to the threshold and sit down with him." Another popular saying comments: "When the husband is a cabbage, the wife requires no lentils for her pot," meaning that she is content with any husband under the present circumstances rather than remain single.[115] The Rabbis assure us, however, that, by putting up with a sexually incompatible husband, she will in no way be able to suppress her need for sexual fulfillment, for "all know for what purpose a bride enters the bridal canopy."[116] She may turn to promiscuity and shield herself with her marital status. Thus, her sexual drive would overcome her natural inclination to faithfulness.

By nature the woman is slower to arousal and to orgasm than the man, and orgasmic privation leads to impairment of health, marital incompatibility, and infidelity. A normally amatory wife whose husband performs in a persistently cursory or deficient manner may feel a need for reassurance of her erotic charms. These needs may develop even when she experiences no actual appetite for additional gratification.

"Infidelity is more likely to occur among sexually unsatisfied women. The sexually satisfied woman has little cause to become involved in extra marital relations," claims Caprio.[117] According to Chesser, "The modern wife who derives no satisfaction from the predictable and unimaginative embraces of her husband is vulnerable to the approaches of a more ardent and experienced lover."[118]

When married to a man she deems satisfactory, but who turns out to be unfaithful to her, she may react in a similarly faithless manner.[119] Further, just as her husband's love and faithfulness brings out the best in her, his infidelity brings out the worst.

Nevertheless, the Rabbis, as a rule, found that faithfulness is inherent to woman's character; wives "reserve sexual intimacy for their husbands, for it is the nature of Jewish women not to be permissive."[120]

One of woman's basic expectations of her husband is his ability to support her needs. In this security lies the most important of all the benefits that a woman attains by marriage.

Since woman's satisfaction is dependent on the man's ability to produce, her fear is in being abandoned, frustrated, while man's is fear of failure.[121]

Woman always feared and felt ashamed of being left single. Worse than the fear of being financially stranded, is the fear of emotional loneliness—being stranded by life itself.

Woman, according to the Rabbis, is willing to endure privation of life's necessities as long as the world knows nothing about it; but when her husband makes an open vow that he is not going to support her, the shame thus caused is greater than she can bear. Such hardship, clearly, is much more intense than that caused by the lack of life's daily needs.[122]

Another rabbinic observation of a similar nature: When her husband has forbidden her to wear jewelry, she hopes that he will reconsider, since she assumes that he abjured her in a moment of anger. Different, though, is the case when she was agitated and so vowed not to bedeck herself with jewelry, and her husband was silent and did not protest. This she takes as a sign of indifference and would not scruple, if necessary, to break matrimonial relations forthwith.

On the other hand, a woman who has lived a long time with her husband, enjoying the comforts and luxuries of life, would not desert him should he become impoverished. Rather, she will say, "In time of riches he supported me, and now, when he is poor, I will not desert him," rebuffing any interlopers with the words, "Mind your own business; he is my husband and has the right to do with me as he wishes." This rabbinic observation can be compared to that of Bell and Vogel, who claim that a wife may feel her husband's sudden anger unjustified in the light of familial values and may state this explicitly, though she may also legitimize his anger because of special consider- ations and not apply sanctions against it.[123]

Although modern researchers feel that economic stress can either intensify the cohesiveness of the family, or disrupt it by providing an arena for marital conflict (i.e., if one of the partners blames the other for not earning enough, causing an unsolvable problem), the traditional woman, once married, is willing to do almost anything to maintain the peace of the home. She will readily renounce all luxuries of her former life in her father's home.

She will not hesitate to sell her marriage deed and give the proceeds to her husband, for she well knows that it will be spent on household necessities, benefiting both of them.

In contemporary American society, "Many city women would rather bring in an income than reduce the need for it . . . the wife's earnings make a big difference in the family's ability to gain its desired standard of living." When circumstances dictate that the wife go to work, she will be rewarded by the man's appreciation and understanding; thus her work "strengthens the marriage bonds." Otherwise, "the economic strain on the family would increase dissatisfaction with the husband, impairing the marriage relationship. . . ."[124]

Every woman who makes a vow does so with the implicit under- standing that her oath is in consonance with her husband's aims; that is, she is loath to do anything contrary to his wishes. Hence the Rabbis concluded that every wife is predominantly loyal to and regardful of her husband; they were also aware that this was due partly to her unconscious motivation of not losing his attentions. So it follows that a "bad wife who always disagrees with her mate" is rather uncommon, clearly the exception.[125]

The Rabbis felt that when the husband has no confidence in his wife, and is always suspecting her of wrongdoing or dishonesty in managing his business, her patience may be taxed, and she may be led to say, "I don't want to live with you since you are so particular with me," for she interprets his lack of confidence in her as a sign that he no longer loves her, and so she resolves to discontinue their marital relations.

"Trust, like love, is only possible as a mutual [sic] relationship; it cannot be the sole property of one or the other spouse. The spouse who trusts an unloving (hence untrustworthy) partner is usually a scared person—not a trusting one."[126]

Tradition has it that there are some husbands who are so niggardly as to demand a reckoning from their wives if, say, they should break a dish or some other household belonging; the frazzled wives, in turn will consider it unbearable to live with such eccentric men.[127]

An overbearing husband will occasion feelings of hatred in the woman and will variously prompt her to oppose him or suffer silently by repression.[128] Bitterness, anger, and disappointment affect the most intimate relationships.

A husband who orally assures his wife of his love and trust, while his behavior betrays selfishness, inattentiveness, irritability, disregard, and impulsiveness, is a poor source of marital trust and accord.

And another exception. When a woman is possessed by a consuming passion for another man, she may become untruthful. Her emotion of love will overcome that of faithfulness and cause her to lie and act against her natural feeling of appreciation and gratefulness toward her husband.

It is known that love is not as strong as hatred in blinding woman's clear thinking and perception of reality; however, love, as well as hatred, can deprive her of her feeling of gratitude.

We find woman identifying with her husband. The Rabbis note that a wife will actively assert herself when it comes to defending her husband's honor, but when he does not merit her respect, she will openly show her contempt for him.[129]

Traditionally, a wife is closer to her husband than his sons and daughters are. She will invariably support him in times of adversity, while the children may not. Marriage-counseling cases similarly substantiate the fact that the woman will rally to her husband's side when he is under emotional or financial stress. "The ideals of American marriage place allegiance between husband and wife on a higher level than parent-child attachments . . . the deepest emotional satisfactions as well as social, financial, and household matters belong to the married couple as an exclusive pair." He and she are united.[130] Mature conjugal love is compatible with realities of marriage and later with family life including children.

Today's husband expects his wife to be a companion, to share in his interests, his job, and profession, in short—to work with him. The biblical concept of *aizer* (helpmate) is expressed by Karl Menninger, who states that it is the wife "who must sustain her husband's courage, bolster his ego, and assuage his disappointments, even if it's only by sympathetic listening."[131]

The personal attachment is undoubtedly the chief bond that conjoins husband and wife. In a broader sense, neither a man nor a woman can be complete alone. It is not that opposites attract but that the two genders are raised to divide the task of living and to complement, modify, and complete one another and to find common purpose in raising their children.[132]

A happy marriage is not a gift but an opportunity. It is an obligation, not an experiment. Best composed of dissimilar material, marriage bridges and unites, complements and completes, the act of creation, where every creature seeks its perfection in another and harmonizes perpetually the song of love and life. Only when men and women work together in understanding and sympathy for the same causes, turning their aggressiveness outward toward a joint threat, can their ideals be realized.

Bemoaning the lot of one married to an domineering woman, the Rabbis state: "Among those who cry but nobody takes any notice of him is the husband who is ruled by his wife".[133]

Lack of cooperation and constant dissension in marriage caused by a negativistic woman were, in ancient times, sufficient grounds for divorce.

In differentiating between a "good wife" as a helpmate and companion and a "bad wife"—a source of perpetual strife—the Rabbis remarked: "It is a meritorious act to divorce a bad wife . . ." Another way of rectifying the wife's surly attitude is by stimulating her jealousy.[134]

In posing the question "How is one to understand the term a 'bad wife'? Abaye said: One who prepares for her husband a meal and has her tongue also ready for him. [Rashi: insulting and cursing him before the meal to aggravate him.] Raba said: One who prepares for him the tray and turns her back upon him." [Rashi: refuses to eat with him at the table in order to annoy him.]*135

R. Menahem Ha-Meiri of Perpignan (d. 1306) depicts a virtuous woman as follows: Our Rabbis have told us: "Do not shame the women of virtue for there are women who are better than men." They have the following attributes: They discard the ways of their fathers and acquire the characteristics of their husbands; their countenances light up when their husbands get angry; they respect them during their poverty as well as during affluence, and their old age as during youth; whose hands are swift in giving bread to the poor; work despite the fact that they have maids; they nurse their own children, listen to those who speak and answer cautiously; flee from quarrelsome people; they say when they are hungry that they are satiated; rejoice when guests enter and serve them. A wise man once said when asked what qualities a wife should have, "One who is perfect without blemish, quick to answer when called by her husband, patient in times of distress, comely, and one who wears modest clothes." (Prov. 31:9)

A king once asked one of his wise men, "Tell me of those type of women who are to be disliked." He replied: "One who rebels against her husband, one who takes pride only in her own work, one who takes credit for things she has not done, one who loses patience quickly, one who easily becomes involved in quarrels, one who is destructive and weak in being constructive."

A distinguished wife is comparable to a vine. One plants a vine in one corner of his house, and after it grows awhile, he will extend one of the branches outside to be in the presence of the sun. Thus its roots will be in the house while its boughs extend outside. Similarly is a distinguished wife; even though she will remain in her house, her deeds will be well known in the public places as the verse says, "and they will praise her by the gates for her deeds." (Prov. 31:31)

Several examples are instanced in the Talmud in reference to our discussion which also reflect the degree of tolerance exercised by the

---

*This may also be a euphemism concerning refusal of cohabitation by her, after arousing him. (M.M.B.)

Rabbis—rather than having recourse to divorce—when they themselves
were saddled with inadequate partners:

> [Rab Hiyya] was constantly tormented by his wife. Nevertheless,
> whenever he obtained anything suitable for her he wrapped it up
> in his scarf and brought it to her. Said Rav to him, "But, surely, she
> is tormenting the Master!"—"It is sufficient for us," the other
> replied, "that they rear our children and deliver us from sin [sinful
> thoughts]."
>
> Rav was constantly tormented by his wife. If he told her,
> "Prepare me lentils," she would prepare him small peas; and if he
> asked for small peas, she prepared him lentils: When his son
> Hiyya grew up he gave her his father's instructions in the reversed
> order [so that his mother would then do the exact reverse and thus
> Rav would have what he really wanted to eat]. Once Rab remarked
> to him, "Your mother has really improved." The son replied, "It
> was I who reversed your orders." The father then said to him,
> "This is what people say, "Thine own offspring teaches thee
> reason; however, you must not continue to do so; for it is said,
> 'They have taught their tongue to speak lies, they weary them-
> selves.' " (Jer. 9:4)[136]

This clearly illustrates how the ethical precept of filial duty was
considered sufficient reason for character training by Rav to accept his
unpleasant lot and tolerate an irascible wife rather than benefit through
his son's transgression, despite the latter's unimpeachable intentions.

Marriage limits the filial responsibility of a daughter, for her energies
are at her husband's disposal and her home is with him.[137] The Bible as
well as the Rabbis expect both husband and wife to honor their
respective in-laws. Moses bows before his father-in-law Jethro (Exod.
18:7) and the Mekhilta states; "Hence a man should always honor his
father-in-law." David, too, calls his father-in-law King Saul "My Father," and the Rabbis again derive the obligation to honor one's father-
in-law as he does his father. Disrespecting one's in-laws is a prophetic
sign heralding the coming of Messiah. Talmudic understanding looks at
such respect more as an expression of extended honor for one's spouse
rather than a form of filial bond to the extended family.[138]

Relating to bereavement, both husband and wife must personally
mourn the death of their in-laws. Though mourning *(avelut)* recognizes
only biological filiation, such mourning represents the humane partici-

pation in the partner's sorrow. Therefore a man rends his garments
(keri'ah) at the death of either his father-in-law or mother-in-law, as a
sign of respect for his wife. In fact, a man is considered responsible for
the disrespect shown by his wife to his aged parents. An interesting
ethical comment is offered by R. Eliezer Azkary. Since husband and
wife are considered "one body," a woman's father is to be considered
her husband's father too.[139]

On the realm of human relations and domestic structure, the Rabbis
were fully aware of the classic tension between the daughter-in-law and
her in-laws when they asserted: "If a lamb can live with a leopard, so
can a bride live with her mother-in-law."[140] It is easily understood,
therefore, why they disqualified the testimony of the mother-in-law and
sister-in-law in some cases, since both are apt to perjure themselves in
the attempt to injure their daughter-in-law and sister-in-law. Similarly,
a daughter-in-law, too, is to be disqualified from testifying against her
mother-in-law. The Sages perceived the wife's animosity as a response
to that of her mother-in-law, while the mother-in-law's hatred is viewed
as stemming from the very presence of her son's wife, for both emotional and economic considerations[141]—due in part to the living
conditions of those times, when both parents and married children
lived together with all the frictions and invasions of privacy due to such
close domiciliary arrangements.

In such cases it was the duty of the husband to protect his wife by
moving her to another domicile or to grant her a divorce with full
payment of her ketubbah, for "a woman is given in marriage for a good
life, and not for a life of suffering."[142]

Protecting the woman from persecution by her mother-in-law was the
husband's prime responsibility and was also decreed by R. Alfasi (11th
c.), whose normal procedure was to appoint a female investigator in the
troubled home to observe and to mediate between the parties and to
have the court remove the party causing the harm (which surely refers
to the mother-in-law and not to the incoming young wife).

Protection from in-law troubles and assuring domestic peace between
husband and wife are reflected in the ruling of Maimonides, who allows
full freedom to either spouse to exclude from their domicile the
partner's parents or siblings who are disturbing their shalom bayit.
Thus, if a man says to his wife, "I don't want your father or mother,
brothers or sisters, coming to my house," he is listened to, and she must
go to their homes; they may not come to her unless something untoward, such as sickness or childbirth, occurs. For we do not force a man

to admit others to his property. Similarly, if she says, "I don't want your mother or sisters coming in to me, and I do not wish to live in one court with them because they harm me and make me suffer," she is listened to. For we do not force someone to allow others to live with him on his property.[143]

Similar to Maimonides' view is that of R. Shlomo Ibn Adret (1235–1310), who states in his responsum that a wife can certainly tell her husband, "I refuse to live with people who harm me" (meaning her mother-in-law), for if her husband may not pain her, she certainly need not live among others who harm her and cause quarrels between herself and her husband.[144]

R. Eliezer Pappo (early 19th c.), discussing the tensions between parents and their married children, advises the son to reprove his wife and appease his parents, but afterward the husband should pacify his wife and show her the right way. However, "the collar of responsibility is also tied around the necks of the parents, who should refrain from causing strife and hatred between a man and his wife."[145]

A man's state of mind and mood depend greatly upon the reactions of his wife and the way she treats him. "All the days of the poor are evil" refers to one who has a wicked wife, "but he that has a merry heart hath a continual feast (Prov. 15:15) refers to him who has a good wife."[146] It is unfortunate that in early patriarchal society woman's role and duties in marriage were taken for granted. She was always expected to be chaste, virtuous, and devoted to her husband; this was required by society to guarantee her fidelity and subordination in marriage, without ever considering her own natural rights as an individual with feelings and ideas on the institution of marriage.

Fully aware that "as men differ in their treatment of their food, so they differ in the treatment of their wives," the Rabbis declared that one must always observe the honor due to his wife, because blessings rest on a man's house only on account of his wife. "Honor your wife that ye may become enriched." Another exhortation: "A man should always eat and drink less than his means allow, clothe himself in accordance with his means, and honor his wife and children more than his means allow."[147] This attitude was incorporated within the Jewish Code of Law.

Great was the praise of a good wife.

Come and see how precious is a good wife, for it is written: "Whoso findeth a wife findeth a great good." (Prov. 18:22) Now, if

Scripture speaks of the woman herself, then how precious is a good wife whom Scripture praises. If Scripture speaks of Torah, then how precious is a good wife with whom the Torah is compared. "How baneful is a bad wife," for it is written: "And I find more bitter than death the woman." (Eccles. 7:26) Now, if Scripture speaks of herself, then how baneful is a bad wife whom Scripture censures. If Scripture speaks of Gehenna, then how baneful is a bad wife, with whom Gehenna is compared.[148]

R. Saadyah Gaon counsels husband and wife to be affectionate and love each other "for the sake of the maintenance of the world, as Scripture says: 'A lovely hind and graceful doe, let her breasts satisfy thee at all times; with her love be thou ravished always.' " (Prov. 5:19) A husband should express "his desire for his wife in accordance with the dictates of reason and religion and to the extent required in order to bind them closely together."[149]

"Never be angry with thy wife" exhorts R. Asher Ben Yehiel (RoSH, 1250–1327) in his will to his son, "if thou put her off from thee with thy left hand, delay not to draw her to thee again with thy right hand."[150]

Further, we hear Rav's appeal: "Be heedful of wounding your wife's feelings. Her tears are frequent and the redress should be immediate."

Intelligent partners should know that to continue love in marriage is a science.

A very logical and instructive lesson in marital relations is found in the fourteenth-century religioothical work named Menorat ha-Maor by R. Israel Ibn Al-Nakawa (d. 1391) of Spain.[151] The author describes the functions of and relationship between a good wife and a good husband. A good wife is one who manages her husband's affairs correctly, watches his money, assists him with all her might, gives him good advice, and does not press him to spend more than is necessary. She supervises the needs of the home and the education of the children and does so diligently. Moreover, she tries to please her husband and is always eager to cheer and comfort him and to free him from worry. She tries to understand his needs, and to study his moods, and takes delight in serving him, because she loves him deeply. Besides, she treats her husband's family fairly, not playing the snob toward them if she herself happens to belong to a higher station.

A good husband must have as high a regard for his wife as for his own self and honor her accordingly. She brings him completion and blessing, and it is his duty to realize it. He must be particularly careful to provide the needs of the home, for lack of these is often the beginning of discord. Let a man sacrifice his personal wants in order to provide the more abundantly for his wife and children. Above all, let him treat his wife with love and understanding, as she is part of him, and depends on him, as he depends upon God. He must never treat her violently, nor abuse her, nor deceive her. Where a man shows deference to his wife, and creates an atmosphere of love and harmony, there the Divine Spirit finds satisfaction.

The concept of marriage exists not only in our world but throughout all cosmic realms. The relationship between a man and woman on the material plane is a reflection of the higher relationship between God and the Jewish people. Marriage is a metaphor that describes the nexus that exists between the Jews and God.

Anthropomorphically, God is considered the groom, the Jewish people the bride. The all-encompassing relationship that exists between a bride and groom symbolically evokes the relationship shared by God and the Jewish people.

The Song of Songs, described by the Rabbis as the holiest book of the Bible, expresses the profundity of this unique relationship characterized by the two youthful lovers.

The maiden, the symbol of the Jewish people, exclaims "Great waters cannot quench the love, nor rivers wash it away." (Song of Songs 8:7) The shepherd, symbolic of God, calls out to her, "Arise my beloved, my fair one, and come with me." (Song of Songs 2:10) The Torah abounds in descriptions of the eternal relationship and inseparable bonds of love which tie God to the Jewish people and the Jewish people to God.

6

The Three *Mitzvot*

> Rabbi Akiva said: "Happy are you, O Israel, before
> whom you cleanse yourselves and who cleanses
> you? Your Father that is in heaven, as it is said
> (Ezek. 36:25): 'And I will sprinkle clean water
> upon you and you shall be clean.' And it says
> again (Jer. 17:13). 'The hope (*mikvah*) of Israel is
> in the Lord'—just as the *mikvah* cleanses the
> unclean, so does the Holy One, blessed be He,
> cleanse Israel."
>
> —*Mishnah Yoma* 8:9

TAHARAT HA-MISHPAHAH—THE JEWISH LAWS OF FAMILY PURITY

Of the three mitzvot ascribed to the woman, two of them, *hallah* and *hadlakat neirot*, may be performed by the man, although they are woman's special privilege; but the third *mitzvah*, which is solely hers, is *taharat ha-mishpahah*. This *mitzvah*, performed through immersion in a *mikvah* (ritualarium), deals directly with the potential of procreation. Procreation represents nothing less than the power of the Infinite that lies within man. The *mitzvah* related to this ability was placed entirely in the care of the Jewish woman.

It is instructive to note that Scripture speaks of cleanliness and uncleanliness not only in respect to woman but also in respect to man. Bodily cleanliness is a prerequisite of ritual purification; the Torah also imposes upon the Jew the need for moral purification.

Jews for twenty-five or thirty centuries have considered cleanliness of the greatest importance. Mosaic sanitary laws of hygiene were unique in the Near East and became a Jewish patent throughout history.[1] So great was the traditional concern with sanitary regulations and purification that the entire sixth section of the Mishnah is called *Taharot*, the laws of purification, lustration, and cleanliness.

The recognition of the *mikvah* ritual and its deeper meaning has elicited a host of remarks from various sources. In the first century C.E., Hillel, the great teacher, remarked: "It is a religious duty to pay attention to hygiene, for if someone is paid to clean the statues of kings, how much more should I, created in the Divine image and likeness, take care of my body, the icon of the Holy One."[2]

Jewish Law is concerned, in addition to the ethicoreligious aspects of human behavior, with the mental and physical hygiene as well. Said, R. Phinehas Ben Yair, "Physical cleanliness leads to spiritual purity."[3] Neglect of such hygiene and bodily health is regarded as a sin. Laws of cleanliness and physical purity are, therefore, integrated within Jewish Law and must be viewed both as sanitary measures, hygienically motivated, and as ritualistic and symbolical ordinances of a high metaphysical nature. Maimonides emphatically states that "physical cleanliness leads to the sanctification of the soul from reprehensible opinions," for "He who is physically unclean has no soul."[4]

The *mikvah* for ritual ablution was, and still is, a *sine qua non*, the sanitary and symbolic process of immersion for the woman after her menstrual period and after giving birth.

The cleansing of the body through the prescribed laws of immersion in the *mikvah*, with all their symbolic significance, remains the basic requirement of the Jewish woman in maintaining family purity.

Some women do not wish to immerse themselves in a *mikvah* because other women have previously immersed themselves, and they feel it would be unhygienic, since the water is dirty. The purpose of the *mikvah*, though, is not to provide renewed cleanliness to a "defiled" woman. We know of the practice of the High Priest during the *Yom Kippur* services who immersed himself in a *mikvah* on five occasions. Surely this ritual was not to remove physical uncleanliness. The *mikvah* is not to be viewed as an anachronistic version of a bath or shower. It is clear that immersion in the *mikvah* is not merely for cleanliness. For this, the preceding bath and preparations are sufficient. The reasons for the ritual ablution are of mysterious meaning and constitute an intrinsic part of the Divine plan for Israel's sanctification.

This symbolic reasoning for the *mikvah* explains why Jewish Law differentiates between a natural stream or well water, which is required, and drawn water, which is humanly transferred, hence invalid. Only through immersion in a proper *mikvah* can a woman be purified and acquire the merit to have righteous children.

It is written in the Torah, "You shall not come close to a woman in her menstrual impurity." (Lev. 18:19) Violations of the laws of *niddah* carries with it the severance of ties with God, the defilement of land, and the exclusion of the soul from the eternal life of *olam haba*.[5]

The Sages ask: "Why did the Torah ordain that the 'uncleanness' of menstruation should last for seven days?" They answer: "Because the husband is accustomed to his wife any time he wishes [Rashi, and he becomes weary of her]; therefore, the Torah states: 'Let her be unclean for seven days' [Rashi, so that he may not get too used to her], so that she will become more beloved [desirable] to her husband as she was when she entered under the *huppah*."[6]

In recognizing the sacred nature of the state of wedlock, Judaism prescribes moderation for the couple. The Jewish ideal of holiness is not confined to the avoidance of the illicit; its ideal includes the hallowing of the licit.[7] It categorically demands reserve, self-control, and temperance in the most intimate relations of life. Judaism ordains the utmost consideration for the wife throughout her monthly separation as a *niddah*.[8] This period encompasses the five (or more) days of menstruation and the seven subsequent "white days" (*taharah*), which culminate in ritual purification through total immersion in a stream, or a "gathering of living water," the *mikvah*. Thus the Torah, in its profound reverence for life, requires water—the source of life—to overcome impurity—the symbol of morbidity. Only natural water, as represented in the waters of the *mikvah*, can offset the forces of death and bring about a state of purity synonymous with life. The actual *tevilah* (ablution) is a spiritual refresher, a creation anew. Within the framework of family purity, marriage is conceived as a celestial blessing initiated by purification, reaffirmation, renewal. By the guidance that these laws afford, Jewish men have been taught respect for womanhood, moral disciplines, ethical propriety. As for Jewish women, they were, on the one hand, given protection from uncurbed passion and, on the other, enabled to view marital life in all its holiness.

The goal of the laws of *niddah* is to combat the malaise and complacency affecting many marriages. It is the Torah's solution to the charge, "Familiarity breeds contempt." R. Samson Raphael Hirsch notes that the Torah places the laws concerning the niddah adjacent to a discussion of laws forbidding relations with one's sister. Perhaps the Torah is suggesting that in the proper marital relationship there are periods in Jewish married life in which husband and wife may live together only as brother and sister, a condition which, far from any lessening of the intimacy of marriage, has the capability of making this intimacy still more intimate and raising it constantly, both spiritually and morally.[9]

This period of physical separation causes the marriage bond to grow in intensity. By controlling his libidinal urges temporarily, the husband learns to appreciate his wife as an autonomous human being and not as an object to serve his own gratification. A man and wife must explore new avenues of communication in the niddah period. Physical affection is to be replaced by a deeper emotional and psychological commitment. The romance is rejuvenated in this period; increased companionship is attained. This period of separation is succinctly summed up by a verse in Ecclesiastes 3:5: "There is a time for embracing and a time to refrain from embracing."

Our Sages were well aware of the difficulty to both husband and wife of the abstinence and self-restraint required during this period. Therefore, as a preventive safeguard, they prohibited various actions which entail a close interaction between husband and wife and which may lead to more intimate contact.[10] Toward these ends, the Rabbis sought to introduce meaningful laws to make the transition period to the state of niddah as emotionally comfortable as possible. They never intended separating or alienating the partners in any other way but the physical.

During the separation period, the couple will make a special effort to communicate orally. There is no chance to let the relationship deteriorate in any sense, since the various aspects of love and friendship must be constantly renewed. However complicated this may be to describe, it is one more beautiful way by which Judaism frees both man and woman from being mere objects to each other; instead, it perceives and respects them as individuals.

The laws of taharat ha-mishpahah have preserved, throughout the generations, the health and well-being of the Jewish people, by preserving the vitality of the Jewish marriage. These laws, assuring the dignity and respect of the Jewish woman in her marital and sexual life, give her a number of religious responsibilities similar to those of the man. The religious duty of the laws of tevilah carry with them definite psychological, physiological, and hygienic benefits to both parties in marriage.

Sexologists like Van de Velde, Stouffes, and others conclude that following the Mosaic laws on sex leads to a happier life.[11]

Condemnation of the laws of niddah generally result from misunderstanding its implications and purposes. "Unclean" is a very poor attempt to translate "niddah." The woman is permitted to enter the synagogue and to function in a normal manner—only the sexual relationship is forbidden. Her state of "impurity" is not wrong or negative in any sense. The kohen also contracted special forms of tum'ah (impurity) in the purification rituals in which he officiated. This tum'ah was accepted without fear and disgust. The terms taharah (purity) and tum'ah signify halakhic and legal categories. They indicate that specific patterns of behavior become obligatory in each case. Family purity is not just a hygienic procedure. Maimonides states that tum'ah is not a kind of adhesion or dirt that is washed off by water. It is a decree of Scripture, and it has to do with the intention in one's heart. Certainly, it is not the function of the mikvah just to cleanse; the halakhah requires that the niddah be thoroughly clean before immersion.[12] On a spiritual level, the very waters of the mikvah seem to wash away any fallacious, psychologically damaging thoughts which carry over from youth and may well imperil mutual love and respect. Mikvah becomes the sacred instrumentality whereby morality and sexuality are reconciled, bringing husband and wife to each other in purity and delicacy, their love undefiled by guilt and shame.[13]

There are those, however, who misconstrue the laws of niddah claiming that they discriminate against the woman. A good deal of this distortion results from the erroneous definition of the niddah and the purpose of the mikvah (ritualarium). According to the halakhah, woman is temayah (impure) for a number of days during and after her menstrual cycle. During this time, she and her husband abstain from sexual relations and direct physical contact. By immersion in the mikvah, the woman becomes tehorah (purified) and permitted to her husband.[14] It is only the uninformed and the ignorant who see the laws of Jewish family purity as discriminatory against woman. On the contrary, these commandments purify and ennoble the outlook of man and woman toward each other and sanctify their relationship.

Adherence to family purity contributes to the sustenance of the family and to the peaceful house, a house of warmth and love, and to immunity to certain diseases. The separation of husband and wife during the period of niddah and the "seven clean days" when they may express to each other feelings of tenderness without any physical contact is equivalent to the period of engagement. The wife undergoes the immersion in a mikvah just as she did as a bride, recites the very same blessing, and joins with her husband in purity and love as she did on her wedding night. In such an environment, where one's anticipation for another is constantly heightened, love does not grow stale.

The laws of *niddah* tone down and control the desire of both man and woman, whose sex drives are revitalized during this self-imposed period of abstinence.

Claims that an Orthodox woman lives with a negative, unhealthy sense of self because of her "impure state" for almost 50 percent of her adult female life are ridiculous and without support.[15] The woman who lives according to the laws of family purity retains her visions and hopes throughout her life. Her rewards are many: among them, the constant rejuvenation of the love relationship.[16] "All of life presents the opportunity of becoming a perpetual honeymoon. Her dreams are not defeated by success and frustrated by fulfillment."[17]

R. Halafta said, "As for every woman who properly keeps watch over herself—happy is she, happy the one who bore her, happy her husband, and happy her purity."[18]

Let us examine now how the physiological changes relate to the laws of *taharat ha-mishpahah*.

The entire period of physiological change of the uterus and hormones continues throughout the menstrual cycle. From ovulation, day 14 (following two days of preliminary swelling, five days of menses, and seven days of the regeneration of the womb) to day 28, there is still uterine buildup and high secretions of progesterone.

The uterine cycle is accompanied by constant hormonal flux and a gradual buildup of the uterine lining. In a twenty-eight-day cycle, following a five-day menses, there is uterine change until ovulation at day 14. The uterine lining continues to grow in preparation for the fertilized ovum. Should conception not occur, the buildup will stop and menstruation will follow. The uterine buildup continues until the time the fertilized ovum would reach the uterus, which is seven to ten days after fertilization (which is within twenty-four hours of ovulation) in the oviduct. The woman is therefore undergoing constant physical, chemical, and emotional changes. Accordingly, "a woman herself is conscious when she experiences a flow, as the guest comes at the usual time" (the regular menstrual discharge).[19] Not only the flow but physical changes prior to menstruating, and even signs of ovulation, are present in a number of women.

Scientific studies have found a toxic combination composed of blood corpuscles, saliva, sweat, tears, urine, and other secretions of women present in the blood serum during the menstrual cycle. It was long ago shown that "menstrual women generate and carry monotoxin throughout their system. Even in their premenstrual state, the onset of the period, they contaminate by contact to such an extent that it retards the development of, and even kills, plants."[20]

The normal menstrual cycle is one of degeneration and regeneration of the womb's inner lining. This lining is relatively thin for the period immediately following the menstrual flow. Intercourse during this return to physiological normality could cause irritation, inflammation, and possibly recurrence of the period. Secretions of an alkaline nature during the woman's recuperative period can produce ill effects in the male as well (inflammation of the urethral canal). The abstinence from intercourse during the niddah period lessens the tendency of vaginal discharges, which are usually aggravated after the period and which may lead to chronic irritation and chronic infections. Physicians and sexologists have recommended the period of marital separation prescribed by the Torah as being desirable.

We are always surrounded by countless germs, many of which cause diseases. The only shield against them is our skin, which does not let them penetrate into our bodies. The internal organs with mucous membranes, however, are not adequately protected by it; as a result of sexual relations there is always a danger of penetration by pathogenic germs to these unprotected internal organs. The Creator, however, devised a prophylactic cure by setting up a "guard" for this: Acidic secretion is always present in the vagina, which serves as a disinfectant against harmful germs. During menstruation this acidic reaction changes into an alkaline reaction, which does not protect against pathogenic germs; instead, it aids in their existence. Without the aforementioned "guard," there is a danger of contracting diseases following sexual relations during this vulnerable period, a fact that is well known to students in gynecology. The sexual organs return to their stability only after ten to eleven days following the onset of menstruation. In addition, the mucus of the womb and adjoining organs are vulnerable then. The tissue is damaged and the thin arteries are open.

The period of niddah is a time for the physical equilibrium of the woman once again to return. Rest gives the woman a chance for physical rejuvenation. This is yet another advantage of the physical separation imposed by the niddah period. In her observing ritual purity, the woman prepares herself both in a physical and in an emotional manner for her monthly "rebirth."

To the Sages, the physiological structure of the woman and the nature of the menstruant's blood was a source of great interest, study, and controversy. The Sages used a metaphor: "There is in her body, chamber[9] an ante-chamber and an upper chamber. The blood of the chamber is unclean. That of the upper chamber is clean . . ."[21]

To protect the physical and emotional well-being and resurgence of energies of both parties, various preventive measures were initiated and encouraged by the Sages. R. Akiva insists that a menstruant continue to use makeup and other cosmetics as well as colorful clothes so that she may not lose favor in the eyes of her husband.[22]

Apart from their purely religious connotation, the importance of the regulations, scrupulously observed throughout the generations, cannot be overestimated. They have proved as favorable to hygiene as to morals. The hygiene of sexual life is surely as important as the hygiene in food, since it strengthens the nation not only in this generation but the future too. If we look at society we find that all traditional Jewish women for hundreds of generations still observe the laws of family purity for their own benefit and the biological good of the Jewish people. Striking testimony has been given by scientists pointing to the fact that, though health is not put forward as the primary purpose of these regulations, such is their indubitable result.

These laws of marital continence are now held by some scientists to accord with the fundamental rhythm in woman's nature. Although medical opinion is not unanimous on this difficult subject, there can be no doubt as to the significance of statistics like the following: An investigation conducted over a number of years at the Mount Sinai Hospital in New York in connection with 80,000 Jewish women who observe the laws of *niddah* and *taharah* showed that the proportion of those suffering from uterine or cervical cancer was one Jewish woman to fifteen non-Jewish women of corresponding social and economic status. According to Professor L. Duncan Bulkey, "The consensus of opinion seems to be that Orthodox Jews observing their ritual are much less subject to cancer of the uterus than the rest of the population."[23]

Aside from the subject of uterine cancer in a greater number of women who do not observe the family purity laws, the number of stillborn births, children born blind, and those who die from childbirth diseases is far less among women who have observed these family laws.

According to Tradition, the menstrual cycle represents a combination of physical-psychic elements, a fusion of matter and spirit, of body and soul.[24] As such, the offense of transgressing the laws of ritual impurity (having intercourse during this period) is also spiritual in nature—

resulting in "the cutting off [of the soul] from among their people." (Lev. 20:18)

By following the divinely ordained life of sanctity and morality, the Jew performs one of the most important motives of the Torah—"Sanctify yourselves and be holy" (Lev. 20:7), the goal of the entire Jewish religion. "I am engaged solely with the purification of Israel," says the Lord. "Divine presence becomes manifest only among those who are pure and holy."[25]

"The whole philosophy of monotheism is contained in this rallying cry of R. Akiva: 'Happy Israel, before whom do you purify yourselves, and who cleanses you? Your Father in Heaven,' " says Hermann Cohen.[26]

The Bible exhorts man to "wash yourselves, make yourselves clean . . ." (Is. 1:16) as a literal and figurative prerequisite for ethical and moral reformation. Concern with tum'ah (impurity) and taharah (purity) was a mark of great piety.

Cleanliness was long considered by Jews as being close to Godliness. As R. Phinehas Ben Yair said, "Study leads to precision, precision leads to restraint, restraint leads to purity, purity leads to holiness."[27]

Cleanliness is an integral part of religion, seen as a purification of the spirit to keep the body clean. This element of cleanliness is, in fact, a prime condition in the niddah laws. "Scripture prescribed uncleanness in respect of both male and female. These laws, as the laws of purity regarding males, are geared to a striving for holiness."[28]

The abusive term "dirty Jew," hurled at the Jew by the Gentile world, has never been more than an anti-Semitic myth. The laws of cleanliness have been instinctively observed by religious Jews since biblical times in their approach to God. The Mosaic Law, striving to elevate man to a higher level of God-like spirituality, has prescribed for the Jewish people a definite code of ritualistic purification which goes beyond atonement offerings, sacrifices, and oblation. These laws must be seen both as sanitary measures, hygienically motivated, and as a ritualistic ordinance of a high metaphysical nature.

The conjugal union, from a Jewish aspect, is wholesome in terms of both physical and mental health. Judaism treats the whole bodily hygiene of sex as an integral part of the couple's regimen sanitatis—to promote happiness and emotional fulfillment in an aesthetic, sanitary sense. Bodily and psychic factors continually interact with and affect one another, especially in a relationship of loving partners.

Rabbinic knowledge and insight of the menstruant's physiological, physical, and emotional state helped the Sages to prescribe sanitary guidelines for the woman's understanding and benefit. This information was imparted to woman to acquaint her with symptomatic explanations and procedures. This further helped her adjust and attend to her personal needs and purification.

Not only does *taharat ha-mishpahah* stand for the very antithesis of the degradation of the Jewish woman, but it serves to protect and honor her. A woman's sexual rights are insured by her *ketubbah*; her dignity is preserved because her consent is necessary for sexual relations with her husband. The regulations of *taharat ha-mishpahah* prevent the wife from being seen as a sexual object, a possession for the fulfillment of her husband's passions and desires. Through the *mitzvot* of family purity a man recognizes that his wife is a person who possesses inner worth, autonomous value, and sacred, inalienable rights (at least equal to his own). To those who question the laws, there is no single satisfactory reason. We observe these laws as we fulfill all other *mitzvot*—because God commanded; but countless Orthodox women attribute their successful marital relations to the religious laws that safeguard their marriage.

"He who loves his wife as himself, and honors her more than himself, to him the scriptural promise is uttered, 'Thou shalt know that thy tent is in peace.' "[29]

The Mosaic Code again stands out as an astonishing example of God-inspired wisdom which should appeal with redoubled force to the enlightened minds of today. Discipline and self-control are the lessons most needed for our disenchanted times.

HAFRASHAT HALLAH

"Go eat thy bread with joy" (Eccles. 9:7) refers to
the law of hallah.
                                        —*Num. Rabbah* 17:2

Among the commandments given solely to the woman we find those of separating the *hallah* and lighting the candles. The Rabbis gave homiletical reasons for the fact that the woman always set aside the *hallah* and always lit the candles on *Shabbat* eve.[30]

The actual reason for her performance of these duties is, of course, that they are household obligations. While man's work kept him out-of-doors most of the time, woman had the privilege of looking after the family; quite naturally, it became her responsibility to set aside the *hallah* and to light the *Shabbat* candles. In her role as the *akeret ha-bayit*, Jewish Law declares that because a woman is fully occupied with the performance of daily duties, she is exempt from all positive *mitzvot* for which there is a fixed time.

Originally, the law of *hallah* applied only to the land of Israel. In order that this institution not be forgotten, the Rabbis ordained that it continue beyond Israel and for all time.[31] It is still kept in observant Jewish households where bread is baked. A small portion of the *hallah* is to be thrown into the fire. It is to be a twenty-fourth part of the dough, no more.[32] The *hallah* is not given any more to the *kohen*, because *kohanim* are today precluded from observing the laws of priestly purity and, therefore, are disqualified from eating anything that is in the nature of a holy sacrifice. The very name *hallah*, applied to the *Shabbat* loaves, actually is derived from this early biblical law requiring of the Jews to "offer a cake of the first of your dough . . . throughout your generations." (Num. 15:18–21) The Rabbis established that the dough, in order to become subject to the law of *hallah*, must consist of at least one *omer* of flour, "about two and one-half kilograms."[33]

Women bake *hallot* to honor the *Shabbat*. Adam, as the "*hallah* of the world" was created on Friday, and so, too, is the *hallah* then separated, which represents the improvement of man through the woman's action.

Woman was entrusted with the performance of the separation of the first of the *hallah* dough, symbolizing her origin at creation. Mother Earth originally gave up a portion of her body, out of which God formed spiritual man. Thereafter man yielded his rib, out of which God created woman as a partner to man, as if she were a *hallah* portion of man. God then gave her back to man as the gift of the Creator in order that they become companions to each other.

By performing the ritual of *hallah*, the Jewish woman is reenacting her origin at creation and, in turn, also sets apart the dough as a symbolic offering which she returns to her Creator. Thus woman hallows the bread and sanctifies her spiritual way of living at home for herself and for her family.

HADLAKAT NEROT

> Said the Lord, "If you will light the candles of
> Shabbat, I shall show you the Menorah candles of
> Zion."
> —*Yalkut Behaalotha* 719

The *Shabbat, Havdalah* and *Hanukkah* candles, just like the *Menorah* in the Holy Temple, indicate that "lights" play an extremely important role in the Jewish tradition. In fact, the prophet Isaiah has assigned to the Jewish people the mission of serving as "a light to the nations." (Is. 49:6) Thus it is not surprising that the Almighty's first act of Divine creation was "Let there be light." (Gen. 1:3) For without light, all that remains is darkness, chaos, confusion. The purpose of creation is simply not fulfilled without light. To illuminate the darkness of alienation, to bring warmth and security into cold indifference, to beautify the mundane: such are the purposes of the *Shabbat* lights.

Light represents inner peace, security, joy, spiritual elevation and mental tranquility, warmth, and blessing. The Lord blessed the seventh day with light.[34] The absence of light is darkness—both physical and spiritual. The candles which usher in our *Shabbat* pierce this darkness and bring light to us, our families, our homes.

The candles lit in the Jewish home are not a communal *mitzvah* but rather family-oriented. The two candles representing father and mother, heads of the household, bring light, hope, and unity to the family. Another reason for lighting two candles on *Shabbat* is that one stands for "*zakhor*" (remember) and the other candle for "*shamor*" (observe), the two principles of *Shabbat* observance mentioned in the Decalogue.[35] (Exod. 20:8; Deut. 5:12) This ceremony is also performed on holidays, with one candle symbolizing man and the other symbolizing woman. In some homes candles are lit for each member of the family, including every one of the children into the fabric of togetherness.

Tradition has bestowed the honor, privilege, and responsibility of this most sacred task to the Jewish woman.[36] In being the first to usher in the day of rest through the *mitzvah* of light, the Jewish woman renews and reinforces her ties with Tradition and teaches her daughters the beauty of such a meaningful and enchanting precept. The Jewish child is able to capture the aesthetic beauty inherent in the "light of *mitzvah*" and to carry the torch of illumination to the generations to come. The peaceful festivity of the *Shabbat* begins with the ritual of blessing the light to be bestowed upon her entire household. She prays for the love and welfare of her husband, and for her children that they may become pious and learned in the Torah, which is called light: "*Orah zu Torah*."[37] So simple an observance, yet one so full of meaning.

Maimonides, in explaining why the lighting of the candles is more the task of the woman than that of the man, states that women are in the house more often than men and, therefore, have the responsibility for home-oriented *mitzvot*.[38]

As the home was characteristically the domain of the woman, the lights marking the beginning of the *Shabbat*, symbolizing peaceful rest and relaxation, were entrusted to the woman. In marked contrast, the lights of *Havdalah*, at the conclusion of the *Shabbat*, marking the beginning of labor and week's hardships, are kindled by the man.

By bringing light into the house and adding serenity and warmth to the festive mood of the *Shabbat* and holidays, the Jewish woman contributes personally to the *shalom bayit* atmosphere of the Jewish home, contributing her feminine touch to the harmony of her family.[39] The benediction for the lighting of the candles is found as early as in the ninth-century *Siddur* of Rav Saadyah Gaon.[40] Without this symbolic and special kindling of the *Shabbat* lights, no one can really partake of the *Oneg Shabbat*, the spiritual delight of the day. In biblical language, *orah* and *simhah*, light and joy, are synonymous.[41]

The Jewish woman renews the initial act of the Lord, who has first bestowed upon His world the gift of light.

The woman kindles the torch of peace and contentment for the whole household, heralding the ray of hope, the beacon of faith in the redemption of Israel and the world at large.[42] *Shabbat*, as the weekly rejuvenation, is ushered in by the *Shabbat* candles. The materialistic life is elevated and ennobled by these rays of Jewish warmth which unite the Jewish people with the Creator. They possess the power to direct one's goals to an inner meaning in life.

7

Motherhood

> And do not abandon the teaching of your mother.
> —Proverbs 1:8.

The concept of "motherhood" is almost synonymous with that of "home." It is in the home that human relations put forth their first demands and babies develop their earliest patterns of response. It is in the home that decency, ambitions, and imagination come to life and are first cultivated. It behooves us as Jews in particular to recognize that of all the historical and sociological factors which have contributed to the phenomenon of Jewish survival, Jewish family life is the most important.

When we contrast the patriarchal order in Oriental society,[1] the woman's position in the Jewish family structure, both as the mother of her children and as the partner of the male head of the family, was not always an inferior one. Though in biblical and postbiblical times she may not have enjoyed an identical position with her husband, in certain legal and ritual areas she was treated as an individual with feelings and emotions. And in the ethical and familial realms she surely occupied the same place as the father.[2] In the confines of her home life and the education of her children, the mother is of equal importance with the father; very often she even selected a bride for her son. (Gen. 21:21)

Abraham was the first man in the Bible to be called "the father of a multitude of nations" (Gen. 17:5); Eve, however, was called "the mother of all living" (Gen. 3:20) long before. Adam was simply known as "the first man"—not as the "father of all living." This would attach to motherhood an earlier, deeper, and, consequently, more lasting mark than fatherhood.

The mother in Israel, far from being the morally and intellectually stunted creature we encounter in Eastern lands, was a woman of position, usually powerful and independent. After the death of her husband she continued as the most important and influential person in the household.

Jewish Law attributed to the woman the sacredness of the family and its centrality for both the gift of reproduction—a creative act of God,—and the role of socializing her offspring, who were solemnly entrusted to her.[3] One can look upon this unique feminine experience as a Divine favor whereby woman is entrusted by the Creator with this special partnership of bringing forth life.

Judaism proclaimed the biblical view that the child was the noblest of human treasures. "O Lord God, what wilt Thou give me, seeing that I go childless?" was Abraham's agonizing cry. (Gen. 15:2)

"Woman was created for children," declares the Talmud; indeed, "Motherhood is the main goal of a woman; it is the most fulfilling experience she may ever have, her greatest creative achievement."[4]

As a woman, she attains a new dimension: motherhood—an additional role to that of wife, which adds to her esteem.

In Sumerian culture a mother was herself regarded as the dwelling place of some divinity.[5]

It is probably true that most children are born as the realization of the instinctual wishes of their mothers.

Both sexes desire children, but women are obviously more concerned—emotionally and physiologically—with the processes attendant thereto.

Woman is biologically closer to nature and to the child than is man. The interests of women may therefore be said to be more closely identified with nature.[6] By virtue of this, she stands in the most fundamental relationship, namely, the support and sustainer without whom the child could not live during its first nine months in the womb. She will always perform the function of a mother, which is to love her child and help in its development and education.

According to Helene E. Deutsch, "Maternal instinct and maternal love are differentiated ingredients of motherliness as a whole. The instinct has a biologic-chemical source and lies beyond the psychologic sphere."[7] Woman's biological purpose seems to require completion through conceiving, bearing, and nurturing children, and strong cultural and educational directives have added impetus to the drive.

Woman is endowed with all the instincts and with keener emotions, with all her virtues and inadequacies directed toward motherhood. Maternal love is the instinctual force converted into emotions. How wisely was it constituted that tender and gentle women shall be our earliest guides, instilling their own spirit in us.

Woman's own inner harmony and intuition give her greater insight into the child's emotional processes, even more than mere pedagogic or psychological training could. Still, woman acquires her so-called maternal instincts from her culture, not from her genes. Bit by bit, from the time of her own infancy, she absorbs the techniques of motherliness in accord with the moves of her own culture. Unlike animals, she has to learn how to be kind and loving and how to want and to care for a child. The full meaning of the complex and rich human nature of motherhood, however, is not automatically determined but is in large part a learned, intelligent pattern of behavior.

The maternal instinct was observed by the Rabbis to be a universal propensity, common to all mammals. The Rabbis delved into the psychology of animals and drew parallels to human behavior.

In early Jewish thought, pregnancy was regarded as the gift of God. According to the Talmud, God never relinquished three keys: the key to the resurrection of the dead, the key to the opening of the womb, and the key for rain.[8]

As the biblical records show, for a woman not to have children was considered traumatically frustrating. In spite of the pains of labor, the longing for motherhood still remains, throughout the centuries, the most powerful instinct in woman; for "no woman wishes to be known as a barren woman." According to Lidz, "The strength of some women's drive to procreate is shown clearly by those who prefer to risk death rather than remain barren." When Rachel saw that she bore no children, Rachel envied her sister; and she said to Jacob: "Give me children, or else I die." (Gen. 30:1) "And Rachel bore a son; and she said 'God hath taken away my shame.' " (Gen. 30:23)[9]

A variety of charms have been employed throughout the ages to induce pregnancy and ease the pain of childbirth. Mention is made in the Torah of Reuben's stone, the ruby, and the mandrakes or "love apples," a fruit still considered in the East as a love charm for the inducement of pregnancy.[10]

Most women want children. When deprived of them, a woman is often willing to subject herself to any hardship to attain them. Bell found that, in childless marriages, the wives are probably more ready to take the necessary steps to resolve the problem than their husbands.

The history of civilization tells us of the tragic lot of the sterile woman who has been despised, ridiculed, disgraced. This is not true in our own culture for the masculinization of women has contributed to the devaluation of fertility. We know, too, that the male partner may be responsible for the childlessness in the infertile couple, and yet, the woman cannot escape intolerant attitudes on the part of relatives and friends, sometimes including her own husband.[11]

Fertility problems and the possibility of childlessness are generally considered more serious both biologically and psychologically to women than to men. It was found that involuntary childlessness represents a more serious problem for women than for men, who, although they may indeed be disappointed by childlessness, appear to feel less deprived and are probably more readily compensated by occupational activity.

An exception to this universal law of nature is the loose woman. She is deaf to the call of her intrinsic nature, does not respond to her maternal instinct, and aims to prevent conception in every way. In some prostitutions, masculinity manifests itself in the negation of motherhood. To them, as women, sexuality has the same meaning as to the men—a pleasurable discharge without the consequence of motherhood.[12]

Woman's craving for sons and daughters—and particularly for the former—was always intensive. Besides her compulsion by the law of nature to propagate and to preserve mankind, she "desires to have a staff to lean upon and a hoe to make her grave."[13] In other words, she is eager to have a son to support her in old age, to provide for her burial, and to be remembered with a "*kaddish.*" However, her paramount aim in life remains motherhood.[13]

It is of interest that in an early Hindu custom the most important function of a wife was doubtless that of bringing into the world a son in order that he might perform the necessary funeral rites for his father and continue the lineage.[14]

Woman's greatest concern is that her child be normal; her greatest fear that it will not be perfect. She tries to do whatever she can to ensure the safety of the child's journey into the world. She takes care that no act of hers will mark her baby or interfere with its growth and development. She scrupulously watches her diet for proper nutrition avoiding both mutagens and carcinogens; protects herself from exposure to X-rays; and carefully monitors her alcoholic and drug intake. All these are precautions against the slightest possible chromosomal or genetic harm to her fetus.

The Rabbis urged the nursing mother to preserve her own health and watch her diet, so that the quality of her milk would insure proper nourishment for her child.

A great desire for food is often associated with pregnancy. This represents the woman's protective mechanism for the infant and is reflected in the myth that "She must eat for two." This saying about "eating for two," though often incorrectly applied, is sound in its implication that what a woman eats affects her own as well as the unborn child's health and development.

The effect of certain foods and odors on the pregnant woman and her unborn child has been amply discussed by the Sages.

The pregnant woman has always been cautioned about the types of foods to be eliminated from her diet and advised about foods beneficial to herself and her child. Certain foods and beverages (e.g., fish, eggs, onions, cucumbers, leeks, beer, wine) were investigated for their possible ill effects upon the pregnant woman and the nursing mother.[15]

Precautions for the pregnant woman were legion. The safeguards prescribed by the Rabbis transcend the most mundane aspects of our everyday life. It was customary for pregnant women to carry a certain stone so they would not miscarry. Prayers and charity, sanitary devices, and symbolic rituals were employed to prevent miscarriage.

The protection of the pregnant woman was the Rabbis' chief concern. In fact, in the Temple at Jerusalem, the High Priest used to include in his Day of Atonement prayer a special supplication "that the pregnant women should not abort."[16]

This attitude is manifest in the psychological observation of the Talmud: No woman wants to be known as one who is never able to carry through a successful pregnancy.

Miscarriage is a traumatic blow to a woman, shattering to her hopes and plans. If she is young or has other children, she may accept it philosophically. But to an older, childless woman it spells tragedy and grief. It indicates to her a profound failure. She blames herself for things she has done or not done, or she suspects some hidden abnormality of her body.

Failure to achieve pregnancy has an effect on her personality that could prove destructive. The woman is not only concerned with her physical misfortune, but, on the emotional level, doubts her status as a woman, her marital relationship and her husband's feelings for her, and even her ability to assume her place in society as a mother. These emotional problems can create havoc with the feelings of a woman who has had a miscarriage or abortion.[17]

The Sages endeavored to understand the workings of the womb. Conjecture led to further contemplation and resolution about the miracle of birth and the tragedy of miscarriage. They stated that "a woman who miscarried, and then miscarried a second, and a third time, is confirmed as one subject to abortions."[18]

But in the case of a woman afflicted by disease, to abort or give birth to stillborn children is no longer a cause of shame, and she is more resigned to the pain, when it occurs. Grief is no longer new to her and her frustration threshold is not easily triggered.[19]

Sometimes a pregnancy, which in itself is normal, is terminated in the interest of the welfare of the mother. This, a therapeutic abortion, for the purpose of protecting or perhaps saving the life of the mother, is, in Jewish Law, a legal and aboveboard procedure.[20]

According to talmudic statistics, most women conceive, and most pregnant women successfully complete the full term of their pregnancy, and give birth to healthy children.[21] The mother's health and well-being during childbirth are of primary import; and, therefore, all is done to facilitate the delivery and insure its fulfillment.

During the period of pregnancy and nursing, the woman is accorded utmost consideration and special care by the Law. She is considered seriously incapacitated and given the rabbinic benefits accorded to a seriously ill person. The restrictions of the Sabbath or the Day of Atonement are waived in special situations.[22]

The duration of the pregnancy was uniformly attested to as being nine months.[23]

There are references in the Talmud to a child that is *yotze dofen*, delivered by a Caesarean section. Such a delivery was not regarded as a genuine birth, and, as such, the child did not reap either the benefits or the duties afforded the firstborn.[24]

A fairly large group of women have one child and then cannot become pregnant again. The reason for this is as yet a mystery—both organically and hormonally.[25] In early talmudic times, however, surgery was not performed successfully for certain complications, such as rupture of the uterus or lacerations of the cervix or of other organs, and these could easily have caused a woman to lose the ability to carry a fetus.

An instance of a woman's inherent adaptability to pain and suffering is clearly seen during the time of giving birth, and later, in the arduous process of raising her children.[26] Yiddish folklore conveys this idea thus: "Woman is like the reed which bends to every breeze, but breaks not in the tempest."

Tradition holds that pious women adjust easily to their travail, which they take in stride because of their submissiveness and devotion to God's will. They accept pregnancy and labor pains naturally and do not allow themselves to become overwhelmed by the physical and emotional trauma of giving birth.[27]

The expectant mother spends long hours daydreaming about the fetus growing within her; daydreaming about whom the child will resemble, its future accomplishments, what the child will mean in her and her husband's life.

The most fascinating aspect of the pregnancy is the unpredictable sex of the unborn child. "It was taught: Seven things are concealed from man. . . . No one knows what a woman is bearing."[28]

From the time she becomes pregnant, up to the time of her confinement, woman is preoccupied by the thought of the sex of the child. Prediction of an embryo's sex is now available with amniocentesis for diagnostic purposes.

To assure a male offspring, various suggestions were advanced. Rabba suggested coition twice in succession. Kabbalah suggests that atmospheric conditions (certain types of air or weather) were more conducive to the birth of a specific sex.

For producing male children, folklore advocates the biting of the etrog (citrus fruit) by the pregnant woman. It was believed that the sex of the embryo could change during pregnancy and that there was no differentiation of sex until the forty-first day of pregnancy.[29]

Talmudical statistics on the sex of children born show that 50 percent were males and 50 percent were females. Nowadays the theoretical sex ratio is one male to one female, but at birth it is actually about 106 males to 100 females. The sex ratio of spontaneous abortions is about the same as the sex ratio of births.[30]

Under normal and usual conditions, Israelite women in biblical times gave birth in their homes with the help of midwives, and only women were present in the house during the hours of labor.[31] Nowadays, women have been turning to midwives again for practical and convenient reasons. The husband's presence nearby is also very helpful and supportive during the delivery.

Let us now view the rabbinic observations on the postpartum state. As a rule, women were expected to breast-feed their children, since mothers are the source of sustenance and survival of their babies.[32] However, the Law forbade any husband to force his nursing wife to breast-feed the child of his friend against her will. The mother's breast, the source of the infant's nourishment, is extremely important to the well-being of the offspring, though nursing mothers are themselves generally of delicate health.[33]

R. Jose stated: In postpartum her limbs are disjointed and her natural strength does not return before twenty-four months. Hence, the High Priest in the Temple also used to pray in behalf of the nursing women that they may be able to nurse.[34]

As to the origin of this nurturing milk, it was taught by R. Meir that the blood becomes turbid and disturbed and the flow of milk begins.[35]

Psychologically, it may be stressed that the origin of love depends upon the first contact with the mother, specifically with the mother's breast. And while the infant benefits from the mother's readiness to nurse and care for him, the mother fulfills her own psychological and emotional needs as a mother.

Scant research and objective data are available concerning woman's functioning, childbirth, her succor, normal mothering, and childbearing. Women's longevity nowadays is extended. Being less needed for their childbearing, and coupled with the development of child care facilities, home maintenance, and homemaker services, women are freer to assume part-time roles other than wife and mother. Similarly, with the advancement of knowledge in the biobehavioral and gynecological areas, women will achieve greater control over their bodies and their health. This is becoming a vital concern for both the scientist and halakhist, who must integrate their disciplines to promote the mental and physical health of the Jewish woman in particular and of the family in general.

Proper transition to motherhood appears to depend on one's having a nonconflicting model of one's own mother and on being in a sufficiently nurturing and protective milieu. Experience and the voluntary full expression of maternal love—the direct affective expression of the positive relation to the child—are the important factors in good mothering.

Until very recently, modern American culture and mores appeared less conducive to successful breast-feeding, which, in itself, was never full proof of successful or sensitive motherhood.

When the mother takes her child to her breast after its arrival, not only does its cry or its touch give rise to an emotional reaction, but a beneficial physical state is established within the woman herself. It is the element of motherliness—her consolidating emotional relationship to the child.[36]

As for the advantages of the breast-fed baby already indicated in the Talmud, we may cite the following modern findings:

1. Breast milk is more easily digested.
2. Breast milk is always available.
3. Breast-feeding yields greater immunity to certain childhood diseases. Antibacterial and antiviral factors are believed to be transmitted in milk.
4. Breast-feeding reduces G-I disorders and food allergies.
5. The baby suffers fewer colds and severe respiratory infections.
6. The baby is less prone to anemia or vitamin deficiency.
7. The milk is more sterile.
8. The baby can regulate its milk intake.[37]

Helene E. Deutsch points out that many women who willingly devote themselves to nursing enjoy a special feeling of contentment having to do with a consciousness of the infant's well-being; the frequent reluctance to breast-feed, conversely, is related to fears of losing attractiveness, freedom, comfort, and vocational achievement. On the other hand, some women who cannot nurse relinquish other aspects of maternal love—having suffered a trauma in the failure to nurse, they take flight from a close relationship with the infant altogether. "Breast-feeding has definite advantages that we know of, and, it may have others that we haven't learned yet," says Dr. Spock, to which child psychologists add that "the breast-fed baby is the best-fed baby, is a lot more than a mere slogan." Most doctors agree that there are ingredients in mother's milk which are not only more nourishing and easily digested than cow's milk but may very possibly also convey all kinds of immunities to later diseases and infection.[38]

A breast-fed baby manifests placidity and absence of frustration, which enable it to progress in a state of uninterrupted good health. Digestive problems or irritability occur only in a small percentage of these children as compared with bottle-fed infants.

Breast-feeding has been advocated because it provides enhancement of the mother-infant relationship and because of its nutritional importance and the sucking pleasure it provides. At times one or other of these factors constitutes the main reason, while at other times all three apply.

Advocates of breast-feeding speak of it as the foundation upon which true maternal feeling rests. One author asserts, for instance, that genuine mother love and maternal care are based upon the pleasure of gratifying a fundamental structural and physiological function in the mother and the suckling. The dimensions and meaning of the mother's love for the child grow for many years after he had ceased to gratify her breast; and, thanks to her humanity, this is true even if, for medical reasons, she was never able to breast-feed him. The fact is that even if she neither conceived, bore, nor suckled him, as with adoptive mothers—who, by quasi-traditional reasoning, ought to be almost incapable of motherly love—they very often succeed in becoming excellent mothers.

The Rabbis advocated that after a maximum of twenty-four months the child be weaned from the mother's breast and accustomed to other eating habits, which include whole foods. The pre-primary age of four or five years is traditionally marked as the beginning of the child's independence of his mother.[39]

They determined that there is no exception to the rule of maternal attachment in humans. They noticed that no healthy-minded woman would do harm to her child for selfish motives. She will suffer and struggle for existence but will never act cruelly toward her offspring.[40]

A woman becomes almost superhuman when her child's happiness or welfare or life is threatened. Her patience and capacity for self-sacrifice are typically feminine virtues and can never be remotely realized by a man. Nevertheless, the mother-child relationship cannot, no matter how skillful and gifted and kindly a mother is, always go smoothly.

On the other hand, the Rabbis were also aware of the fact that nobody would renounce his own pleasure in favor of another person: narcissism is a universal instinct in all human beings.

On this subject, psychoanalysis shows that in the normal cases the mother's sexual instincts are sublimated into tenderness for her baby and her aggressive instincts into protective activity in its behalf. Through tender and protective acts she facilitates the gratification of her own narcissistic needs to be loved. The process of mothering, though apparently a natural and biologic one, involves difficult tasks, especially in view of the many conflicts that take place between the mother's personal interests and those more strictly related to the child.

A mentally disturbed woman—one with a Medea complex or who is immoral—would forgo her maternal love for selfish purposes and even give away her offspring; so, too, a woman who is madly in love, who does care for her children but disregards their legal status.[41]

Similarly, in a traumatic crisis, hunger as well as shyness are powerful enough to override the maternal instinct. In years of famine, many mothers cast away their children. This was done in the hope that they would be found and provided for by others, for the mothers could no longer bear their babies' heartrending cries for nourishment.[42]

We now turn to another aspect of motherhood—tenderness. This makes the mother-child relationship among the most important and exciting that the human being ever experiences.

When a particularly tender relation is pictured by the biblical writers, a mother's love is often invoked to symbolize the thought. "God could not be everywhere, and therefore He makes mothers," says a Jewish proverb. God himself is comforting his people "as a mother comforts her son." God will not forget them [the persecuted] "even as a mother cannot forget her child." (Is. 66:13; 49:15)

Living for children means living through children. Parents identify with the child, whose welfare becomes their concern. Indeed, motherhood is a complex and an ambivalent role; it is the single most demanding and rewarding aspect of the traditional Jewish role. Every woman is an extraordinary being to her child; she carries the greatest share and burden of parenting her children. In meeting the primary social expectations of womanhood, woman devotes the productive years of her life to caring mainly for others.

The Midrash relates a story that illustrates a mother's compassion for her child. A distressed widow appeared before a judge in order to complain about her son. As she saw the harshness of the sentences being passed on others, she feared for her son's fate and decided not to disclose her son's culpability to the judge, lest he sentence him to death. She waited until he finished the other cases. When he finally asked her, "What is the nature of your son's offense?" she replied, "Your Honor, when my son was in my womb he used to kick me." "So," the judge replied, "does he do you any harm now?" "No," she answered. The judge dismissed her.[43]

The mother's concern for her child, say the Rabbis, displays a unique attitude in human weaknesses, resulting from her love. As a rule, the mother will worry over her child's reluctance to eat, drink, or go to school.[44]

The mother is the child's source of comfort, nourishment, protection. She fills the role of surrogate ego for her child, selecting what is useful and harmful and providing the guidance that the child is not yet able to provide for himself.

In the light of the unflinching stress accorded to education in Jewish tradition, it is not surprising to find that great recognition was given to the task of imbuing the child with the love of learning. This was exclusively the mother's role—a role highly appreciated by the Rabbis.

PERPETUATION: THE MOTHER AS TEACHER

The mother is the child's first—and often best—teacher. One can surely note that educating a man means educating an individual, while educating a woman leads to the education of a family. Similarly, Clare Booth Luce gives the following insight into the mother's role as educator:

> Modern man when faced with contemporary questions has been prone to ask: "Is it good for business, or for my Labor Union, or my Political Party?" Woman asks, rather: "Is it good for the family, the children?" For she knows better than man "that the ultimate economic and spiritual unit of any civilization is still the family, and all questions should be answered with respect to the well-being, happiness and solidarity of the individual family unit.[45]

The Jewish mother inspires and encourages Torah learning, while the father is responsible for the actual teaching. This facet of the mother's role in the upbringing of the children is probably one of the most strenuous of all the hardships in the training of children; in the words of Emerson: "Men are what their mothers made of them." Children are what their mothers are; no father's fondest care can so fashion the infant's heart or so shape his life. It is believed that the capacity for attaining satisfying motherhood is based upon the kind of identifications a woman has had with her own mother.[46]

Tradition asserts that the mother, attached to her children with such devotion, will even forgo the familiar pleasure of celebrating the festivals at her paternal home, which she loves, if she cannot bring her children along. She will prefer to remain with them.[47] Truly, a mother "lives only for her child." She devotes her life to it and is uncomfortable whenever she is away from it.

The four mothers of the Jewish people, Sarah, Rivkah, Rachel and Leah, are the paragons of virtue, the Matriarchs *par excellence* who represent the ideal of motherly love, faith and reverence. They are symbolized by the four cups of redemption at the *seder* night on *Pesach*. Our ancestress Rachel weeps and pleads for her children of Israel that they are no more, slain or driven into exile. In the words of the prophet, "a voice is heard on high," Rachel's lamentation has ascended to the heights of Heaven. (Jer. 31:14–16)

The Midrash states that her love for her children is more intense than that of the father. Among parents, the mother loves the children more than the father and is emotionally far more involved with them, particularly when the children are beset with troubles. While father pities, mother consoles.[48]

A mother usually feels her daughter is weaker and hence needs more help and support than a son might need. The mother's memory of her own pubescence psychologically constitutes a factor in her relation to her maturing daughter. The mother tries, successfully or not, to protect her daughter from repeating her own mistakes; she projects her own repressed striving onto her daughter.[49]

For her travail she receives her just reward, the faithful devotion and respect of her children. She is remembered and lauded for her most important role, for which she continues to be extolled throughout the generations.

Daughters relate to and identify with their mothers more than they do with their fathers, claim our Sages. And the sons—who are loved by the father much more than the daughters—respect and love their mother even more than they do their father.[50]

In young children we find how the instinctive growth of this feeling of affection may be observed from day to day. Thus we see them cling to their mother's skirts when danger threatens. As a rule, it is the kindly mother, who forgives and provides everything, to whom the child turns, and who is seen by the child in sharp contrast with the strict and comparatively aloof father. Is it, then, not perfectly natural that the child's affection should be concentrated on the mother rather than on the father?

Robert Bell feels that children will generally perceive the mother in a different light from the father, since the mother role tends to be anchored between the family and the mother-child systems; the father role between the family and the extra-familial systems. The fact that the mother is involved in a variety of role activities means that her children see her role as more extended than the father's. The evidence appears to clearly illustrate that the mother is the major parental influence for both sons and daughters before puberty.[51]

"A boy's mother is the first object of his love," says Freud, "and she remains so too during the formation of his Oedipus complex and, in essence, all through his life. For a girl too, her first object must be her mother."[52]

In contrast to the midrashic view of mother-daughter identification—which could be explained in terms of the Oriental culture and its patriarchal setup, with separate living quarters for each sex and less paternal involvement with the daughters than with the sons—the classical Freudian view is that the conclusion of the infancy period is marked in the child by his becoming emotionally attached to the parent of the opposite sex. The relationship is pleasurable to both partners, but social standards ultimately interfere with it. The boy must, eventually, identify with his father, his appropriate role model, if he is to assume the adult male status successfully. It seems probable that it is more important for the boy to give up his Oedipal tie with his mother than for the girl to relinquish her ties with her father. Assumption of the adult status requires from the man relative independence, dominance, and initiative in social interaction and the taking on of responsibility as head of the family. He cannot move directly from being mother's little boy to being his wife's little boy without social reprobation and loss of self-esteem. It is, however, acceptable for a girl to move from being father's little girl to being her husband's little girl, with less censure. In reality, a large percentage of people never resolve their Oedipal ties, and the psychodynamic consequences arrest their adult functioning. Nowadays, many intelligent women show growing awareness of and objection to being father's little girl.

The Rabbis point out that daughters will confide almost everything to their mothers. Only if the mother is dead does the father take her place in this regard. Children feel closer to the father when there is a stepmother than when their own mother is present. This might be compensation for the loss of the mother's love.[53]

In defining the essence of maternal and paternal love, Fromm claims that a mother's love by its very nature is unconditional. Mother loves a newborn baby because it is hers, not because it has fulfilled any specific conditions or expectations. Fatherly love is conditional love based on the principle of fulfillment of expectations. The mother's and the father's attitudes toward the child correspond to the child's own needs. Mother's unconditional love and physiological and psychical care are needed by the infant. After the child reaches age six, father's love as well as his authority and guidance become necessary.[54] Mother's function is to provide the child with security; father's function is to teach and guide him.

The supreme self-sacrifice of a mother is well illustrated in the classical biblical story of the two harlots and King Solomon's sagacious judgment. (1 Kings 3:16–27)

Maternal love is the purest, and at the same time the most efficient form of love because it is the most compassionate, most sympathetic, most understanding, and the least censorious.

The Rabbis observed that a mother's love is not only confined to her children but extends to those who are fond of them. Even enemies become friends when their children befriend each other. An old English proverb declares: "He that would the daughter win, must with the mother first begin." Ignace Lepp remarks that detachment from the children by their father is resented by many women as a sign of a lack of love for themselves. This frequently results in their growing farther apart from their husbands and directing their affection more and more to the children.[55]

A mother's love for those who care for her child certainly includes her sons-in-law, and especially her first son-in-law. Yet this fondness for her son-in-law can sometimes be so extreme as to lead her into falling in love with him. The Rabbis advised the father-in-law to be on guard against such a possibility.[56]

The mother, say our Sages, always endeavors to help her daughter to win the respect and love of her young husband; to achieve this, she would even give away her husband's savings to her son-in-law, in order to requite her son-in-law's affections for her daughter. She offers her counsel based on her experience to her daughter in the hope that she will heed it.

The mother's love for her son is demonstrated to a higher degree and more freely than that of a wife for her husband. He is the only male other than her husband toward whom she may halakhically display affection.[57]

An example of motherly love for her child is depicted in the
following eighteenth-century *tehinah:* A Mother's Prayer on the
Wedding Day of Her Son

Almighty God! Thou hast proclaimed that "man should leave his father and mother and cleave to his wife," that he should live with her and pursue by her side the pilgrim paths of this earthly life. Thanks be unto Thee for this day, this solemn day, on which my son shall enter into the sacred covenant with the wife of his choice, with the dear being he has chosen as the consort of his life. Thanks be unto Thee, above all, that Thou hast preserved him, that Thou hast ever surrounded him with the wings of Thy grace and love, and hast saved him from the numberless dangers of this life. O, be Thou further with him in all his ways and prosper his undertakings. Do Thou, who art the source of all blessings and love, bless the union of love which he shall conclude this day before Thy countenance, that he may find the blessing for which he hopes—a wife that shall always create joy for him and never cause him grief or woe, a companion that shall persevere with him in all the chances and changes of life. Grant, O God, that concord and contentment may ever dwell between them, that not the smallest cloud may darken the horizon of their matrimonial happiness.

All gracious Father! One more thing I ask of Thee, in whose hands are the hearts of man, who directest them as streams of water. Grant that though my child shall leave the house of his parents, filial love may never leave his heart. Grant that his devotion for his consort of life may not weaken or deaden the feelings for those who gave him life and educated him, that he may continue to be our joy and delight and preserve that love and reverence in his soul, for Thou has promised long life here on earth and full Divine reward in eternity . . . Amen. [From an 18th-century *tehinah* in Yiddish]

The mother exercises strong influence over her daughter; hence the mother is usually held responsible for her. When the daughter is indecent, people blame the mother and call her a "bad mother," even if she (the mother) is innocent. As the talmudic saying goes: "Ewe follows ewe; a daughter's acts are like those of her mother," or, in the words of the Kabbalah: "The daughter is the heiress of the mother."[58]

Traditionally, parents do not hesitate to consider their sons and daughters-in-law as their own children.[59]

As to the relationship toward the stepmother, classic folktales seem to confirm that, in the eyes of the stepchildren, she is always the wicked one, while the stepfather is not necessarily wicked; this seems to be true of both female and male children. As a rule, stepmothers have difficulty winning their stepchildren's affection, their attitude is often hostile, for they resent the stranger's intrusion vehemently. The psychological task of the stepmother is even more complicated when she brings children of her own into her new marriage.

Hysterically predisposed stepmothers with exaggerated emotions, who display an enthusiastic readiness to love their stepchildren, feel disappointed and discouraged by the children's distrustful attitude and withdraw their readiness to love and become negative in their relation. The warmth and tender solicitude formerly fantasied by the stepmother in her relationship to the children is gone. Instead, she experiences a frustration reaction, and the good foster mother becomes the wicked stepmother.

Affection for stepparents is extremely low compared with affection for one's own parents. Studies show that the level of affection by children toward stepfathers is usually much lower than toward real fathers, but the lowest level of affection was found to be by children to their stepmother. Stepfathers fared better than stepmothers in terms of affectional bonds.

The child may be even more uncertain of his relationship to the various members of the family, when half-siblings and stepsiblings are added. The stepparent may discriminate against his stepchildren if he sees in the stepchild a rival for the spouse's affection.[60]

If, as shown, a mother is capable of going to extremes in her self-sacrifice and devotion for her own children, how unpredictable is her behavior in relation to children that are not her own when she is required to act in a maternal role and carry fully the responsibilities of motherhood! A stepmother may tyrannize her stepchildren; as good as she is to her own child, so she may tend to be bad to her stepchild. A Yiddish proverb claims: "There is as yet no chair in Paradise for a good stepmother."

THE MOTHER OF TODAY

There are undoubtedly deep roots nourishing the concept of motherhood. Today's concept of motherhood is a changed one, different from those of previous generations. Modern woman is fascinated by the classic image, yet fearful of the effect on her future sex life, her figure, and her career.

The stereotypical "Jewish Mother" who compulsively overdoes her job has become, sadly enough, a literary model of overcommitted mothering. To the modern American mother, the task of motherhood is fraught with uncertainty and anxiety.

Attendance at maternity classes given by clinics and hospitals, the strong interest in child care, education, and the growth of PTA's and parent clinics all evidence the strong desire of modern woman to be a competent, informed mother. Yet the air resounds with Portnoy-like complaints charging the Jewish mother with the castration and sissification of her sons; with secretly rejecting her children; with psychologizing about them instead of mothering them; and with either coldly abandoning them to a maid or suffocating them with an excess of maternal devotion and overprotection. What an injustice committed against mother.

The Jewish mother is totally involved. She is at work, and yet is the one who is trying to be at home during the child's formative years— even if it involves much sacrifice on her part, not only taking her child out into the world but making sure that the world is brought into the home.

She is in almost total charge of ego-building discipline and the physical, moral, and psychological welfare of her children. She is determined and zealous to provide her children with the best and most constructive home atmosphere of which she is humanly capable. She instills in her offspring a love of learning, the first in the Jewish hierarchy of values, a reverence for knowledge, compulsively pushing them toward accomplishment.

One factor that is most clear about the Jewish mother is that of her commitment. This mother cares, tries to give the best to the child. What this commitment entails can probably be seen in the form of intense stimulation of the child in the earlier years. The mother's intensity no doubt invokes reciprocal intensity in the child and is constantly stimulated and directed in terms of superego pressure when the child grows older.

This concern at times hurtles into overprotectiveness; yet it is this genuine concern which ensures the child's strength, the sense of identity, and the healthy value of the self. Modern Jewish woman, like her earlier counterparts, is extremely cognizant of the major facts of Jewish family life, one of which is that the family generally is very closely knit. Primary responsibility for keeping family ties close falls on the shoulder of the Jewish wife. She is expected to entertain, visit, send cards, telephone, and do other communication chores. She controls the social balance.

Women should indeed involve themselves in their homes and families, but the attitude that through this self-abnegation alone are they expected to find fulfillment is psychologically damaging. If a woman's sense of worth is dependent solely upon the accomplishments and worth of her family and not on her own merits, she is more vulnerable to feelings of isolation and loss than a woman whose sense of worth comes from her own interests, successes, and merits.

8

Woman and Sex

> Sex is a two-faceted experience; it can be the
> expression of earthiness or that of spirituality.
> —M. Brayer

The Rabbis fully acknowledged the power of the sexual drive upon man's ideation, stating that a man is constantly preoccupied with two thoughts, the thought of women and the thought of money.[1] Therefore, they said, no one is immune to illicit attractions, for "even the most pious of the pious cannot be guardians against unchastity."[2]

Sexual *yetzer hara*—the tempting desire incited by woman—is overpowering, as seen in the story of R. Hiyya bar Ashi.

Frequently, R. Hiyya Bar Ashi would fall upon his face and cry, "O Merciful One; save us from the Tempter." One day his wife overheard him. "What could be the meaning of this?" she reflected. "It is so many years that he has held aloof from me. Why, then, should he pray thus? Surely he can restrain his passions." One day, while he was studying in his garden, she adorned herself and repeatedly walked up and down before him. "Who are you?" he demanded. "I am Harutha [a well-known prostitute of that town], and I have returned today," she replied. He desired her. Said she to him, "Bring me that pomegranate from the uppermost bough." He jumped up, went, and brought it to her. When he reentered his house, his wife was firing the oven, whereupon he ascended and sat in it. "What means this?" she demanded. He told her what had befallen him. "It was I," she assured him, but he paid no heed

121

until she gave him proof (the pomengranate). "Nevertheless," he said, "my intention was evil."[3]

Purity of mind was viewed as crucial in stimulating proper conduct. A strict code of sexual morality exists in definite terms in the Bible. Even in those early biblical times, the Jewish people firmly believed in the institution of marriage, sanctioned sexual intercourse only within the legalized framework of marriage, and prohibited it otherwise.

One of the reasons that today's Jewish laws and customs are so particularly interesting is that many of them represent an unbroken continuation of Jewish religious tradition as practiced in the ancient Middle East society. Many of these ancient laws and customs are the foundations of Western morality and ethics.

The early foundations pertaining to the control of sex were related to the milieu of the ancient Hebrews. The Jews of the First Commonwealth had a relatively uncomplicated legal view of sex; it was not a social problem for them.

Early preexilic admonitions on sex were directed mainly against the sex orgies related to heathen rituals and phallic worship. There were denunciations more against idolatrous paganism than sexual immorality.

During the First Commonwealth, sexual matters were viewed realistically as a natural human need, and the Pentateuchal laws regulating sexual morality were often not enforced except in cases of flagrant public violations, such as incest, rape, or adultery.[4]

The biblical terminology used for sexual morality was also employed for other transgressions (with the exception of the sexual term *zimmah*—libidinousness, showing further that the pretalmudic Jew was not overly conscious of sex matters but viewed them as a normal function of human life.

Both men and women were seen as interdependent, and it was believed that a man discovers himself only through union with a woman. By virtue of becoming one flesh, man and woman were led to the building of the family. (Gen. 2:24) The ideal in the sexual act was propagation of the species through the institution of the family, the stability factor of society. Sex offenses were not regarded as a unique category of sin but were subsumed with other transgressions of the Law.

In the postexilic period, Jewish attitudes toward sex morality changed basically. Commerce developed in Judea, and the Jewish society changed from one that was agricultural in character to a commercial urban community. Cities then, as cities in our day, tended to be centers of immorality; and in a sincere effort to minimize the influence of immorality among their people, the Rabbis instituted additional laws. These laws resulted in the curtailing of the woman's freedom outside her home and in the restricting of her social status.

Coincidentally, a more rigorous moral code was developing among the sophisticated Jews returning from the Babylonian exile. Thus, more and more, new restrictions came into being in the private relations between the sexes, and highly strict standards of sexual morality were enforced.

A new concept was developing in which woman was seen as the fountainhead of temptation, and man was conceived as a weak, helpless creature overwhelmed by inborn impulses.[5] It came to be understood by some sects, as expressed in the Apocryphal writings, that Evil engulfs man, and one of its chief manifestations is the sexual drive. Besides leading to stricter sexual codes in Judaism, this new view brought about an increasing emphasis toward asceticism and nazirite philosophy and eventually did much to mold Christian doctrines.

The Apocryphal and pseudo-Apocryphal literatures abound with negativistic echoes about woman. They warn against the free mingling of the sexes and urge segregation.[6]

FROM THE TALMUD, THE KABBALAH AND RABBINIC TEXTS

On the heels of the destruction of the Second Temple and the Jews' dispersion among nations came the exposure to the Gentile society. Assimilation and disintegration were real dangers. In early Greece and Rome, sexual behavior was an expression of pagan taste and custom. In order to safeguard, solidify, and discipline the internal integrity of the people and assure the survival of Jewish customs and traditions, numerous legalistic restrictions —takanot—were instituted. Hence we find during that period still further constraints upon social relations between Jew and Gentile, between man and woman.

During the talmudic period, the Rabbis dispelled the earlier fear of woman and denied her putative Satanic role. They held that a moderate restriction of women's freedom was sufficient and that isolating them and denying them social freedom was unfair and cruel. It is related that when Papus Ben Yehuda, upon leaving his house, locked his wife in to prevent her from wrongdoing, he was strongly rebuked by the Rabbis.[7]

The talmudic Weltanschauung was humanitarian in its outlook. It opposed earlier asceticism, which regarded the flesh as evil. The Rabbis taught that man has the ability to control his passion and that, if properly directed, man's sexual drive becomes the source of energy for sublimated activities. Accordingly, the goods of the physical world were to be enjoyed—but in moderation and in accordance with the prescribed laws. Thus the Amora Rava (d. 352 C.E.) openly defended the *yetzer hara*—our sensual passion—as a positive and vitally necessary factor which "was very good" (Gen. 1:31) because, without it, "no one would build a house, nor take a wife and beget children."[8]

The *yetzer hara* was to be kept in balance and controlled by man. It is credited with helping humanity by keeping the human race alive, as reflected by R. Shimon ben Lakish, who gave thanks for the "sin" of our parents which resulted in our coming into this world.[9]

So marriage represented a healthy social institution, the foundation of ethnic life whereby the libidinal drive is formally channeled and socially accepted as a normal function of life. In this state, man and woman can fully partake of the unique relationship of love and sex with the full sanction of God and society alike. The Rabbis advocated for the normative Jew the pietist concept of *kadesh atzmekha be-muttar lakh*—"sanctify yourself [even] within the permissible realm." Unlike Paul, they never condemned the sexual drive as evil and certainly did not condemn woman as the source of evil. Rather, they looked upon sex as a normal function of life, to be indulged in within the marital union, rather than in any form of unchastity or licentiousness, in order to perpetuate the human species and thus regenerate the Jewish people.[10]

This rabbinic attitude afforded woman much more freedom than before. It relaxed her previous confinement to the house and allowed her more social contacts with the outside world. It permitted her to engage in business pursuits both at home and in the market. She participated in social affairs, in Bible study, in ritual matters, as well as in relations with the neighboring cultures (Greek and Latin).

Concerning woman's sexual behavior, the rabbinic morality of the talmudic period strove toward aesthetic purity and spiritual upright-ness, as will be seen later.

Though it may seem that sexual morality in *aggadah* differs with that codified in *halakhah*, the truth of the matter is that both express the various rungs one must ascend on the way toward saintliness—a person's closest proximity to God.

If the *aggadah* homiletically shows the ideal, *halakhah* deals more with one's workaday behavior, regulating and refining sexual conduct.

Both these rabbinic teachings became the norms for the medieval codifier; hence a new pietistic-moralistic sexual regimen was developed during the Middle Ages in the Jewish ghetto in which disciplined standards of everyday conduct were implemented by strict guidelines to moral perfection. This trend of ascetic control of sexual proscriptions to achieve elevation of the soul was inherent in the spiritual *Zeitgeist* of the Middle Ages, and it is, therefore, no surprise that traces of it found their way into Jewish laws and customs of the time.

This dichotomy between one's bodily desires and his/her spiritual needs led the medieval Jewish philosophers to conclude that the human being embodies two eternally warring entities: one, the animalistic, physical entity manifested by one's orgiastic sexual appetite; and, two, the immortal, sublime aspect, or soul, manifested by the yearning for holiness.

According to the Talmud, one should strive to sublimate and master one's instinctual drives to the supernal morals and ethical demands of the soul.[11]

Sublimating the sexual drives through intellectual endeavors, study of the Divine Law, religious contemplation, and spiritual fulfillment, while enjoying the worldly goods (which one ought not to ignore but indulge in moderately), became the moral code of conduct for the medieval Jew toward self-realization and the attainment of the two worlds, the here and the hereafter.

The Jewish outlook during the Middle Ages, as expressed by the pietists and moralists, was, essentially, a belief in the dualism of the human personality, where the body coalesces with the soul, which they termed "Reason." To them, reason is the core of the universal reality, the highest human attainment. A person's physical needs and desires are merely a conduit in the process of one's spiritual self-fulfillment. Similar views are echoed in the works of early Jewish philosophers.

R. Saadyah Gaon (882–942) is his *Book of Beliefs and Opinions*, discusses sexual intercourse and its therapeutic value as an antidote against melancholy. According to him, its greatest values are that "it is the cause of the coming into being of the rational being endowed with intelligence [called] 'human,' and that it forms the unique basis of "human sociability, and friendly relations."[12]

Sexual union, he contends, could not be inherently reprehensible or shameful; otherwise the Lord Himself would have restrained His prophets from engaging in it. The sexual appetite, therefore, should be satisfied, not abused, for the purposes of procreation and for establishing a close bond between husband and wife.

R. Bahya (second half of the eleventh c.) suggests that G-d implanted the sexual instinct in human beings for the purpose of procreating other individuals to take their place in the world. The pleasure that comes to a person during the sexual act is actually G-d's gift for the human being's part in the procreation process. Reason and understanding should thus predominate over the physical inclinations, and one is exhorted against libidinous excesses. In the rabbinic literature of the Rhineland, the stress on abstinence and pietistic continence is echoed throughout the Crusade and post-Crusade periods.[13]

R. Yehudah Halevy (1085–1142) also suggests a compromise between the Senses and Reason. He declares sexual satisfaction in moderation to be wholesome and psychologically beneficial. But he urges that it, as well as the other bodily appetites, be limited and controlled by Reason. This prevents the nurturing of one appetite at the expense of others, "making them all active in the service of his reason, permitting none of these faculties more than specifically belongs to them while neglecting others."[14]

Based on the talmudic adage that "There are eight things which in large quantities are harmful, but in small quantities are beneficial, and one of them is sexual intercourse," and being that they are therapeutically beneficial for the body, it is better that we indulge in them a little than totally deny them.[15]

Maimonides (1135–1205) sets up two categories of behavior: one; the lawful and unlawful, and the other the worthy (or ideal) and the unworthy (or nonideal). In his medical treatise *On Sexual Intercourse*, Maimonides introduces the idea that sexual intercourse is not just a physiological process, uncontrolled by the performer, but basically a psychological activity, "a process of the soul," which depends greatly on the emotional state of the persons involved.

Maimonides felt that in order to attain truth and a better understanding of the ultimate and Divine attributes of G-d, one has to exercise one's intellectual faculties. The bodily needs, however, must be satisfied in moderation as a vehicle to spiritual elevation and Divine knowledge.

In general, then, one's activities, including the sexual ones, have, as their keynote, the preservation of a healthy body in order to serve G-d better. But the sex act has still another purpose, notes Maimonides, the propagation of the species: and, in cohabitation, one's mind should be set on producing a G-d-fearing, intelligent child.[16]

Maimonides counsels sexual moderation, as long as one does not deny his wife's conjugal rights. "The Sages have found no pleasure in the man who indulges in sexual intercourse to excess and is as frequently with his wife as a cock is with a hen. Such conduct is a serious blemish, and brands him as a boor . . ."

He also urges against sexual excess and explicitly regulates coition in terms of the need, and he stresses "consideration of timing and position, which will promote the mental and physical health of the couple and of ensuing offspring."

According to Maimonides, "the law about forbidden sexual intercourse seeks in all its parts to inculcate the lesson that, ideally speaking, we ought to limit sexual intercourse altogether, hold it in contempt and only desire it very rarely . . . the act is too base to be performed except when needed."[17]

This disapproval of sexual activity was countered a century later by another rabbinic medical scholar, Nachmanides. This great and authoritative spokesman for Judaism, in commenting upon Maimonides' statement, made the following rebuttal:

> It is not true, as our Rabbi and Master asserted in his *Guide For the Perplexed* in praise of Aristotle, that the sexual urge is a source of shame to us. G-d forbid that the truth should be in accordance with the teachings of the Greek! . . . . The act of sexual union is holy and pure. . . . The Lord created all things in accordance with His wisdom, and whatever He created cannot possibly be shameful or ugly . . . When a man is in union with his wife in a spirit of holiness and purity, the Divine Presence is with them. (Sot. 17a)

Through the sexual union between man and wife they become partners of G-d in the perpetual creation of man and of the universe. Sexual union in biblical Hebrew is called "knowledge," and it is evident that if it were not a matter of great importance it would not be called "knowledge." The best proof is the narrative in Genesis 3 and 4. Mystically, man and woman are sublime symbols: "man is the foundation of Wisdom and woman is the foundation of Intelligence, and their pure union is the foundation of Knowledge."[18]

Yehuda Alharizi (1170–1230) stresses the hygienic and therapeutic view. He maintains that sexual intercourse is a means of strengthening the body and the vitality of the psyche. Engaging in intercourse moderately is a sound, preventive health measure, while its excess breeds unwholesomeness and will cause both psychical and physical deterioration and even shorten the life span. A similar view was expressed by another rabbinic doctor, Shem Tov Falaquera (1225–1295), in his poetical work.[19]

As we have seen, sex attitudes and practices in Jewish life can hardly be generalized. Nevertheless, all historical rabbinic data and indications point to the fact that sex was viewed as a normal, healthy need in human life to be approached, not rigidly or puritanically, but in a natural and wholesome way, yet controlled by self-discipline.

Judaism teaches neither perversion of nor aversion to sex and considers sex to be neither evil nor base. Rather, it is considered essential for cementing a healthy relationship between a man and his wife, the entryway into the community, an affirmation of the material world. It is a legitimate element in nature, vital to normal life. To truly understand Jewish attitudes toward sex we need only accept natural views and our physical constitution as bestowed upon us, our emotional patterns as experienced, our spiritual growth and maturity as God-given and Divinely inspired. What we feel and see and experience is Divine and should be used as a blessing, for God cannot create anything that is ugly or obscene.

In different periods, therefore, sexuality was viewed as being noble and positive. Even those who stressed its possible negative aspects credited it with benefits related to the family, love, and mutuality. Inherent in the approach to sex was both a recognition of its biological or instinctive basis and an acknowledgment that it must be socialized to fit in with the needs of society, i.e., a primarily ethical view of sexuality.

Based on the biblical verse "And Adam knew Eve his wife" (Gen. 4:1), kabbalistic thought viewed "knowledge" as implying the sublime erotic expression and interpreted it as the realization of union applied to both wisdom (reason) and intelligence, the symbolization of God and the Shekhinah.

Kabbalah endeavors to discover symbolically the mystery of "union" within God Himself and views marriage not as a concession to the weakness of the flesh but rather as a most sacred mystery ordained by God and representing the union of two different aspects of the Divine.[20]

The sexual symbolism in the Zohar reflects a positive attitude toward sex within traditionally ordained limits. It upholds the healthy Jewish Anschauung, which rejects the notion that the sex drive is intrinsically shameful or sinful. Instead of being repressed, this libidinal drive should rather be sublimated.

The Kabbalists believed that since God's world was created as being (very) "good" (Gen. 1:31), it follows that the individual's worldly activities must necessarily be a reflection of the ultimate and infinite Divine "good."

A person, relates the Kabbalah, is a microcosm (*olam katan*) echoing the union of the Physical and Spiritual; through total concentrated direction of the deepest emotions (*kavanah*) toward the infinite Source, one can actually bring about a union of those physical and spiritual worlds one represents. Kabbalah, therefore, does not consider the sex drive a shameful passion to be expelled from one's life experience but rather a God-given, natural impulse, worthy and good, when satisfied in loving union within the sacred bond of matrimony.

In contrast to most forms of non-Jewish mysticism, which glorified asceticism and injected eroticism in the relation of man and God, sexual asceticism was never accorded any true religious value in Kabbalah, since great importance was attributed to the first Divine Commandment of *peru u-revu*—"be fruitful and multiply." (Gen. 1:28)

Considering the human body as the vessel for the divinely infused soul, Nachmanides[21] views the sex organ like all other organs of the human body as being noble, a vehicle of "good," when involved in a loving act of purity. Only when given to orgiastic sensuality does such an act become obscene. To regard the sex organs as vile is to deny the perfection of God's creation.

The quality of the mental intent—*kavanah*—during the sexual union between man and woman is what determines its cosmic outcome. If the union is a loving and noble one, its intent pure and holy, then it bears the power to harmonize and actually strengthen the cosmic unity. If, however, the act is no more than a vulgar, ignoble act of carnal pleasure, it can form a negative force potent enough actually to harm the world of God and man.

To be sure, sexual pleasure is of ancillary importance according to the kabbalistic purview, and the fact that this is a holy union of sublime meaning is to be kept in mind throughout the act of coition. In this respect the kabbalistic view adheres to R. Yehuda's advice in the name of Rav: "One is to hallow himself during intercourse so that holy children will descend from him. For it is written, 'And you shall hallow yourselves and you will be holy.' "[22] One's indifference and lack of inward *kavanah* in regard to the sexual act can cause discord to the cosmic order, just as visual and verbal licentiousness or lascivious thoughts can regress and adversely affect the Divine harmony and spirituality of the universal creation as well.

THE STATUS OF SEX

Sexual relations are not to be viewed as an abuse or a punishment but as a total comprehension of the human composition. Judaism reveals foresight into the emotional obligations of an individual and deals directly with his or her maturity and stability.

Judaism attempts to lead the human being along the path to holiness and sanctification. For Israel to be a holy nation it must imitate G-d, who, at one and the same time, is immanent and transcendent—a part of the world and yet beyond it. Holiness, according to Judaism, implies a capacity to be part of nature and yet to be capable of transcending it.

Judaism encourages people to enjoy life and nature and to derive pleasure from all that is G-d-given, even pleasures of the body. In this way, Jewish discipline primes man and woman for holiness. Rav Kook sees no conflict between body and soul when he says: "Spirituality is not cultivated in our generation without the fulfillment of the bodily attributes."[23] Clearly, holiness is achieved by self-control and transcendence vis-à-vis nature. Sex *per se* is pictured neither as demonic nor godly but rather as a basic instinct which, by means of the *mitzvah* of *kiddushin* (marriage sanctification), is sublimated into the service of God. A good source for understanding Jewish attitudes to sex is the wedding service. *Kiddushin* implies rising to G-d's will and sublimating human desire through a Divine *mitzvah*.

Historically, Judaism encompasses the various attitudinal trends and influences that affected the development of traditional law throughout the generations. Like other codes of Jewish conduct, the code of sex morality in every age remained a sound guide for refined and pure sexual conduct, organically related to man's normal psychobiological needs of finding fulfillment through marital love and mutuality.

Prudery was unknown in the Talmud. To the contrary, the Rabbis were very outspoken in all matters of sexual education and techniques enhancing our knowledge and mastery of the subject in the spirit of Tradition.

With one's own marriage partner, sex is viewed in Judaism as natural—not to be glorified and exaggerated or denigrated, nor to be overindulged in, nor to be abstained from for prolonged periods. Judaism never advocated the extremist paganistic position nor the sex motifs in mythologies. It has never held to the classical negative Christian view of sex. Quite a chasm exists between Jewish acceptance of sex and the early Christian disapproval of it. Early Christian philosophy maintained that sex was evil and sinful. Procreation meant the transmission of sin from one generation to another. Christian theology called for abstinence and celibacy. To enter the celibate world of a nun or priest was considered the highest level on which a person can serve God.[24] Christian practice does allow marriage only if the individual cannot conquer his passion. This negativism was a reaction to the permissive and sex-glorified pagan world.

Judaism does not hold with either the extreme laxness of paganism or the asceticism of Christianity. The Rabbis were fully aware of the moral laxity present in an urban society (i.e., Rome), where materialism and hedonism were regnant. Instead of angrily repudiating this world and perceiving woman as diabolic, they called for controlled moral conduct and spiritualization and sublimation of the libidinal drives. "One who causes himself pain by abstinence from something he desires is called a sinner."[25]

Much confusion stemming from ignorance of the Jewish Law surrounds the realm of sexual activity in Judaism. Misconceptions and distorting inhibitions based on fear and religious insecurity becloud the Rabbis' truly humanistic and reality-oriented philosophy of sex. Sex is not simply tolerated by Jewish Law. Jewish Law views sex as encouraged and ordained by the Creator Himself in His very first commandment to man. Elucidation of the subject is therefore imperative.

Sexual abnegation is disapproved of by many Rabbis. R. Yitzhak said: "Are not the things prohibited to you in the Law enough for you, that you wish to forbid yourself other things?"[26]

From statements of the Rabbis found in the Talmud and Midrash, one can see that not only were the Sages acquainted with the intimate details of sex, but that it was for them an important part of behavior.

The mishnaic section of *Nashim* and the talmudic tomes called *Niddah*, *Yevamot*, *Kiddushin*, *Ketubbot*, *Gittin*, *Zavim*, and others abound in realistic detailed discussions and lore relating to the sexual realm in all its ramifications.

We may discern two major trends in Judaic thought in reference to sexual pleasure: one, the pietistic—representing the extreme restrictive view, under kabbalistic influence—which calls for self-restraint from purely hedonistic or orgiastic pleasure during coition, directing the entire experience to spiritual motives; and the other, the more moderate and liberal attitude, which holds that the pleasurable element in coition is perfectly legitimate and natural.

Lest one assumes incorrectly that the family and procreation of children are the only objectives in sexual relations, the second, more moderate approach maintains that a husband and wife have every right to enjoy sex and derive pleasure from the sexual act. The sexual union need not only be for specific purposes such as procreation; pleasure and companionship are legitimate ends in themselves. For it is written: "It is not good for man to be alone." (Gen. 2:18) Through marriage, man must hope to attain emotional and social fulfillment with his wife. Marriage should bring two people together, and, thus, bring them closer to God. Sexual fulfillment is not discountenanced by Judaism but is encouraged. In marriage no subject is taboo and no desire is secret.

Contrary to the popular belief that it is solely the woman's duty to give pleasure to her husband, his duty to fulfill her sexual need is clearly stated in *halakhah*: A Jew transgresses a commandment of the Torah if he fails to provide his wife with her conjugal rights. If his inability to satisfy her is caused by health problems, a period of six months is granted to him for possible recuperation. After this period, she may either remain patient or he must give her her *ketubbah*, that is, marriage settlement (through divorce).[27]

According to modern sexologists, whatever else it may be—culturally, socially, economically, financially—marriage is still basically a sexual relationship. The pleasure of sexual intercourse, the satisfaction it brings, the release from tension it confers upon the individual are all the reason needed for indulgence in it, and each member of a married pair has the responsibility of seeing that the other partner is sexually satisfied.

Many of the viewpoints expressed in the Jewish tradition are now being corroborated by modern sexology. Kinsey seems to be saying "Amen" to traditional Judaism when he affirms that "marital coitus is socially the most important of all sexual activities, because of its significance in the origin and maintenance of the home . . ."[28]

Jewish Law acknowledges the sex drive in people. This is confirmed today by the Masters and Johnson report, that the desires of the woman are manifold and it is man's responsibility to fulfill them.

When the Talmud states that "A man shall not abstain from the performance of the duty of the propagation of the race unless he already has children," the implication is simply that once a man has begotten children, his sexual activities are no longer required to be directed toward procreation—but the requirement of his having sex with his wife is no less in effect. This implies that in the case where one has no children, he must marry a woman capable of procreation, but if he has children, he may marry one incapable of procreation.[29]

A man is expected to have sexual relations with his wife not only after the rites of purification but also while she is pregnant, when nursing, and even after menopause, when she is no longer able to conceive.

The Kabbalist R. Yitzhak Luria was asked if one is exempt from sexual cohabitation during his wife's pregnancy or nursing period, and he replied: "Only if the wife voluntarily renounces. Nonetheless, it is advisable to offer it to her."[30]

Renunciation is permitted only if one has already fulfilled the commandment of procreation; otherwise, one is not allowed to skip any of the opportune times (onah) for conception until the commandment is fulfilled.

These times of intimacy are for pleasure and personal satisfaction for both the husband and the wife. The woman is not placed on this earth exclusively to bear children. Since conception occurs only during the twelfth to sixteenth day of the twenty-eight-day cycle, the question arises: Wouldn't it be meaningless to engage in intercourse on any other day? Yet, halakhically, intercourse is allowed, which points again to the fact that Judaism credits sex with multifaceted aspects.

It is recorded that R. Yehuda was once punished for denying his wife her conjugal rights owing to preoccupation with his studies, for he who deprives his wife of her conjugal rights during her night of tevilah (ritual immersion) frustrates her and is breaking the Law. Similarly it is considered a sin if a wife deprives her husband of his conjugal rights in order to extort from him money or jewelry or simply to frustrate him. The Rabbis recognized the growing intensity of the woman's sexual cravings before being separated from her husband and so obligated the husband to fulfill her needs before and after lengthy voyages.[31]

The husband is required to satisfy his wife's sexual needs prior to her regular menstrual period, although at prescribed intervals he must keep away from her. This abstention takes place during the twelve hours before the expectation of her menses; yet, if this happens to coincide with the time immediately prior to his embarking on a journey, then not only is he allowed but is required by Law to satisfy her sexual needs (onah—conjugal duties), thus leaving her in a contented and fulfilled state of mind.[32]

As to frequency in sexual activity, Jewish tradition allows for sexual intercourse at regular intervals and considers it the basic right of husband and wife. There was no antisexual or ascetic tradition in the mainstream of Jewish thought. As would be expected in a patriarchal society, men had more rights, but women were also duly regarded. Hebrew society was fairly stable, and sex was not at all conceived of as a problem. Even polygamy, which was practiced throughout the biblical period by rich and important men, was a crucial source of solidarity, since it provided every woman with some kind of family structure in which to function.

As to the proper timing of sex, our Rabbis stated that Friday night is reserved for conjugal relations. Nachmanides justifies this tradition on mystical grounds, since a holy act should be performed on a holy day. The Shabbat and *Yom Tov* are special occasions on which marital duties must be observed. Nachmanides considers these duties so holy that he encourages the reciting of a blessing (*berakhah*) before engaging in intercourse, as these are the only times that one can unite with another both physically and spiritually. Man and woman fulfill their share in the Divine partnership of creation (through the creation of an offspring) both physically and spiritually, as God created them in two facets, body and soul.[33]

Rabbinic literature appears to understand man fully and carefully considers his needs. The Rabbis incorporate all facets of life into their understanding of *yetzer hatov* (the good inclination) and *yetzer hara* (the evil inclination). When they refer to the sexual impulse as *yetzer hara*, no disparagement is inferred. They are simply acknowledging the sexual impulse as a possible source of evil. It becomes evil and sinful when the *yetzer hara* is not coupled with Torah principles, morality, and self-control, causing the man to violate common decency and reason. It is these consequences of the *yetzer hara* to which the Rabbis are referring. Judaism teaches that man is perfectly capable of sublimating his impulses and living in moderation.[34]

The *yetzer hara* is considered part of the child's personality from birth. It has been said that the *yetzer hara* precedes the good inclination by thirteen years, for it grows with and accompanies the child from the moment it comes forth from the mother's womb. After thirteen years, however, the *yetzer hatov* is created. Rav Shimon Ben Eleazar declared: "To what is the *yetzer hara* compared? To a piece of iron which is cast into the fire. As long as it is in the fire, one can make of it whatever vessel he wishes. So it is with the *yetzer hara*—there is no remedy for it except the study of the Torah which is likened to fire."[35] Though man is always beset with the conflict between his two natures, by keeping his *yetzer hara* properly balanced by his *yetzer hatov*, he is able to give pleasure to the absolute *Yotzer*, his Creator, through his free choice in mastering his fate.

The moral quality of the Jew must be based upon inward acceptance of virtue by an intrinsic, voluntary appeal, not upon an external, imposed authority. This is psychologically valid only when man is master of his thoughts; otherwise he weakens and causes dissolution of morality.

In their emphasis on character training, rabbinic ethics teach man to control his *yetzer hara* and make it serve the *yetzer hatov* by employing the stimulus and energy of *yetzer hara* to perform good deeds.

Judaism civilizes, rather than represses, passions and harmonizes the powerful cravings with the potent moral yearning by sublimating the egotistic drives into transformed creative good. This can be achieved not only in the sex act *per se* but in various other activities, such as work and play. There are sexual components in many of our interests and activities which are apparently unrelated to the quest for direct physical satisfaction. All of these can reach sublimation. *Halakhah* comes to us as a code of discipline designed to contain man's sexual appetite, control and balance his actions, and elevate sexuality to a holiness it deserves.

ON SEXUAL HYGIENE

Maimonides deals with this subject in great detail. He places the hygienic meaning of reproduction in its proper perspective. In his recognition of erotic needs, he remains an impressive admonisher against excess and a caring teacher for a more ethical comprehension of love, about which many of us are, alas, not too particular.

The following is a quote of Maimonides' medical observations regarding the physical and psychological elements of coitus:

> It is known that this [sexual] act is not merely instinctive, meaning that erection would depend upon the nature of activity represented by nutrition of growth, so that the processes of the Soul would have to be discounted. Rather, in this respect the condition of the Soul either runs counter to it or is beneficial to it. Grief, sadness, sorrow, or the repugnant character of the woman chosen for sexual intercourse greatly weaken sexual intercourse, while, conversely, there are certain conditions of the Soul which stimu-

late strong excitement. Physicians have already made mention of the factors which especially weaken sexual performance: sexual intercourse with a virgin, an old woman, a young girl who has not as yet attained sexual maturity, a woman who has for several years abstained from sexual intercourse, a menstruant, or one who is sick, and particularly one who is disliked. Even if man's nature gets accustomed to the act under any of these conditions, nevertheless, listlessness is introduced into the act and this becomes habitual in the person so that if he feels desire, he may become impotent. Therefore, a man should make sexual contact his habit, whenever his soul demands it, and use this treatise of mine to learn what is to be striven for or avoided in order to stimulate desire.

And know that all which makes the body or the genitals cold and likewise all which makes the body and those parts dry, does great harm, and that if something warms and moistens moderately, in food, medicaments, and conduct, is very beneficial to the body as a whole or the genitals in this respect. And so, joy, merry-making, jubilation, rest and not overly long sleep are very beneficial in this respect, whereas, on the contrary, the following are very harmful: worry, grief, sadness, continuous silence, exertion and waking: all this frustrates erection and renders the man impotent. The frequent mention of sexual intercourse, conversation about it, and directing one's thoughts toward it further it.

Abstention of thought from it causes the membrum to become dry and its activity to be weakened. So the exercise of sexual intercourse which is desired is such that the membrum is strengthened and it furthers the increase of sexual intercourse, whereas the exercise without desire is such that it causes the membrum to become weak and dry, and lessens erection. All the more so if one connects elimination of thoughts with elimination of practice, for this is the very first thing which monks and ascetics do in order to remove themselves from unchastity.[36]

Maimonides investigates, primarily, the question of the hygienic meaning of sexual relations. He points to the hygienic advantages in cohabitation and its influence on physical well-being. It removes glutting and has a healing effect, when moderately practiced, on headaches, rheumatism, stomachaches, and sciatica. Coitus also quiets insomnia and excessive stimulation and hyper-activity. Psychologically it is of great value. Through it, anger is appeased, melancholic thoughts and moods are banished, and passionate love is soothed. By comparison, when excessive, the harmful effects are extraordinarily greater.[37]

While evaluating the performance of coitus, Maimonides also groups those individuals who are fit and unfit for sexual intercourse.

Those who are fit are those powerful in body, full-grown and sanguine, who possess a lively temperament, live a life of pleasure and lead a life of luxury, are well-fed and stout, and are without worry. The larger group, those for whom coitus is not beneficial, comprises people who are weak in body, are not too hairy, are thin and slightly built, and are narrow-chested. Likewise, those who are encumbered with the worries of existence, who are taxed and overworked, and whose brains are weakened by their being busy with minute scientific questions; they may also incur tuberculosis, emaciation, and other maladies. Youngsters whose bodies are still too fragile, old men whose bodies are too weak and too old, and, above all, the sick and the convalescent should likewise be dissuaded from copulation. Among the sick, the following are especially mentioned: those bitten by animals, the consumptive, the emaciated, those with heart conditions, those with bowel and intestinal ailments, those who are weak-eyed, dropsical, and affected with strong heart palpitations. Maimonides emphatically warns the sick or convalescents against engaging in coitus.

The choice of a wife should also, naturally, conform to hygienic views. Preferably the following sex partner should not be chosen: one weakened by sickness, who is feverish or obese, or is very frightened, or one over forty. Likewise, one should avoid coitus with one who is menstruating, recovering from childbirth, suffering from vertigo, or one with inflammation of the uterus. It is not advisable to have relations with too young and naïve a girl, even if she had already reached puberty, also not with one who has no feeling for the person in question or, in reverse, one for whom the person has no feeling, and also, not with one who feels no shame. Obesity, for practical considerations, was not considered an impediment to sexual compatibilty because love "compresses" the flesh. (Rashi: since our wives' sexual desire is stronger than ours, our bodies push into each other leisurely and we cohabit.)[38]

Sexual hygiene was required by Tradition as a necessity for practical cleanliness, carrying also symbolic meaning. The couple was urged to wash their hands before and after intercourse.

One is warned against getting up immediately after intercourse for reasons of health. This implies that the couple is to extend their postcoital embrace until both have had ample time to relax after their sexual activity.[39]

Concerning the hygiene of the menstruant woman, the Mosaic Code had early instituted detailed hygienic regulations. This was amply developed by the rabbinic tradition upon which the concept of family purity is based, and which is still practiced among traditional Jews.

MORALITY AND SEXUAL PURITY

Throughout the Bible, nudity was basically considered an act of shame and humiliation rather than a breach of sexual mores. This is seen in the case of slaves, war captives (Is. 47:2–3), and the *sotah*—the unfaithful wife. The uncovering and disheveling of the *sotah's* hair (*u-fara*) during her trial in court served to shame and humiliate the guilty woman.[40]

To the Israelite shepherd and farmer in their pastoral milieu, nakedness was seen as shameful rather than obscene, and, therefore, it follows that a person who exposes his nakedness willingly is beneath feeling shame.

Unlike other neighboring nations, the Israelites were very sensitive to bodily exposure. By talmudic times the belief that bodily exposure constituted shame was still accepted in the man, though the scantily clad woman was labeled "immodest." Throughout talmudic literature, when mention is made of woman's sexuality, it bears reference to the concept of *tzeniut*—modesty—rather than to that of *bushah*—shame.

From the Tannaitic period on, nakedness was ruled as a barrier to the performance of certain religious practices, such as the recitation of the *Shema*, the daily prayers, learning, or meditation upon the Torah. The few instances of nudity during the talmudic period were considered by the Rabbis as immodest, an affront to human dignity.[41]

The Roman custom of mixed communal bathing was abhorrent to the Tannaim—contemporaries of the Romans—and inconceivable to the Amoraim. During the thirteenth century, or later, it was apparently acceptable to be bathed by a Gentile maid when no sexual intentions were involved.[42]

The social requirements for modesty and decency related mainly to woman's bodily exposure, while exposure of nonsexual parts of the body by the man was not considered a breach of sexual morality.

Since a woman's unclad body was always considered tantalizing to the opposite sex, even partial exposure of usually unrevealed parts of her body was considered by social standards to be sexually suspicious. In this way, nakedness came to be related to sexuality. This is seen in the biblical text which refers to incestuous relations as "uncovering the nakedness" in a purely genital sense. (Lev. 20:17) The display of woman's nudity thus came to be considered a provocative threat to social-moral norms, since it fostered impure thoughts and indecency and implied immodesty. A handbreadth (of nakedness) in a (married) woman constitutes sexual incitement. Similarly, Jewish women would not do their wash at the laundering brook, so as not to reveal any part of their body.[43]

A wife could be charged with misconduct if she revealed the usually covered parts of her body or bathed in a nonprivate bath; indeed, for her to bathe in the company of men was considered grounds for divorce.[44]

The psychological phenomenon that continuous exposure to certain parts of the woman's body tends to lessen its sexual suggestiveness and eliminate the element of indecency was acknowledged at a later period by the Gaonic Rabbis, who permitted such exposure within limits, when required by fashion or style.[45]

During the Tannaitic period the Jewish woman's failure to cover her head was considered an affront to her modesty. When her head was uncovered, as related in the story of R. Akiva, she might be fined four hundred zuzim for this offense.[46]

In early Oriental tradition the veil symbolized a state of distinction and luxury rather than feminine modesty. From the Assyrians to the early Hebrews it personified in the noble woman an element of dignity and superiority. It bespoke woman's inaccessibility not so much in a sexual sense but as a sanctified possession of her husband.

In the postexilic period, a period which apparently was burdened with a sense of morbidity in matters of sex, the symbol of the veil acquired a new connotation—that of modesty. It became a socially accepted feature among Jews and, by Philo's day, was mandatory for every Jewish woman.[47]

Another form of modesty concerned the intimacy of sexual relations—discussion of which was to be kept private. Such discussion in public was considered a breach of modesty and good taste and served as grounds for divorce. Similarly, it was considered tasteless immodesty for a wife to raise her voice during intercourse and thus be in danger of being heard by her neighbors. This betrayed a lack of inhibition, poor emotional constraint, and tactlessness.[48]

It is virtuous for a wife to ingratiate herself with her husband and to show her desire for him, as Leah did with Jacob. (Gen. 30:16) It is meritorious for a woman to demand her conjugal rights.

A Jewish woman was encouraged to take the initiative in matters of sexual union with her husband, not by oral demand but by flirting and coyness. "A woman who actively encourages her husband in sexual congress will have children the like of which did not exist even in the generation of Moses."[49]

Even though the trait of modesty (tzeniut) is praiseworthy for all, and especially so for woman, still, anything she does to make herself more desirable to her husband and induce him to perform the commandment is not immodesty but rather zeal and a good trait, and her reward awaits her.

One of the most subtle phases of female psychology with respect to her normal erotic life is her shyness: the natural demureness or coquett-ish sexual caution of woman. This characteristic has been variously emphasized, distorted, and perverted to appear as something of an affectation. However, it is so deeply rooted in the feminine constitution that it is typical of the woman of all races and cultures. It is biologically substantiated and evident in the females of many species. In woman it is closely associated with modesty, yet it is something quite different— more inherent in nature and less a socially acquired quality. It has a dual biological motive: one of guarding the sexual centers against the undesired advances of the male, and one of exciting the sexual ardor of a prospective male by making the object of his desire more difficult to attain.

It has been often shown that coyness is really the sign of a sexual emotion becoming an invitation. Montaigne speaks of the "artifice" of virgin modesty, claiming that nothing whets our taste so much as rarity and difficulty. Stendahl asserted that modesty or coyness "is the mother of love," considered a natural stimulus to sexual excitation, both for the man and for the woman.[50] It makes the man more passionate and the woman more enticing and, by retarding the sexual congress, increases the secretions of the sexual glands—promoting tumescence, assuring the most complete preparation for intercourse.

Ellis describes the primary female role in courtship as the playful, yet serious, assumption on the part of the hunted animal, luring on the pursuer, with the object of finally being caught—not escaping. The primary role of the male, on the other hand, is a display of energy and skill in the capture, or arousal of his mate to an emotional condition that will lead her to surrender herself to him (a process that heightens his own excitement).[51]

PREMARITAL SEX

Premarital contact between the sexes during the ultramoral and disciplined period of the Second Commonwealth constituted grounds for public condemnation, despite the fact that no clear legal stand was taken until the early Tannaitic period. To R. Eliezer, any sexual relation between man and woman in which there is no marital intent is an act of prostitution. The Tannaim, however, distinguished between the motives of a prostitute who seeks pecuniary or sexual gratification with any man, and the naive maiden who indulges in sexual activity with her seducer. The latter are not punished in the Bible for prostitution, though they are censured for immorality.[52]

Throughout the annals of Jewish history, no evidence of communal approval of premarital-sex relations can be found. This is true from an halakhic stand and from the haggadic standards of ethical conduct as well. These standards received public acceptance and sanction as much as the Law itself and strongly influenced the public attitude toward sexual morality. Such attitudes engendered severe restrictions.

The concept of entering into marriage in full chastity and moral purity was the ideal, both for the bride and for the groom. This special purity of Jewish girls, compared with its lack among their heathen sisters, was extolled by the Rabbis as a special virtue.

The Jewish foundation for the sex education of young girls was to set high standards for their modesty. The guiding principle was the avoidance of behavior that might be sexually arousing. "It was the custom of Jewish girls to remain domestically modest and not to indulge too much outdoors": "A garden inclosed is my bride, a spring inclosed a fountain sealed." (Song of Songs 4:12) "Jewish daughters are chaste and innately pure . . . They are virgins marrying sexually modest bridegrooms, as both did not indulge in premarital sex." Thus were the daughters of early Israel, as viewed by the Rabbis.[53] Girls were also to avoid being alone with men and even at public gatherings, including the synagogue, were to sit in the *Ezrat Nashim* (women's section). Premarital chastity was the great ideal, exemplified by the girl who prayed that no man might fall into sin through her.[54] Young women were to look forward to early marriage and to rely on their father to find a suitable match. Nowadays the traditional standards of modesty still prevail, although a freer and more relaxed encounter of the sexes exists. Education and other social factors play a role in the flexible and more informal dating and selection of a mate.

Historical evidence of the behavior of chaste Jewish daughters who entered their nuptials in complete purity, matched by similar chastity in their bridegrooms, was attested to by Philo two thousand years ago.[55]

Despite a persistent element of laxity on man's part—male premarital-sex indulgence was not held to be as dishonorable or scandalous—chastity remained the ideal.

According to Kinsey, most cultures throughout history have accepted a double standard in the premarital-sex code. He claims that this stems from the fact that, for the majority of males, the prevention of premarital coitus has been impossible, while females are more controllable, since they are less often sexually responsive at early ages and less often stimulated psychologically at any age.

The woman has been imputed with having a lesser sexual drive than the man; culturally, therefore, she was expected to remain a virgin and practice abstinence more than man. Kinsey shows "that the male is conditioned by sexual experience more frequently than the female. The male more often shares, vicariously, the sexual experiences of other persons . . . He may react to objects associated with his sexual activities. . . . In all of these respects, fewer of the females have their sexual behavior affected by such psychologic factors."[56]

Still, the conditions leading to strong sexual stimulation can be limited. The Rabbis assisted in this restraint by considering the checks imposed on man's social environment and by enforcing the punitive measures taken by the community.[57] This severe enforcement of the moral code of premarital-sex behavior persisted throughout the centuries until the "new morality" became a fact of social life.

Chaperonage is one of the earliest forms of society's control of the private life of men and women. The Midrash ascribes to Boaz the rule that at parties and festivities, young people should be chaperoned, because they are often oblivious of decorum. According to Tradition, chaperonage existed during the Davidic reign and was instituted because of the violation of King David's daughter Tamar by her halfbrother Amnon. (2 Sam.13) The *Bet Din* (court of law) legislated against unchaperoned meetings—yihud—between a man and (even) an unmarried Jewish girl. The Midrash uses the story of Lot and his daughters as a warning to men, to avoid being alone with women.[58]

The schools of Hillel and Shammai extended this prohibition to include meetings between a Jewish man and a non-Jewish woman.[59]

Relatives, too, were subject to the law of chaperonage.[60]

The prohibition of *yihud* applies only to private places, not to public ones where groups mingle, and it does not apply to a house with an opening to a busy street, or in the city or in the daytime.[61]

From the early Tannaitic period, betrothal legally placed the couple in a husband-wife relationship (with the exception of sex relations, which were to be consummated after the marriage ceremony) and exempted them from the laws of chaperonage. Prior to the betrothal, both in Judea and in Galilee, couples could not hold private meetings, except under strict surveillance of the family, since they were considered as strangers. After the betrothal, this was no longer the case in Judea, where the recital of nuptial blessings was offered at the betrothal ceremony—which automatically sanctioned sex relations thereafter. In Galilee, however, these blessings were recited only later at the wedding ceremony; chaperonage was therefore required during the betrothal period, and sexual relations were not condoned by the Tannaim.[62]

In the Amoraic period the Babylonian Rabbis reinstated the practice (which has in fact been kept alive in the Galilean communities throughout the preceding period) of reserving the nuptial blessings for the marriage ceremony itself. It was at this point in Jewish history that the phrase "And He prohibited to us our betrothed" was incorporated into the betrothal blessing.[63] The young couple were then left alone in the chamber, prior to the wedding, so that they might get acquainted with each other, which would help them to overcome their inhibitions at their first sexual union following the wedding.

Every new communal enactment needs strict legal enforcement in order to gain acceptance. Thus we find that violation of the new enactment by either spouse was punishable by flagellation. In time, there was less and less need to prove the efficacy of the enactment, and by early gaonic times we find that the few violators of the rule were no longer even punished.[64]

But times changed once again, and again the Rabbis were alert to the situation. When they noted that more and more infractions on the part of couples were becoming dire reality, they reinstituted the early Judean custom of reciting the nuptial benedictions at the time of engagement in order to lessen the possibility of the couple's sinning, lest they be overcome by their desire for sexual contact.

This rabbinic action was reconsidered in later Gaonic times. The Gaonim felt the situation demanded a return to withholding of the nuptial blessings and the sexual rights they conferred until marriage.[65] This decision, demanding chaperonage for the betrothed, was further reinforced with the talmudic laws. Eventually, as a realistic attempt to avoid temptation to sin, prohibition against any betrothed couple dwelling in the same house was decreed; but, when even this was not feasible, the earlier, Judean custom (reciting the nuptial benedictions at betrothal) was again implemented.[66] It seems that the Central European communities left the issue to the moral conscience of those involved, trusting the bride and groom to conduct themselves in the spirit of the moral law, and did not take recourse in *takkanot*—communal enactments—to restrict the social activities of young couples and the mingling of the sexes.

From the time of the Talmud on, rabbinic sources are a vivid picture of the attitudinal fluctuations in the realm of sex morality and premarital sex. Reality proved that the libidinal drive is immune from legal restrictions and communal enactments.[67] The Rabbis, fully aware of this universal element of the human libido, actually succeeded in their exegetic flexibility in adapting the Law to human needs. One example of this adaptability is the early Judean practice of the Tannaitic period of reciting the nuptial blessings at the betrothal ceremony, which was invoked repeatedly by later Rabbis in order to give halakhic sanction to those who would otherwise be considered sinners. The Rabbis suggested early marriage, in acknowledgment of the positive elements of the *yetzer hara*, and so forth.[68]

By the time of R. Yehuda Ha-Hassid of Regensburg (d. 1217), separation of the sexes was urged for all ages and for all activities.[69] The law thus attempted to preserve public morality with great rigor, punishing anyone who flouted that morality. In individual cases, however, the law dealt leniently, in order not to jeopardize a girl's future chances for marital success.

Various rabbinic responsa, throughout the ages, show the swing of the juridical pendulum between rigid enforcement of the Law and restricting all social activities between the sexes, and the more moderate approach.

By the fifteenth century, Germany, as a Sephardic scholar states, was a country where prenuptial lovemaking was popular, while another scholar reports from Egypt that couples were "encouraged" to get together privately before the wedding so that they could get acquainted with each other and eliminate some of their inhibitions.

In old Romania, as well as in the Byzantine empire and in Italy, the old Judean custom was revived, but according to the famous Rabbi-traveler Ovadyah Bertinoro (1450–1516), unfortunately more laxity developed.[70]

In Prague, in the sixteenth century, we find betrothed couples engaging in love play, with parental approval, at family gatherings. While the community seemed to give its tacit approval, the Rabbis were at all times most vehement in their opposition to such moral lawlessness and let their voices be heard.[71]

Restrictions on premarital encounters between the bride and groom were reenacted and continued throughout European Jewish communities.

Some takkanot were directed toward strict separation of the sexes. A takkanah in Prague in 1611, threatened to expel any young man found flirting in the street or a young girl strolling without a chaperone. Several communities tried to prohibit mixed dancing, since they feared it would lead to sexual intercourse. These takkanot appeared throughout the seventeenth century and duly testify to the difficulty the Rabbis had in combating certain types of moral laxity. Thereafter, however, the practice of separating the sexes until marriage seems to have been accepted within the community and continued to serve as the norm until modern times.[72] Traditional communities nowadays still follow the old norms.

With the later rabbinic enactment of combining the betrothal and marriage ceremonies into a single ceremony the entire problem of postbetrothal laxity of morals vanished, since the doubt of matrimonial status at betrothal was now removed. With no prior and separate betrothal blessings performed, there could be no more misunderstanding as to the status of the prospective bride and groom, who are considered legally strangers prior to the wedding ceremony and thus are subject to the restrictions of chaperonage.[73]

Instances of premarital sex in Jewish history involved prostitution. Although condemned morally, prostitution appeared during biblical and talmudic times and into the Middle Ages and was viewed as an existing evil.[74] A brief discussion in the Talmud concerning the marriage of a kohen (who is forbidden to marry a prostitute) centers on the question of who is considered a prostitute. R. Eleazar stated that if a man has intercourse with a woman without intending to marry her, he renders her a prostitute.[75] Others disagreed, asserting that a prostitute is a woman who is available to any man for sexual relations or is being remunerated for her services. If, though, she is discriminating, or cohabits with anyone whom she is not permitted to marry by Law, or must be coaxed or seduced before she will agree to intercourse, she is not considered a prostitute.[76]

All these rabbinic discussions were really concerned with practical, and not solely moral issues. Maimonides worried lest promiscuity spread and result in children of unknown parentage. In his *Sefer ha-Mitzvot*, he found a basis for prohibiting casual sex in the passage "And the land will become full of lewdness." (Lev. 19:29) He further stated that any man who has intercourse with a woman without first giving her a marriage contract and wedding ceremony should be severely punished by the Jewish community.[77] The Rabbis in the Talmud hesitated to label a woman a prostitute, lest she be disqualified from marrying a kohen (priest). A nonvirgin could marry freely without legal stigma.[78]

The attitude of Jewish Law, while far from being permissive, was concerned with several purposes: first, to protect the woman so that no one may treat her frivolously—Jewish daughters are not hefkair (abandoned to unbridled lust)—and even if she has such illicit sexual relations, to permit her then to marry and thus to rehabilitate her; second, to prevent promiscuity in the Jewish community—because of moral scruples and, more so, because of the danger of illegitimacy and the birth of children of unknown parentage.

A sexual escapade was not viewed as severely as one might think. If a man had intercourse with a woman, he was liable for flagellation; but if the incident happened only once, and accidentally, then the girl was not condemned and the matter was forgotten. Only if the relationship continued, or if the parties were openly promiscuous, or if the girl's behavior was sanctioned by her father, did the community take punitive action.[79]

Another halakhic problem concerned the act of marriage. Technically, in earlier times, a woman who cohabited with a man was thereby married to him. The Rabbis enacted the rule that the act of intercourse alone not be considered sufficient grounds for marriage, and meted out flagellation to any man who did not go through a proper marriage ceremony.[80] There were several reasons for this order: to prevent hasty, ill-conceived marriages, as well as to lessen the chances of promiscuity; and to allow a woman who has had a sexual relationship to marry without having to obtain a divorce. A concubine, for example, did not require a divorce if she wished to marry.[81]

The halakhic authorities frowned on "casual marriages," where a man gave a woman a trinket at a party, and she was thenceforth considered married to him. So many disputes recorded in the Responsa resulted from such "marriages"—especially when the parents had not previously agreed to the match—that takkanot were passed to require a marriage contract signed in front of witnesses and the bride's family in order for it to be valid. Girls were advised never to contract a marriage without their parents' approval, for without a proper ketubbah the girls had little protection and could make no claim on their husbands.[82]

Laws pertaining to sex and marriage, therefore, gradually developed in the direction of greater rigidity in conformity to the moral ideals of the community. The Talmud and Shulhan Arukh decreed flagellation for premarital intercourse, for visiting a prostitute, for living with a woman without a ketubbah and wedding ceremony, for cohabiting with one's betrothed before the wedding, and for violating the codes against nonassociation with women.[83]

The incidence of premarital relations is higher today than it has ever been in history. Yet today's couples are no happier than their elders. Many of them find themselves frustrated in refraining from sexual intercourse but by no means entirely happy or conscience-free if they indulge.

Society and education assign divergent sex role images to both sexes. Boys are raised with the image of being aggressive, direct, and virile. They may desire to display these manly traits through sexual involvement. Girls, on the other hand, are raised with thoughts of love, devotion, and the social aspects of interpersonal relationships. They are generally more cautious abut sexual expression. Premarital sex to them is more an emotional involvement than a quick biological release. The fundamental difference, then, is that boys are body-centered as opposed to girls who are person-centered. A girl wants to be loved, not just made love to. Personality involvement rather than mere physical involvement is required by her to insure true mature love.

A person's education is directly related to the responsibility he brings into his sexual life. One who is capable of exercising restraint in the pursuit of his educational and professional goals will deal restrainedly with other vital problems. The goal of future fulfillment and mature expectations would prohibit the kind of activity we would expect from less actualized people. Maturity implies the ability to postpone gratification, not the impulsive acting out.

One salient element in middle-class norms is the deferred-gratification pattern. Primarily, it involves deferring economic rewards through prolonging the period of education, but it also includes postponing sexual gratification. Premarital chastity has practical value, especially for members of the middle class, since sexual gratification endangers education through early forced marriages.

Deferred gratification is especially emphasized by men who are upwardly mobile. Concentrating their efforts on occupational success, they are even more conservative sexually than many of their peers. People who frequently engage in the most intimate behavior seem to have stronger impulses and weaker inhibitions; they lack the self-control that comes with successful socialization at home and at school.

Insecurity and a desire to be loved can make anyone vulnerable. When boys and girls feel lonely, rejected, or neglected, they become easy prey for their own neurotic needs and so they delude themselves into thinking that making love is synonymous with being in love; after the sexual release, however, the lovers are left with a sense of emptiness, dissatisfaction, and, often, of having been used by the other partner.

Perhaps the most common cause of premarital sex is that the young couple may truly believe they are in love. By impetuously not waiting until marriage, they show that they have not yet matured, nor, of course, have they allowed their love for each other to ripen.

What distinguishes true love from "puppy love"? Building a deep interpersonal relationship which does not rely on physical intimacy for support. Getting to know each other in a variety of interests and situations allows both partners to experience each other's personality. Out of such a relationship love grows. Love cannot simply be physical attraction and infatuation, for sex alone is not a strong bond at all. Each one of us must learn to enhance the ability to love and cultivate it. One's ability to love deeply can easily be stifled by premature sexual relations. What is simply an enhancement to true love is often mistaken for true love itself.

The strength a couple's developing love causes a considerable disarray in their daily lives. They are too precipitate to be able to control the biological, psychological, and emotional concomitants of premarital sex.

Engaging in premarital sex also evokes different psychological responses from the partners. Because a girl, by nature, becomes more emotionally involved, she invariably is more possessive of the man and may view premarital sex as a commitment on his part, but this is not so. This "uneven commitment" is sensed by both partners. Such a meaningless relationship cannot last because the couple have become too sexually involved before marriage. In the great majority of cases, premarital sex complicates matters and places an enormous strain on a young couple's love.

Living together should not be equated with marital partnership. Research suggests that cohabitation leads to marriage in one out of four cases. Those who finally decide on marriage are probably mindful of its social, legal, and religious implications. Yet the inevitable psychological changes come as a surprise to many couples. In order to achieve full intimacy, a couple has to learn not only how to get along but also how to share life's values, higher goals, and levels of aspiration and also how to deal with conflict. They must manage how to stay married together during very stressful periods while still maintaining their individual identities.

The proponents of premarital sex who argue that the experience serves as a good foundation for marriage are deluding themselves in the "try before you buy" fallacy. This specious argument is easily refuted by reality. Burgess and Wallin have found that marital love was favorably associated with premarital chastity. In another study, Harvey Locke compared married versus divorced couples and found that a higher percentage of divorced couples engaged in premarital sex. Virginity, therefore, appears to contribute to marital happiness.[84]

Marriage, too, can also suffer from sexual permissiveness. Companionship, fidelity, idealization, and romance are all threatened by loose and easy sex. Loving and fine understanding of your partner's needs is what enhances sex in marriage. Unfettered and casual premarital sex makes it very difficult to experience mutuality and companionship later. Restraint, not promiscuity, provides greater harmony between the lovers and even greater fulfillment. The prelude to complete expression of marital guilt-free love can be enjoyable almost as much as the sexual act itself.

Finally, marriage is not simply a civil ceremony but an act of Divine sanctity under Jewish Law. Sexual expression finds full meaning only in marriage; to practice it outside the marital bond of love thereby desecrates the holiness of marriage. The beauty and truth of this philosophy is fortified and confirmed by the survival of the Jewish family for millennia.

THE KISS

This brings us to a manifestation of love in which gustatory, tactile, and olfactory sensations combine: the kiss. Many mammals, birds, and insects exchange caresses which remind one of the human kiss. "Love birds" seem to spend much of their time kissing each other.

Eastern races, on the other hand, do not seem to relish the caress which Western people call a kiss. In China, for example, a form of affectionate greeting corresponding to our kiss consists of rubbing one's nose against the cheek of the other person, after which a deep breath is taken through the nose with the eyes half shut. In some primitive races the equivalent for our "kiss me" is "smell me."

In other races the kiss is a symbol of respect rather than a proof of love. Thus Anglo-Saxons on certain occasions kiss the Bible. In the early Christian and Arab civilizations the kiss was a ritual gesture and has remained so in certain Catholic customs: kissing the Pope's foot, relics, a bishop's ring, and so on.

In certain races, kissing is a proof of affection but not of love. Japanese mothers kiss their children, but Japanese lovers do not exchange caresses of the lips.

The people of Africa are ignorant of the kiss; so are the Malays, the aborigines of Australia, and many other primitive tribes.

It appears that even among the kissing races, the kiss is a relatively recent development. It is rarely mentioned in Greek literature. In the Middle Ages it was a sign of refinement, being almost unknown among the lower classes.

Some psychoanalysts have concluded that the kissing habit is derived from a baby's sucking the mother's nipple. But if this were the proper explanation, all the races would instinctively indulge in it.

The kiss is infinitely more complex. The psychoanalytic explanation should not be discarded entirely, though even it is not complete. The kiss has grown in importance, what with societal restrictions placed on sexual activities. The more primitive the race, the more promiscuous they are, the less they are the more they kiss. The kiss seems to have become an act of possession and a sublimation of intercourse in more sexually inhibited, more developed cultures.

If the kiss on the lips is preferred by lovers, it is because the moist mucus of the lips is a better conductor of electrical current than the skin. In very passionate kisses, the lovers' tongues play a double part: a symbolic part, which represents the mother's nipple, and a physio-chemical part, which secures a closer connection.

In that Anglo-Saxon fiction which does not countenance descriptions of lovers' embraces, a very passionate kiss is always symbolic of complete surrender. Physiologically, this symbolism is quite accurate.[85]

THE KISS IN JUDAISM

The kiss as a mark of affection, favor, or a form of salutation made its mark in social life in antiquity, especially in the East.

In the Bible, we find the kiss expressing various emotions related to particular social circumstances:

1. The kiss as a token of domestic affection toward both law and blood relations alike.[86] Kissing and embracing relatives of both sexes was an asexual, accepted social formality among Semites. An example was Esau's greeting to his brother, Jacob, and Moses' greeting his brother, Aaron, with a kiss. Naomi kissed her two daughters-in-law, Orpah and Ruth, and Jacob kissed his young cousin Rachel; the male cousin had the same affectionate rights in this case as the brother, a custom still adhered to among Bedouins.[87]

We can distinguish among three types of kisses enumerated in the Bible: (a) parents kissing their sons, daughters, grandchildren, daughters-in-law; (b) children kissing their parents; and (c) siblings kissing.[88]

It appears that the custom of greeting relatives with a kiss continued throughout the ages. Rashi thus records the Jewish custom of people kissing their father and mother and older relatives on the knee or on the palm of the hand (as a sign of honor, a practice evidently borrowed from the Babylonian Jews) immediately upon leaving the synagogue.[89]

2. The kiss as a mark of condescension, as when Absalom kisses the people to gain their confidence, and when David kisses Barzillai.[90]

3. The kiss as a mark of respect leading to reverence, as when the prophet Samuel seals the annointing of David as a king with a kiss.[91] The deferential kiss is age-old and seems to have been quite customary

throughout the land of Israel. The kissing of the Torah scroll in the synagogue, the *mezuzah*, or the stones at the Western Wall of the Temple and the reverential kiss of the Tzaddik's hand by some Hasidim are later applications of this type of kiss.[92]

4. The kiss as a sign of friendship, when meeting or parting, as when David and Jonathan (the classical friends) kissed each other. Such kissing was usually accompanied by weeping—an expression also of the strongly emotional Orientals.[93]

In the same category we may list the kiss of reconciliation.[94]

5. The kiss of love between the sexes, as poetically mentioned in the opening verse of Song of Songs: "Let him kiss me with the kisses of his mouth for thy love is better than wine." Since, in the Rabbis' allegorical interpretation of the Song of Songs, this is referred to as God's love for Israel, it marks the kiss by mouth as the expression of the highest degree of love.

In contrast to this pristine kiss of tender love, the Bible also mentions the promiscuous kiss of the prostitute.[95]

The biblical text differentiated between the purely innocent kiss of relatives, devoid of lustful intent, and the sexually immoral kiss or embrace of the luring harlot, as depicted in the Book of Proverbs. (7:13) "She caught him and kissed him . . ." From this text, however, the Tannaim and, later, Maimonides infer biblical prohibitions, not only relating to actual sexual congress but also concerning all forms of embracing and kissing. Nachmanides, in milder form, subsumes these under a purely rabbinical restriction.[96]

The Second Commonwealth, with its rigorous sophistication in sexual matters, introduced a stricter moral code, which became more austere with each generation. The ever-constricting rules for moral standards were aimed not only at deterring mere sensuality but also at establishing and guarding exceptionally high standards of chastity and virtue.

"All kisses are considered frivolous except for the following three: A kiss of dignity (as homage to one elevated to prominence), a kiss of occasional greeting, and a farewell kiss."[97]

Another kind of kiss not considered frivolous is the kiss of relatives, and the kiss of a brother and a sister.

The Talmud relates concerning Ula, a Babylonian Amora, that he would greet his sisters with a kiss on their hands or chest.[98]

While the Talmud speaks in general terms, Maimonides and Karo specify that a brother may kiss his sister if she is still a minor and unmarried, although a truly pious Jew refrains from even such affectionate expression.

Kissing or caressing other female relatives, strangers, or married women, regardless of age, even without sensual desire became unconditionally forbidden.

"Just an innocent harmless little kiss" is often far less innocent in the accepted sense of sexlessness, than it is conventionally assumed to be," says Van de Velde. "For many adults . . . who attempt to be honest with themselves, have found that the innocence . . . of a kiss on brow or hand, has proved quite fictitious—whether the fiction was profitable or harmful in its further states."[99]

Strict medieval morality made itself felt even in the realm of intimate family relations. In differentiating further, Maimonides declares that "hugging or kissing" any woman who falls within the forbidden relations listed by the Torah—such as an adult sister or aunt and so forth—even if it be without lustful intent or pleasure at all is exceedingly indecent and prohibited and constitutes foolish behavior. For except in the case of a son kissing his mother, and vice versa, or a daughter kissing her father, and vice versa, one is neither to kiss nor to embrace any relatives to whom marriage would be forbidden according to the law of incest.[100]

The *Shulhan Arukh*, however, which became the accepted word in traditional Judaism, ruled that a father may kiss his daughter or granddaughter at any age, even when she was married. The same applies to a mother and her son or grandson.[101] Extolling sexual modesty and mutual respect between the sexes, Judaism abhorred all forms of incestuous relations. With such a structured regimen of sexual morality, the Jewish people can pride themselves on being on the lowest scale of the explosive statistics of contemporary incest activity.

Jews have traditionally abided by the old code of refraining from any expression of affection, oral or physical, toward strange women.

To illustrate the seriousness with which this prohibition was held, it is recorded[102] that in seventeenth-century Germany a young Jewish woman trying to cross the border, which was permissible only to couples, received a stranger's permission to do so. She claimed to be his wife, a fact duly recorded on his passport. A suspicious guard, though, bent on disproving the truth of their claim, ordered them to kiss, and by their refusal to do so, the ruse was exposed and the couple penalized.

The kiss as a symbol of union and togetherness is also referred to in the Bible metaphorically.[103]

ON TOUCHING

Touching a woman with innocent intent, as a sign of fondness, was considered indecent among traditional Jews, because it might lead to erotic arousal.

No direct reference is made, in the Babylonian Talmud, prohibiting the touching of a woman's hand; nevertheless, no permission is granted to touch a woman's body. In the Palestinian Talmud, however, we do note that the touching of a woman's hand is deemed immodest. This prohibition was fully applied throughout the thirteenth and fourteenth centuries, and even later in Europe.[104]

Traditionally, pious Jews refrained from touching the hand of a woman and even wore gloves to avoid such contact. Strict adherence to the laws of *negiah* (touching) is still prevalent among Orthodox and hasidic Jews as well as Oriental Jews, while some of their modern brethren show a more liberal approach.

The entire idea of *negiah* stems from the Pentateuchal prohibition of touching a woman during her menses. Such contact is categorized under the prohibition of incest.[105] Hence, all sexually mature women from twelve years and a day are considered *niddah* until they are purified in a ritualarium *(mikvah)*. The *Shulhan Arukh* categorically prohibits all bodily contact between the sexes.[106]

Drinking a toast to a woman was also prohibited, since wine was always viewed as an inducer of levity and frivolity. Wine and sexual immorality were always related since early biblical times. The temptation of both leads to unwholesome morals.[107]

Secular social gatherings, where women indulged in singing and playing instrumental music, and where there was a bacchanal, were similarly prohibited as immodest and a violation of the moral code.[108]

Flirtation of all kinds was always seen as offensive to Jewish morality. Winking, exchanging of come-hither glances, smelling a woman's perfume, or looking at her while she was bent over the wash was prohibited. Attracting her attention, admiring her beauty, or paying her effusive compliments were considered displays of levity.[109]

As early as mishnaic times, flirtation was strongly discouraged and decreed immoral. Said R. Jose ben Johanan (during the Maccabean period): "Indulge not in chatter with woman" since idle talk with women "will ultimately lead you to unchastity."[110]

The sayings of the Sages are replete with maxims stressing the high esteem in which womanhood should be held. The respect and honor due one's wife, and particularly the great importance a husband should attach to her views, opinions, and counsel, clearly reveal the status of the woman. R. Jose ben Johanan's observation need not be construed pejoratively. In fact, this very statement may well be founded on genuine appreciation of the vital role played by both husband and wife in the task of creating a home. *Sihah*—"talk"—according to R. M. Ha-Meiri, does not mean serious conversation but merely idle talk and gossip, such as *sihat yeladim*, or children's talk. A man who truly respects his wife will have more to offer her than just trivial talk and idle banter. He will want to discuss with her the serious concerns of life and will derive enjoyment from the resulting exchange of views. Moreover, engaging in trifling talk with other women and other men's wives may imperil moral purity—the mishnaic statement was, after all, conditioned by the prevailing laxity in sexual behavior characteristic of many ancient peoples.

Chatter may lead to lascivious thought and impure conversation—even with one's own wife. This is a waste of precious time, time which one ought to devote to the study of Torah.[111]

Greeting a woman intimately is prohibited; it breeds familiarity, leading the man's and the woman's thoughts to dwell on the other person.

This prohibition extends also to relaying greetings by messenger, even through her husband.[112] But one is permitted to ask others, or the husband, about his wife's health. Thence derives the custom of inquiring at the beginning of a letter about the wife's well-being. It is, however, permissible to be solicitous, by mail, of a woman when she is ill.[113]

"The heart and the eye are two agents of sin; the eye sees, the heart desires, and both lead the body astray."[114] This talmudic dictum is based on the Pentateuchal exhortation "That you search not after your own heart and your own eyes, after which you use to go astray." (Num. 15:39) Gazing at a woman was also considered immodest.[115]

Ben Sirah warns: "Gaze not upon a maid lest thou be trapped in her penalties. . . . Turn away thine eyes from a comely woman and gaze not on another's beauty." Not only is an adulterous act a sin against the Lord but even mere watching was considered unchaste.[116]

The Talmud, though, revealingly records the case of Rabban Gamaliel II, the Nasi (Prince), who, upon seeing a beautiful Gentile lady, pronounced a benediction praising the Lord who fashioned such a beautiful creature. A similar story is related of R. Akiva. Nonetheless, the law never acceded to such leniency and forbade gazing at a beautiful woman, even when she was unmarried, or at a married one, even when she was homely.[117]

Numerous instances of unusual visual and emotional control by the Amoraim are recorded as examples of pietistic restraint.[118] The prohibition of looking at a woman encompasses not only her face and body but even glancing at her little finger, or her clothes—even when they are not on her body—lest the man become possessed by thoughts of her.[119]

The only exception to this rule was the long-accepted tradition of viewing the bride on her wedding day, when she was expected to expose her face to public view, as if to say, "let all testify as to my virginal purity."[120] This custom extended for the entire seven days of nuptial celebration, as stated by R. Jonathan. The only time a man was permitted to look at an unmarried woman and to appraise her beauty was when he sought to marry her, as long as he did not look at her lasciviously.[121] The Law, in fact, advised such behavior.

The Rabbis' custom was to sing songs of praise about the bride's beauty and meritorious character, a tradition derived by the early Tannaim Shammai and Hillel.[122]

Halakhah insists that the groom see his bride prior to the marriage, so that he may not enter into matrimony blindly.[123] This may also explain the Orthodox custom, traced back to the Bible (Gen. 24:65), of having the groom, escorted by the Rabbis and his male friends, cover his bride's face with her veil (called *badeken die kallah*) prior to the *huppah*. He was, therefore, able to see the bride before the ceremony.

Halakhah surely permits a husband to look at his wife (even during her menstrual period), though within the limits of modesty and refinement.[124]

During talmudic times, for reasons unrelated to Oriental etiquette, the Jewish woman, as a rule, followed the man when walking. This was also a form of sexual morality. The Rabbis decided that a man should not walk behind a woman along the road, nor should a married woman meet him on a bridge (a narrow pass). They were of the opinion that walking behind a woman gave the man an opportunity for visual excitation, which, in turn, might lead to sexual temptation and lewdness. Consequently, the authorities suggested: "It is better to walk behind a lion than behind a woman."[125] As a precautionary measure, they prescribed that a man who finds himself walking behind a woman should either turn in another direction, hasten to overtake her, or remain behind her, at a distance of four ells or more, in order not to be exposed to her figure. Four things were listed as lending to a scholar's shame; among them was following or walking behind any woman in the marketplace,[126] an act which may give rise to suspicion.

ON SEXUAL MATURITY

The age of a woman's sexual maturity was the subject of much talmudic debate. Some scholars set the age at nine years and a day for girls, twelve years and a day for boys; others prescribed the higher ages of twelve years and a day for girls and thirteen years and a day for boys.[127] On the average, the latter became the accepted rabbinical view for the respective ages of pubescence, although still another group of Rabbis argued that, for girls at least, no age could be set as a true criterion, since, they felt, the advent of sexual maturity varies with each individual. Rather, at whatever age a girl becomes ashamed to stand publicly exposed, that is when she has reached sexual maturity,[128] according to this group of scholars.

It may be conjectured that the differences in these three points of view are due to the fact that the Rabbis' opinions stemmed from the individual differences in their studies of adolescents. They had to consider different climatic conditions, differing conditions of health, and differing balances of nutrition. Indeed, physiologists tell us that even a distance of a few short miles will influence the sexual development of the child.

The Rabbis considered the appearance, length, color, and location of the physical marks as signs of sexual maturity in both sexes.[129]

The Talmud teaches that, physiologically, a woman matures earlier than a man.[130]

The Mishnah uses figurative terms to describe the stages of a woman's sexual development. She is compared to a fig or a berry in its three stages of development:

1. The unripe fig, *pagah*, or hard berry, is the prepuberty stage termed *yaldut*—childhood—from three to twelve years.
2. A fig in its early ripening stage called *bohal* is the stage of pubescence termed *naarut* or maidenhood—between twelve and twelve-and-a-half years.
3. The final stage is that of complete sexual maturity of a woman termed *bagrut* or womanhood—after twelve years and a half.[131]

They observed also that a girl who had never reached sexual maturity was quite capable of deriving pleasure from intercourse with a male,[132] a fact also reported in the modern psychological studies from Freud to Masters and Johnson.

As soon as she gives birth to a child, the minor is assumed to have passed out of the age of minority into that of puberty. It is pointed out by the Sages that even a minor is capable of bearing viable children.[133]

Another mark of sexual maturity is the appearance of two pubic hairs. Any time after the age of twelve years and one day, she becomes subject to all the commandments enjoined in the Law.[134]

This sign is the more correct one physiologically because a child's looks (appearance) can sometimes be deceiving. She might look much younger, or much older, than her chronological age.

Medical evidence concurs with the importance of pubic hair as an indication of the onset of puberty but disagrees about the age factor. Doctors claim that at the age of ten or eleven the first anatomic evidence of puberty is the development of pubic hair and a small increase in the size of the breast. These changes are the result of ovarian estrogen stimulation, accompanied by the increase in the size of internal and external genitalia. Others say that the biological variation of the time of the onset of puberty in the United States varies between ages nine and seventeen. The onset of puberty after the age of eighteen would be considered delayed puberty.

The overt physical signs of womanhood, the Rabbis observed, are protrusion of the breasts, the darkening of the ring around the nipple, and the resilience of the nipple.[135]

WOMAN'S SEX LIFE

Woman's appreciation of sexual intercourse is so keen that even though it may entail keen suffering, she cannot refrain from indulging in it. While undergoing the indescribable pains of childbirth, she determines to renounce sexual love, but no sooner has she recovered than she willingly gives herself to her husband. In fact, according to the Bible, an offering is to be brought to the sanctuary by the woman after childbirth. (Lev. 12:6) The Sages understood its purpose to be to atone for a vow she never meant to keep. While undergoing the pangs of birth, she presumably vowed "never again," but this oath she soon forgets. The strain and violence of muscular effort is swept from the mother's memory by the sound and touch of her newborn child.[136]

The sexual drive is so strong that "she does not want to live with a husband who will not gratify her sexual longing from time to time," and when she is deprived of this gratification, it causes her immense suffering.[137] The fact that woman's capacity for sexual pleasure is bountiful is documented by recent clinical reports.

Yet, even though abstinence from sexual pleasures with her husband causes her to suffer, it is in no way as painful to her as to the man. Woman's desire for sexual gratification is covert and she can control herself with less effort, because her sex drive is the more passive.[138]

Woman's desire is deep in her heart; her self-control was considered a virtue and was greatly praised by the Rabbis.

Today, despite the lessening of sexual inhibitions, the arousal of the woman's natural desire is less spontaneous than with a man and depends, to a great extent, upon her husband's expression of love, his desire, insight, understanding, and skill as a lover.

A woman's repression of her sexual needs is effective because her sexual being is not as physically obvious as the male's (i.e., erection, nocturnal emissions, and the like). Her sexual thinking is repressed more strenuously because of her social role and her fears of what sexual freedom might cost her.[139]

Though she can resist her sexual impulses with greater ease than the man, she is unwilling to do so for any considerable length of time. This is explained by the fact that her sexual experience is emotionally deeper, her involvement more profound. She therefore derives—in all probability—more pleasure from intercourse than does the man.[140]

Masserman explains that this is so precisely because most males are so easily aroused and satisfied, they can often go through the same monotonous sex procedures and not complain. Developmentally, the male is interested especially in the biologic act of sexual gratification.[141] Many women, with their less imperious sex urges and their greater sensitivity to the romantic aspects of life, have much greater need for unusual surroundings and situations.

Woman cannot understand sexual intercourse without love, and this love is the dominating factor in the life of the woman; it is, in fact, the whole of her life, the essential purpose of her life. This is what makes her a woman.

Kinsey holds that marriage, love, and sexual outlet are usually seen by woman as inseparable and explains this by the fact that "the female is generally conditioned to believe that love is a pre-condition of sexual behavior." The male and female are closest together in their response to erotic stimuli, items involving some "love," and farthest apart on those items related to "pure sex." A woman derives pleasure from giving herself to the man she loves. This pleasure is as remote from the man's experience and understanding as the physical aspect of his experience is unfathomable to her.

The cultural values of our society have led to different sexual concerns and fears on the part of men and women. Kinsey and his associates failed to find any anatomic or physiological basis for the oft-repeated emphasis on the supposed differences between female and male sexuality.[142]

Differences in sexual behavior between men and women therefore appear to be the product of learning and conditioning. One may claim, as a consequence, that "our sexual behavior is essentially the result of our attitudes toward sex; and these attitudes, in turn, are a product of how we have been brought up."[143]

Woman prefers a scanty living with a husband who will be with her all the time and gratify her libidinal longings to a life of luxury and wealth when such a life presents restrictions on chastity and forbearance. She may, therefore, give preference to a poor man, whose business does not necessitate his going away from home and who is able to fulfill her sexual needs. We can find, perhaps, a secondary psychological motive for her being conditionally discriminating in the selection of her mate: since woman is known to suffer acutely from fear of loneliness, her strong wish to avoid this situation will prompt her to easily accept the man who is willing to offer her companionship and warm shelter.[144]

In stating that it causes woman less suffering than man to abstain from sexual pleasure, it must be understood that this is not the case when she is in the throes of passion with the man she desires. When she finds her sexual advances rejected, it causes her such great distress and shame that she feels she would prefer leaving to living with a cold, indifferent husband. This is consistent with our studies today. Actually, an aroused woman is no less responsive to the sex urge than a man. In many cases she is more responsive.[145]

The rabbinic observations on the libidinal force prefigure much of Freud's emphasis on the libido. Obsessive sexual relations and frustration-fantasy not leading to sexual gratification are destructive—even more damaging than improper sex. The Talmud was fully aware of the sexual drive and the continuously potent sexual imagination. The Rabbis knew that unfulfilled desire intensifies with time.[146]

Woman's strong desire for sexual gratification leads her to fantasizing and dreaming, which enhances and satisfies her sexual longings.

Spiritual and educational preoccupation, as with the study of Torah, was prescribed by the Sages as a means of controlling one's sex drive.[147]

Discussion of sexual matters between partners was considered a strictly private matter. A sexually importunate wife, who makes her sexual claims publicly known, thereby provides her husband with legal grounds for divorce.[148]

As for woman's self-control, the Rabbis observed that when she is intoxicated she becomes bold and brazen (because her inhibitions are lowered); as the proverb runs, "what a sober man bears on his lung, the drunkard carries on his tongue." But this happens only when her husband is not with her;[149] his presence causes her to repress her libidinal impulses. This restraint is probably due to the fact that she might either be afraid to act in such a provocative way in his presence or because she might feel ashamed to have him witness her shamelessness. The influence of liquor on sexual behavior, in both sexes, is erratic: it may heighten passion, especially in women, or lower it, depending upon the quantity absorbed and the mood of the individual.

Owing to a woman's difficulty in exerting full control over her sexual cravings, she needed, psychologically, a husband's protective guardianship: (in addition to her need for economic security and for children) as the rabbinic adage puts it, "woman's desire to marry is considered stronger than man's." The Rabbis advised a father whose daughter had reached maturity to marry her off quickly.[150]

Age is a sociobiological factor that has a definite influence on marital choice. Evidence shows that a young woman should not marry "an old man."

On account of her pronounced sexual needs, "woman renounces an old mate, even if he is opulent, and will be satisfied with a young one, even if he is poor." The Rabbis enjoined the father not to marry off his daughter to an old man, because he will not be able to satisfy her needs and she might be driven to adultery.[151]

Woman's antipathy toward an aged husband is so great, she tries to keep him young; on the other hand, a woman does not want her husband to appear younger than she. As the talmudic parable goes: "A man had two wives, one young and one old. The young one desiring her husband to appear young, used to pluck out his white hair, whereas the old one, desiring her man to appear old, used to pluck out his black hair. Between the two of them, he ended up bald."[152]

The Rabbis observed that not only is the husband a fair guardian of the wife's moral conduct but that the wife's presence exerts a stabilizing influence over the husband; she is just as much of a stabilizer for him as he is for her. In her presence he will curb his sexual desires for other women. In his presence she will suppress her sexual longing, even when intoxicated, for other men.[153] But this holds true only with righteous men or women. The immoral ruffian does not care about the chastity of his wife, and neither does a woman of loose morals care about the purity of her husband.[154]

It was noted that the woman enjoys discussing erotic subjects. In Freudian interpretation we could say this is because of her pronounced sexual longing, which has not been fully gratified. In this respect she is like one who is fond of wine and cannot get it (who will, though, continuously talk about it).

Letorneau pointed out that in various parts of the world women have taken a leading part in creating erotic poetry.[155]

A surprising proportion of the women sampled by Kinsey indicated that they enjoyed erotic stories because of the stories' intrinsic humor. Sometimes this was true because the stories represented a defiance of social convention. There is even some indication that there is an increasing delectation of such stories among women in the United States. Kinsey, however, in comparing the psychological differences between men and women in susceptibility to erotic stimuli, found that 16 percent of men versus 2 percent of women respond to stimulation by erotic stories. Some 95 percent of the women studied have heard or read erotically stimulating stories. His findings point to a higher erotic response by men to almost all sexual stimuli.[156]

A unique aspect of verbalized eroticism relates to the use of salacious sexual terminology, pertaining to and during intercourse. Its range encompasses three stages: (1) an intrinsic distaste for vulgar terms, which subverts the desired erotic effort; (2) a neutral reaction, whereby the vulgarisms have neither a stimulating nor a distasteful effect; and (3) a strong desire to utter, hear, and actually experience such terms as an integral part of sexual stimulation and gratification.[157] However, Jewish morality and sexual modesty encourage the couple to refrain from vulgarities and use only loving and endearing parlance.

The Talmud claims that "A woman does not make a covenant [bond] except with the man who is her first love," and, by the same token, a man can only achieve peace of mind from his first wife. Upon this, R. Akiva advises his disciple, "You should not cook in the vessel your neighbor used," meaning, he should not marry a divorcee during her husband's lifetime or even a widow, for she may remember her former love, especially if her second husband does not satisfy her sexual needs as the first one did. In such a case, she would feel only contempt and hatred for him.[158]

Another interesting psychological observation of the Rabbis was that the gratification of the woman's sexual desires is dependent to a great extent upon her mental attitude. When she engages in sexual intercourse in a halfhearted manner, she does not derive the pleasure or gratification out of it that she would have had she actively, willingly, and gladly given of herself in her own characteristic way.

Frame of mind is of vital importance. Often it lies at the root of frigidity in women; weakness or impotence in men. Mental readiness is a significant prelude to the sexual act. A virgin, then, feels pain when forced into intercourse but will feel only slight discomfort when she willingly consents to it. Then the irritation caused is no more than that caused by the puncture of the lancet.

It is noteworthy how the Rabbis analyzed this phase of "pain sensation." They questioned their open-minded wives, to find out the exact degree of pain felt by them during their first sexual experience.

On the other hand, Tradition was fully aware of the power of sexual passion, making the sexual act, though initiated by controlled intromission, conclude with the woman's tacit consent and enjoyment.[159]

Another very telling rabbinic example of the influence of the mind on the sex instinct is seen in the following observation: If a widow abandons the idea of ever remarrying, or indulging in sexual intercourse, for a period of ten years or more, and then decides to remarry, the union will be childless. If, however, her mind was set all along on marrying, she will conceive.[160]

The Rabbis observed that by social activity and domestic labor the woman finds sexually sublimated gratification, while idleness leads her to acts of immorality.[161]

This principle of sexual sublimation is further exemplified by R. Yohanan's assertion that, before Jerusalem was destroyed, boys and girls played together until they reached the age of sixteen or seventeen, without being conscious of any sexual attraction for each other or of the need of sexual gratification. This story seems to confirm the modern theory that erotic impulses can be successfully regulated through proper guidance and intelligent training. Deferring the whole matter till the time is ripe works well with many a youth or maiden. Combined with social interests, the sex motive finds sublimated satisfaction in a great variety of activities as well as in business associations between the sexes.[162]

THE SEXUAL ACT

The regulations of the *Shulhan Arukh* about the frequency of sexual relations allow for the recognition of two hygienic *leitmotifs:*

1. The knowledge that the too frequent discharge of sperm will weaken the body.
2. The acceptance that the spiritual, mental, and physical condition of the couple is able to influence their offspring favorably or unfavorably. This would tend to protect them as much as possible against the transmission of parental vice, defects, and infirmities. This consideration, as well as the regard for the health of the couple, is contained in the regulation: "One does not cohabit while standing up, in the bath, on the day one is bled, nor on the day one sets out or returns from a fatiguing journey, also not immediately before or after.[163]

Maimonides cautions against sexual abuse, suggesting control and mental distraction from sexual ideation. "Whoever wants to be continuously healthy, should remove all thoughts of coitus out of his mind with all his power."[164]

Other conditions considered by Maimonides to insure optimal physical fitness of the couple for congress are as follows: avoiding coitus after enjoying spicy foods, fresh fruit, greens like cucumbers, Indian melons, "portulaca, cabbage, garlic, onions; likewise, after excessive excitement, an upset stomach, diarrhea, during a famine—except for childless couples; when one is sated, or hungry, or thirsty. Cohabitation is considered most advantageous when the digestive process has already concluded; not after staying awake, after tiring, after gymnastic exercises, or after being drunk. Coitus is also hygienically unsound whenever there is bodily fatigue, or incapacity, or when physical or psychological depression exists to which personal hatreds are linked.[165]

The couple's state of mind, as well as their physical well-being, were taken into consideration when the Rabbis suggested the frequency and appropriate timing of coition; hence, one's occupation was a highly relevant factor.

Aphrodisiacs have always been in vogue—especially in the Orient—and were also known and recommended by the Rabbis, in order to increase the seminal flow both quantitatively and qualitatively as a prime factor in procreation. Eating garlic was believed, along with other foods, to increase the spermatic flow. (This led to the popular custom of eating garlic on Friday nights.) On the other hand, the seminal flow is believed to be diminished by the use of salty foods, skin disease, hunger, too much weeping, sleeping on the ground, being flogged, and because of the growth of premature pubic hair.[166]

The frequency of conjugal duty prescribed by the Rabbis, in consonance with the Torah, was regulated by time, availability (determined by vocation or profession), and the potency of the man.

The suggested frequency is as follows: for men of leisure, every day; for laborers, twice a week; for mule drivers, once a week; for camel drivers, once in thirty days; for sailors, once in six months. Scholars were expected to perform their marital duties every Friday night, and during the week when returning from a journey, or, if the wife demonstrates her desire for him in any way, even during pregnancy or lactation; indeed, all these occasions are considered as important as on the night of tevilah.[167]

As for the adequate timing for sexual activity, the night was considered best. Darkness is imperative for sexual relations even during the day, according to the Law; one of the reasons being modesty and consideration for the woman. Kinsey, too, attests that very few of the women studied preferred light during sexual activity. He attributes this "to represent the greater modesty of the female."[168]

Maimonides suggests that, although one is free to cohabit with his wife at any time he wishes, it is pious practice to control oneself and sanctify oneself during intercourse, keeping in mind its main purpose: procreation.

Midnight is viewed by the Rabbis as the ideal time for cohabitation. "Son, when you awaken from your sleep in the middle of the night converse with your wife in holiness," says R. Eliezer the Great. At this hour no outside interference or voices will disrupt, "and one will not drink out of one goblet, and think of another."[169]

The early Rabbis were very knowledgeable in matters of sexuality, and the codified Jewish Law never glossed over these issues, the sexual experience being perceived by the Sages as a normal function of vital human need. Especially so since "sexual desire brings peace between man and wife"[170] and was chosen by Providence as the only vehicle for the Divine command of procreation.

Great latitude was accorded by Jewish Law to the married couple in order to enhance their relationship through love, consideration, and understanding for each other's needs. Respect for the partner's scruples is fundamental. It is as important to know one's partner's mind as it is to know his or her body.

Notwithstanding the Christian code, which considers any unconventional sexual activity as biologically abnormal and perverse, the Jewish code, in the words of Maimonides, states:

> Since a man's wife is permitted to him, he may act together with her in any variety of ways. They may have intercourse whenever so desired, kiss any organ of her body he wishes, and he may have intercourse naturally or unnaturally, provided that he does not expend semen to no purpose. Nevertheless, it is an attribute of piety that a man should not act in this matter with levity and that he should sanctify himself at the time of intercourse . . . A man should not turn aside from the normal way of the world and its proper procedure, since the true design of intercourse is fruitfulness and multiplication of progeny.[171]

One should not indulge with his partner in frivolities or foul language. It is permitted, however, to discuss all matters relating to coition in order to become sexually aroused, provided one can control himself from premature ejaculation.

It is told of Rav that he used to converse freely with and stimulate his wife, arousing her sexually before intercourse.

Women are more susceptible to the stimulus aroused by the hearing than are men. Proof of this is afforded by the power of the "love-whisper" on women, which may, in an instant sweep away their reserve.[172]

Jewish tradition required the loving couple to perform the sexual act in complete nudity, while covered with a sheet.

After an argument, one should amiably converse with his wife to pacify her, before engaging in sexual intercourse. According to R. Menahem Ha-Meiri (1249–1316), "While modesty is proper for a woman even with her husband, she is permitted to talk to him desirously in order to make herself beloved to him."[173]

The man, in turn, should engage in matters which pacify his wife's mind, excite her, cause her enjoyment, through erotic conversation which stimulates love, agreement, and togetherness, in order to combine her mind and intention with his. The couple should be neither apathetic toward each other nor in depressed moods; they should talk to each other and engage in foreplay to relax each other's minds before a mutually fulfilling union.

There must be harmony to achieve the maximum sexual satisfaction. A wise husband will make it his business to treat his wife with kindness and understanding; she is more apt to be sexually cooperative if she feels loved and wanted.

Since people's sexual needs are not necessarily similar, understanding between husband and wife is important. One cannot approach his partner abruptly and always expect her desires to match his own. Once husband and wife begin to believe that their desires are no longer respected, they look upon their sexual relationship as a denial, rather than as a confirmation, of their love.

"Even a king", the Zohar states, "when he desires to visit his consort, should coax her and use words of endearment, and not treat her as a mere chattel, etc." There is such a thing as "bedroom manners."[174]

An experienced husband never exhibits an overly aggressive approach to a sex relationship. He restrains himself from any behavior which overemphasizes his mood. A refined woman expects her man to control his passion and repudiates any crude overtures. Even in the privacy of her bedroom, a woman feels entitled to expect sexual dignity on the part of her husband.

Just as words of affection and kisses precede coition, "endearments should be uttered by the husband after coition, in order to gladden his wife's heart and show her that her pleasure is as important to him as his own," counsels Tradition.[175]

The Jewish husband was exhorted to display tact and genuine consideration in approaching his wife for sexual relations. He was urged to woo her, promise her gifts, entice her by endearments and demonstrations of his love and affection, and so build up in her a sexual desire and reciprocal cooperation, without which he should not embrace her.[176]

No intelligent male will force sex upon his wife. How, after all, could a coerced relationship be a pleasurable experience for a man when he knows that his mood will not be reciprocated? The enjoyment of his wife's passion should be his foremost concern; a vital element to a satisfactory relationship is lacking when a woman performs in a merely perfunctory fashion. Any man who insists upon his rights as a husband at the expense of his wife's rights as a human being is thoroughly deserving of contempt. Hence, the husband must show lovingkindness, patience, and understanding. He should endeavor to satisfy the wife's sexual longings and needs and give her sexual pleasure and fulfillment.

Sexual intercourse is sometimes considered a masculine right and feminine duty. This attitude was more common in the past, but it has not yet disappeared. This duty-right is cold, one-sided and unchallenging, an imposition of rights and the unwilling performance of duty. Any man who enters marriage with the intention of demanding his rights shows plainly the shallowness of his attitude toward his wife. He is old-fashioned and boorish. A woman should participate in and encourage the responses of her husband. On the other hand, where a woman feels that her role in sexual relations should be completely passive and expects the husband to be the sole active partner, her attitude becomes a burden to the man, who usually loses interest and can become impotent.

A wise wife will help the husband in the various kinds of love play. The ability to experience sex in this assisting way will come to her gradually. A woman who advances from the immature state of "being in love" to the mature state of "loving" will acquire the knack in time and will find that it leads to a true and fulfilling union.

Whoever cohabits in a sanctified spirit with the intention of prolonging coitus by self-control, concentrating lovingly on his wife, and extending coition in consideration of the woman so that she may enjoy him fully and climax first is rewarded with sons. Similarly, if one is aware of his inability to control the seminal emission, and therefore goes through the act without delay, in order to avoid *ejaculatio praecox* he, too, fulfills the commandment and is similarly rewarded.[177]

The husband should not subject her to intercourse through intimidation or force, or while he is in a state of inebriation, or if he intends to divorce the wife, or when the wife is ill or asleep. Neither should he abuse his wife with excessive coition, unless she fully agrees to a second sexual embrace. He should refrain from burdening her. When one injures his wife during coitus, he is punishable by Jewish Law, because he abused his obligation to be considerate to his mate.[178]

Every man ought to be punctilious to fulfill his wife sexually in the night of her ablution in the *mikvah*. Even when she is nursing, if he recognizes that she is enticing him, wooing him, and adorning herself for him in order to get his attention, he should lavish upon her sexual pleasure, although it is not in the set time of *onah*.[179]

One of the most common sources of sexual dissatisfaction for the woman is the abruptness with which her husband's passion subsides. Much energy goes into the heightening of an orgasm, only to be followed by a change in his mood. On the other hand, a woman's passion rarely ends with the orgasm and tends instead to recede more slowly than it does in the man. She feels hurt and dissatisfied by the sudden change of her husband's mood and his physical removal from her. Oral indications of love, satisfaction, or appreciation—though brief—and prolonged physical contact after detumescence will make her love experience fuller and more rewarding.

The sex act, then, should leave the woman feeling calm, at peace with the world.

In view of the biological differences between the sexes, it would be very surprising indeed if women's sexual reactions were identical with those of men. Women's approach to sex is more indirect. They take longer to be aroused, longer to complete the act. For a woman, sex is seen more as a part of her whole nature than as purely an isolated excitement which can be forgotten as soon as it is over.

The real difference is that in the woman, the duration of the several stages of sexual satisfaction is not the same as in the man, who reaches his climax at ejaculation, followed immediately by lassitude. The woman requires not only the sexual act itself but also preliminaries leading up to it and the events following it, the prologue and the epilogue.

With the orgasm, the man experiences complete relief, but the desire of the woman for proof of love is by no means ended. There begins in her the "after-sensation," as we might call it. She still desires to be kissed and embraced—and more strongly than ever, to feel that her husband truly loves her.

The absence of reserve and the freedom of mutual expression during the sexual union of man and wife were encouraged by the Rabbis in order to give unimpeded and natural pleasure to the loving pair (as long as the laws of modesty are not offended). Indeed, sexuality may be a God-given gift, but it may become degrading unless it is accompanied by love and mutual dignity.[180]

The implication is that all positions are permitted, "provided that one does not expend semen to no purpose."[181] This attitude in Judaic law points up the fact that the sexual union within marriage, with all its variations, is an accepted natural expression of man's ability to give and take pleasure as an aesthetic manifestation of love within the boundaries of modesty.

There were, however, some rabbinic admonitions on the matter.

The face-to-face position, with man above and woman supine beneath, was thought of as the most usual and accepted one. This is still widespread in European and American cultures. It was also recommended by the *Zohar* for kabbalistic reasons.[182]

The converse position (the woman on top of the man) is not, on the other hand, considered advisable during the first *tevilah* night, since the main objective then is conception, but on other occasions disapproval appears to be less.[183]

The standing position was discouraged because of the fatiguing and uncomfortable effect, as well as impracticability for conception. Equally discountenanced were sedentary positions. R. Yehudah Al-Harizi recommends the reclining-on-the-side position.[184]

Since sexual congress was viewed as an intimate and aesthetically Divine experience for the loving couple, the proper setting and milieu were required in order to assure them full privacy and a relaxed atmosphere for the act of love. The bedroom was always seen as the most natural love "nest." One was admonished against cohabiting in public places (i.e., marketplaces, streets, parks), or on the ground, lest the act be debased; also when one was a guest, unless complete privacy is provided. Similarly, intercourse is prohibited in front of a Torah Scroll, or the Sacred Books. Piety requires that cohabitation not be performed in front of living beings.[185]

Education in sexual manners and techniques appears to have been supplied during the talmudic period. This is even more a case of curiosa when one considers that intimate dialogue took place between father and his daughters. We note this in the case of Rav Hisda, who taught his daughters how to excite their husbands sexually before coition, by telling them metaphorically that when a man is holding a precious stone in one hand and with the other something less precious, and his friend asked him for both—if he shows his friend the hand with the precious stone and does not show him the other, his friend will be frustrated and will desire the second more than the first. This implies that the most pleasant and beautiful feature in the woman's body should be revealed to her husband at the end, after he has become ablaze with desire; only then should the sexual union take place.

The Moslem traditionalists (who lived within two or three generations of Mohammed) claimed that Mohammed exhorted his disciples: "Do everything opposite to the Jews, except what concerns copulation."[186]

The experience of the centuries has shown that Jewish domestic happiness is enhanced when the traditional sexual code is observed.

People can cast aside sexual stereotypes and learn to relate to each other as individuals. Because of their mutual respect, husband and wife become flexible enough to respond to each other's inclinations. At times, a woman will allow her husband to stimulate her sexual interest enough to match his, and, at other times, he will allow her lack of interest to postpone his. Every kiss or caress need not necessarily lead to the sex act. A normal sex life in marriage is varied, ranging from deferring the release of desire, to routine satisfaction, to the most sparkling and rapturous experience imaginable.

In our day the range of sexual experience in marriage has widened owing to the emancipation of women, the egalitarianism of marriage, and increased education for both sexes. Experimental attitudes are increasingly common. While marriage manuals may encourage variety for variety's sake, mutual respect for the partner's feelings is still a must.

An individual's pattern of sexual behavior will depend greatly upon the long-standing religio-social codes concerning the various types of sexual activity. The social attitudes may force one to confine overt display to sexual expressions that are acceptable to his particular culture. The formula for an enjoyable, wholesome sex life requires the right attitude, namely, an unadulterated appreciation and favorable opinion of it.

In our culture, woman is not always certain of her husband's intimate approach in the areas of tenderness, patience, and care. She may anticipate the initial union with mixed emotions of hope and fear. He must overcome her fear by trust and love for him, so that her full sexuality will be expressed.

Sexuality is an expression of one's total personality and physical identity. A woman's first sexual encounter is her initiation into the most intimate and profound kind of contact, when her body takes on a new meaning for her—by its erotic response to another person. Her first sexual experience is a harbinger her future sex life, helping her conceptualize her own sexual identity by a fuller sense of awareness and reliance on her own body.

Woman usually does not separate emotional feelings and sexual satisfaction. Since her body responds together with her partner's, she involves herself completely in this most sensitive act of love. The assurance, therefore, that she can trust and rely on her husband's emotional involvement and his genuine feelings for her needs is paramount for her sexual gratification and emotional fulfillment.

The Rabbis counseled for the husband a positive, respectful, and caring approach toward his wife, which would, ultimately, result not only in a physical but in a spiritual wholesomeness of *Shalom bayit*.

OTHER FORMS OF SEXUALITY

Sexual taboos and prohibitions were instituted by the Sages in order to guard against the free-flowing id impulses and orgiastic urges in man, and thus to help him attain self-discipline.[187]

Sexual deviation in talmudic terms was primarily related to the wasting of the seed, since the essential purpose in sex, according to Tradition, was procreation. Sexual activity contravening this traditional intent was considered a deviation.

Masturbation, or the deliberate self-stimulation which effects sexual arousal by man, is strongly condemned in rabbinic law and considered a sin. The rationale, from a religious standpoint, is obvious: indulgence in masturbatory activity may result in substituting this sexual form for regular intercourse, thereby foregoing the commandment of procreation, and is hence synonymous, religiously, with unlawful killing.[188]

The Rabbis believed that the first intercourse with a virgin does not lead to conception; it is told that all women of the house of R. Yehuda, the Prince, exercised digital friction to break their hymens, in order to be capable of conception from the first sexual contact like Tamar, the daughter of King David, and the daughters of Lot.[189] It was taught, however, that a young girl's genitals should not be thoroughly examined by other women, lest she be taught the enjoyment of digital manipulation and develop such habituation.

To prevent premarital unchastity or masturbation, a great number of noteworthy and extremely subtle regulations were espoused: spiritual diversions through earnest study, moderation in eating and drinking, abstention from stimulating foods (meat, eggs, cheese, spices, hot drinks), not sleeping on one's back or stomach, involvement in sports, and so forth.

Various forms of sexual activity are amply expounded in the Talmud, showing the vast rabbinic knowledge on the subject.[190]

LESBIANISM

Judaism is unequivocally committed to higher moral practices and *tikun olam bemalkhut Shamayim*. The Law treats the practice of lesbianism as an unseemly, delinquent, immoral act. Maimonides advises exclusion of women known to be addicted to this vice from the company of decent women. Women involved in lesbian activities, however, are permitted to marry *kohanim*.[191]

The practice, though, was not specifically prohibited in the Bible; the Rabbis however find it implied in the general Levitical injunction: "The practices of the land of Egypt wherein you dwelt shall you not follow; and the practices of the land of Canaan whither I bring you shall you not follow, neither shall you walk in their ordinances." (Lev. 18:3) Although, theoretically, laws against homosexuality can be applied to lesbian behavior, perhaps because no actual coitus takes place between two females and no seed is actually "wasted," society has almost invariably taken a more permissive attitude toward lesbianism than it has toward male homosexuality.

The *halakhah* condemns the act and imposes disciplinary penalties but recognizes no restrictions against private nonsexual association between two women. The Talmud calls lesbianism "delinquent" while Maimonides and Karo forbid it on moral grounds requiring rehabilitation and *teshuvah*.[192]

During the talmudic period the Rabbis tried to protect the sexual morals of their children by not allowing their daughters to sleep in one bed. This was adhered to even more rigorously concerning single men in order not to encourage mutual erotic stimulation.[193] Indeed practitioners should bear in mind that a real difference exists between homosexual transitory encounters and homosexual preference.

DISTINCTION OF SEX IN APPAREL

The pagan sexual deviations and unnatural lusts of the Near Eastern people surrounding Israel affected even the Israelites.

The biblical prohibition of transvestism proclaims: "A woman shall not wear that which pertaineth unto a man, neither shall a man put on a woman's garment; for whosoever doeth these things is an abomination unto the Lord thy God." (Deut. 22:5) An interchange of attire between the sexes would foster immodesty and sexual immorality, since transvestism also involves a desire to assume the role of the opposite sex in the social organization. Surely, such a law is directed against homosexual practices.* The Mosaic Code, though not mentioning such deviation

---

*Although transvestism and homosexuality are different phenomena and Kinsey shows that only a portion of the transvestites have homosexual histories.

as pathological in nature, does stress its immoral aspects as a gross human degradation.

Sexual disguise in apparel was seen by Philo and Josephus as a degrading and cowardly technique of warfare, as practiced by the warriors of Yohanan of Gush-Halav, who indulged in sexual transvestism for military debaucheries during the Roman occupation.[194] Women, though, were always kept out of the battlefield, since carrying weapons by women was considered a distortion of their feminine, tender nature.

According to Maimonides, the biblical prohibition against wearing garments of the opposite sex refers to a primitive heathen ritual where masquerading in disguised garments of the opposite sex was part of the religious sexual worship. The Mosaic Code condemns such sexually immoral practices connected with idolatrous worship.[195]

The *halakhah*'s concern for public morality interprets the biblical injunction as a precautionary measure to distinguish and separate the sexes, who, if clad in a sexually equivocal manner, might engage in deviant sexuality and debauchery. The Law extends the primary prohibition of full intersexual disguise to other forms of costume.[196]

It should now be clear why, as we mentioned earlier, women were prohibited to bear weapons in war.[197]

For the same reason, woman could not wear a turban or cap—the customary headgear for men. Women could not clip their hair in male fashion, since their long hair was characteristic of femininity. Likewise, men could not shave their hair on the hidden parts of their body, as women do, or dye their hair or pull out the gray and leave only the black hair.[198]

Men were also forbidden to wear feminine, brightly colored clothes or jewelry, or ornaments in a feminine fashion. Karo prohibits men from dressing in front of a mirror, as women do—except for shaving or for adjusting the phylacteries on the head.[199]

Nonetheless, some of these interdictions were gradually eased, as custom and fashion for both sexes changed or when valid reasons for the discontinuance of the prohibited practices were cited.

R. Judah Ha-Hasid, of the twelfth century, permitted Jewish women on the road to disguise themselves as men in order to deter any attack on them by Gentiles. Similarly, since medieval times it has been customary for men to disguise themselves in women's costumes on Purim for masquerades (*farshtelen*), for Jewish weddings, for traditional celebration, and for merriment.[200]

SACRED PROSTITUTION

The ancient religions of Babylonia, Syria, Egypt, and Phrygia worshiped an omnipotent feminine power, personified as a supreme goddess of fertility.

In Phrygia, and throughout Asia Minor, Cybele, the Great Mother of the gods, was worshiped by orgiastic dances, fertility rites and human sacrifices. This cult later spread to Greece and Rome. In Babylonia the mother god, Ishtar, yearly mourned her dead lover, Tammuz. The women wept over the corpse of Tammuz and tore their hair. This ritual was in vogue even in Israel, prompting the prophet Ezekiel to protest vehemently against it. (Ezek. 8:14) In Phoenicia, Ishtar became Astarte or Ashtoreth, as she is called in the Bible; in Greece, Tammuz became Adonis along with his beloved Aphrodite.

None of the forms or derivatives of sacred prostitution were of native Jewish origin. This practice strayed into Israel's life under perverted kings who borrowed from their idolatrous neighbors, or it was introduced by foreign rulers. Legislators, prophets, preachers, and warriors were relentless in their fight for religious and sexual purity and fought continuously with their neighbors and their pagan revelry.

The Code of Hammurabi records the existence of "sacred servants"— religious officials whose functions included enactment of the sexual rite. They had legal status and enjoyed greater inheritance rights than any other women. These "women of Marduk," as they were called, were known by other names too—Ninan ("woman of god"), naditum ("vowed woman").

The Hebrew people encountered cults of sacred prostitution from the earliest days. Among these cults were women votaries, who were regarded as married to the deity they worshiped and who performed the duties of priestesses. They gave themselves up to the worshipers as part of the temple rite. (Men performed the same service for female or male worshipers.)

The ancient Hebrews reacted variously to the practice of sacred prostitution which flourished in the Orient. Sometimes they succumbed to the lure and adopted their heathen neighbors' practice in the worship at the sanctuary of God. (They called the woman engaging in this act kedeshah, and the man, kadesh.)[201] Recall what was said about the sons of Eli ". . . lying with the women that assembled at the door of the Tabernacle of the congregation."(1 Sam. 2:22) The author of the first book of Samuel records their conduct with sharp criticism and attributes to this transgression the defeat of Israel by the Philistines, the capture of the Ark of the Law, the death of Eli, the High Priest, and of his sons. During Saul's, David's, and Solomon's reigns there is no mention of sacred prostitution, but Rehoboam, son of Solomon, influenced by his Ammonite mother, introduced the practice into the Temple at Jerusalem. The kings Asa and Jehoshaphat tried to eliminate it, but it never really disappeared. Under Manasseh it flourished again. Josiah assailed all pagan practices in the Temple, and it was then finally ended. "There shall be no *kedeshah* among the daughters of Israel, neither shall there be a *kadesh* of the sons of Israel" (Deut. 23:18) is the Deuteronomic injunction that applied so fittingly to this period. Thereafter sacred prostitution as part of the Temple worship does not rear its ugly head again, though it is likely that individuals still took part in lustful activities at the heathen shrines of their neighbors.[202]

Another form of sacred prostitution in early Mideastern societies was not so much a religious ritual as a sanctuary practice. "Pious" women would indulge in harlotry and dedicate their earnings to the sanctuary.

In Phoenicia, women would sometimes sacrifice their hair or prostitute themselves for a day. In such a case, temporary harlotry was a sacred service. This practice, common among the Canaanites, wandered into the lives of the Ancient Hebrews as well. Although the Hebrew term for this kind of harlot is also *kedeshah*, she is called more often *zonah* or, simply "harlot," and she is denied sacredness, regardless of her devout intent. Again we find a Pentateuchal ruling intended to preserve Israel's morality. "Thou shalt not bring the hire of a harlot nor the price of a dog into the house of the Lord thy God for any vow; for even both these are an abomination unto the Lord thy God."(Deut. 23:19)[203]

Sex orgies as part of the idolatrous celebrations of heathen festivals constitute yet a third kind of sacred prostitution. This whoredom, "at mountain tops and under green trees" (Jer. 2:20), accompanied by the pouring of oil and offering of sacrifices, was considered particularly dangerous, since such orgies were not part of God's worship. The Jew who craved for orgies could only indulge in them at heathen festivities. The appeal of idolatry was powerful, which explains the intolerance with which the Bible treats the early Canaanites. Since their practices presented such a grave moral and national danger, Moses felt justified in commanding that all the adult women of the harloting Midianites should be annihilated.

The ritual defloration of a virgin by the head of the pagan tribe, the priest, or a number of guests at the nuptials is also related to sacred prostitution. We hear of it in the East, where it was an accepted rite for a long time.[204] In the Western world this primitive ritual developed into the jus primae noctis, the law granting the governor or his official the privilege of the first night with every virgin bride.

Despite the esteem for virginity throughout the Bible, this foreign influence also crept into Jewish life. The word halalah in the Bible also suggests that this practice was not an unknown or uncommon practice among the Jews.[205] The extent to which this practice was accepted by the Jews during the biblical period is unknown, but evidently there was enough of it to warrant various injunctions from the Torah.

During the rabbinic period, with the exception of the jus primae noctis, which the Jews opposed, such defloration seems to be unheard of. At the end of the Amoraic period the Palestinian Jews, following the example of their neighbors, performed, when necessary, artificial defloration, without male contact.[206]

SECULAR PROSTITUTION

In the Middle East, prostitutes have always been considered as part of society, in rural and in urban life. (Josh. 2:1; 6:25; Judg. 16:1; 1 Kings 3:16–27; Hos. 2:47; Ezek. 16:37–38; 23:29) The prostitute was called zonah—the faithless one—a term used in the Bible for condemnation.[207]

Like all other cultural groups, the Jews were not exempt from this social evil. Jewish Law speaks out against this practice. The Levitical injunction prohibits the kohanim from marrying harlots or divorced women and prescribes the death penalty for the daughter of a priest who becomes a harlot. (Lev. 21:7–9) Israelite daughters were also admonished not to become prostitutes. (Lev. 19:29)

Even so, Jewish prostitution was not widespread; indeed, from the total lack of laws regulating it, we may deduce that the Jewish brothel was virtually nonexistent as a social institution. There is hardly any mention in the Bible, Talmud, or Midrash of a Jewish prostitute maintaining a brothel. Social condemnation of harlotry was so harsh that few women would defy the social and moral opprobrium.[208] Philo's belief that a harlot was not even allowed to exist is justified by the rarity of prostitution in Jewish society, a scarcity that continued until post-talmudic times.[209]

During the fourteenth century a Jew who visited a brothel of Christian prostitutes was publicly burned at the stake by decree of the Church. Some Jewish communities, especially in Italy, brought the matter before the rabbinate. When the question of establishing Jewish brothels was debated, the Rabbis would not allow the community to approve the plans, because the recrudescence of Jewish prostitution could in no way be squelched.[210]

In recent centuries we find that even though their number is proportionately smaller, professional Jewish prostitutes are unfortunately no longer a rarity. With all the anti-Tradition liberalization and the rationale of the "new morality," there is still no justification for this frivolous approach to sex. It is dehumanizing to make use of one's own or another's body as a mere object for perfunctory sensual gratification. Something priceless—the sexual faculty—the source of total intimacy, the enhancement of human togetherness, is lost in casual sex.

In terms of the still predominantly exploitative attitude of men in this most intimate of human interactions, a perusal of the halakhic sources shows no sanction by Tradition of such one-sidedness.

Rabbinic attitudes throughout Jewish history point to Judaism's positive view of sexuality and its advocacy of it within the context of marriage as central to Jewish life. Judaism long ago recognized the "wife's conjugal rights" as a prime requirement of the husband, together with his biblical duty to provide for his wife's food, clothes, and shelter. The Mishnah further stipulates that even if the wife agrees to forgo food and clothing, she cannot renounce her sexual pleasure. In fact, the Talmud describes coitus as an act in which "one body derives pleasure from another" and that the husband is required to be sensitive to the woman's desire. He has to indulge in coital prelude using "words of tenderness," for husband and wife are like one flesh. Man is not considered man until he is united with woman.[211]

In her struggles for equality with man, the modern Jewish woman has gained ground in terms of self-affirmation and role assessment. She surely can gain more by drawing from her traditional resources in order to understand truly her rights and value in society.

ON CONTRACEPTION

Jewish Law is outstanding among the extant ancient and medieval legislative codes in its pursuit and support of eugenic regulation and counseling.[212]

It was always a deep concern of Judaism to promote progeny, both quantitatively and qualitatively speaking. For this purpose it sanctioned matrimony, encouraged early marriage, insisted on sexual purity of the marital partners and the regulation of conjugal coition, extolled maternity, and sought to protect the living embryo in any way possible. Jewish eugenics promoted the improvement of a healthy nation, physically, mentally, and morally, by prescribing a canon of protective behavior for the safeguarding and preservation of future generations.

Children were always considered a blessing in Jewish tradition. (Ps. 127:3) But when innumerable human lives had been sacrificed in wars, pogroms, and all sorts of persecutions, rabbinical wisdom formulated many a precept promoting the twofold purpose of marriage, namely, the welfare of the individual and the preservation of the human race.

By the same token, in earlier times, marriages which had proved themselves sterile might (after a ten-year period) have required dissolution. This precept serves also as a proof that the Rabbis did not favor bigamy. In such an instance a divorce is enacted for the mutual benefit of both husband and wife—enabling the husband to satisfy his obligation of procreation and allowing the wife to remarry, presuming her to be blameless for their barren marriage.[213] The Midrash recognized this and drew upon the barrenness of Sarah to exemplify this situation: "And Sarai, Abram's wife, did not bear to him." (Gen. 16:1) R. Judah said: "To him she did not bear, but had she married another she would have borne."[214]

Jewish religion regards procreation as a God-given duty. It may, however, be set aside when it conflicts with the supreme Divine imperative, "He [the Jew] shall live by them—and not perish by them" (Lev. 18:5)—which commands us to preserve existing human life and enhance it.[215]

The morality of contraception was long ago a pressing issue in Judaism, both in the legal and in the philosophical sense. It recognized that sexual relations are not for reproduction alone but are, indeed, necessary for the physical and mental fulfillment of both sexes. If conception proves to be a danger to the health of the woman, she is not only permitted, but advised, to use some means of birth control.

According to halakhah, man is under the scriptural obligation to fulfill the precept "be fruitful and multiply." (Gen. 1:22) Refusal to do so is equated with the shedding of blood and the diminution of the Divine spirit in Israel. (Gen. 9:6) Since the duty is placed basically upon the man, it is he who is forbidden to undergo any means of contraception or sterilizing treatment; the woman, however, is permitted to employ only the halakhically acceptable contraceptives.[216] Although the mitzvah of procreation is not directly incumbent upon the woman, she performs a separate *mitzvah* through her participation in the process of procreation.[217] The castration, surgical sterilization, and maiming of the genital organs of man and animal alike were long condemned by Judaism.

While Catholicism prohibits the use of contraception, the Jewish view on birth control is much more liberal. In Jewish tradition its utilization is confined to medical exigency, based on a talmudic affirmation which prescribes the practice of contraception for three types of women: a minor who would use contraception for fear of becoming pregnant and die; a pregnant woman, so that her embryo be protected; and a nursing mother, whose child could be endangered through premature weaning owing to the mother's pregnancy.[218] These women are permitted to utilize intrauterine contraceptives.

The Rabbis seem to agree that birth control by the woman is permitted if pregnancy endangers the health of the woman or child or if one expects a defective child.[219] There is considerable warrant in Judaism for regarding a halting of the procreation of children as permissible, even obligatory, in cases where the mother's health is in danger or if she is to be exposed to extraordinary pain, or where the health of a child, born or unborn, would be jeopardized through the pregnancy.

Four methods and techniques of contraception used by women are discussed in the Talmud: the safe period, the postcoital gyrating movement, an oral contraceptive, and the use of an absorbent tampon during coition.[220]

The Talmud permits nonsurgical sterilization of a woman after she has had the traditionally prescribed number of children. This is seen from the case of Judith, the wife of R. Hiyya, who drank a "cup of sterility" to render herself incapable of childbearing, because she could not bear the extreme pains of childbirth.[221] This is echoed in the contemporary rabbinic sanction regarding the use of oral contraceptives. The liberal ruling regarding the cup of sterility is subsequently qualified by R. Shlomo Luria (1510-1574), who limits the sanction to women who fear the pain of further childbirths.[222] Luria also added that a woman was permitted the potion "if her children do not follow in the right way, and she fears she may bear more such children."[223] An 1821 responsum by R. Moses Schreiber declares that the use of a sterilizing treatment necessitates the compliance of the husband, since he, too, would be deprived of any future offspring. However, if the wife's thoughts and actions are upset by fear of pain or the danger of child-birth, she may ignore his protestations and continue her sterilization process, since "she is not bound to torment herself on account of her submission to her husband . . . one need not destroy oneself in order to populate the world."[224]

While according to Jewish Law the birth of two children (a son and a daughter) fulfills the minimum duty of procreation, parents were encouraged to have as many children as possible with the hope that many, if not most of them, might survive the tragedies brought about by physical hazards such as pogroms and persecutions. With the continuous decline nowadays of the Jewish birthrate in the post-Holocaust generation, however, one wonders whether the *mitzvah* of *peru u-revu* does not gain additional meaning in terms of *hemshekh* and *kiyum*—the continuity and existence of the Jewish people.

Although the Talmud permitted family limitation if the mother's and child's health were at stake, these provisions as the sole ones were disregarded by later authorities. The classic tenor of the Jewish traditional opinion remains clear. With only intrauterine devices available until recently, Jewish legalists could not as easily allow birth control for reasons other than some threat, whether more or less remote, to the mother's life. But the advent of the oral contraceptive has eased the situation somewhat, although the side effects inherent in long-term use of the "pill" seriously impugn its use both medically and halakhically.[225]

Oral contraceptives (or other devices) are not sanctioned by Tradition prior to the fulfillment of the *mitzvah* of procreation. In short, Judaism reaffirms the obligation to procreate where the medium of the family is considered the basic goal.

The rabbinic consideration of the legality of contraception is limited only to medical cases. In this respect, Judaism's blend of idealism and realism proves once again its deep concern with the human being—the centrality of Divine creation for whom a *Torat hayim* remains the guiding light.

ON ABORTION

The problem of abortion was always one of major interest in the theological, legal, and social-science literatures, its subject being vast and controversial. Religious attitudes concerning this intricate issue differ and influence the thinking and legislation in various countries regarding the liberalization of abortion. Before introducing the Jewish view on the topic, it is of interest to view the Catholic Church's attitude, which has always regarded therapeutic abortion as worse than murder, relating such action to the concept of original sin.

Already in the sixth century, Fulgentius[226] stated that the soul of the fetus is tainted with original sin from its very conception. Therefore, in case of a difficult birth, the Church rules that the mother (who was already baptized as an infant) should be left to die and thus "go to her reward" rather than be saved by abortion. Not so the fetus, who should be given a full chance to escape perdition in hell through baptism. Accordingly, the welfare of the soul of the innocent unborn child is paramount; no human society or authority can destroy life.

Catholic theologians at the Sorbonne in the nineteenth century even suggested the use a baptismal syringe which would be inserted in the uterus to baptize the fetus with holy water in case of a miscarriage. Code 2350 of the Canon Law penalizes, with the threat of automatic excommunication, any person who undergoes an abortion.

The Protestants differ with the above view. The Baptists, the Methodists, and the Lutherans consider abortion a medical problem. The Presbyterians accord first consideration to the life of the mother, while the Unitarians consider the judgment regarding therapeutic abortion to relate solely to the domain of the patient and the physician.

Out of the traditional reverence for life and the image of God imprinted on humans, the act of abortion is viewed in Judaism as morally and religiously wrong. This is to say that artificial termination of a pregnancy involving the death of the fetus any time before the full birth of the child means the destruction of an innocent life. Most rabbinic authorities have concluded that, although woman is not involved in the prohibition of *hashatat zera* (frustrating the reproductive process by contraception) as man is, still, destroying the fetus after conception is another matter altogether; therefore, no similarity can be found between contraception and abortion.[227]

The problem of abortion is closely related to the legal status of the fetus, which is accounted by the Talmud as the loin of its mother (*ubar yereh imo*).[228] Therefore, in a therapeutic abortion there are Rabbis who tend to be lenient, because, as in any surgery, we sacrifice the part for the whole.

The basic reasons given by the rabbinic authorities for prohibiting therapeutic abortion upon demand where no threat to the mother exists are as follows:

1. The unborn fetus, although not a viable person, does have some status.[229]

2. A woman submitting to an abortion, or performing one on her own, is considered as intentionally harming herself, which *halakhah* prohibits.[230]

3. Destroying the fetus, although not legally criminal, is, nonetheless, seen as an accessory to murder.[231]

Maimonides rules that deliberate murder includes the killing of an adult male or female or of a day-old baby provided that the child is born after a full-term pregnancy. [Isserles states that we consider it a full term pregnancy after the beginning of the ninth month.] Before that time, it is regarded as an abortion until it has lived for thirty days. If one kills it during these thirty days, one is not put to death on its account, although such an act is certainly prohibited.[232]

Tradition considers the fetus a *nefesh* in the sense of a soul-filled person only *ex utero*—after the baby is born and becomes fully viable (*bar kayyama*) and only thirty days postpartum. Prior to that we deal with doubtful viability, *safek hai*.[233] Rashi holds that the fetus *in utero* is not viewed as a full human being, has no independent life system, but, rather, the status of "potential human life" and not just "mere tissue," and, therefore, anyone harming the fetus is thwarting potential life.[234]

Therapeutic Abortion

While Jewish Law considered unnecessary feticide by a non-Jew as homicide, abortion, by a Jew, although forbidden, was viewed as a noncapital crime.[235] Abortion was already a legal and moral concern cited by Philo and Josephus and later by the Samaritans and Karaites.[236] Abortifacient drugs are mentioned in the Talmud as *samma denaftza* (a scattering drug, which destroys the semen in the womb) given by Cleopatra to her pregnant bondwomen.[237] Famous Jewish medical authorities have also denounced the practice of abortion: among whom are Assaf Harofe[238] (7th c.), Amatus Lusitanus[239] (16th c.), and Yaakov Zahalon[240] (17th c.).

The Talmud cites the mishnaic ruling for therapeutic abortion as follows:

> If a woman is in hard travail, one may cut up the fetus within her womb and extracts it limb by limb because her life takes precedence over its life; but if the greater part of it was already born, one

may not touch it, since one does not set aside one life for the sake
of another.[241]

Most interesting is the rabbinic stand which views the principle of
abortion and its morality more out of maternal consideration than fetal
concern. It is the mother's physical and mental welfare that takes
precedence in considerations of abortion. The humane concern of the
Rabbis in protecting the health of the Jewish mother because of the vital
role she plays in the life of the family and the perpetuation of Jewish
existence has prompted them to abide by the principle "her pain comes
first."

Once the fetus begins to emerge from the womb during parturition
into "the air of the world," it has its own identity and the same
unforfeitable right to life as its mother. Seen as a living being—*nefesh*—
it enjoys an inviolable sanctity of life of its own.[242]

If one assaults a woman, even unintentionally, and her child is
thereby lost, he must pay the value of the child to her husband and the
compensation for injury and pain to the woman. This Torah decision,
later codified by Maimonides and Karo, does not concern itself with the
unborn fetus, since it is not yet considered a person, and its destruction
cannot be called murder.[243]

The talmudic concept of the fortieth day of gestation as a crucial
break-off point is found in Aristotle[244] who believed the rational soul to
be infused in a male the fortieth day after conception, the eightieth day
in the case of a female—evidently the selfsame view of the Catholic
Church which forbade all abortions. The Stoics, followed by the
Romans, believed that the soul entered the body at birth. Therefore, in
common law the penalty of taking a life is liable only after there has
been complete extrusion of the child from the mother's womb. Medical
science, however, declares the fetus a living thing from the moment the
ovum is fertilized.[245]

Inspiriting, or soul-infusion, of the fetus is more of a theological-
philosophical problem related to the attribution of life to the fetus, but
not directly to the issue of feticide versus homicide. From a talmudic-
midrashic dialogue, we know about the Tannaitic view of soul-infusion
into the embryo. When the Roman emperor Antoninus asked
R. Yehuda, the editor of the Mishnah, "From when is the soul
(*neshama*) endowed in man, from the time he leaves his mother's
womb, or from before that time?" he replied: "From the time of

formation." The midrashic version reads: "From the time he leaves his mother's womb." "Can meat remain three days without salt and not putrify? [i.e., between coitus and impregnation]. You must concede that the soul enters at conception." And the Rabbi agreed: "From the time of conception [beginning of gestation]."[246]

Although much of the rabbinic disputation in the matter of the legal status of the embryo refers to the concept of *nefesh*, or personhood based on viability, the above aggadic dialogue and similar ones relating to the soul and its immortality in the *aggadah*, which remain "the secrets of God," are not cited by the rabbinic responsa dealing with abortion or with the legal problems of feticide.

The Talmud states that forty days after conception fetal formation has occurred. A fertilized egg, prior to forty days after conception, is nothing more than "mere fluid."[247] Based on this talmudic principle, R. Yair Bachrach[248] permitted abortion prior to forty days of pregnancy because the fetus is lacking any status of a person and is considered "mere fluid." While others support such a view, R. Unterman[249] opposes it on the grounds that such a fetus, even prior to forty days after conception, has the status of a potential person—*safek nefesh*—which, if left to nature may become an actual person and destroying it, therefore, is akin *(abizraihu)* to murder; also, on the grounds that the Noahidic prohibition of "shedding blood of man in man" (Gen. 9:6), which is interpreted to mean a fetus, applies to the Israelites as well, even though their penalty is different.

In all areas relating to the woman, such as birth control, abortion, sterilization, and so forth, Jewish Law bends toward maternal consideration.

Therapeutic abortion, therefore, because of the gravity involved, that is, saving the life of the mother—whether prepartum or postpartum—when the life of both mother and baby are in danger is clearly mandated by the Mishnah. Therapeutic abortion was declared legitimate when no other means are available to save the mother's life. It is in such cases that most rabbinic authorities permit the termination of the pregnancy on medical grounds. However, when the mother's life is not in danger, destroying the unborn fetus is prohibited on religious and moral grounds.

Rabbinic authorities still differ in the interpretation of "maternal needs." Some are stringent, some more lenient. However, most of them agree that pregnancy may be terminated in instances where docu-

mented medical evidence shows that the continuance of the pregnancy
may threaten the physical or mental health of the mother. These include
cases of *pikuah nefesh*, dangers to mother's life; rape, incest,[250] the birth
of a defective child which would prove harmful to the mother,[251] social
stigma, or any other health dangers. Exposure to German measles,[252]
ingestion of thalidomide,[253] deafness, mental-health risks, "extreme
mental anguish, hysteria, suicidal tendencies,"[254] or other psychiatric
disorders,[255] are also causes for abortion.

Abortion is also permitted where the pregnant mother is nursing and
the change in her milk threatens the suckling's life.[256]

As seen, abortion, then, is condoned under extenuating circumstances which bespeak the woman's physical, spiritual, and emotional
well-being. Again, the abortion, when sanctioned, is free of any homici-
dal connotation; it is prescribed not only to save the mother's physical
life but also to save her spirit from debilitating effects and needless
suffering. With all the rabbinic tolerance and humane concern for the
mother, however, almost every responsum cautions against indiscrimi-
nate and unnecessary operations which ignore the potential life involved and interfere with the Divine design of procreation.

9

ON SINGLEHOOD

Jewish daughters should not become deserted
wives.

—*Gittin* 19b

THE *AGUNAH*

The *agunah* is a woman who is legally barred from marriage. The
term is derived from the Hebrew verb *agon*, meaning "to be shut off" or
"to be chained." (Ruth 1:13) A woman is not free to remarry unless she
receives a *get*, a writ of divorce, or brings proof of her husband's death.[1]
Otherwise, she remains what the Bible calls a "living widow." (2 Sam.
20:3) A woman may become an *agunah* either through her husband's
accidental disappearance or through his willful desertion, although
accidental disappearance constitutes the main source of difficulty. For
example, in the case of a man lost in a shipwreck, even though a
survivor of the shipwreck testifies that he saw the husband drown,
Jewish Law does not consider him dead so long as the witness does not
testify unequivocally that he saw him lying dead. Similarly, in the
battlefield, the man is not legally considered dead unless the witness
averred, "I saw him dead and I buried him."[2] To protect the woman
against willful desertion by her husband, a common occurrence during
the Middle Ages, Rabbenu Yaakov Tam ruled a ruling partly incorporated in the *ketubbah*—that the husband in search of livelihood be
forbidden to stay away from his wife for a duration of twelve months

187

without reporting to the nearest *Bet Din*. On his return, the husband was compelled to remain at least six months with his family before contemplating his next trip. A man was also prohibited, without the court's permission, from leaving his wife as a result of a quarrel. If the husband refused to give his wife the *get*, the *Bet Din* was empowered to compel him to grant her a divorce.[3]

Since early talmudic times the Sages tried to mitigate the hardships arising from cases of desertion or a suspected death of the husband. Tradition deems it important to free the woman from *igun* (desertion) even if only one witness testifies to her husband's identity and death.[4]

Freeing a woman from "the chains of *igun*" is considered a very great *mitzvah* and, therefore, even hearsay evidence or the testimony of a woman or the testimony of an otherwise incompetent witness is considered acceptable: equally competent were any written documents, even non-Jewish, attesting to the husband's death.

Igun became a very complex problem in *halakhah*, especially during periods of persecution and particularly after the Holocaust. The Rabbis tried to be lenient and relax the laws of evidence, to help the woman regain her freedom and remarry.[5]

The stringent aspects of the Law are also for the woman's protection; namely, to prevent the risk of having a married woman, while considering her first husband deceased, contract a second marriage, thereby exposing herself to bigamy and adultery and her children from the second marriage to the stigma of being illegitimate.[6]

After being permitted by the *Bet Din* to remarry, the *agunah* is entitled to the payment of her *ketubbah*.[7] With the establishment of the State of Israel great strides were made by the Rabbinical Courts to help resolve the deplorable status of the *agunah* and to free her finally from the trammels of despair.

THE DIVORCÉE

Judaism realizes that divorce is antithetical to the stable family unit toward which religion and state strive, though divorce is a way out for the individual who feels that he or she wants to or must break the marriage agreement. Judaism recognizes that relationships change and, so, permits divorce and remarriage. Judaism frees people when the chains of matrimony become fetters of anguish. As a holy creature endowed with freedom of choice, the individual is too sacred to suffer degradation or dehumanization. When all avenues of marital reconciliation have been exhausted and the marriage must be dissolved, divorce, as the necessary evil, is the only remedy. In the words of the last prophet, Malachi, "I hate divorce, said the Lord" (2:16). R. Eleazar said: "If a man divorces his first wife, even the [very] altar sheds tears because of him."[8]

The old patriarchal pre-Mosaic law in the Bible had, as its main principle, the absolute authority of the husband to divorce his wife whenever he pleased. This is evident in the story of Abraham, who "sends away" Hagar—his concubine—at his wife Sarah's behest. (Gen. 16:6)

The requirement of a written bill of divorce was instituted in later biblical times.[9] This formal measure is the central feature in the biblical passage regulating divorce procedure: "That he writeth her [i.e., his wife] a Bill of Divorcement and giveth it in her hand." (Deut. 24:1–4) The bill dissolved that which had been sealed in the marriage contract: "She is no longer my wife and I am no longer her husband"[10] (Hos. 2:4); the woman was free to remarry. A bill of divorce was peculiar to the Jews; other ancient Near-Eastern nations did not incorporate it in divorce proceedings.

While the Torah granted the husband alone the right to divorce his wife, the Oral Law drastically circumscribed this absolute right by requiring justification for his divorce. Jewish Law granted woman the right to be a plaintiff in a divorce action, thereby automatically authorizing the courts to represent her and enforce their decrees against the husband, the defendant.[11]

In the first pre-Christian century the Rabbis were engaged in an exegetical controversy over the text in Deuteronomy 24:1. The school of Shammai argued that a marriage could be dissolved only if one found his wife guilty of adultery[12] (similar to the New York State Law effective until September 1966). The Shammaites interpreted the Pentateuchal meaning of *ervat davar* (something unseemly) in the strictly literal sense of "the nakedness of the matter" and viewed adultery as the only legitimate cause for divorce.

The more moderate school of Hillel held that divorce should be permitted for any reason that entailed a disruption of the principle of companionship—the basic purpose in marriage.[13] This liberal view of Bet Hillel was accepted in later *halakhah*.

Rabban Gamaliel, the Elder (40 C.E.), deprived the husband of the power to annul a *get* at whim. In order to check the husband's hasty intention to divorce the unprotected wife, additional barriers were

legislated, such as requiring the divorcing husband to return to his wife
all her premarriage property in addition to the apportioned money
granted her as alimony in the *ketubbah* and that the *get* be carefully
written and executed in the presence of a Jewish Court of experts.[14] Or,
if there linger any doubt as to who provoked the dissension, the
husband who blithely blames his wife for inciting the quarrel is not to
be believed by the court, since, the Talmud states, "All women are
presumed to be lovers of domestic harmony."[15]

Jewish Law also permits divorce by proxy, since an agent is allowed
to act on behalf of another.[16] Rabbinic stringencies in favor of the
woman gradually eroded the popular misguided notion that the old
patriarchal right of divorcing one's wife at one's whim still prevailed.
The Law was really directed toward greater equality between man and
woman.[17]

The Bible does not speak of the wife's right to divorce her husband.
However, the Jewish colony at Elephantine, Egypt, did allow a woman
to divorce her husband. In Palestine itself the custom is attested to in a
second-century C.E. document from the desert of Judea.[18] A unique
clause inserted in the *ketubbah* specifying a divorce price is reported in
the Palestinian Talmud, whereby the privilege for divorce is given to
both husband and wife.[19]

The Mishnah and later rabbinic law established equal divorcing
rights for the woman and her husband; the Jewish Court enforced her
rights upon the husband. Naturally, the Jewish court cannot itself
perform divorce; it can only compel the husband to divorce, if such a
court has legal jurisdiction and its force is effective.

If a non-Jewish court compelled the parties in any way, the divorce is
invalid even if it contains rabbinic stipulations, because it would then
be an instrument of coercion rather than one contracted by free agents.
Even when Jewish courts later lost their authority, they could appeal to
the civil courts to carry out their mandate; of course, the traditional *get*
would still be issued by the *Bet Din*.[20]

The Amoraim added the right of the wife of compel her husband to
grant her a divorce, if she stated, "My husband is repulsive to me and I
cannot live with him." The reason for this offered by Maimonides is that
"She is not considered a captive woman that she should be forced to
consort with a man whom she hates."[21]

In the year 1000 C.E., Rabbenu Gershom of Mayence decreed it
unlawful for a Jew to divorce his wife without her consent. The decree
of equality became law in the West (except for the Sephardim) and was
later incorporated in the Code by Karo.[22]

The Jewish Attitude to Divorce

> R. Eleazar said: "If a man divorces his first wife,
> even the altar sheds tears."
> —*Gittin* 90a

In essence, then, a woman may, at times, compel her husband to grant her a divorce, while a man cannot compel his wife to accept one. These rabbinic reforms were all incalculable benefits to the Jewish woman, granting her rights which are protected by the *Bet Din* to divorce her husband. In the words of G. F. Moore, "The woman's legal status under Jewish Law compares to its advantage with that of contemporary civilizations."[23]

The Jewish Court, while it disparaged divorce, could compel the husband to divorce his wife in the following cases: when witnesses officially testified to the spouse's misdemeanor and brought to their attention suspicion of adultery; when there was a breach of moral deportment; refusal of marital intercourse; refusal of the wife to move to her husband's domicile; or violation of the religious code of behavior in the management of the household. Adultery was not reckoned only as infidelity to the conjugal partner but also as a violation of the Divine order.

An interesting eleventh-century responsum from Troyes in France illustrates the rabbinic concern for woman's right.

A man had ordered his wife out of their home, trying to divorce her without paying her the amount stipulated in the *ketubbah*. He charged that she had been afflicted with a repulsive skin disease already before her marriage. Rashi (1040–1105), with humane warmth and understanding, leniently ruled that the man was unworthy of belonging to the children of Abraham, who, as a rule, are known to be full of compassion for all people, especially for their wives:

Had he set his mind on keeping his wife, as diligently as he had on getting rid of her, her charm would have grown upon him. The Sages have said: "Every locality has a charm for those who live in it!" The same is true of the charm exerted by a woman upon her husband. [Sot. 47a] Happy is the man who has been fortunate to obtain such a wife and thus acquire through her a share in life everlasting. Even among disbelievers of God, there are many who do not reject their wives and their wives act similarly toward them, but this man has acted cruelly toward the wife of his youth, violating the covenant of our Heavenly Father. Both Law and decency decree that he is obligated to treat her as prescribed by custom for all daughters of Israel. If he refuses to reinstate her in his affection in accordance with the dictates of kindness and self-respect, let him divorce her, but then be obligated to pay her the full sum stipulated in her *ketubbah*.[24]

Conditions and Grounds for Divorce

In general, as if to offset the virtual free reign regarding divorce bestowed upon the husbands by the court, the Rabbis formulated the following two principles:

1. The woman has the right to demand, in certain contingencies, a divorce from the husband, and the *Bet Din* is obliged to compel the husband to grant her request.
2. The Rabbis have the right to annul any marriage, directly or retroactively. The Rabbis interpreted the words *ke-dat Moshe ve-Yisrael*—"and Israel" (from the bridegroom's marriage declaration)—to mean, "the sanction of the Rabbis."[25]

Compared with Catholic law, *halakhah* is favorably inclined toward permitting divorce. While the early Christians prohibited divorce, an attitude upheld by the Catholic Church, they also prohibited marrying a second wife so long as the divorced wife was still alive. Judaism was never that rigid; indeed, when a marriage is consummated illicitly, such as in cases of consanguinity, divorce is made compulsory by law. Incestuous marriages need no divorce since they were, *ab initio*, a void relationship. While the Catholic Church and many modern states, as well as English common law, refuse to allow divorce when both parties—even when they are blood relatives—mutually consent, Jewish Law always agreed to the granting of a divorce in such a case.[26]

There are several categories of divorce. The first is divorce by mutual agreement of the parties, whereby the wife receives her full dowry in the *ketubbah*. The husband can petition for divorce, and if the wife is found to be the guilty party, she loses her *ketubbah* rights. Divorce enacted by the court without petition of either of the parties is another mode of divorce.[27]

The Jewish attitude toward divorce has both legal and moral implications. The Rabbis frequently denounced divorce, claiming that the act of bringing together, and making peace between, husband and wife was one of the loftiest deeds. In fact, the *raison d'être* of the *ketubbah* is to deter divorce.[28] The marriage bond is holy; but while it is inviolable, it is not indissoluble.

Valid grounds for divorce were carefully defined, the court being the final arbitrator in these matters. Dismissing a wife without just cause was cruelly wrong; restrictions were imposed upon the husband who sought the easy way out.[29] For example: the husband was punished for falsely accusing his wife of premarital incontinence and was, by dint of his slander, deprived of the right to divorce her. A similar penalty was placed upon a ravisher. (Deut. 22:13–19; 28–29) By losing his free power to divorce, the man's freedom was curtailed.

Sterility is regarded as sexual incompatibility; hence, unless otherwise proven, sterility is not attributable to a defect in the wife and can be affirmed only after a period of ten years. Sterility may justify divorce if the husband has had no children by another wife. The woman's statements about her husband's sexual fitness are believed against his. In reality, the Law disapproved of childlessness as grounds for divorce.[30] It is curious that barrenness, one of the most frequent grounds for divorce in the Middle East, is not mentioned at all in the Bible as a cause for divorce.

The Tannaim considered it morally unjust to divorce a sick wife. It was necessary to wait, instead, until recovery. In the case of mental illness, the wife cannot be divorced, since she is unable to take care of herself.[31] Not fully aware of her actions, she cannot consciously and in good faith receive her *get*. The wife cannot be divorced while she is in captivity, a victim of war, or a pogrom, or in any other oppressive situation. The husband must ransom her and cannot escape his obligations by divorcing her.[32] To protect the minor wife, who is too young to understand the meaning of a *get*, a divorce is not granted.[33]

The wife's rights were protected by the Jewish Courts as long as they had legal jurisdiction to enforce their decrees by fines or by other punitive measures.

The elementary obligation implied in marriage, in addition to companionship, is conjugal union. An agreement between husband and wife to forgo sexual union is legally void because it is contrary to biblical ordinance and physiological functioning. Denial by the husband of conjugal rights to his wife or inability to fulfill his sexual obligation constitutes grounds for divorce.[34] Such willful neglect classifies him as a *mored*—rebellious. A woman is called *moredet* only if she refuses to cohabit with her husband out of malice. When the wife persists in such rebellion, divorce is advised, and, she takes with her whatever part of her dowry she possesses.[35]

There are a number of other sexual grounds for divorce. Included are unnatural sexual acts insisted upon by the husband, admitted impotence, contraction of chronic diseases from the husband, abhorrent trade engaged in after marriage making sexual union intolerable, and unattractiveness of the husband due to physical defects, loss of limb, or to his vocation which is unbecoming. In practice the Tannaim prescribed a one-year separation for reconciliatory purposes.[36]

Wife beating is considered an assault to be recompensed by a court, which may chastise the husband for disrupting domestic discipline.[37] The Law requires the husband to adhere to standards of love and affection, kindness and considerate treatment. Posttalmudic Rabbis compelled the husband to divorce his wife for shameful un-Jewish treatment (recorded by German Rabbis) and cruelty—for example, the husband's refusal to permit his wife to visit her parents. Any criminal action compelling him to flee the country, any acts of bigamy—these constitute valid grounds for divorce. This last item applies mainly to the Ashkenazic Jews, who are under the authority of Rabbenu Gershom's prohibition of polygamy.[38]

If the husband severed the wife's support by vow, prohibiting her the use of his possessions, or by actual nonsupport, the wife is entitled to a divorce, if no reconciliation is possible. Restrictions upon the wife's social liberties or management of the household, ordering her to do useless labor or to indulge in total idleness, are grounds for divorce. If his vow restricts her rights, and the husband does not annul it, the Law grants her the right to ask for a divorce.

The wife is also entitled to domicile rights. If the husband wishes to move to a new city, she may object and, upon persistent refusal, is entitled to a divorce with full payment of the *ketubbah*.[39]

Another legal innovation safeguarding the woman was the conditional divorce. It was granted during the Middle Ages and is still utilized for wives whose husbands are absent for a long period of time, as in war or in the case of willful desertion. In such instances the husband, before departure, is compelled to give his wife a conditional divorce to the effect that if he does not return within a certain period of time, and there is no proof of his death, the divorce will take effect. Such procedure is traditionally accredited to the biblical court in the times of King David and his Jewish army.[40]

The right to demand or refuse custody of the children was usually the woman's. If the wife requested custody, the husband was required to pay for the support of the children, even if she remarried. She could retain the sons against her husband's wishes only until the age of six, when the father became responsible for teaching them Torah, a trade, and so forth, but she could keep the girls with her indefinitely. In general, the court used its discretion in acting in the best interests of the children.[41]

Once the parties were divorced, Jewish Law favored remarriage. The divorced woman has a *sui juris* status and can freely remarry. A waiting-period of three months after the divorce is required so that paternity may be ascertained in case of possible pregnancy.[42]

Jewish Law condemned the easy transfer of a woman between one man and another. This was considered degrading to the matrimonial ideal and was prohibited because it might lead to a deliberate, even a formally legalized, exchange of wives for orgiastic purposes. Woman is a moral personality and not an object, that a man may hand over to another and then take back again at pleasure. A woman may not marry her ex-husband after she has been married to someone else. (Deut. 24:1–4)[43]

Divorce and Its Causes in Contemporary Society

The view in America today is that it is immoral to continue a nonfunctioning marriage. It is a well-known fact that one out of four marriages ends in divorce. Two-thirds of the divorced women and three-fourths of the men remarry. Among the adjustments during the first few years of the new marriage, there are usually children who are involved.

Many factors undoubtedly combine to account for our high divorce rate. These factors include conditions in the social setting as well as characteristics of the two persons involved and of the pattern of interaction between them.

Some of the causes of divorce involve emotional immaturity, in-laws, unemployment, illness, and financial stress. Other causes reflect changing views about the self, spouse, and marriage. These views can increase the feeling of insecurity and cause personality conflicts. Both parties become very independent, they repel each other, and seek greater satisfaction outside the home. This can be called the disintegration process in marriage.

One study shows that, compared with happily married people, divorced couples knew each other for less time, had shorter engagement periods, more conflict, and fewer expression of affection during engagement. Among the divorced couples there were forced marriages. The happily married couples were more patient and tended to overlook disagreements. Divorced couples displayed more anger and criticism.

Instead of solving the problems together, they would separate for a short time. A primary distinction in attitudes toward marriage was found among the two groups. Individuals were more independent of each other among the divorced couples. They were more ego-centered and rigid; the happily marrieds were extroverted and flexible. The greatest number of divorces occurred in the early years of marriage. The frequency of divorce among childless marriages was almost double as compared with those with children.[44]

Marriages are often built on premises which later prove tenuous. Often the marriage is an escape from an unhappy home or from feelings of loneliness. The marriage might be flimsily entered into to gain status or money from the mate; or, on the rebound, as an escape from being single. It seems to us legitimate to interpret the recent and seemingly ever-increasing divorce rate in this light. It is not an index that the nuclear family and the marriage relationship are rapidly disintegrating and losing their importance. The truth is, rather, that, on the one hand, these two institutions—marriage and divorce—have been changing their character; on the other, their specific importance—particularly that of marriage, whose standing has actually been on the upsurge. Both these aspects of the process of change impose additional stress on the family and marriage as systems and on their members as personalities. We suggest that the high rates of divorce are primarily indices of this additional strain and that adjustments are extremely complex and far-reaching.

The Roman Catholic Church, relying on early New Testament teachings of the absolute prohibition of divorce, still refuses, in most cases, to recognize divorce; the Protestants not only recognize adultery as a basic ground for divorce but also allow for other causes of family disruption that contribute to the dissolution of marriage, such as drunkenness, felonious acts, and contraction of disease. According to American law, such grounds are granted for divorce to both the husband and the wife. Other grounds are variously recognized and interpreted in most of the other states; the grounds include impotence, felony convictions, drug addiction, separations, insanity, pregnancy at marriage, bigamy, fraudulent contract, and violence.[45]

How does a woman feel during and after the divorce? It is usually believed that the readjustment will be easier for the woman if she is the one who originates the divorce proceedings. Adjustment to a divorce is, usually, difficult. Divorced people are greatly burdened emotionally; they must come to grips with lingering emotions and attitudes from their marriages. They now have to restructure their self-concepts, a reappraisal which includes adjusting their personal habits, finances, and social life. The following attitudes by the divorced person may cause conflict: the individual may still love the spouse. The divorcée may glorify marriage as being better than the divorced state. Hostility toward the former spouse may be a defense mechanism to cover up for feelings of guilt and a sense of rejection linked to feelings of personal failure. The individual can become more disturbed when the ex-spouse remarries. Hopes that the marriage relationship can be restored may cause the person to wait for the remarried mate to return, or, conversely, or despair may cause him to start a new relationship prematurely.

Studies indicate that divorced individuals usually prefer other divorced individuals. About one-third marry people who are single. In order to make a successful adjustment to remarriage, the individual must change his deep-seated, stereotypic notions of the roles played in marriage. Perhaps the best way for the divorced person to regain his status is to remarry. Divorced individuals are usually less romantic and more pragmatic about marriage as they face the reality that there are mutual obligations.

The hardships of the divorced in American society are a growing problem as the number of divorces continues to rise. The divorced woman is particularly afflicted with financial troubles. She must face a difficult job market to support herself and usually her children as well. Many housewives are untrained in pursuing a career. Having just undergone the trauma of divorce, the woman now experiences the additional emotional strain of being adrift in an increasingly impersonal society.

It is estimated that more than 20 million Americans are directly afflicted by divorce; the problem obviously extends to more people than the couples involved. Marriage counseling is being increasingly sought. With the rapidly rising divorce rate, both society and government must share the responsibility of dealing with this very pressing situation and help the divorced and their families cope with the problem of the aftermath of divorce.

A recent, unpublished study by Brodbar-Nemzer of Brandeis University (1981–85), based on a sampling of 4000 Jewish households in the New York area, revealed that the rate of divorce for Orthodox Jews is only one fourth that of unaffiliated Jews. It also showed that any kind of synagogue affiliation or strong ties to the Jewish community sharply reduced the incidence of divorce.

The divorced Jewish woman may suffer even more than others, since Jewish society is very marriage- and family-oriented. Many times the husband refuses to give her a get and the woman cannot remarry; if she does, the offspring of the new marriage are considered *mamzerim* (loosely translated as "illegitimate"). The Jewish community and rabbinate cannot ignore the problem and must find ways of integrating the socially displaced woman and compelling the man to issue a get. *Halakhah* has responded to the problems of divorce in the past and solutions must be sought to ensure the fulfillment of the prophetic declaration that "The wife of one's youth is not readily discarded." (Is. 54:6)

A 1983 ruling by the New York State Court of Appeals considers the *ketubbah* as a binding civil contract as well as a religious covenant. The court's decision would force recalcitrant spouses to honor contractual obligations and would make it easier for Jewish couples seeking divorces to do so within the faith. While in the past some husbands have effectively prevented their mates from obtaining a get simply by refusing to appear in person before a *Bet Din*, the new ruling should allow traditional women to obtain a get without the kinds of litigation and harassment imposed by their spouses. "This agreement—the *ketubbah*—according to the court's ruling, should ordinarily be entitled to no less dignity than any other civic contract to submit a dispute to a nonjudicial forum, so long as its enforcement violates neither the law nor the public policy of this state."[46]

THE WIDOW

> The Lord cares for orphans and widows. He is
> their Father and Protector.
> —*Exodus Rabbah* 30:5

Why does God love orphans and widows, asks the Midrash? Because their eyes are turned only to Him, as it says, "The Father of orphans and judge of widows." (Ps. 68:6) "Therefore, whoever robs them is considered as if he robbed the Lord Himself."[47]

The widow is mentioned about sixty times in the Bible. In all cases she is described as a destitute, weak, and helpless person in need of protection, understanding, love, and fair treatment. The prophets often admonished the people to plead for the cause of the widow with righteousness and justice. (Is. 1:17, 23, Mal. 3:5; Ps. 94:6; Job 24:3; 31:16)

The Lord, in His immense compassion, is described as the "One who executes justice for the fatherless and widows, and loves the stranger in giving him food and raiment." (Deut. 10:18) He displays from His exalted Heavens condescension in vindicating the cause of the helpless, in caring for their needs.

Perverting the justice due to the widow is reprehensible to God (Deut. 27:19), who is the protector of the oppressed and defender of the defenseless. The Torah repeats the prohibition of acting unjustly toward defenseless persons as well as the obligation to care and provide for the poor woman, to treat her with respect and compassion, and to give her priority in litigations, "for God restores the boundaries of the widow." (Prov. 15:25)[48]

To rejoice the heart of the widow and to be beneficent to her was a most humane quality, a deed attributed to Job, the pious. (Job. 29:13)

The mere fact that the Law has to remind us of the inherent rights of the widow and our obligation to treat her with fairness and warmth points to a grim social reality—the widow perceived of herself throughout history as being in a state of shame and isolation. The prophet Isaiah compares the desolated land of Israel and its homelessness in the Diaspora to the reproach of the widow's lack of sovereignty, waiting for full restoration of her status. (Is. 54:4)

The Widow and Her Status

Protection of the widow was a policy common to the Near East. The basic conception of Mesopotamian and Egyptian literature is that the protection of the weak is the will of God.

The widow and the orphan in Israel's culture received special consideration as ordered by the Mosaic Law in the command: "You shall not afflict any widow or fatherless child." The implication is—"If you afflict them in any way, for if they cry at all unto Me, I will surely hear their cry." (Exod. 22:21–22)

The plights of both the widow and the orphan are usually quoted together. It was always the obligation of the community to provide for them the necessary sustenance and not to ignore their ill-treatment. The Bible exhorts the Jewish people to protect the helpless widow, whose voice and cry will ultimately be heard by the Lord, who will then bring punishment upon those exploiting her and her children; the exploiters must not forget that they themselves "were once strangers in the land of Egypt." (Exod. 22:20) This admonition is repeated several times in the Torah. Its echo throughout the Bible is a constant reminder of the humane treatment required for the widow. Her raiment is not to be taken as pledge (Deut. 24:17), for the Law requires "justice, justice shall you follow." (Deut. 16:20)

A widow's status in Judaism differed according to her particular family. A young, childless widow returned to her father's house and could remarry after a time. She continued as a member of her husband's family by accepting, when possible, a levirate marriage. (Gen. 38:11; Lev. 22:13; Ruth 1:8) The Jewish contracts of Elephantine, Egypt, allow a childless widow to inherit from her husband. In other Near Eastern societies, a widow had no direct family ties and, therefore, had to return to her father's house and protection.

In early biblical times, a widow with a grown son lived with him. (Judg. 17:1–6) The mother of King Solomon, Bat Sheva (1 Kings 2:19), is an example of such a status.

The widow occupied a rank similar to that of a divorcée—she was her own mistress, and was bound by her own vows, without the consent of her father or husband. (Num. 30:10) She could not marry a *kohen gadol.* (Lev. 21:14) A common *kohen,* though, was permitted to marry a widow.[49] The prophet Ezekiel insisted that a *kohen* marry the widow of a *kohen.* (Ezek. 44:22)

The fundamental rule in succession and inheritance gives to sons alone the right to inherit, except where there are no sons—then the daughter is the heiress.[50] A classic example were the daughters of Tzlofehad. (Num. 36:8-12) Job's three daughters are another notable exception—they received a share of the inheritance along with their seven brothers. (Job 42:13–15) A widow had no right to the inheritance. She retained what she had contributed to the marriage and the gifts she had received from her husband. Still, a part of the husband's property was, under Jewish Law, hers.[51] R. Judah Ha-Nassi instituted by his own example a further privilege. The heirs could not sell the house as long as the widow wished to dwell in it; and her right to be attended by the servants of the house was inviolable.[52] She could even claim an exaggerated sum for sustenance and no one could dispute her right.[53] The levirate marriage shows further consideration of the widow in that it provided for her as soon as possible a protector to enable her to continue to live honorably and be socially accepted.

Since, in most cases, the widow had no direct support, the Torah provided for her—just as for the stranger and fatherless—to receive from the tithe of the poor. This was reserved for the poor every third year so that they "shall eat and be satisfied." (Deut. 14:29) Jews were required to share their bounty with the widow, and to rejoice together in the freewill offering from the crops, during the festivals, especially on *Shavuot* (Deut. 16:11), together with the Levite, the stranger, and the fatherless. "These four, God says, are Mine, corresponding to the four who are yours, viz.: son, daughter, man-servant and maid-servant. If you make my four happy, I will make your four happy."[54]

In addition, the widow was accorded the right of *leket, shikhah,* and *payah*—the abandoned sheaves in the field, the gleanings, the remains of a corner of grain, that is, the portion of the harvest left in the field for the poor, which includes also grapes of the vineyard, olives, and a quantity of fruit on the trees. (Deut. 24:19–21) All these are legal obligations of every Jew.

Psychological Considerations

The role of the widow in our society is one without definition; she is socially and culturally ignored. It is estimated that there are about 12.5 million widowed people in the United States. Every year, some 237,000 new widowers and some 506,000 widows join the ranks of the bereaved.

Widowhood is one of the major crises in life, a turning point, a readjustment process. It is a time in life when grief and despair, a total sense of loss, overtake the person with brutal impact. After the initial shock, when reason and caution block the perspective and the full grasp of reality, one gradually accepts a new status—that of being alone, or, in the words of the Talmud, "the world turned into a blackout, where the loss of the beloved is manifest by weeping and bereavement. Tears are shed, memories are screened, questions are asked, answers are not forthcoming."[55] Consolation is sorely needed and yet not easily accepted. The intensity of despair and the feeling of physical emptiness and emotional destitution are the signals of loneliness, fear, guilt, and self-reproach.

It is high time that we appreciated the enormous problems of widowhood, the frustratingly bitter realization of being left alone that is so very traumatic. The conflict between the widow's feeling guilty and responsible over the tragedy and the painful emotion of anger toward the deceased, who has left the living party bitter, and often even hostile, without support or shelter, drowning in self-condemnation, is very strong.[56]

Morbid brooding, regret, and despair dominate the life of the bereaved. The experience called "grief work" is a natural process which must be understood and worked through. Facing the grim reality of death and trying to recover and regain one's equilibrium is a most unpleasant and difficult task. The community has a religious and moral obligation to help the widowed person integrate into society and share again experiences with friends in new affiliations, in new meaningful relationships, for both personal and social adjustment.

Having to reach out for new roles and greater social mobility after overcoming her grief, the widow generally has difficulty in cultivating new relationships and in acquiring new companionships. She sees herself as an outsider, a fifth wheel to the wagon. She feels every reason to be unmotivated in reaching out socially.

On Living Alone

The average American wife can look forward to about ten years of widowhood. Woman outlive men by about five years, and husbands are four years older than their wives. Widows outnumber widowers by five to one, though both categories face and share the same problems: to rearrange one's life and regain happiness, develop fresh interests, and get through life with a minimum of stress after an emotional upheaval.

Statistics show that nearly two-thirds of older women are living without a man, since most of them are widowed. Divorcées, too, share many of the widow's problems in the new and difficult challenge of being single.

The widow usually camouflages her unspoken anger at the deceased partner for dying and leaving her alone, often unsheltered and insecure from the storms of life. It is, indeed, easier for her to feel guilty about being partly responsible for his death than to feel angry. It is, therefore, an absolute necessity to prepare oneself for widowhood—ideally, to prepare together for the eventual death of one's spouse. This should be done in a sound, frank, and open discussion as a preventive measure for the unexpected season of grief, when pain will have to be confronted and life restructured.

There is, unfortunately, an unspoken stigma to widowhood, which the single person must learn to overcome. Sympathy and verbal reassurance cannot resolve the grief work of the mourner.

The best cure for loneliness is people. Learning to relate to people after weaning oneself away from the emotional dependence on the departed mate insures the single person social acceptance and redirection toward a creative life. It is not pity and sympathy that the single woman needs but rather an invitation by the community, synagogue, sisterhood, clubs, and centers to reenter the world of belonging—perhaps with a late career or volunteer work—and help to reestablish a healthy identity and ego strength. It is the Jewish concept of hessed (lovingkindness) which we are required to cultivate for the disadvantaged, the lonely, and the poor, to make them feel needed and important.

We ought to distinguish between aloneness and loneliness. In our fast-moving society, most of us are very often subjected to periods of aloneness—a condition that often can be desirable. Loneliness is a painful feeling of emptiness and deprivation. One way of dealing with loneliness is to make the effort to communicate our feelings to other human beings and show that we care about their well-being, a process called "creative loneliness."

Singlehood implies a critical change in one's life when adjustment and reorientation are necessary for the surviving to survive and adopt a new life-style by necessity. Reflecting on the past may help us reassess our actions so as to learn from our mistakes; living in the past is neurotic. Bridging the past and future through faith and renewed hope will make the present more meaningful and fulfilling. A reaffirmation of life and trust in the human potential will help dispel the shadows of loneliness and despair, and where darkness once reigned, light will once more shine.

APPENDIX A

Psychophysical Characteristics

PHYSIOLOGY, CONCEPTION, AND CHILDBIRTH

> Every organ the Lord has created in the woman's
> body was not created in vain.
> —*Berakhot* 31b

In order to fully appreciate the observations of the Rabbis on the distinctive physical features of the woman, it is necessary to make a survey of those characteristics which have a direct and indirect influence upon her mental makeup. In many cases, the findings of the Rabbis are supported by modern medical and scientific knowledge. There are instances, however, in which a scientifically acknowledged fact is in marked contrast to what has been recorded in the Talmud and in the *Midrash*. In this regard, contrasts and similarities will be noted as we follow the development of the woman.

According to the Talmud, one of the first characteristics peculiar to woman is the number of her limbs: she has two hundred and fifty-two joints, while the man has only two hundred and forty-eight. The disciples of R. Ishmael once dissected the body of a prostitute who had been condemned by the king to be burned. They examined her and found two hundred and fifty-two joints and limbs. They came and asked of R. Ishmael: "How many joints has the human body?" He replied: "Two hundred and forty-eight." Thereupon they said to him,

205

"But we have found two hundred fifty-two." He replied: "Perhaps you made the post-mortem examination on a woman, in whose case Scripture adds two hinges [in her genitalia] and two doors of the womb."[1]

The physical formation of woman, the Rabbis claimed, is far more complicated than that of man. They attributed this to her childbearing function. Furthermore, woman is built differently; she is wide below (in order to carry the child) and narrow above, while the man is broad above and narrow below.[2]

Modern science describes the female pelvis as differing from that of the male in those particulars that render it better adapted to pregnancy and parturition. It is more shallow than the male pelvis but relatively wider in every direction. The inlet and outlet are larger and more nearly oval, the bones are lighter and smoother, the coccyx is more movable, and the subpubic arch is greater than a right angle.[3]

The physical condition and structure of the pregnant woman were of great concern and interest to our Sages. Regarding her internal structure and the safety of her unborn child, the following was said:

It is the way of a beast to walk with its body in a horizontal position, its embryo in its womb in the form of a bag. A woman walks erect while the embryo is in her womb, and the Creator guards it that it should not fall out and die.[4]

The Rabbis correctly understood the role of the uterus, for its flexibility and its size are important in terms of conception and viability of the fertilized ovum.

Further, R. Simon said:

The abdomen of a woman consists of many cavities, many coils, and many bands, so that when she sits on the travailing chair she does not cast out the fetus all at once.[5]

Indications of pregnancy and noticeable physical changes in the pregnant woman prompted the Sages to document their findings as follows: Because of the bulk of her embryo, a pregnant woman has difficulty sitting. Pregnancy is discernible in the woman's walk.[6]After the first three months of pregnancy her condition can already be distinguished. Aside from the aborning fetus, other physiological changes take place during the pregnancy. The Sages noted that the first three months after a woman has conceived, her face turns faint and pallid. In addition to her outward appearance, a pregnant woman feels heaviness in her head and limbs.[7] She does not menstruate, and according to R. Meir:

> All the nine months that a woman does not menstruate, she really should do so; but what does the Creator do: He directs the blood upward to her breasts and turns it into milk, so that the fetus may come forth and have food, the more of it, if it be a male.[8]

While primitive man's knowledge of the functions of the procreative man and woman was based largely on myth, rabbinic observations surprise us with their experimental approach and keen observations.[9]

The origin of the embryo, the participants in its creation, and their respective roles also prompted much investigation and writing by the Sages. The Midrash illustrates an example of their speculations:

> R. Simlai said: In the past Adam was created from dust and Eve was created from Adam; but henceforth it shall be "in our image after our likeness." (Gen. 1:26) Neither man without woman nor woman without man, and neither of them without the Divine Spirit.[10]

As to the process of fertilization, they said:

> There are three partners in the creation of the human—the Creator, his father and his mother. The father supplies the sperm of the white substance, out of which are formed the child's bones, sinews, nails, the brain in the head and the white in the eyes. The mother supplies the substance out of which is formed the skin, flesh, hair, blood and the black of the eye. The Creator gives the spirit and the breath, beauty of features, eyesight, the power of hearing, the ability to speak and to walk, and the ability to comprehend.[11]

Another midrashic statement presents this process from a different standpoint—the physiology of woman.

> A woman's womb is full of blood, some of which goes out by way of her menstrual flow; and, by the favor of the Creator, a drop of white matter enters and falls into it and immediately the fetus

begins to form. It may be compared to milk in a basin; if one put *meso* [curdling or stiffing agent] into it, it congeals and becomes consistent; if not, it continues to be loose.[12]

"A spermatic emission," noted Samuel, "that does not shoot forth like an arrow cannot fructify."[13]

Knowledge of the genetic elements (i.e., genes and heredity) involved in the process of reproduction was also discussed:

R. Jeremiah raised the question:—Do we say that each limb of the progenitors produces the identical limb in the offspring . . . or not. It obviously does not, he decided, for otherwise the blind should produce a blind offspring, and the crippled a crippled offspring. We, therefore, must say that the seed is admixtured.

R. Simeon Ben Lakish said: "Moreover, God does not allow any drop of sperm to go to waste: He throws off part of the drop to form the brains, part thereof to form the bones, part thereof to form the sinews."[14]

"R. Judah says: The blood vessels of the afterbirth of the woman are full of the seed of the man, which has all the elements of the fetus."[15]

The following are the circumstances, according to the Sages, under which conception may or may not result: immediately before the woman's menstrual period and immediately after the ritual immersion. Conception may also result from two men simultaneously before the sperm decomposes.

Conception cannot occur from the first intercourse, because the woman's doors (or inward part) are not completely open till the second intercourse;[16] from coitus performed in the standing position;[17] and from conception until the termination of the pregnancy.[18]

The rabbinic view noting the feasibility of conception following the ritual immersion corroborates modern medical findings, for ovulation takes place fifteen days before a period, when the egg starts a journey through the Fallopian tubes, and it must be speedily fertilized or it dies.[19]

The Rabbis were aware of the climax and secretions in the woman's body which occur during coitus and affect sex determination. "If a woman emits first she bears a male child. If they both discharge simultaneously, twins [possibly one male, one female] result." "R.

Hiyya Bar Abba said: [It may be likened] to two artists each of whom executes the likeness of the other; thus it is always that the female is formed from the man and the male from the [emission] of the woman."

"Twin brothers are the product of one drop of semen that divided itself into two."[20]

Studies have shown that there are two distinct types of male sperm, one carrying the female sex chromosome (X), and weighing more than the other, and one bearing the male sex chromosome (Y). The different DNA content in the two sex chromosomes may cause a mass difference. The lighter, Y-bearing sperm, therefore, have greater mobility than the heavier, X-bearing sperm.

Y sperm are more delicate in nature and so survive best in an alkaline environment, which exists at ovulation. Following ovulation, the environment changes to an acidic one, killing the lighter, more motile Y-bearing sperm, allowing for X-bearing sperm to reach the egg.[21]

According to the *Halakhot Gedolot*, a ninth-century gaonic code, the first forty days of pregnancy have a special legal status. During their duration, the embryo is considered to be in a precarious, "mere liquid" state. Talmudic lore, as well as Aristotelian and Roman jurisprudence, considered the fortieth day as the first in the real stage of "embryonic formation."[22]

Pictures of the embryo at about day forty seem to show the first stage at which the embryo begins to take on some "human physiology." Scientific evidence concurs in this: that although the distinction between embryo and fetus is essentially arbitrary, it is customary to refer to the human conceptus from fertilization through the first eight weeks of development (or from week four to week eight) as an embryo and from eight weeks until the end of its term as a fetus. During the embryonic period, the major internal and external organ systems are formed. During fetal life, histogenesis or differentiation of the tissues occurs.

The Sages maintained that the fashioning of the male and the fashioning of the female take the same course, each lasting forty-one days.[23] Modern medicine maintains that before the seventh week of embryonic life, the gonads of both sexes are identical in appearance, precluding separate structural examinations and sex diagnosis. Both gonads evenly begin to differentiate into separate recognizable structures.[24]

Embryological development is similar in the two sexes. In the female embryo, however, the primitive germinal epithelium (from which the ovary or the testis develops) remains neutral and under the hormonal influence longer. It appears that the female embryo is slower in taking on its sexual identity.

Concerning the stages of the fetal development, the Rabbis state: "It begins with flesh and skin and ends with sinews and bones."[25]

The following descriptions illustrate how the growing fetus and its properties were perceived by the Rabbis:

> R. Simlai said, "The embryo is an organ of the mother, what does a child in its mother's womb resemble? A slate that is rolled up . . . he eats from the same food that the mother eats, and drinks from that which the mother drinks; and he does not give off any excretion, for it might kill the mother. And as soon as he comes into the world, the parts that were closed are open [the mouth, for instance] and the open parts are closed [the navel]. But for this, he would not be able to live for an hour . . . "[26]

R. Eleazar further compared the fetus in its mother's womb to a nut that is lying in a vessel of water; when a person puts his finger on it, it floats from one place to another.

In its primary stage (when it is merely a sac, though the limbs are fashioned), the Rabbis say, a fetus resembles a locust, and its two eyes are like drippings of a fly, far removed from each other. Its two nostrils are like drippings of a fly, and they are near to each other. Its mouth is as narrow as a stretched hair, its membrum is of the size of a lentil, and in the case of a female has the appearance of the longitudinal slit of barley grain; it has no shaped hands or feet. Its two thighs and two arms are like two silk threads.[27]

They further said that during its first three months the fetus occupies the lower level of the womb. During the middle three months of the pregnancy it moves to the middle section of the womb, and during the last three months it lives in the upper level. A male embryo was thought to lie on the right side of the uterus, a female on the left. When the time comes for this baby to be born, it turns itself around, descends, and goes out. While in the mother's womb, the baby resembles

> folded writing tablets, its hands rest on its two temples respectively, its two elbows on its two legs, and its two heels against its buttocks. Its head lies between its knees, its mouth is closed, and its navel is open.[28]

Hence we note that the Rabbis' understanding of the placenta is similar to what we know today, namely, that by means of the placenta the baby's nourishment is provided and its life maintained. In the womb, the fetus is protected by "three bags; one, the womb of its mother; two, the placenta; three, a thin skin." Modern medicine tells us of three cavities present between the embryo and the exterior. The embryo is surrounded by an amniotic cavity, which contains amniotic fluid. The amnion is itself contained within the uterine cavity. Finally, the uterus is contained within the abdominal cavity.[29]

When the woman sits on the travailing chair, every string, every compartment, and every coil in her abdomen is stretched.

The manner in which woman gives birth prompted the Rabbis' observation that the position assumed at childbirth is one in which the woman kneels and presses her heels against her thighs; while in this position her limbs become stiff and rigid, so that the new life should not bring about the death of the mother.[30]

The woman's pain during childbirth was, the Sages noted, a result of the changes of position and turning of the baby before its emergence into the world. They claimed that the pains of the female birth were more intense than those of a male birth, offering a symbolic rationale: the female emerges in the upward position she assumes during intercourse, the male in the downward position he assumes then.[31] Medical findings, though, show that the pain is not due to the child's turning over in the uterus; and there is no proof that the pains of a female birth are more intense than that of a male child.

The talmudic views do not concur with medical knowledge that

Alone among physiologic muscular contractions, those of labor are painful . . . The cause of pain is not definitely known but the following hypotheses have been suggested: (1) hypoxia (lack of oxygen) of the contracted muscle cells; (2) compression of nerve ganglia in the cervix and lower uterine segment by the tightly interlocking muscle bundles; (3) stretching of the cervix during dilation; and (4) stretching of the peritoneum.[32]

Protracted labor in its various forms was discussed and compared by the Talmud to "the heavens when they are shut up so that neither dew nor rain can fall. It is like a woman who is in labor but cannot give birth."[33] When protracted labor endangers the health of the woman, halakhah allows it to be terminated and the baby aborted.[34]

The Rabbis observed that once the baby leaves the mother's womb, all blood and fluids are excreted from the womb. The umbilical cord is severed and knotted. The question is also raised whether the placenta can be thrust out until many days after the baby is born.[35]

The Sages studied and provided therapeutic advice in the event of postnatal difficulties or other abnormal conditions besetting the baby.[36]

A multiple birth (twins) is no different from a single birth, except for an additional element of time—that span of time between the emergence of the first and the birth of the second child. There is no foretelling the chances of survival of any one of the children in a multiple birth.[37]

OTHER PHYSIOLOGICAL CHARACTERISTICS

While she shows remarkable strength and endurance throughout the entire process of conception, pregnancy, and childbearing, the woman is even more deserving of credit when we consider her physical condition of fragility compared with man's physical strength. For this physical frailty, the Talmud acknowledges a greater need for medical care. In addition, the Talmud was most sensitive to the delicate condition of the woman in labor: When she is asked to do a man's hard labor, it causes her stress and pain. This reaction can be seen even in our early history: when the Egyptians forced the women to do the physical labor of the men, it "made their lives bitter."[38]

The woman was unafraid of highwaymen and robbers, for "she carried her weapons with her at all times," meaning that her physical delicateness is her protection against murder. Not being a warrior or a fighter as man is, her life was usually spared.[39]

Because of woman's lack of strong physical stamina, the Rabbis felt that she is unable to resist the intoxicating effect of alcohol.[40] Moreover, the Rabbis viewed woman to be too sensitive to bear the sight of blood, or the sword, or even the wounding of an animal.[41] Perhaps this may explain the absence of women in the front lines of the battlefield, as well as the rarity of women *shohetot* in the Jewish Community. Nevertheless, we find that in talmudic days, women did perform the task of ritual slaughtering. According to Karo, "All persons, including women, have the right to [ritually] slaughter." Records show that in Italy from the sixteenth century women were actively engaged as *shohetot*. [42]

BEAUTY AND THE POWER TO ATTRACT

The daughters of Israel are beautiful . . .
—R. *Ishmael* in Nedarim 66a.

Let us consider the sphere of beauty, in which woman stands sovereign. Here we shall see the effect of adornment upon her psyche.

Traditionally, "The woman was created only to represent beauty."[43] That is the basis of her appeal to man. The woman is the epitome of beauty.[44] Thus, not only was Eve the first woman portrayed as very beautiful, but her successors, the reigning beauties of each generation, were endowed with the same physical beauty as Eve. The Midrash states: "Eve's image was transmitted to the reigning beauties of each generation."[45]

How did the Rabbis view woman's beauty? What were the criteria of their evaluation? How did they describe woman's physical charms? The Rabbis noted that all women are invested with the basic elements of beauty at birth.

First and foremost were the eyes, which were often called the windows of the soul. The eye confers what we may call "life." The eye exercises its influence through its expression. So much value was attached to the eyes that if, while examining a bride-to-be, the groom's family found she had beautiful eyes, they would relinquish their right to proceed with any further examination.[46]

"The eye and the heart are the agents of sin. The eye sees and the heart desires."[47] "Passion is a master," so runs a Yiddish proverb. A woman through her wiles and charms can subdue the most powerful man to do her bidding, all women being heirs to Mother Eve.

The hair, woman's crowning glory, was another important feature of feminine appeal. Woman's hair can appeal to men to the extent that it may lead to sexual seduction and fetishism. When a woman braids her hair and ties it back, it is considered an additional charm. From a psychological point of view, according to Havelock Ellis, after the eyes, hair is sexually the most generally noted part of the feminine body.[48]

Woman's speaking voice may be noted for its sweetness and appeal. In addition, her singing voice can be aphrodisiac and can create an eroticizing effect. A harsh, bass voice in a woman was regarded as a blemish in her beauty.[49]

"A noble man is led far by women's gentle words," says Goethe. A man will be attracted by a woman's voice because it is in accordance with his early impressions of his mother. Havelock Ellis states that a man often associates his early ideas of love with women singing and playing, adding that the fascination is romantic and sentimental and not specifically erotic.[50]

In various periods of history, the emphasis of feminine physical characteristics caused many societies to become body-worshiping cultures. In the ancient Far East, in Imperial Rome, and even in Judaism, woman's swelling breasts were regarded as the "glory and pride of her sex." The Rabbis went further in stating that swelling breasts in the male were infelicitous, even a blemish.[51]

Woman's legs always had the sexual power to attract. The Rabbis also considered the following feminine features to be ideal: a symmetrical head, delicate ears and nose, full lips, a slender neck, and small feet.[52] Even the sound of her name was euphonious, a part of her charm.[53]

R. Israel of Ruzhin said: "There are two types of beauty in a woman." He observed beauty in terms of her physique and when woman herself is not physically beautiful but a chord of grace mystifies her. The difference between the two is the following: The first type is intrinsic beauty. The woman always remains beautiful; she does not change even in times of stress or danger. But the woman who is lacking in physical beauty is beautiful only because of the chord of grace she possesses. When the grace has a reverse effect, she may not appear beautiful. This can occur in a dangerous situation when a woman seeks safety from danger. This is the meaning of Abraham's statement to his wife, Sarah: "Behold now, I know that thou art a fair woman to look upon" (Gen. 12:11), stressing the word "now" to connote that she is beautiful, possessing intrinsic beauty by her own merit; if, however, she were beautiful because of the chord of grace, she would have hardly been beautiful in a physical sense.[54]

While man concerns himself with, and sets value on, woman's external beauty, woman does not set great store by man's physical endowments.[55]

The Rabbis observed some innate characteristics in woman's mental makeup. The more pronounced included a strong creative desire for children, a feeling for beauty, and a love for cosmetics and adornment, each of which is complementary to the other.[56] As soon as the girl reaches puberty, she is compelled by a desire to be beautiful. Thus the female adolescent reverses her childhood behavior of neglecting her personal appearance. She begins to devote much care to her body and concerns herself by greatly caring for her physique. Cosmetics were always a necessity to the average woman. She uses them to improve her appearance, to increase her self-assurance and her sense of well-being.

The concern for attractiveness and display may be seen as a prelude to sexual communion, or as an appeal to the opposite sex. According to H. L. Mencken, "A woman never so much as buys a pair of shoes or has her teeth fixed without considering the effect upon some unsuspecting candidate for her 'reluctant affections.'"[57]

When the woman is stimulated, her fascination with sexuality is extended into parasexual areas. Dress is not the antithesis of nakedness, but rather its accomplice. The sex motif has brought into fashion a state not unlike that of the erotic impulse and its satisfaction. The ability to attract is often so overwhelming that it sometimes leads to the girls exhorting the boys. "Direct your eyes to our beauty."[58]

It is possible that the young woman may be unaware of her ornate proclivity; subconsciously, however, her inclination for display may certainly be a fillip. Indeed, without this instinct, the human race would no longer survive.[59]

This phenomenon, furthermore, has narcissistic connations. The woman is elated when she sees herself dazzling in her jewelry and clothes.[60] Feminine extravagance, though, was condemned by the prophet Isaiah, who depicted the woman's sense of beauty and attractiveness in his colorful account of twenty-one feminine ornaments and articles of exquisite apparel worn by the "the daughters of Zion." (Is. 3:16–24)

The Rabbis observed that some women's desire for display was so strong, they would forego the necessaries of life in order to possess colorful dresses and to dwell in beautifully decorated homes.[61]

This inclination is so much a part of woman that the gratification of her desire for cosmetics and lovely dresses has a powerful influence upon her complexion and facial expression.[62] "A pretty face costs money," notes the proverb. A beautiful wife is among the "three things which increase a man's self-esteem."[63] Hence, the husband who desired his wife to look beautiful was admonished to provide her with perfumes, cosmetics, and stylish dresses.[64] Happiness is the greatest cosmetic for beauty.

During the festival week when most work was prohibited, the woman was permitted to beautify herself. She would plait her hair, paint her eyes with kohl, apply her facial makeup, manicure her nails, and remove her body hair. The love for beautifying herself accompanies woman from "May to December." As the talmudic saying goes: "At sixty as at six, the sound of a timbrel makes her nimble." Furthermore, the Rabbis observed that when she was in the company of her rivals or her friends, this inclination toward attractiveness was heightened.[65]

Another view was expounded by the psychoanalyst J. C. Flugel. He claims that general sociological considerations, combined with our knowledge of male and female psychology, show that "women dress much more to please their own vanity and to compete with other women than to satisfy the more immediate desire of men . . . " Also, men are not interested in the changes of fashion that seem of such importance to women themselves, for all the follies of competition in which women indulge are absolutely unnecessary for the purpose of attracting men.[66]

According to the biblical exegete Ibn Ezra (1089-1164):

> It is the nature of all women to beautify themselves and look every morning at their reflection in their copper or glass mirrors, to arrange the ornaments on their heads . . . for the custom of Israel in Bible times was similar to the Arabian custom in those days. There were some devout women, however, who yielded up their mirrors as a token of self-dedication to God, since they felt no more the need for the physical beautification, and assembled at the entrance of the Tabernacle for daily prayer and devoted their time to the enhancement of the Holy.[67]

As in displaying her jewels and clothes, a beautiful woman can also easily derive satisfaction from displaying her natural beauty. This leads to a strengthening of her tendency to display and beautify herself. An old English adage states, "It is as natural for women to parade themselves in fine clothes, as it is for a peacock to spread his tail."[68]

The use of perfume, a primitive practice, plays a similar role to that of facial paints and powders among women. "Perfumes have a definite sexual significance . . . being used consciously and unconsciously, either to enhance the natural charms by stimulating the olfactory sense, or to disguise unpleasant bodily odors. It has been argued that the use of perfumes has developed a genuine estheticism in itself—i.e., a pure delight in perfume for its own pleasantness."[69]

A woman's love for perfume is so deep-rooted that Jewish Law compels the husband-to-be to assure his bride a separate allowance for perfumes and cosmetics, since woman is fond of them. This explains one of Ezra's oldest regulations, which states that the peddlers of spices and perfumes should, at regular intervals, offer their wares at the doors of homes. According to the Midrash, "Any city that does not establish a basket for spices [i.e., perfumes], a scholar may not dwell there."[70]

Jewelry and cosmetics are vital to a woman. Though she is devoted to her home, and will exert herself to maintain peace in it, she will not brook her husband's refusal to buy her dresses and cosmetics. One might even insult him openly for depriving her of these necessary embellishments.[71]

Women and children cherish their adornments, says Rashi. Woman's emotional distress is so strong when deprived of them that an outburst of anger followed by tears and sobs is likely to result.[72]

The average woman sometimes tends to be an inveterate show-off. She will endure the pain of being temporarily uncomfortable for the chance to apply cosmetics to herself, as long as she believes they will enhance her beauty.[73] Seventeen hundred years later, Montaigne makes almost the identical observation: "There is no torture that she will not endure to enhance her beauty."

In talmudic times the woman would wear a wig to give the impression of having an abundance of hair. Unlike the conception of the ideal feminine figure nowadays, plumpness was the fashionable style in the Near East. In her zeal to display her charms, the woman would tighten her neckband, almost to the point of strangulation.[74]

The custom of using cosmetics was not ecumenical: natural beauties disdained the use of paint and rouge;[75] the very poor could not afford cosmetics.

The married woman was concerned with her appearance. This included her manners and dress since she wanted to attract her husband. This fastidiousness was given her by the Creator Himself. According to Tradition, "The Holy One brought Eve all beautified into the presence of Adam, and they joined together face to face." In fact, R. Meir of Rothenburg (1220–1293) states: "Cursed be the woman who has a husband and strives not to be attractive."[76]

A woman's charm is appreciated by her husband. The husband's love will, sooner or later, fade if the wife no longer thinks it important to dress herself tastefully and make herself attractive and desirable.[77]

The bride uses every means at her disposal to attract the bridegroom. This explains why it was customary for her to have twenty-four kinds of ornaments.[78] Jewish Law showed consideration for the bride by allowing her traditional immersion to take place several days before the wedding; an immersion closer to her wedding day might spoil her cosmetic preparations on that special day.[79]

Feminine display is at its height on holidays. Women are free from work; everyone is out to attend services and visit friends. Though the feast and other festive events may be enjoyable, one of its most delightful parts for the women is the opportunity they have to display their dresses and jewelry. Hence the Law stipulated that the dress her husband was required to buy her should be bought for the holidays,[80] in order to fulfill and enhance the *mitzvah* of *ve-samahta be-hagekha* ("you shall rejoice on your holiday.") (Deut. 16:14)

The Law, in fact, was so sympathetic, that it allowed the woman to be smartly dressed constantly. A male mourner is not permitted to have his garment basted after the *keri'ah* until thirty days after his father's or mother's death. A woman mourner, on the other hand, may have her garment basted immediately, out of regard for her dignified appearance.[81]

The obsession with beauty (among other things), brings with it the fear of old age, which is considered to be the disease of our day. Men, as well as women, are desperately fighting against old age, seeking rejuvenation with the help of plastic surgery, cosmetics, massages, clothes, and hair dyes. The results of this drive to carry on a pretense of youth are often a pathetical absurdity, which fools only the stricken victim himself.

As long as the woman looks young, claim the Rabbis, she will resent being called "grandmother." This is owing to her desire always to appear young and beautiful. Women marry, on the average, before age twenty-one and begin bearing children soon after; some women become grandmothers by age forty, many more by age forty-five. There is evidence that some of these women are ambivalent about their new status. They refuse to be branded with the epithet "grandmother" by their grandchildren, opting, instead, to be addressed by pet names. The grandchild, moreover, may be virtually ignored by the grandmother, who concentrates, instead, on envisioning herself as the picture of youth. Today, however, there seems to be less of a craving among the "Jewish grandmothers" for rejuvenescence.[82]

Woman's instinctive desire for display is related to her native love for music. She is fond of dancing and enjoys wearing wide dresses. "A woman of sixty like one of six runs at the sound of music," say the Rabbis.[83] One reason why women love dancing is because it enables them to give harmonious and legitimate emotional expression to the neuromuscular irritability that might otherwise escape in more explosive forms. Music satisfies the same craving, for in a muffled but harmonious manner it exercises the whole of the emotional keyboard.[84]

The knowledge of foreign languages enhanced a quality of feminine refinement. Jewish daughters were always taught to be versatile in languages and music, literature and art, with the exception of the ultrareligious families who wouldn't expose their daughters to secular influences.[85]

The Rabbis made a profound study of the conflict between the traits of display and of modesty. They concluded that, in the refined woman, modesty subdued display.

The Rabbis fully appreciated woman's need and love for self-adornment and display as necessary to enhance her self-image, which would make her more desirable to her husband. While this love and need may be the keynotes of woman's characteristics, vanity, in the Jewish tradition, was never deemed praiseworthy. Indeed, Judaism looks askance at valueless conceit and inflated pride; it stresses, instead, humility.

APPENDIX B

Personality Features

EMOTIONAL DEVELOPMENT

A woman is more compassionate than man.
—*Rashi* 2 *Kings* 22:14

Were it not for our emotions, human life would be quite drab indeed. Emotions are essential to life, and describing or classifying them is still problematic in psychology.

Much of our emotional behavior is learned. Aside from being a by-product of a particular activity, emotion is also a goal in itself.

Satisfying emotional goals are normally sought by an intelligent human being. Such an individual will neither abuse nor repress his emotional expressions, but, rather, channel them in a mature and fulfilling way.

Emotion is a "complex state of the organism, involving bodily changes of a widespread character" physically. Mentally, it is a "state of excitement marked by strong feelings and usually an impulse towards a definite form of behavior."[1] It is accompanied by characteristic motor and glandular activities—excitement.

Phenomena such as joy, anger, pity, affection, fear, ecstasy, and so on are classified as emotions.

Certain behaviors may be described as emotional. Emotion is also interchangeable with a system of feelings such as sentiment.

A mood, passion, feeling, or interest is a variety of emotion. Emotional behavior and development are strongly determined by particular events, experiences, and the routine of living through perception and appraisal.

It has been suggested that we use the term "feeling" to refer to the milder states and "emotion" to the stronger ones. It is obvious that sensations from internal bodily changes play an important role in emotion. A complete emotional experience consists of a cognitive integration of external stimuli and internal bodily sensations.

Instinct

From the Latin *instinctus*, instinct is one of the oldest concepts. It is generally described as a natural or congenital impulse with responses characteristically involving innervation of the autonomic nervous system.

For Freud, the primary drives or instincts consisted of two categories: Eros (love), or life instinct, which contributed to the survival of the person and of the species; and Thanatos, or death instinct, involving the self-destructive forces that produced aggression and war. Freud regarded instinct as a kind of response to a situation that was brought to an end by some external disturbance. His theory of personality was built around the transformations within the sexual and aggressive drives, the fruits of living in a social world. Allport feels that love and hate are really postinstinctive. In fact, our mores, our loyalties, and antipathies always rule our behavior; it is not, as Freud believed, ruled by the instinctual instructional forces.[2]

In early psychology, instincts were thought of as inborn tendencies to respond in certain definite ways without previous experience or training. As a result of having become so misused, the word "instinct" has been dropped by psychologists who, instead of labeling certain forms of behavior "instinctive," try to discover what environmental or biological conditions produced the activity in question.

When a woman becomes infuriated she goes from one extreme to the other; she is difficult to calm and is overbearing. Why is a man more easily pacified than a woman? The metaphoric answer, provided by the Rabbis, is, "Because man was made out of the soft earth, and woman out of a hard rib."[3]

The average woman can be tempestuous. We find that, when vexed or infuriated, she may not hesitate to betray a confidence or make a false accusation. Sometimes she cannot control her temper or her loquaciousness.

The Rabbis observed that women are compassionate. Unlike men, they tend to sympathize more with the distressed.[4] Their tears express strong identification with the sufferer. It is for this reason that the Rabbis spoke of woman's frequent crying spells and warned man to be considerate. Woman's "tears are frequent" because of her sensitivity and vulnerability. Even today, crying, perhaps wrongly so, is more accepted in women. They can, therefore, be lachrymose with less shame or none at all.[5]

As psychologists today affirm, tears and crying are wonderful cathartic mechanisms in their ability to bring out repressed drives. A person whose repressed drives are evoked in a socially acceptable manner is better able to adjust to problems. Freud relates crying to hysteria—a symptom known mostly to women. Hence women are more prone to get rid of inner conflicts by crying and are therefore, able to bear more burdens.[6]

Traditionally, if the woman was not allowed to take part in a banquet or even a funeral, it caused her much grief. Attending a funeral was considered a religious duty. The Rabbis were puzzled by her predilection for funerals. They questioned it thus: "It is natural that not going to a banquet should cause her unhappiness, but why should she consider herself as being locked up [and deprived] when kept back from going to a funeral?" Their answer was that she reasoned, "When I die, no one will bewail me and no one will come to mourn at my funeral since I never came to theirs; people will pay me with my own coin."[7]

The psychological explanation for this suffering is that the woman desires to go out and satisfy her gregariousness; she wishes to participate in what others are doing. She sees a crowd and immediately wants to join it, regardless of its nature. Not only does she desire to follow a cortege, but she likes to participate with the men in performing the religious ceremonies and feels herself part of the required rituals, though she is halakhically exempted.

Tradition viewed the chief merit of attending a funeral as an occasion to lift up the voice in lamentations to elicit cathartic crying by the mourners.[8] Ancient Oriental funeral processions and even modern ones among Arabs always comprised keening women. These women beat their breasts and their mouths in great sorrow. Women were skillful mourners at funerals owing to their ability to emote and wax elegiac in prodding the mourners to give vent to their grief. Customarily, at funeral processions, the women would precede the men. This is also depicted in ancient Egyptian bas-reliefs.[9]

In biblical times, the women were experts in eliciting tears and in helping to heighten grief and mourning. Like their Egyptian and Chaldaic sisters, the Hebrew women were known as "weeping women" (mekonenot), who pulled out their hair and mimetically filled the air with lamentations. The Bible abounds in illustrations of "weeping for the dead," pointing up that the mourning was performed both for women and by women.[10] The same trend continued throughout the Second Commonwealth and later in talmudic times.

Fear

Fear is a response that assists man to cope with life with the maximum chance of survival. Fear is emotionally desirable as long as its responses are within normal bounds. It keeps one from impulsive behavior.

One of the most primitive of human emotions, fear is the basis of modesty. This is evident in the biblical story of Eden where shame and fear were ushered into the world; Adam feared God because he was naked. This very ancient association of modesty and fear is also found in the fragments of Epicharmus. "Modesty is, indeed, an agglomeration of two important and distinct fears; one of much earlier than human origin and supplied solely by the female; the other of more distinctly human character is the social rather than sexual origin."[11]

It has been observed that woman, from a very early age, is more fearful than man: this may be suggestive of her more highly developed sensitivity and generally superior adaptation to her environment. Modern studies have shown that from childhood on there is a difference in the kinds of fears exhibited by girls and boys. At night, states the Talmud, for example, she would not go more than a distance of fifty cubits from her house alone. While girls fear the dark, being alone, strangers, and strange situations, boys more often fear physical injuries.[12]

To the feeling of fear in woman, shyness is closely related.*

Religiosity

> Women are diligent in fulfilling the command-
> ments of the Torah.
> —*Exodus Rabbah* 28, 2

Let us now turn to woman's feelings and religious faith.

Religiosity is one of the most sublime experiences of mankind. Some psychologists assert that a special human need necessitated religion;

---

*See *infra* on Modesty and Woman and the Home in this chapter.

others disagree.[13] All concur, however, that emotions play an important role in religion. Their prominence is observable in prayer and in numerous rituals and ceremonies.

Woman, the Rabbis noted, was vested with more faith than man. There is in woman's nature a craving for religion and an inborn reverence for Rabbis.[14] She seems to possess a degree of optimism alien to man. A possible reason may be that the woman is more emotional. Of course, the validity of this conclusion is based upon a psychological thesis that belief and emotion are symbiotic.

In this sense, religiosity is not native in her, but it is exceedingly fortunate that she is able to develop it, since the natural events in a woman's life, such as childbearing, require extraordinary belief that all is divinely ordained.

The Rabbis noted that woman is more zealous than man in performing her religious duties. This is true, in fact, in most religions. The Lord commanded Moses, in giving to the world His Divine precepts, to address the women first and then the men, for "women are more prompt in fulfilling the commandments." A reason for this is offered by Scheinfeld, who asserts that, having been more conditioned to conform and to accept discipline, the woman is less likely to question her religion and does not usually take the initiative in breaking away.[15]

In matters of religion, woman is more alert than man. Furthermore, we find that she is more observant than him; hence the admonition, "A curse lieth upon the man whose wife or children have to say Grace for him."[16] How shameful, indeed, it is for an ignorant man whose wife and children supersede him in the knowledge of the Law. Traditionally, the Jewish woman would not do any labor the night following the Sabbath, nor on Mondays or Thursdays, nor on *Hoshana Rabba*, nor in the Nine days of the month of *Av*, nor on the festival of *Rosh Hodesh*, which, according to Tradition, was given to the Jewish women, as reward for their refusal to offer their jewelry for the making of the golden calf.[17]

Another reason why *Rosh Hodesh* was assigned to women as their special festival is offered by the Or Zarua: Woman renews herself with every monthly cycle, and desires to unite in love with her husband as if she starts freshly as a new bride, similar to the reborn moon which is seen anew every month. Therefore, was *Rosh Hodesh*—the first day of the new moon, significantly assigned to woman.[18] The intent of observing *Rosh Hodesh* by abstaining from certain weekday activities was not so much to sanctify these days as days of rest but rather to mark them as a festival through the distinction conferred by this limited observance.

The Rabbis were always opposed to extremes. They felt that unadulterated sybaritism and narcissism were reprehensible. Excessive piety was also considered odious. An excessively devout and zealous maiden was thought to be unnatural since such religiosity was at odds with all her other womanly inclinations; such an individual was dubbed by the Rabbis "a prayerful maiden" or "a self-afflicting girl," as a false Pharisee. Another type of false Pharisee was one "who sits down and quotes biblical phrases in a squeamish manner"; that is, she criticizes certain biblical expressions, pretending that they offend against her sense of decency.[19]

From these extreme cases we return to what we term "the average woman." Woman wishes to participate in all religious ceremonies, including those in which she is not obliged to take part (such as dwelling in the *sukkah*, reciting the blessing over the *etrog*, etc.). The only two exceptions of unduly pious women cited in the Talmud were King David's wife, Michal, who is said to have donned *tefillin*, and the wife of Jonah, the prophet, who attended the festival pilgrimage to Jerusalem.[20]

Usually, the woman will join forces with her husband against a religious foe. The wife of a nonobservant man, however, will not follow his views; rather, she will align her sympathies with the husband's religious opponents.[21]

Because chance plays a very important part in their lives, with so many aspects of their existence depending on the vagaries of fortune and with so much of their destiny controlled by others, women are more prone to superstition than men. They are drawn to the miraculous and supernatural, to fortunetellers and horoscopes. The woman's naiveté and belief in the occult and the superstitious are a result of her lack of exposure to academia (owing to the fact that she was not required to devote herself to study as the man was), and they render her gullible to sorcery.* Because of her credulity, she lapses into accepting everything.[22]

Jealousy

> Jealousy is cruel as the grave; the coals thereof are
> coals of fire.
>
> —*Song of Songs* 8:6

Just as in the realms of religiosity, love, hatred, and benevolence, the Rabbis observed a tendency in the woman to go to extremes when confronted by jealousy.

---

*See *infra* chater 14.

Jealousy is a complex emotional state. Its nucleus is hate or resentment by one person for another.

Women, claims the Midrash, are inclined to have a jealous disposition.[23] When there are two women in the house, there must be strife. Freud remarked that women are generally more jealous than men. According to Freud, "Jealousy is one of those affective states, like grief, that may be described as normal." Its apparent absence in a person is only a sign of repression in the unconscious. Abnormally intense jealousy cases encountered in analytic work reveal themselves in "three stages: 1) competitive or normal; 2) projected; and 3) delusional jealousy."[24]

To Karen Horney, woman's jealousy of other women is a neurotic reinforcement resulting from the "unerring unconscious feeling of a lack in the sexual sphere."[25]

Studies of childhood have shown that the pattern for greater jealousy in the female sex appears to be established very early. Envy of boys, leading to envy of others, may extend into later life. As time goes on, a woman may have more reason than a man to be jealous. Since the security of the woman and her children depends upon her husband's economic support, the threat of losing her husband is a serious matter.[26]

The basis of jealousy, a destructive emotion, is fear—fear of losing the love object. Other emotions, such as anger, envy, pain, vanity, and a sense of inferiority, also figure in the problem.[27] Many examples of a wife's rivalry and jealousy in the early Israelite polygamous family are cited in the Bible. It is of interest that the Hebrew word kin'ah connotes jealousy, envy, and passion. Consequently, the tendencies of jealousy in the human relationship are almost entirely harmful. It can blast love more quickly and irretrievably than almost any other force. The jealous person, actuated by a blind desire to retain the love and affection of the loved one, fails to realize that jealousy invariably defeats its own ends.[28]

When her security is menaced, woman's aggressiveness, previously veiled, asserts itself, at times even sadistically. "The sadism of woman is in no way less cruel than man's, it merely chooses another form of expression . . . In her attitude toward her rival—there is no room for pity or generosity."[29]

Woman is a Draconian judge of her sisters; she is more critical of them than man, since she compares their motives with her own. Her "rivalry," or emulative instinct, is very pronounced. Woman will endure disgrace or exposure, regardless of the consequences, rather than allow a rival to surpass her in any respect.

Her jealousy could swell so that she may adopt Samson's tactics, "let me die with the Philistines" (Judg. 16:30), meaning that she would not scruple to endure infliction in order to inflict pain upon her rival.[30] Woman wants to do everything to degrade her rival morally or physically.

When woman is in love, the emotion of jealousy intensifies. The psychologist McDougall felt that full-blown jealousy is only developed where some sentiment of love or attachment exists.

The same psychological principle is couched in a rabbinic saying: "There is no real jealousy but among lovers." "Love without jealousy is not true love," explains the *Zohar*.[31] Woman, in her natural wish to keep her man's love pulsating for her, will feel hatred toward her rival.

She will strive to remain as beautiful as she can in order to preserve her love object or to reconquer it. The amorous woman cannot endure the thought that her beloved might be attractive to another woman; she will suspect betrayal in her inamorato's fleeting glance at another woman. Or, in the words of the Talmud: "A woman is made jealous only by the thigh of another woman." Woman will not be surpassed by her rival, as instanced by the rabbinic proverb: "Reforming a bad woman by giving her a rival will be more effective than thorns."[32]

Jealousy encompasses all human relations. "Wrath is cruel and anger is overwhelming, but who is able to stand before jealousy?" (Prov. 27:4)

"In jealousy," claims Rochefoucauld, "there is more self-love than love of another." Jealousy is, in many ways, rational and just; it aims at the preservation of a good which we think belongs to us. It is in this light that the Rabbis speak of a woman's antipathy toward her mother-in-law—another phase of jealousy common in woman.[33]

It is said that jealousy is love, but though it may be produced by love as ashes are by fire, jealousy extinguishes love, as ashes smother the flame.

CHARACTER

> Kindness in women, not their beautiful looks,
> shall win my love.
>
> —*Shakespeare*

Character consists of distinctive traits, encompassing both the moral and the mental qualities of an individual. It is the sum of these characteristics that makes one human. (The word "character" is of Greek derivation, meaning "engraving," and it was used mainly by Theophrastus, Aristotle's disciple.) Today it is used synonymously with "personality" (Freud spoke mainly of "character structure.") There are many psychological treatises that offer diverse definitions of the human character.

Character implies a moral standard, a value judgment. Gordon Allport calls it "personality evaluated," while personality is "character devaluated." Some psychologists define it as "the degree of ethically effective organization of all the forces of the individual." Others, as the "enduring psychophysical disposition to inhibit impulses in accordance with a regulative principle."[34]

In the standard current psychological usage, character is "an integrated system of traits of behavior tendencies that enables one to react, in a relatively consistent way in relation to mores and moral issues . . . It is distinguished from personality by its emphasis upon a) the volitional aspect, and b) morality."[35]

A. A. Roback defines character as weak or strong, and he explains when and how it is manifested. "Character is inhibition of the instincts."[36] Primarily, then, the difference between one quality of character and another is that of a mental condition in which the range and degree of behavior is curtailed and the instinctual process is prevented from coming into consciousness by the restraining activity of the superego. It is the difference of one psychical inhibitory activity upon another.

In observing the character of woman, the Rabbis remarked: "If a woman is good, then her goodness is unlimited; if she is bad, her wickedness is boundless."[37]

They also considered the woman to be of a weaker disposition; that is, she does not possess the power to resist or inhibit her strong instinctive propensities.[38] Perhaps this is a result of the intensity of her impulses and complex responses or of her physical frailty. Here we can only rely upon the philosophical views of the Rabbis rather than on empirical evidence.

Because of her fragility, it was taught that man should not be too strict with woman, lest he harm her. R. Shimon Ben Elazar enjoins: "A woman should be kept at a distance with the left hand and drawn near with the right hand." Recognizing that the right hand symbolizes supremacy in Judaic and Oriental tradition, the quotation means that the reproof ought to be mildly administered by the left hand only—while the loving reacceptance be proffered with the right. This implies that one should relate to woman with equilibrium: neither by total rejection nor by smothering her to death with love.[39]

Temptation—as a human frailty—was amply discussed in rabbinic literature. Woman was considered to be easily influenced by and sometimes unable to resist temptation.[40] This view was also shared by Freud, whose theory of female sexuality affirmed that sexuality should not be thwarted or denied, but mastered. Since woman's capacity for the sublimation of her instincts is lesser, she lives dangerously close to the "archaic heritage." The antiwomen implications Freud drew from his beliefs have been criticized by others, most recently by Kate Millet.[41] There was sharp disagreement among the Rabbis about woman's reaction to outside influences. Just how far can character be influenced by environment?

A case cited in the Talmud is emblematic of the fluctuations in woman's character. The wife of a scholar was accustomed to help in tying the phylacteries on her husband's arm; but, after the death of her husband, she married a robber and assisted him in his lawless undertakings. This case touched off much discussion among the Rabbis, and it was finally concluded that this woman was the exception, for an honest woman remains worthy of trust, even under changed conditions.[42] This propensity is what Freud, in his essay on the feminine character, calls "psychological rigidity."[43]

Let us examine another phase of woman's character: her sense of justice, her integrity and her reputation, as set down in the talmudic and midrashic literature. In all instances the Rabbis were exceedingly frank in dealing with women. They were not in the least hesitant to give credit where credit was due. Woman was credited with possessing virtues superior to man's, but she was never credited with virtues in which she was lacking.

Freud believed that "women have little sense of justice." In Jewish tradition the woman was not permitted to sit in judgment.[44] This, no doubt, on account of her very compassionate nature. Sometimes, influenced by her emotions, she cannot judge objectively. Likewise, she cannot differentiate between circumstantial and real evidence. Furthermore, she was considered incapable of rendering a decision on halakhic questions, with the exception of being fully reliable in matters of *niddah* and *taharat ha-mishpahah*.[45] At times she is unable to control her imagination when relating events. Jewish Law always believes the woman, though, when she claims she has been raped.[46]

Let us now consider other aspects of woman's character and behavior.

Cleanliness

The question in psychology as to whether cleanliness is instinctive or is the result of education and habit is a moot one.

The relation of cleanliness to emotion is already manifested in early childhood where troubles about cleanliness are an expression of the child's feelings about people and should never be understood as merely a physiological matter. Early discipline in ordering the training in cleanliness by parents was long known to be guilt-inducing. Any emotional upset could result in a temporary breakdown in cleanliness.[47]

The high regard in which Jews held cleanliness is reflected in their attitudes and deeds. The Talmud states that "physical cleanliness leads to spiritual purity" and enjoins man to "Wash your face, hands and feet daily in honor of your Maker."[48]

The role of woman in Jewish tradition was especially related to the concept of cleanliness and purity, for in her hands was entrusted the master key of taharat ha-mishpahah.

The Rabbis observed that woman showed a strong desire to maintain a high degree of physical cleanliness. One reason may be her dermic sensitivity and concern for bodily freshness.

Currently, according to Gesell and Ilg, the woman's tendency toward cleanliness is already present in adolescence.[49]

Sleep

Woman's chemistry strongly influences her mental and psychological makeup. Even before puberty, the production of estrogens makes the little girl less aggressive and noisy. At puberty, with the increase of hormonal production, her character softens more and, during pregnancy, this process continues and she becomes more subdued. Studies show that, from infancy, women on the average sleep and rest longer than males. This may also be the result of inner conflict, as reported in medical research. The Rabbis, too, agree that women sleep longer than men.[50]

Oral Tendencies

Another characteristic attributed to woman is her loquaciousness. In the following excerpts the Rabbis' observations are apparent:

Women are talkative.
Ten measures of talk came to this world and nine of them were taken by women.
While she handles the shuttle, she continues to talk.
Very early in the morning she starts talking with her husband.[51]

One explanation of this trait is offered by Theodore Reik, who traces it "back to the evolution of the two sexes." Theoretically, "woman retains much more of the emotional character traits of the child than the man." She finds it hard not to blurt out trivial thoughts. On the other hand, woman is known to be more secretive than man if she needs to withhold information. In reconciling this trait with her childlike talkativeness, Reik assumes "that her mental psychological development moves on two separate tracks." In one she remains childlike and on a lower evolutionary level than man; in the other, she shows more maturity than he does. When concealing something, a woman is not necessarily silent. "Many women are especially talkative when they are anxious."[52]

One of woman's greatest assets is speech. Since a girl is smaller and physically weaker than a boy, and society dictates that she should not be pugnacious, she develops a trait that she carries into womanhood—tongue-lashing: her way of relieving pent-up anger and frustration.

Perhaps the reason for woman's loquacity is that she may find speech the most available satisfying form of releasing tension and anxieties that result from her having been alone in the house. Throughout history she has searched out the company of her friends and neighbors.

Women are inclined to gossip, elaborating and exaggerating the most ordinary occurrences. This gossiping trait in some women is a classic theme in many cultures, particularly in the Orient. In the words of Ben Sirah: "A silent woman is a gift from the Lord."[53]

Still, one of her many contradictions is that, while she often seems to talk abundantly, she is sometimes reticent, modest, reluctant to speak out; the explosive candor of the male distresses her. She may act mischievously, but in the presence of other women she will, through her strong desire not to be outdone or humiliated, inhibit her natural impulses.[54]

Woman is very fond of sweet things and likes to taste everything. This trait is already discernible in early childhood and becomes most pronounced in adolescence. According to H. Deutsch, "The intensification of many oral tendencies serves as an aggressive gratification of the appetites, which is increased by the process of growth."[55]

Gregariousness

Woman's intuitive response to other people was duly noted by the Rabbis. Her intense love of home symbolizes the "family instincts" and, at the same time, illustrates her need for social interactions. This may explain her strong feeling of patriotism, love of home, and devotion to country.[56]

This gregarious predisposition was manifested, according to the Rabbis, in woman's pronounced desire to visit her neighbors, especially her female friends. Such a characteristic was not so apparent in man, they observed. Nathan Ackerman, too, feels that within the modern family group it is the "wife who maintains the active social life and who wins friends and arranges dinner parties."[57]

This inclination, coupled with others, explains the woman's willingness to stay married to a man, even if he does not satisfy her sexually, a view also shared by Ignace Lepp.[58] This tendency reflects the woman's deep-seated fear of and aversion to remaining single.

Even in modern times some women may be willing to compromise their early romantic expectations in favor of more realistic considerations. In choosing a husband they might even relinquish some of their more fanciful notions.

The Need for Acceptance

The need for approval and reassurance is inherent in the woman. This was illustrated in the Talmud by the conduct of the bride. On being found pleasing in her husband's paternal home, she is eager to report this to her father's house.[59] The feeling that everyone likes her usually occurs at the first festival after marriage, since, at that time, she can exult in her newly found status. (This may have been the origin of the custom for a bride to dine at her father's house on the first festival after the wedding—it was called the "festival of the anxious."[60] If, for some reason, she was prevented from going to her father's house on the first festival, she would go on the second.)

Devotion to Parents

Woman's dependence on parents seems to be different from the man's. Parental love is, indeed, a stronger emotion in woman than in man.[61] Before a man marries, he may be very devoted to his parents; but after marriage he leaves them and seems to bestow all his love and affection upon his wife.[62] This is in line with the first biblical advice: "Therefore shall a man leave his father and his mother and shall cleave unto his wife." (Gen. 2:24) Traditionally, throughout her life woman feels the need to visit her parental home on holidays and other occasions. Indeed, it was felt that she could not bear to be absent from her parental home for more than one holiday.[63]

Self-Assertiveness

> Honour not a woman for her possessions; honour
> her for the right use she makes of them.
>   —proverb

Woman has a keen appreciation of her worth and refuses to lower herself in any respect. She would never give herself in betrothal or accept the customary "betrothal money" if she felt she was not being accorded the respect that her dignity deserves.[64]

On the other hand, she would say: "I want no shoe larger than my foot." She may not desire a husband superior to her in rank, lest, by dint of his lineage, he pull rank and thereby deprive her of her ability of self-assertion.[65]

In some cases, a woman would refuse a wealthy suitor from her own class, fearing that she would have to assume additional responsibilities and show him greater consideration.[66] She would prefer to forego the comforts of life rather than jeopardize her social position.

The mistress of the household would often choose to employ a dull maid, before whom she could act without inhibitions. She was afraid that an educated one might gossip about her to the neighbors. Thus she often refused the professional services of a hair dresser, who might be indiscreet.[67] Such was woman's self-assertion that she displayed no weakness in the presence of her domestic staff, lest she undermine her authority over them.[68]

There is a rabbinic statement that woman's influence is so great that everything depends on her. If she is a good woman, she can convert a wicked man to righteousness; if she is wicked, even if her husband is a saint, she can influence even the most pious husband and change him completely. This point is illustrated as follows: "A pious man was married to a pious woman; their marriage was childless, and they divorced each other. He married a vicious woman, and became evil also. She married a wicked man and converted him to righteousness." A woman can make a man follow a righteous or evil path.[69] An early Renaissance proverb states: "A good wife makes a good husband."

It is an accepted fact that woman inspires man. She encourages him to work and to succeed because she loves him. The means at her disposal is in man's own nature: the average man enjoys having his ego inflated. The ego may be likened to the skeletal structure of the body. Every man possesses a mental skeleton—his ego. When man's ego collapses, everything suffers. Woman's influence is so great that, because of it, man is no longer a primitive hunter. She has, in her subordinate position through her constructive forces, made man her instrument for building the world. "When a man's work fails, his hopes fall and ambitions sink; cynical friends inquire, 'Who is she?' " Every woman knows how to create a favorable impression upon her husband. Since she was able to persuade her husband to follow her advice, she was considered his adviser. Upon her death, the husband was left bereft of counsel; for without a wife to plan and share his thoughts, he was truly pitiful. On the other hand, if the wife was domineering and denied her husband his position as head of the family, his life was considered valueless.[70]

Modesty

> Nothing is more dear to the Lord than modesty.
> —*Pessikta Rabbati* 45

R. Phinehas Ben Yair said: "Holiness leads to humility; humility leads to the fear of transgression; fear of transgression leads to saintliness; saintliness leads to the Holy Spirit." The insistence on humility distinguishes Jewish from Greek ethics. "Everything heroic in man is insignificant and perishable, and all his wisdom and virtue unable to stand the crucial test, unless they are the fruits of humility," says Hermann Cohen.[71]

The absence of arrogance is related to modesty, the quality of freedom from conceit or vanity, stressing the propriety of dress, speech, and behavior. *Tzeniut* as a concept of humility encompasses both attitude and practice. First used by the prophet Micah (6:8), *Ve-hatzneya lekhet im Elokekha* ("and to walk humbly with thy God."), *tzeniut* is considered as one of the three cardinal principles of Jewish faith. It implies constant awareness of the Divine presence by avoiding all unseemly actions of trespassing the limits and instructions given to us. *Tzeniut* relates to indecent speech or action, dress and appearance, covert or overt behavior. It is conceived as humility and human decency in counterdistinction to *peritzut*—the frivolous breaking of the moral code of conduct.

Modesty in Judaism is seen as a human quality. It implies concealment of natural functions, sexual relations, and nudity and leads to a camouflage of the reality for the sake of delicacy.

Since the days of Aristotle, man's propensity to cloak certain parts of his body has been discussed. The issue is as old as Adam and Eve in the Garden of Eden. Modesty is the first inward stirring of morality, which the human being does not learn until he begins to depart from the heedlessness of the brute.

It is of more than passing interest that the Rabbis' attitudes to this problem, to this day, remain moot. They observed, however, that woman is sensitive to shame to a far greater degree than man.[72]

Modesty and delicacy were required by the Rabbis of both man and woman. We are told that Eve was created from the side, a hidden part of the body, symbolically indicating that woman has the quality of being demure, modest, and prudent, and attached to her home.[73]

A woman who conducts herself with prudence (though she comes from nonpriestly stock) deserves to be married to a *kohen* (priest) and to bring up high priests.[74]

A woman's embarrassment in remaining single is more intense than man's.[75] Based upon this psychological fact, Jewish Law ordered that when a male or female orphan had to be married by the court or the community, the preference was to be given to the female.

Because of her instinctive modesty and shyness, the woman, despite her great need, will not go to the doorsteps of others to ask for alms. Similarly, when a man and a woman are standing in line to receive charity, the woman feels more shamed than the man. Hence woman has to be attended to before man. This was the basis for the law stipulating that when a man and woman are both in need of clothing, or must be ransomed from captivity, the woman takes precedence.[76]

This psychological insight compelled Rava, a judge in talmudic times, to change his *modus operandi* when a man and a woman had appeared in court in separate cases. Originally, he would hear a man's case first, since the man was the provider and was required by law to fulfill certain obligations and duties to her. Yet, being aware of woman's greater sensitivity, Rava later implemented the principle of "ladies first"; this in order to save the woman from the unnecessary pain of inordinate exposure to the galleries of the court.

According to the Rabbis, woman is bashful, sometimes to the extent that she will even dismiss her rightful legal claims if people treat her kindly. A widow, in earlier times, would not seek out her deceased husband's properties, for a woman would rather forego her legal rights than attend a court enforcement.[77]

Sometimes woman's shyness may even impede her from engaging in business, avoiding involvement with the employees.[78] This ancient feminine trait is a far cry from her business involvement in later periods, especially in our present industrial era. Hence the Rabbis, knowing the acuteness of her feeling, wondered whether a woman would prefer being insulted to being inflicted with bodily pain. One opinion was that no matter how much a woman suffered physically, she found it preferable to the humiliation of public exposure. The other view was that the average woman would not react in this manner.[79]

Singularly bashful was the bride. In her paternal home she was extremely timid when her bridegroom visited her, but by the time she was taken to her husband's parental home, she had become accustomed to him and was more at ease.[80] During the time of her betrothal, a bride was still shy in public and was known to avert her face from onlookers.[81]

The Rabbis did not elaborate upon whether there was a natural reaction of modesty and shame in man or woman. But from a thorough search of talmudic sources, it appears that the woman was especially susceptible to these traits. At the same time, it is evident that many manifestations of bashfulness in the Jewish woman were direct results of the rituals and precepts of modesty dictated by religion, such as Ezra's ordinance that woman shall wear a *sinar*[82] (petticoat).

Some authorities held that there is a natural impulse in women to be more modest. Various anthropological studies, though, challenge this view, claiming that modesty and bashfulness are purely artificial qualities deliberately assimilated, not inborn traits. These studies show that, among many primitives, women are no more modest than are males and that often, in fact, the males are more reserved in their behavior and more careful about observing the prevailing rules of propriety in conduct and attire. Havelock Ellis sees modesty as "something acquired by education and increased in later life by many agencies of incalculable importance which are not sufficiently appreciated."[83]

The retiring disposition of the woman was always pronounced. A verse in Psalms was interpreted by the Rabbis to illustrate the modesty of the Jewish daughter: "All gloriously attired awaiteth the King's daughter in the inner chamber." (Ps. 45:14) This was expounded in the Midrash to mean that "It is the nature of the woman to remain in her home." Maimonides views "The glory of the woman to be in the home."[84]

The close relationship of the woman to her home was already

extolled in biblical times. When Abraham was asked by his angelic guest: "Where is Sarah thy wife?" he replied, "Behold, in the tent." (Gen. 18:9) The Talmud sees herein praise of Sarah, the highest excellence of a wife, her domesticity and her privacy.

The Rabbis also discouraged men to be waited upon by women and to be ministered by them. Samuel, the famous Amora, declares that one must not subordinate or make unnecessary use of a woman, whether adult or child, in order not to accustom her to be in the company of men, lest she become frivolous and be taken advantage of.[85]

Nevertheless, the Rabbis observed a certain natural modesty in the woman. Even in the animal kingdom, they maintained, it was very unusual to see a female running after a male.[86] This feminine passivity is not quite so observable today. It was once thought entirely proper for only the male to pursue the female, or, as the French say, "*cherchez la femme.*"

During early childhood we notice a natural sense of retirement and seclusion in the girl, in contrast with the boy. Young boys, for instance, had to have a special governor watch over them and prevent them from running into the streets, where they might meet with an accident. Whereas girls, on account of their extreme modesty and reservation, did not require such protection.[87]

It was not thought seemly for a woman to be found in the fields, as may be adduced from the proverb: "What has a woman to do between reeds and bulrushes?" Extreme fear of being alone or exposed to strange situations and people was, surely, a cause for her avoidance of deserted fields or places.[88]

What we consider modesty is often merely a form of fear. Modesty in behavior or dress may be prompted by the fear of violating a social or religious code, or a taboo. This fear is usually developed in woman to a greater extent than in man. To some extent, modesty in behavior should remain one of woman's defenses against unwelcome advances and undesired sexual relations. Modesty in dress and in speech has always been the traditional hallmark of the Jewish daughter.[89]

Quite often the taboo of modesty, which originally applied only to the sexual organs, came to include the whole body. Psychologists agree that the tendency toward libido is more prevalent in woman than in man. While in man the libido is more definitely concentrated upon the genital zone, in woman the whole body is suffused with sexuality (erogenous). This is true both subjectively and objectively—showing or looking upon her body. The exposure, therefore, of any part of a woman's body is more charged erotically than the exposure of the corresponding part of the male's, with the exception of the genitalia.

Let us now consider woman's behavior based on her sense of morality. Throughout the Orient, woman's unwillingness to expose her body is a timeless tradition. In the Japanese theater the role of the woman is played by men because it was not thought morally decent for a woman to exhibit herself publicly. Women, therefore, were banned from the Kabuki stage. Chinese women were as reticent in exposing their feet as a European woman her breasts. Modesty is a matter of convention, dependent on the culture one lives in.

Woman's modest character does not easily permit her to wage war, although today the brave daughters of modern Israel enlist in the ranks of the Israeli Army and shoulder their share of the country's defense.[90]

It was the custom of the Jewish woman never to expose any part of her body. Hence she did her washing on her own premises, lest men might see her legs and arms. Neither would she bake in the presence of men, since it was necessary to bare her arms in the process of baking. She would, however, not scruple to grind wheat in the presence of strange men, since it was not necessary to uncover her arms.[91] Woman's sense of modesty was so distinct that she would not even welcome male guests at the doorstep of her house with bread and water.[92]

Consideration for women's right to privacy and modesty was given them in relation to the law of mourning. Women in mourning are not required to bare their chests. They may either rend the outer garment or tear an inner garment first and then cover it up so that the naked skin is not exposed.[93]

This aspect of her character was further reflected in the woman's dress. When she walked in the street, the train of her dress would trail behind her. The Midrash actually compared the overhanging curtains of the Tabernacle (Exod. 26:12) to the trails of a woman.[94] This custom is still preserved today in many cultures, for example, with the bride's wedding gown.

Modesty may be intimately connected with education and custom. There is a distinct difference between urban and rural populations, between different social classes. In the towns, where there was a great deal of entertainment and immorality, the painting of the eyes was a sign of immodesty. In view of this, it was customary for modest women to veil their faces, leaving only one eye unveiled; in the villages, however, where life was more simple and wholesome, the women were free to go about unveiled.

According to Rashi, one derives two important concepts about modest dress. There is no universal code of modest attire, and certain types of people do wear more modest apparel because of their personality structure and makeup.[95]

During talmudic times it was considered improper for a townswoman to go barefoot for more than a day, while it was entirely proper for the women in the villages to go barefoot for months.[96] Another custom discountenanced women who appeared in public with their heads uncovered, because of the seductive nature of their hair. This was one of the strictest customs among Jewish women; any violation was considered indecorous.

Similarly, it is told of the Kimhit woman that she credited the honor of being the mother of seven high priests to the fact that the ceiling never saw her hair nor the hem of her undergarments.[97]

The Rabbis considered modesty to be innate in woman's character and a controlling element in her behavior. Even a prostitute, they said, cannot sink to such depths of degradation that she will sit where the masses go by and barter herself in public.[98]

The modesty of Jewish daughters was particularly evident in their carriage, which they strove to make light and graceful, and in their manner of speech and laughter, which was always subdued. If she were lacking in elegance, the woman would acquire the reputation of being "shrill and noisy." Likewise, she loathed a haughty husband. The average woman was not haughty; indeed, it was widely felt that arrogance and frivolity were unbecoming to a woman. As the old talmudic saying goes: "That which wisdom makes the crown of her head, humility makes the shoe of her foot."[99]

WOMAN AND THE HOME

The Home is the fulcrum on which woman moves the world.

—Warner

In the Bible, as well as in comparative Oriental literature, the woman is likened to a tent,[100] meaning that she is all-encompassing, indispensable. We find the biblical *eshet hayil*, preoccupied with her home, epitomized in the thirty-first chapter of the Book of Proverbs.

The Rabbis, cognizant of woman's powerful love for the home, regarded the wife and the home as identical. On the Day of Atonement the High Priest used to make atonement for himself and for his "house," which was traditionally understood to mean his "wife." Said R. Yossi: "I always called my wife 'my home.' " Rashi interprets R. Yossi's statement in terms of the woman's being the foundation of the house.[101]

R. Eliezer called woman "the house" of the family. The woman was also referred to in the Midrash as "the house of the nation."[102]

Wife and home were also equated by the Jewish philosopher Philo, who said:

Why does Moses call the form of a woman "building"? Everything is altogether imperfect and destitute in a home which is deserted by the woman. Man is committed to the public affairs of the state, but the domestic affairs of the house belong to the woman, her absence will be the destruction of the house, but her presence brings order to the house.

From this the Rabbis conclude that prosperity would not exist in the house of a man were it not for his wife.[103]

It is the nature of woman to remain within her own household, states the Midrash. During the talmudic period the Jewish woman was not encouraged to go out to do business but rather to stay at home and supervise her household.[104] Subsequently, we find woman's role historically changing from that of the private and passive guardian of her home to one of an active financial supporter of her household, through labor, the professions, and business.

The Rabbis asserted that idleness in a woman leads to folly, and even immorality, but they assured us that it was not the habit of woman to be idle at home.[105] It is worthy of note that the Rabbis advocated labor as the vehicle for a healthy mind. The woman's dislike of sitting idle was very keen, and we are told that she would even resort to playing checkers, just to keep herself occupied. Checkers was an established, traditional indoor game, played by women throughout the late Middle Ages.[106]

Woman is so industrious in her various responsibilities at home that she can perform two, three, and sometimes four tasks at once, finding herself always usefully employed. Since time immemorial she handled the shuttle while she talked. Her talkativeness did not impede her ability to fulfill her tasks. She would watch the vegetable garden while she spun the flax; would give a lesson in singing and warm the cocoons to make silk. She spun and made the garments for the family; ground the grain, kneaded the dough and set apart the *hallah;* prepared and served the food. She sent the children to school and looked after their hygienic needs and welfare.[107]

The Talmud observes that only the decent woman cared for the household. It stressed woman's importance within the household: the woman is disloyal to her husband only if she neglects her matrimonial duties and does not assume her share of the burden.[108]

Woman always endeavors to see that everything is supplied and in its place. Therefore, when a woman has no provisions in the house it devolves upon the man to provide them. The wife is never ashamed to demand from her husband the necessities of the household. For this reason, the Rabbis advised that a man should always take pains to provide the grain for the house, since no strife is more frequent than that about food. "When the barley is quite gone from the pitcher, strife comes knocking at the door."[109]

Another interesting talmudic observation was made about the facility with which woman adapts herself to the environment. Wherever a woman goes, she feels at home. Being away from home causes greater suffering among men than women.[110]

"An old man [grandfather] in the house is a burden, an old woman [grandmother] is a treasure in the house."[111] Since a man is engaged in activities outside the home, he loses his usefulness when old. Not so the woman, who is still able, and continues, to perform her daily housework. Rabbinic lore posited that a woman over sixty is able to earn a third of what she did when young, but a man is not. An old Hebrew dictum reflects: "When we were young we were treated as men, whereas now that we have grown old we are looked upon as babies."[112]

It was customary during the talmudic period for the man to situate his bedroom far from the dining room for fear that otherwise, he might expose himself to the danger of violating the old medical adage: "Whoever does not walk after the meal is going to suffer." The woman, who was accustomed to serving at the table and cleaning up after the meal, did not need to have her room thus removed.[113] Likewise, she was exempted from the ordinance to eat while recumbent at the *seder,* since she could not sit at one place, being busy with the serving. The one exception was the woman of rank, who, having servants at her beck and call, was accustomed to reclining during the meal in the same manner as the man.[114]

Although woman more adaptable to change, she attaches more importance to her hallowed haven than to the most appetizing foods.[115]

The modern attitude to this adoration of the home remains unchanged: "Be it ever so humble, there is no place like home." The dreams of many a young woman are still to be a wife and assume the obligations of a home.

Woman was considered extremely meticulous. She would examine the borders and folds of garments before putting them into the wash. This punctiliousness made her appear so sluggish that her work was not conspicuous. Thus some women acquired a reputation for laggardness. For this reason, according to Tradition, Ezra's ordinance requires that women should rise early on Fridays, to tend to the baking of *hallah*.[116]

The Jewish woman was traditionally praised for her hospitality and charitable deeds. Her home was always open to the poor.[117]

A married woman is permitted to give small amounts to charity without her husband's knowledge or permission. Nowadays, since the household finances are customarily in the wife's charge, she may even contribute larger amounts to charity commensurate with her overall budget and can make loans to others, too, without her husband's permission. If the wife has a job or owns her own business, she may contribute from her earnings, even if the husband disapproves. Tradition expects every husband, however, to grant his wife carte blanche to contribute to charity whatever amounts she wishes, for the charities dispensed by women are more favorable in the eyes of the Lord than those given by men.[118]

The "Jewish home" represented the life-giving sustenance of faith, fortitude, and hope, which have always been the hallmark of the Jewish household. It served as a viable model for the Jewish heritage and spirituality; it was the haven for the ideals and aspirations of the Jewish family. The Jewish home, though physically small and its quarters restricted in the cramped ghetto, was nevertheless the rich and encompassing habitat of Jewish culture and nurture. It was the intimate and warm source of Jewish education and character-training of the Jewish child; its walls echoed the cradle songs and the intonations of Torah study—the substance of which inspired and gave hope and perpetual faith to Jewish existence for generations. It was the living witness of Jewish joy and sorrow, of *hakhnasat orhim* for the traveling poor and stranger. It was the sanctuary of the proverbial "true house of Israel."

Although woman loves her home, and is devoted to her household, she does not like to feel as if she were incarcerated. She needs a respite from her domestic duties, continual demands of being a housewife, and involvement with her children. And when her husband restrains her comings and goings, visiting, attending affairs (even of a religious nature), she feels frustrated, suffers, and is legally entitled to her freedom.[119]

The educated woman in our society nowadays faces a dilemma. She is taught, on the one hand, to be a dutiful homemaker. But, on the other hand, apart from being a devoted wife and mother, she wants to participate significantly and use her abilities outside the home. It has been traditionally held that a married woman is the wife of her husband and that her duty is to look after the family, while the husband's duty is to provide for them. Many married women, and particularly the educated ones, find the traditional view of the occupational roles of husband and wife too one-sided. Certainly a wife should fulfill the traditionally expected obligations, but no one should deny her a right to a life of her own. If a married woman wishes to work, she should be given the chance to do so. Her being employed outside the home is in no way incompatible with her being a good wife and mother, as millions of married working women prove.[120]

According to C. Gilman, restricting woman's range of duty and service to the home and family hinders her continually. This arrests her spiritual expansion, the social love and service on which our very lives depend.[121]

APPENDIX C

Psycho-Intellectual Makeup

The wisdom of women built her house.
—*Proverbs* 14:1

The Lord has given woman greater maturity of judgment than man.
—*Niddah* 45b

INTELLIGENCE

When we consider the level of woman's intelligence, we are fortunate in being able to draw upon the Rabbis' careful observations. Their views and findings are in consonance with modern thinking on the subject.

Opinions differed whether the woman reaches the peak of mental development at an earlier age than man. Some Rabbis maintained that boys matured before girls. Since the boy went to school and often frequented the home of his teacher and friends, they claimed, he acquired mental acuity prior to the girl, who was scarcely known to leave the house. Moreover, even if he did not attend school, he was always in contact with other people and, as a result, developed more quickly. The general rabbinic consensus, however, was that girls matured, both mentally and physically, earlier than boys.[1]

As far as anatomical and physiological rates of change, studies reveal that growth is relatively gradual during the years from five to ten. An upsurge in growth starts between ages ten and eleven in most girls, while, in the majority of boys, this takes place between the ages of twelve and thirteen. We find that girls at this later age begin to look like young women, while most of the boys are still immature. Hence girls experience the preadolescent period of accelerated growth and reach maturity about two years sooner, on the average, than boys do. On the whole, boys and girls develop comparably, though girls tend to accelerate in physical growth and in social development.[2] With this classification, the Rabbis fixed the attainment of religious majority and legal status in Jewish Law at the age of twelve and one day for girls and at thirteen and one day for boys.[3]

What are the factors that contribute to woman's intelligence? Since they are complex and varied, there is no simple answer. We shall try to examine those qualities which are outstanding: reason, imagination, and intuition.

The early patriarchal societies of Orientals, Greeks, and Romans believed that a really complete and noble psyche was not to be found in woman, whose intelligence was regarded as greatly inferior to that of man. Woman, according to Aristotle, has a "sort of natural deficiency. Accordingly, woman must be regarded on a far lower level than man, her sole function being to fulfill the pleasure of men and to provide for the reproduction of the species."[4] This view, alas, has influenced man until just recently.

Although in early Judaic literature one may find similar belittlement, such as "There is no wisdom for woman except at the distaff," this was not the opinion of the preponderance of the Rabbis, in whose work we find for every derogatory statement on woman, two of praise. It is quite possible that R. Eliezer, the only Sage who made this pronouncement in reference to woman's intelligence, was echoing Philo, who said: "In general, the women are found to suffer a mental weakness. They comprehend only such things as are concrete."[5]

In general the Rabbis felt that women were very intelligent and were not to be relegated to a lower class. R. Yehudah Ha-Nasi, the editor of the Mishnah, declares that "Woman was endowed with greater maturity of judgment than man."[6] When we find a midrashic expression, "Poor is the generation whose leader is a woman,"[7] we must not interpret it as derogatory. It infers only that an exclusive involvement in public life would necessitate the surrender of her indispensable duties in the home.

Let us now turn to some of the modern psychological views on the matter.

Psychometric results of modern intelligence tests show girls to be as intelligent as boys, albeit in different ways. As shown on achievement tests, girls tend to excel in verbal ability, boys on quantitative or spatial problems. Academic grades almost universally indicate superior achievement for girls. On vocational aptitude tests, boys score higher in mechanical skills and girls in clerical pursuits and aptitude.[8]

It is now important to cite some related studies in the field. Up to and during puberty, girls develop physically and mature faster than boys. They are also less physically active and more sedentary from birth.

Girls are verbally more precocious when compared with boys. (Kagan, 1969a) This was found to be true in all cultures. (Mead, 1958) Girls begin to talk somewhat earlier than boys, to form sentences earlier, to use a larger vocabulary, and to show superior articulation. They retain a slight edge in verbal facility even as adults. This would imply that girls can communicate effectively earlier than boys. (Tyler, 1965) Girls have fewer speech and reading problems. Women are superior in tasks requiring fine hand movements and clerical skills, but their reaction time is slower. Maccoby (1966b) concluded that impulsiveness is a disadvantage for boys but advantageous for girls in role-fulfillment.

In addition to verbal precocity, at least in the United States, there is evidence that girls are advanced in a variety of ways affecting their reading skills. (Sapir, 1966) Girls learn to read earlier than boys and, in the first grade, are superior in reading readiness and achievement. (Balow, 1963)

Findings like those of Ljung (1965) suggest that there is mental acceleration in girls paralleling general physical acceleration. Quite possibly these advantages stood women in good stead in the beginning of civilization. Beard (1930) supposes that women originated culture and civilization. It is noteworthy that the Greek deity for wisdom was a woman—Athena. Even more so, the foundation of home and family is attributed in the Bible to the intelligent woman and wisdom to sisterly relationship. (Prov. 14:1; 7:4) Men are said to have an analytical (field-independent) cognitive approach, while women tend to show a global (field-dependent) one. (Witkin, Dyke, Paterson, Goodenough, and Karp, 1962)

Bennett and Cohen found strong similarities between male and female thinking (correlation of .90). However, male thinking was less intense, more self-oriented, more concerned with achievement than with love and friendship; and men preferred rough-and-tumble competition, whereas women preferred autonomy in a friendly, pleasant environment.

According to Freud, whose theories about woman originally referred to the Victorian type, the woman's lower capacity for moral strength and integrity than man's is a result of her inability to develop a strong superego of her own; she would rather adjust to and integrate the convictions of those men who had recently influenced her life.

Related to this issue, it was found that fewer girls suffer brain injury at birth. (Knoblock and Pasamanick, 1963) Based on the fact that unlike boys, intelligence in girls developed almost unaffected by maternal behavior, it has been suggested that girls are less fragile in their intellectual and physical growth. (Bayley, 1967; Bayley and Schaefer, 1964) Girls were also found to be more mature in their responses to a variety of tests, including the Rorschach, during ages five to nine. (Ames and Ilg, 1964)

There are also indications that boys and girls succeed for different reasons. Girls seemed more motivated by approval and affiliation than simply by the need for achievement. (Romer, 1975)[9]

Freud points out in his biopsychological description of women that they are intellectually less capable; and, in the psychomoral description, he assumes that they should not preoccupy themselves with mental activity since this interferes with the performance of their sexual function. In addressing the problem caused by the emancipation of women, he states that "intellectual training" may cause them to deprecate the feminine role for which they were intended. Sexuality, for Freud, is a relatively fixed datum, especially so for women, whom he conceives of as "ethically and intellectually limited by their complex libidinal development," a most divisive charge by today's standards.[10]

Jastrow remarks that women have more interest in the concrete than in the abstract. Man's intellect seems detached, nonmoral, and independent of individual character, while woman's is subordinate to her character, more personal, less abstract. This results in a lesser degree of tolerance in woman than in man. Tolerance and sound judgment generally relate to breadth rather than to depth of keenness of vision.[11]

According to Bauer, there is a certain amount of superficiality and levity that must be ascribed to the woman. Woman, despite her intelligence, cannot refrain from attaching undue importance to externals.[12]

Viola Klein points out that women tend to shun rigid rules, or abstract propositions, since they feel they can behave just as correctly spontaneously. They are restive under the rigid order which man is inclined to obey upon principle. Women also dislike the intellectual process of analysis. They instinctively feel that analysis may destroy the emotional faculties by which they are largely motivated. Philo observes that Moses calls "sense" a woman, suggesting "mind" to be a man.[13]

Intelligence of High Order and Sex Differences

When we discuss the factor of intelligence and its development, we find that almost all the copious entries in encyclopedias are for men. Ernst Kretschmer, in his studies on genius, observed that "the great women [like Joan of Arc, etc.] achieved greatness because they were 'great men.' "[14]

The question has traditionally been posed: Why are there so few women geniuses? Genius is a high-status position determined by social value judgments based on genetic and other possibilities. Man and woman adhere to different values, and male values are dominant in our culture. (Smith, 1963) For genius to result, many factors—such as individualism, recreation, energy, and education—apart from intellectual ability must interact.

Kretschmer denied that genius is hereditarily linked to masculinity. Marks held that female characteristics are essentially recessive in the production of genius. Hirsch differentiates between the artistic genius, which is dominated by instinct and the unconscious through the influence of the mother, and the scientific genius, representing objective intelligence—a genetic result of the dominance of the father.

H. Ellis found only 55 women among 1030 British geniuses, while Cattell found only 32 among the 1000 most eminent people in the world; and the majority of those women gained recognition through physical beauty, tragedy, or accidents of heredity. Ellis concluded that women were the stable, conservative element in evolution, while man had the wider range of capacities.[15]

Experimental evidence, however, does not indicate appreciable sex differences in the area of intellectual endowment. One can easily explain male predominance here by the fact that social customs have favored men in appointments to positions of prominence. Cultural differences between the sexes in areas of expectation, education, and recognition are too varied and complex to be conclusive.

"Women," claims Mencken, "are not only intelligent, they have almost a monopoly of certain of the subtler and more utile forms of intelligence."[16] The Rabbis asserted long ago that woman possesses certain feelings which enable her much more quickly than man to recognize intuitively the character of people with whom she comes in contact.[17] Women are wiser than men because they know less—and understand more.

Helene Deutsch believes that women's intuition of other people's minds stems from an unconscious process through which the subjective experience of another person becomes one's own by association and, therefore, is immediately understood. She contends that it is the "inner perception" that women possess to a greater degree than men; the understanding of it is important because intuition, the most striking feminine characteristic, can be derived from it.[18] What we see in each intuitive experience is the emotional and unconscious reexperiencing of another person's mental state.

Ashley Montagu feels that women are, on the whole, more quick-witted than men, "because culture has forced them to develop a keen attention to small detail quite unnecessary to the male." Thus woman's intuition supersedes man's transparency, constituting a comment, possibly, on man's comparative opacity.[19]

Woman's perception is most keen, according to rabbinic observations, since "G-d gave greater understanding to woman than to man." This does not refer only to the development of her comprehension but to her actual superiority in her discernment: she can infer one thing from another more readily than man. This explains the Rabbis' appreciation of woman's counsel.[20]

Schofield found perception and apperception far stronger in women than men. Women are much sharper in observation and retention as well as in thought. Their use of mentation is more rapid within a limited range. Women are also quicker at drawing conclusions; but men, perhaps more confident.

Erikson argued that women do not develop an identity in quite the same way as men (1968). Marcia's work found that women are not supported in a search for identity, and are content to remain foreclosures (1980).[21]

When we described woman's capability for exerting influence upon man, particularly her husband, we presented only half the picture, since "women bear rule over king and beggar alike."[22]

The Rabbis relate a story concerning Alexander the Great, who, in his expeditions, reached a country ruled by Amazons. In answer to his ultimatum to surrender, they confronted him thus: "If you conquer us, what will people say? 'Oh, here we have a great king, he fights women.' This will not be to your advantage; but in case we kill you, the people will say: 'He was a king whom women killed.' " Alexander later admitted, before the entire world, that he had learned a lesson from women. When he was ready to leave their country, they presented him with a loaf of golden bread. Baffled, he asked them: "Do you eat golden bread here?" "No," they replied, "we don't, but if you desired only bread, why did you come all this distance? Have you no bread at home? Certainly you came here for the sake of gold!" When leaving the country, he engraved upon the gate of the city: "I, Alexander, the Macedonian, was a fool until I came to this country of Africa inhabited by women, and learned a lesson from them."[23]

We see that, though to wage war on woman was odious, it was not considered beneath the dignity of man to take counsel from her. Her thought is different from his, acting upon man as a stimulant or inspiration.

Before the Revelation to the people of Israel on Mount Sinai, the Lord commanded Moses: "Go and speak to the daughters of Israel as to their willingness to receive the Torah, for it is the nature of men to follow after the mind of the women."[24]

Another laudatory instance of woman's counseling ability may be cited in the case of the great Sage R. Eliezer ben Azariah. When he was approached by the elders of Palestine, who wanted to elect him their Nasi, he replied: "I want to go and take counsel with my wife . . ." In fact, the Rabbis actually advised, "If thy wife is short [beneath you in intellect], bend down and listen to her."[25]

Imagination depends on the power of the mind to build up mental images and project them into the future, even as memory images are projected into the past. Reason, imagination, and calculation are inextricably interwoven in a woman's makeup. Besides these three factors, woman is endowed with persistence. Woodworth showed that persistence is an important part of intelligent behavior. It is probably the same as the mastery of the self-assertive instinct. Once woman's mind is set, she knows no doubt. She may still have fears, though, and display shyness. She does not doubt what she wants, although she sometimes hankers for what she is not sure she ought to have. Woman is pertinacious, as revealed by her assiduity and her signal capacity for work.

There appears to be a certain singleness of purpose in woman, which admits of no compromise. While man, for the sake of convenience, may prefer the spiraling approach of "reasoning out" all the possible consequences before acting, woman will always take the direct route.

As far as reasoning, the Rabbis observed that when a woman considered marriage, she was quite circumspect. She was cautious about the lawfulness of her relation with her husband and was not hesitant to clarify his standing in the eyes of the Law.

As to her reputation for being calculated, on occasion the woman will not be too inquisitive. When she resents her husband and he is reported dead, (which legally sets her free to remarry since Jewish Law requires, even today, in such a case, clear circumstantial evidence of the husband's death), she will not exert herself to verify or contradict the report. She will be happy to believe it and will not scruple to remarry. She is, of course, aware of the untoward consequences should the report prove to be false and the husband returns home.[26]

Yet another case: Would a woman, if in love with another man, exert herself to confirm the news brought to her about her husband's death? Would she rush recklessly into marriage, thus laying herself open to reproof and shame should the husband return? The decision in the Talmud is that her calculative power is strong enough to control her feelings of love and prevent her from being led astray.[27]

The Tosafists offer a wonderful rationalization of the woman's behavior when in love and of her reaction when she hates. Hatred, they say, is far more absorbing than love. It robs the human faculties and leaves no chance for deliberation. Love, however, does not preclude logical thinking. When the woman is in love, her common sense tells her that she cannot be confident that she will always be loved; her beloved may some day relinquish his love. Her imagination and her reasoning work hand in hand, the romanticism of the one prudentially coming to terms with the pragmatism of the other.[28]

The prudent woman is symbolized in the following talmudic proverb: "The duck bends its head down in walking while its eyes look all around."[29] The woman talks of present matters but examines future possibilities. She is much more wary about falling in love, she is cautious and circumspect.[30]

NOTES

CHAPTER 1.

   1. Shab. 62a.

   2. Tertullian, *Apology*, L. 12.

   3. D. S. Bailey, *Sexual Relations in Christian Thought* (New York: Harper, 1959), chap. I. V. L. Bullough, *The Subordinate Sex* (Baltimore: Penguin, 1974), p. 101, Eusebius, *Ecclesiastical History*, IV, 23, 7 8.

   4. Nahida Remy, *The Jewish Woman* (New York: Bloch, 1916), p. 43.

   5. Maimonides, Yad, Ishut 13:17; Karo and Isserless, Eben haEzer 75:1.

   6. B.M. 59a.

CHAPTER 2.

   1. Zohar 5:79a.

   2. Jer. 2:2; 31:3; Mal. 1:2; Mekhilta Yetro 19:4; Exod. Rabbah 28:2.

   3. San. 39a.

   4. From the daily Kedusha deSidra in the Siddur.

   5. Tanhuma Metzora 9, Tur and Moshav Zekenim to Yetro 19:4, also Lekah Tov and Torah Shelema ad loc. 49.

   6. Ber. 5b.

   7. Elyahu Rabbah 9.

CHAPTER 3.

   1. See Freud's essay in the *New Introductory Lectures on Psycho-Analysis* (reprint ed., New York: Norton, 1964).

   2. See J. A. Sherman, *On the Psychology of Women* (Springfield, Ill.: Charles C. Thomas, 1971); also J. M. Bardwick, *Psychology of Women* (New York: Harper & Row, 1971). Compare infra "Emotionality," note 4.

   3. Clara M. Thompson, *On Women* (New York: Mentor, 1971), pp. 125–134.

   4. See supra note 2.

CHAPTER 4

   1. Max Brod, *Paganism-Christianity-Judaism* (University, Ala.: University of Alabama Press, 1970), p. 5.

   2. John Chrysostom, *Homilies sur les statues*, in vol. 3, *Oeuvres*, ed. J. Bar-le-Duc (Nantes, 1866), homily XV. Thomas Aquinas, *Summa Theologica* (New York: Benzinger, 1947), 2, pt. 2, 152, "Of Virginity," 4:153.

3. K. Horney, *The Neurotic Personality of Our Times* (New York: Norton, 1937), p.109.

4. E. Fromm, *The Sane Society* (New York: Rinehart, 1955), p. 33; *The Art of Loving* (New York: Harper & Row, 1956), p. 121.

5. Avot 5:19.

6. P. Rieff, *The Mind of the Moralist*, pp. 158–160.

7. Zohar Gen. 101b. *Tzavaat haRivash* (Jerusalem. 1948).

8. *Meor Enayim* (Warsaw, 1889).

9. Avot 3:13.

10. *Ohev Yisroel, likutim* (Jerusalem, 1962).

11. Z. Rubin, *Liking and Loving: An Invitation to Social Psychology* (New York: Holt, Rinehart & Winston, 1973).

12. T. Reik, *Of Love and Lust* (New York: Straus & Cudahy, 1957), pp. 32, 66.

13. See Taan. 4a, Yoma 54a, Exod. Rabbah 49.

14. Avot De R. Nathan 26:5; Tosefta Sot. 5:11; Zohar Gen. 133.

15. Introduction to the Zohar, letter 11; Zohar Gen. 153, Ibid. Lev. 108; Tikunei Zohar 142. See also Yer. Peah 1:1, Suk. 49b, Shek. 5:3, Lev. Rabbah 34:12.

16. Deut. 6:7, Ber. 6b, Kid. 2a, Lev. 19:9–10. Maimonides, Hilkhot Matnat Aneeyim. See supra 16.

17. Maimonides, Deut. 6:3, Lev. 19:17, Gen. Rabbah 54:3, Ber. 31a, Shab. 119b, B.M. 31a, Zohar Lev. 46.

18. Exod. 21:10 Ket. 47b; Maimonides, Ishut, 12–14; Sefer haHinukh 46.

19. Ber. 19b, B.K. 79b, Sifrei Shoftim 192.

20. Gen. 1:27; 2:21–22.

21. It suffices to mention the classic romance of R. Akiva, the shepherd, and his lovely Rachel, the daughter of the wealthy Kalba Sabua, which ended in R. Akiva's crediting her for his rabbinic knowledge and famous achievement. A similar case is reported of her daughter, who accepted betrothal from the Tanna Ben Azzai on the same condition that he should go forth to study. "As the mother did, so did the daughter." Another such case is related about the son of R. Yossi ben Zimra. See also Ket. 62b, Ned. 50a.

Isa. 54 54:5–6, 62:4–5, Hos. 2:21–22; the Song of Songs in its entirety was interpreted as a symbolic projection of the love of God and Israel.

The cherubs in the Holy of Holies symbolically represented the embrace of man and woman, and the pilgrims were told, "Behold and see how great your love is before the Almighty, as the love of man and woman." Yoma 54a, Gen. Rabbah 80, Exod. Rabbah 49.

22. Rabbenu Joseph Bekhor Shor, *Perush al haTorah*, I (Jerusalem, 1956), p. 32. Nachmanides, commenting on Gen. 29:30, "And he loved Rachel more than Leah," states as follows: The reason why Scripture mentions that Jacob also loved Rachel more than Leah is that it is natural for a man to have more love for the woman with whom he first experienced physical love, as the Sages stated: "Woman makes a firm commitment only to he who marries her first" (San.

22b). Thus Jacob's loving Rachel more than Leah was unnatural. This is the sense of the word *gam* ("more") in the text.

23. Kedushat Levi in the name of the Maggid R. Baer of Mezritch (Jerusalem, 1958), p. 53.

24. Rabbi A. J. Heschel of Apt. *Ohev Israel, likutim*, pp. 302–3.

25. S. Y. Agnon, *Days of Awe* (New York: Schocken, 1948), p. 18.

26. Sifra Kedoshim 19:18; compare Shab. 31a, Avot. 3:18.

27. Fromm, op. cit., pp. 4–5, 47.

28. Avot, 4:1.

29. Yer. Ned. 9; see Pnei Moshe ad loc., Kuzari 3:9.

30. Shab 31a.

31. San. 27b, Sheb. 39a.

32. Gen. 9:5, B.K. 91b, San. 57a. See also S. Ykarim 11:15.

33. Avot 1:14; compare San. 9h, Yeb. 28b, and Mekhilta Beshalah.

34. Avot De R. Nathan 12:7, 16; compare Shab. 151b, ibid. 6:1.

35. Shab. 31b, Yoma 86a, Mekhilta Beshalah 15, Eliyahu Rabbah 28.

36. B. Stendhal, *De l'Amour*. (Paris, 1853).

37. Baeyr haHasidut, Sefer haBeSHT, ed. E. Steinman (Tel Aviv), p. 305.

38. Yadaym 3:5; Songs Rabbah 1:10, 2:13; Tanhuma Tetzave 5; see Rashi Ber. 57b. s.v. *Shir* and to Songs 1:1.

39. Sefer Hasidim 953, 1096.

40. Martin Buber, *I and Thou* (New York: Scribner's, 1943), p. 154.

41. Yeb. 62b.

42. Ruth Rabbah 6.

43. Pirkei De R. Eliezer 32. This phenomenon was reflected in the biblical story of Abraham's son Isaac, who after his mother's death brought the young Rebecca "into his mother Sarah's tent, and took Rebekah, and she became his wife, and he loved her and Isaac was comforted for his mother" (Gen. 24:67). The biblical exegetes Ibn Ezra and RaShBaM comment on the literalness of the Hebrew text *haohela—Sarah immo*—"into the tent, his mother Sarah," that he brought her into the tent installing her as the mistress of the household, and behold, she was his mother Sarah! i.e., the young Rebekah replaced his mother Sarah in all respects, as he found in her the qualities and traditional characteristics that were his mother's. Gen. Rabbah 60:15. "A man is attached to his mother during her lifetime, and upon her demise takes comfort in his wife." Rashi ad loc.

44. *Pele Yoetz* (Wien, 1898), part 1, see full discussion on marital love, Letter Aleph, pp. 5–8.

45. *Maaseh Book*, based on Keth. 62b, Zohar Gen. 55b.

46. Emunot veDeot, On Eroticism, treatise 9, chap. 7, trans. S. Rosenblatt (New Haven: Yale University, 1958), p. 377.

47. Leone Ebreo, *The Philosophy of Love: Dialoghi d'Amore*, trans. by F. Friedenberg-Seely and Jean H. Barnes (London: Soncino, 1937), p. 28.

48. San. 1056 based on Prov. 10:12.

49. S. de Beauvoir, *The Second Sex* p. 605.

50. Ibid., p. 609.

51. San. 7a.

52. Deut. 4:4, 11:22, 30:20, where the same term *dbk* is employed in connection with man's cleavage to God, compared to man's love for woman in Gen. 34:3.

53. Avot 5:16, Avot De R. Nathan, end of chap. 40.

54. Zohar Exod. 216a.

55. Buber, op. cit., Chap. 3.

56. Sotah 17a, B. M. 59a, Hul. 84b, (RaBaD. Introduction to Ba'alei haNefesh. R. Eliezer Papo advises the husband as follows: It is part of love that he should not wander long distances for beside the harm he does to himself, there is personal pain for his wife, "for love is as strong as death." For when her husband is separated from her, she is an unfortunate, living a life of sorrow and at least he should try to console her with a letter to strengthen the bonds of love. And if he has the means, he should send her presents and desirable objects from time to time to make her happy and to ease her sorrow. See loc. cit.

57. San. 22a

58. Yeb. 63b, Ber. 32b.

59. See N. Remy, *The Jewish Woman*, pp. 54–44.

60. To a questionnaire "on the essence of love beyond the realm of sex," Freud answered, "My dear Sir: It is quite impossible for me to fulfill your request. Really, you ask too much. Up to the present I have not yet found the courage to make any broad statements on the essence of love, and I think that our knowledge is not sufficient. Very truly yours, Freud" (quoted in T. Reik; *30 Years With Freud*, pp. 175–76).

CHAPTER 5

1. Cowley, *The Aramaic Papyri* (Oxford 1923).

2. Yeb. 63a, Ned. 74a; man receives a wife according to his own actions, Sot. 2b.

3. Sot. 2a, Nid. 30a.

4. Sanh. 22a.

5. Gen. Rabbah 68:4, compare Zohar Bereshit 89a—"God creates new worlds constantly. In what way? By causing marriages to take place."

6. Sefer Hasidim (13th c.), 19.

7. Mencken, op. cit., p. 87.

8. Meg. 27a.

9. Gen. 2:24, Rashi ad loc. See also Pesikta Hadeta (ed. Yelinek 6), Zohar 13:12. Nachmanides (ad loc.) observes that a major difference between the animal and the human kingdom consists in the fact that "the cattle and the beasts have no attachment to their females, but the male will copulate with any female he finds who will bear his children, but the female of the man was 'bone

of his bones and flesh of his flesh' and he cleaved unto her and she clung to him as his own flesh, and he wished to have her continually with him. And as this was the case with Adam, so was his nature implanted in his offspring, so that the males among them should cleave to their wives. Leaving father and mother, he looks upon his wife as though he and she were one flesh. . . . Thus, man should leave the kinship of his father and his mother and his female relatives, and he should see to it that his wife is closer to him than they are."

10. Yeb. 59a, compare San. 58a, Exod. Rabbah 1:14 and 18. The monogamous family had long been the general rule, even before it was formally accepted by the Jews of Northern Europe about the year 1,000. This, indeed, was taken much more seriously than by the Christian neighbors, where even wife beating was quite customary and permitted by Canon Law during the twelfth and thirteenth centuries. In the Judengasse, adultery, concubinage, and prostitution were a rare phenomena. The Rabbis codified in fact that "such behavior is a thing not done in Israel" and such practice serves as justifiable grounds for divorce, for "nowadays all Jewesses are women of surpassing merit, and are to be regarded with honor and respect since they are credited with the purity and warmth of domestic life. They are the dispensers of education, charity, and hospitality." Mordekhai to Pes.108a and Keseph Mishnah Hametz uMatzah 7, 8 and Rama O.H. 472, 4.

11. Avot De R. Nathan 2, 5a.

12. Code of Hammurabi #145 and #146.

13. At times distinction is made between wife and concubine (Gen. 30:4), pilegesh, amma are other terms used synonymously for "concubine." There is no strong Semitic etymology for the word pilegesh; see J. Hastings Dictionary of the Bible. Its form suggests a Greek origin (Latin pellex). See Ibn Ezra, who interprets pilegesh as meaning "half-woman" (in status). The term was originally applied to a foreign slave-concubine. References in Gen. 35:22, Judg. 19:1, 2 Sam. 15:16, 20:3, suggest that the pilegesh was a second-class individual and lax in morals. The wife's claim (Gen. 21:10) that a servant's son held no share in inheritance was never sustained by the later Mosaic law. All of a man's acknowledged offspring were legitimate regardless of the mother's status. The case of illegitimacy involved the offspring of an adulterous or an incestuous union (Deut. 23:3; compare Lev. 18 and 20). Thus we read: "If a man have two wives, the one beloved and the other hated, and they have borne him children, both the beloved and the hated, and if the first born son be hers that is hated, then it shall be when he maketh his sons to inherit all that he hath, that he may not give the son of the beloved first born precedence, but he shall acknowledge the son of the hated for the first born, by giving him a double of all that he hath" (Deut. 21:15–18).

The wife was the husband's favorite, she would enjoy superior consideration and wield greater influence over her husband. Her children's claim to their father's inheritance was substantially larger than a concubine's offspring (Gen.

21:10). Slavegirls who became concubines remained the property of their mistresses (as in the case of Hagar).

In a polygamous family, each mother and her children formed a subfamily. Unlike the Assyro-Babylonians, the management of each subfamily and the early education and training of the children was done mostly by the mother. There also exist situations contrary to the above mentioned, where sons of concubines rank as ancestors of the tribe (Jacob's sons) Exod. 1:2, 4, Num. 2:2–32). In Graeco-Roman culture there was no difference of legitimacy between sons of wives and sons of concubines. Compare Gen. 21:10.

14. Samuel's father had two wives, one of whom was barren (1 Sam. 1:2). According to 2 Chron. 24:3, the priest Yehoyada had chosen two wives for King Joash. It is hard to say whether bigamy of this kind, referred to in Deut. 21:15–17 was very common. See also Otzar haGeonim to Yebamot, ed. Levin, p. 156.

15. Pirkei De R. Eliezer 32; see Yeb. 61b, Zohar Gen. 136; compare Is. 45:18. Tekanot deRabbenu Gershon Meor haGolah, Ginzburg Ms., tekanah 2.

16. Kid. 41a, Yeb. 107a, B.M. 59a, Responsa Asheri 42:1; compare Yeb. 62b.

17. "Any man who has no wife is no proper man." Yeb. 63a, Sanh. 22a–b, Zohar Gen. 55b on Gen. 5:2; also Shevet Mussar 24. In early Hindu custom a wife completes a husband and is half of his self. *Brahadiranyanyaka Upanisad,* I, IV, 17; *Satapatha Brahmana,* V, 2, 1:10.

18. Tradition attributes to woman the following qualities; that she prevents her husband from sinning, that through her, he ratifies his obligation to increase and multiply, she raises the children, she helps him always and as a result he is free to study the Torah and to engage in the fulfillment of the commandments, and she aids him also in the service of the Creator. Ber. 17a.

19. Parsons and Bales, *Family, Socialization and Interaction Process* (Glencoe, Ill., 1955), pp. 9, 16–17.

20. Yeb. 63a, Ber. 25a, Eccles. Rabbah 4; a woman is her husband's fortress, Recanate, Taamei haMitzvoth. The mutual completion and fulfillment of man and woman is expressed by R. Samuel Bar Unya in the name of Rab. Woman, before marriage, is an unformed being (i.e., of undetermined character) and concludes a covenant only with him who transforms her into a useful entity. Sanh. 22b. See Maharal's interpretation of *aizer kenegdo* (Gen. 2:18), as being similar and equal to man. Beair haGolah 4. p. 84. Jerusalem, 1972.

21. Yeb. 62b; Otzar Midrashim, ed. Eisenstein, p. 224, and Eliahu Zuta 9; for mutual respect see Otzar haGeonim, ed. Levin, p. 425. And even though a woman is obligated to subordinate to her husband, nevertheless he should not treat her as one of the maidservants but treat her as the house mistress and be subordinate to her to fulfill all the conditions of his obligation to her. Sefer haHayim by R. Hayim, brother of Maharal of Prague.

22. B. M. 59a, Hul. 84b, Yeb. 62b. "Said the Rabbis: He who has no wife is denied five things: He lacks blessings, life, joy, support and good." See Midrash Shochar Tov 2.

23. Maimonides, Yad, Mamrim 6:6, re: Kid. 30b; Sot. 44a; compare Zohar Hadash Gen. 1:4b. On the equality of sexes, see R. Ezekiel Landau, NodabiYehuda, II, Even haEzer 45; also Resp. Giveat Pinehas, 3.

24. Zohar Gen. 122, compare Gen. Rabbah 8; "What is love? The inclining and joining of two hearts together." Yedayah Bedershi in Mivhar haPeninim.

25. Meg. 5b; "All know for what (purpose) a bride is brought into the bridal chamber." Keth 8b.

26. Pes. 113b.

27. Shab. 119a and 133b; Deut. Rabbah 1:3.

28. All unions between the sexes that are repellent to the finer feelings of man, or would taint the natural affection between near relations, are sternly prohibited. Primary prohibited marriages are (a) blood relations; mother, sister, daughter, granddaughter, father's sister and mother's sister; and (b) cases of affinity, the wives of blood relations and of the wife's blood relations. These unions, whether temporary or permanent, between persons belonging to these groups are closed as "incestuous."

An impediment of consanguinity exists in the direct line between father and daughter, mother and son (Lev. 18:7), father and granddaughter (Lev. 18:10), and in the collateral line between brother and sister (Lev. 18:9, Deut. 27:22). Marriage with a half-sister, which was permitted in the patriarchal age (Gen. 20:12), and even under King David (II Sam 13:13), is forbidden by the laws of Lev. 18:11, 20:17; marriage between a nephew and aunt, like that from which Moses was born, is prohibited (Lev. 18:12–13, 20:19). The impediment of affinity exists between a son and his stepmother (Lev. 18:8), between father-in-law and daughter-in-law (Lev. 18:15, 20:12; Gen. 38:26), between mother-in-law and son-in-law, between a man and the daughter or granddaughter of a woman he has married, between a man and his uncle's wife, between a brother-in-law and sister-in-law. Marriage with two sisters which might be sanctioned by the example of Jacob, is forbidden by Lev. 18:18.

According to Lev. 21:7, Kohanim could not marry a prostitute or a divorcee. The prophet Ezek. 44:22 adds also widows, unless they were widows of a Kohen. The rule was even stricter for the Kohen Gadol: he could marry only a Jewish virgin.

All societies have their own traditions regarding marriage between close kinship. As biblical examples, we have Nahor, who married his brother Haran's daughter; Isaac, who married his father's brother's daughter; Jacob, who married his mother's brother's two daughters; Amram, who married his father's sister; Hezron, who married a paternal second cousin; Rehoboam married his father's brother's daughter. See Tosefta Kid. 1. Hebrew law apparently permits a man to marry his niece, but definitely not a woman to marry her nephew (Lev. 20:19). In ancient Palestine and among the Phoenicians, marriages between half-siblings were both legally permitted and actually practiced.

Abraham asked Sarah to say she was his sister, not his wife, in the occur-

rences with Pharaoh (Gen. 12:15), and Abimelekh (Gen. 20:2), presupposing
that the mores of both Egypt and Gerar adjudged it a far graver crime to take the
wife of a living husband than to kill the husband beforehand. Marriage between
paternal half-siblings was legal in Israel down to the tenth century B.C.E., but
was regarded in subsequent centuries as incestuous. During the days of King
David, Amnon raped his half-sister Tamar in spite of her entreaty II. Sam.
13:12–13, 23–29. In the sixth century the prophet Ezekiel (22:11) bitterly
accuses Jerusalem of various sexual transgressions, among them union between a man and "his sister, his father's daughter." Levitical law forbids
marriage between half-siblings under penalty of death (Lev. 20:17; 18:9, 11).
The Code of Hammurabi prohibits relations with four kin: daughter, daughter-
in-law, mother, and stepmother. See E. Neufeld, *Ancient Hebrew Marriage
Laws* (1944), p. 207; S. A. Cook, *The Laws of Moses and the Code of Hammurabi* (1903), p. 100.

The Hittite Code too prohibits intercourse between near relatives. There is no
punishment for living with his stepmother after the death of his father. Perhaps
due to the fact that sons inherited their father's wives (except their own
mothers). See Yeb. 21a; O. R. Gurney, *The Hittites* (London, 1952), p. 102, E.
Neufeld, *Hittite Laws* (1951), p. 188.

Forbidden degrees were few in Greece, the practical working of the laws of
inheritance and adoption being to encourage marriage between near relatives,
and even to enforce it (Plato, *Laws* 838). According to Roman Law, the parties
must not be within the prohibited degrees of relationship *(cognatio)*. From the
time of the Punic Wars it seems to have been possible for first cousins to marry.
The Emperor Claudius married his brother's daughter by obtaining a decree of
the Senate.

29. Yeb. 59b, A man should never, in searching for a wife, seek one older
than he, maybe, because of her advantage over him she will also dominate him,
and surely she will not listen to him in family matters (Yeb. 63a). Compare Avot
5:24, Kid. 30a, Pes. 113a, Nid. 45a, and Elyahu Rabbah 2.

30. Shab. 25b, B.B. 109b: a pleasant, calm personality was one of the traits
sought in a woman. "Be prudent when you marry a woman" (Rashi). Wait until
you check out her deeds so that she may not be bad and quarrelsome" (Yeb.
63a). In the same vein it is said that "two who quarrel constantly should not
marry one another (Kid. 71b). It is told of Ulla, who visited Rab Judah in
Pumbeditha, as he saw R. Isaac, the son of R. Judah grown-up and yet
unmarried, he asked him why he had not taken a wife for his son; R. Judah
replied that he did not know one of pure descent. Ulla then advised him to go
after one from a peaceful family, "as the Palestinians make a test: When two
quarrel, they see which becomes silent first and say, 'This one is of superior
birth.' Rab said: silence (peacefulness) in Babylon is the mark of pure birth."
Ibid.

Much emphasis was placed on genealogy, *yihus* (nobility), and fine upbringing. Marriage of a Kohen's daughter with a common Israelite, or a scholar's daughter with an ignoramus, was considered "not a beautiful marriage." Pes. 49a. "One could disqualify his descendants and tarnish his family's reputation by marrying an unworthy woman." Tosef. Derekh Eretz 3:2 and Kid. 70a. How stringent this concern for qualified and distinguished relationships before entering marriage during the Talmudic period is seen in an illustration of *Kezazah*. When one of his brothers has married a woman who is unworthy of him (of ill-repute), the members of the family come together and, breaking a cask full of fruit in the middle of the street, say: "Brethren of the house of Israel, hear, our brother so-and-so has married a woman who is not worthy of him, and we are afraid lest his descendents will be united with our descendents. Come and take for yourself a sign (to remember) for future generations, that his descendents shall not be united with our descendents." Keth. 28b, compare Gen. Rabbah 9:4. One can easily understand, in light of the above concern for genealogical purity and worthy descent, why R. Eleazer ben Pedat advised marriage into a good family to ensure good offspring. B.B. 109b, Yer. Shab. 8:8. "One cannot compare someone who marries a 'queen' with someone who marries a simple woman." Zohar Vaykra 107.

31. Israel ibn AlNakava (1391), Introduction to *Menorat haMaor*, ed. H. G. Enelow (1932), part 4, pp. 54–55.

32. Joseph Ibn Kaspi (1297–1340), Abrahams, *Jewish Wills*, I. p. 145. See I. Al-Nakava, loc. cit.

33. Pirkei De R. Eliezer 12.

34. Sifra Lev. 19:18, Avot 2:15, 2:17. One should not marry with the intention of later divorcing his wife. Yeb. 37a.

35. Sot 17a, R. Akiva mainly poses the problem on status of woman. His attitude towards woman was classic. When it was asked, "What is wealth," R. Tarfon the rich landowner replied, "The possession of 100 vineyards and 100 slaves to work them." R. Meir said modestly, "Contentment and satisfaction with one's riches." But R. Akiva replied, "A wife who is comely in her deeds." His severity with regard to incestuous and forbidden unions which he declared void, thus making the offspring illegitimate, stems from his concern regarding infidelity and disintegration of family life. Suitability in marriage wasn't based only on compatibility and love, but also on the absence of legal and moral impediments to the union. R. Akiva continuously defended the rights of the woman and opposed the tradition of woman's inferiority before his patrician colleagues. Even when conceding that a married working woman's wages should be turned over to her husband, he nevertheless ruled that if her earnings exceed his expenses of maintaining her, the difference belonged to her.

36. Ruth Zutta, ed. Buber, IV 2, 24b; Yalkut Ruth 606. Whoever marries a woman strictly for the sake of God, it is considered as though he engendered her. Sot. 12a.

37. R. Akiva said: "He who marries a woman not suited to him violates five precepts: (1) thou shalt not avenge; (2) thou shalt not bear a grudge; (3) thou shalt not hate thy brother; (4) thou shalt love thy neighbor as thyself; (5) and that thy brother may live with thee. For if he hates her, he wishes she were dead." Avot De R. Nathan 26.

38. Pes. 49a–b.

39. Kid 70a. A man should always be careful, when contemplating marriage, to examine the woman's character; is she pedantic or bad-tempered, or calm and peaceful; for there is nothing more bitter in the world than a bad woman, but nevertheless, he to whom (such a woman) fell should be tolerant as much as possible and leave room for peace. R. M. Meiri to Yeb. 63a.

40. Kid. 49a, Yeb. 63a. R. Papo advised deliberation in taking a wife (Yeb. 63b): careful selection and investigation of background and personality. In the case of a young levir and an old widow, or the reverse, he is told, "What would you do with an old woman? Go to one who is of the same age as yourself and create no strife in your house" (Yeb. 44a). The Rabbis understand the verse, "Profane not thy daughter, to make her a harlot" (Lev. 19:29) as referring to one who marries off his (young) daughter to an old man (Rashi: for since she won't accept him she will cheat on him) (San. 76a). Compare also Elyahu Rabbah. "Whoever wishes his wife's death so that he may inherit her, in the end she will bury him." Ben Sirah 7:25; See also Bek. 48b, Kid. 70a, Pes. 49a and 112b, Ber. 34b, Nid. 70b, Mishnah Kid. 1:7, Num. Rabbah 3:4, Elyahu Zutta 3, 10; Midrash le'Olam, Zohar Tissa 52a.

One was encouraged to "acquire" a scholar for his daughter, even if one has to pay out all the money he possesses. For marrying the daughter of a scholar will bring forth scholarly children, exemplified by good winegrapes with good winegrapes. Yalkut Yithro 268. Conversely, claims the Zohar, "whoever is meritorious and marries an intelligent woman is rewarded with everything (Zohar Lev. 52).

41. Tana deBei Elyahu 9, Sot. 12a, compare Elyahu Zutta 3.

42. Spinoza, *Ethics*, IV, Appendix 20. For the custom of betrothal in early Israel, see Gen. 24:67, 29:15–21; 1 Sam. 18:17–19, 18:26–27. Legal texts show that engagement was recognized custom with juridical consequences, similar to the state of marriage. According to Deut. 20:7, a man who is engaged, though not yet married, is excused from going to war.

43. Yeb. 64b, Yalkut Yithro 268; compare Sot. 27a. Hereditary and physiological differences or other anomalies were other important factors one ought to consider. "A man should marry a woman who is fit for him, since the sons follow the mother and the daughters follow the father" Pesikta Zutta, Tazria. "He who wishes to take a wife should inquire about her brothers . . . most children resemble the brothers of the mother" B.B. 109b–110a. "A man should not take a wife either from a family of epileptics, or a family of lepers (Yeb. 64b)." "Said Resh Lakish: An abnormally tall man should not marry an

abnormally tall woman, lest their offspring be like a mast. A male dwarf should not marry a female dwarf, lest their offspring be a dwarf of the smallest size. A man abnormally white-complexioned should not marry an equally white-complexioned woman lest their offspring be excessively white-complexioned. A very dark complexioned man should not marry an equally very dark complexioned woman lest their offspring may be pitch black" (Bek. 45b). "And Joseph was of beautiful form and fair to look upon, because Rachel was of beautiful form" (Gen. Rabbah 8). R. Akiva said, "A son resembles his father in five ways: build, strength, wealth, knowledge, and life span." The Rabbis say when the son matures, everything depends on his actions, etc. (Eduy. 2a, Tosef.1:10).

44. B.B. 109b; see Num. Rabbah 1:5; compare Sefer Hasidim No. 1097 regarding marrying into a family of pure, kind, and honorable proselytes as preferable to marrying into a Jewish family but lacking such qualities.

45. See Gen. 24:57; Keth. 102b, and Gen. Rabbah 60.12. However, in Greek and Roman cultures neither bridegroom nor bride had much voice in the selection of a partner. The parents arranged the match often with the aid of a match-maker.

Parental guidance and consent to a shiddukh was always the traditional norm. The Jewish ethos requires of a father that he see to it that his child find a proper mate. Joshua, the High Priest, was punished, according to tradition, because he did not object to his son's improper marriages (Kid. 29a–30b and Ket. 52b; see San. 93a).

In thirteenth century Spain we hear R. Solomon ben Adrat "Praise the Almighty that in these areas our generation is moral and the daughters of Israel are chaste so as not to take for husband those whom they might fancy without the consent of their father." (Resp. of RaShBa I, 1219). We hear a similar echo in the 15th century Germany from R. Moses Mintz (Responsum 98). And yet, halakhah did offer the young the freedom of their matrimonial choice overriding their parental objections. Such was the rule by R. Solomon ben Adrat in thirteenth-century Spain and by R. Joseph Kolon (1420–1480) in Italy (Responsum 272, erroneously attributed to Nachmanides and Resp. of R. Joseph Kolon 164:3), and R. Elijah Kapsali, based on the Maharik, see H. H. Ben-Sasoon in Sefer Zikaron le-Gedaliah Allon (1970), pp. 278–283. See also Resp. of TaShBatZ, III, 130, 5, and R. David Pardo in Mikhtam le David, 32. For an opposed view see R. Naftali Zvi Berlin in Meshiv Davar 1–2, 50. For a more detailed discussion on this subject see G. Blidstein, Honor Thy Father and Mother (New York: Ktav, 1975), pp. 85–94. Thus, R. Moses Isserles of Cracow rules that a son is not obliged to listen to his father who objects to his son's woman of choice in marriage (Yoreh. Deah, 240:25 gloss).

46. Kid. 29b, Avot 5:21.

47. Kid. 30a, Avot 5:21. The age of eighteen is the proper age for marriage. "He who is twenty years of age and is not married spends all his days in sinful

thoughts," Kid. 29b; the conclusion in the Gemara is that between sixteen and twenty-two, according to others between eighteen and twenty-four is what we mean by "youth," and that is the period when one is obligated to marry. Kid. 30a. For girls, the age after twelve years and a half, *bogeret*, was the proper for marriage. Pes. 113a. A case in point is related of Justinia, the daughter of Asuerus the son of Antonius, who once appeared before Rabbi Judah and said to him: "At what age may a woman marry?" "At the age of three years and one day," he told her. "At what age is she capable of conception?" "At the age of twelve years and one day," he replied. "I (she said to him) married at the age of six and bore a child at the age of seven; alas for the three years that I have lost at my father's house." Nid. 45a. Similar cases of birth at the age of seven and eight are recorded in medical literature as having occurred even in our days. R. Hisda states: "A woman who marries under twenty years of age begets till sixty; (at) twenty, begets till forty; (at) forty she needs a miracle to conceive." B.B. 119b.

48. Kid. 30a to Deut. 4:9.

49. Kid. 29b–30a; Yoma 72b; see Yeb. 63b.

50. Keth. 62a.

51. Yad. Deoth. 5:11, based on Sot. 44a.

52. Ben Sirah, 7:23–25, Lev. Rabbah 21.

53. Sanh. 76a, re: Deut. 29:19.

54. Mishnah Kid. 2:1, compare Pes. 113a. See Nid. 13b, "Men who are frivolous with young girls are responsible for the delay of Messiah." see Rashi ad loc.

55. Shab. 150a. See I. Abraham, *Jewish Life* (London, 1932), p. 193, based on Talmud Kid. 13a, also Israel Halpern, *Takanot Medinat Mähren, 1650–1748* (Jerusalem, 1952), pp. 54–55.

56. Rab ordered chastisement (*makkath marduth*) of any person who betrothed a woman by cohabitation without preliminary negotiation, regarding such an act as immoral. Yeb. 52a. See Resp. Tzitz Eliezer 13, 78 and RaMa Y.D. 140–141, Resp. Noda Be Yehuda II, E.H. 46, Resp. Torah 266 and Sefer haMeorot haGadolim relating to the Hafetz Hayyim shiddukh.

57. Keth. 102b, Kid. 41a. See Gen. 29:15–30; 1 Sam. 18:25–27; Josh. 15:16; Judg. 1:12. (Hittite law contained similar provisions). In some cases the girl's consent was obtained, in others it was complete disregarded. Laban asked Rivkah for her personal wish (Gen. 24:51, 57:8). The Manalul and some other tribes of the Hadramaut in Southern Arabia required only the consent of the girl herself while the father expressed no opinion.

58. See supra note 42.

59. Kid. 41a.

60. B.B. 168a. "No man drinks out of a cup unless he has first examined it." Bek. 85b.

61. Exod. 20:17. Moreover, in Deut. 21:13, 24:1, "to marry a wife" is expressed by the verb *ba'al*, the root meaning "to become master."

62. *Mohar* is mentioned only three times in the Bible: Gen. 34:12; Exod. 22:16; 1 Sam, 18:25, the same custom is found in the Mesopotamian Code of Hammurabi, J. B. Pritchard, *The Ancient Near East* (Princeton, 1958), pp. 159–161.

63. Keth. 82b, 11a; Yer. Git. 3:2.

64. "A woman cannot be acquired by less than a *perutah*'s worth." Kid. 12a, 13a: Keth. 82b, 39b and Tosaf. ad loc.; Keth 84a and Tosaf. 97b, Git. 49b.

65. M. Gaster, *Maaseh Book*, vol. I (Philadelphia: Jewish Publication Society, 1934), pp. 83–84.

66. Keth. 57a.

67. R. de Vaux, *Ancient Israel*, (New York, 1961), p. 19. Evidence of a fratriarchate society has been found among the Hittites and Hurrites, whose influence on the customs of Aram Naharaim is a strong probability.

68. Compare Gen. 38:8–19, Ruth 2:20, 3:12.

69. "If a levir marries his sister-in-law on account of her beauty, or in order to gratify his sexual desires, or with any other ulterior motive, it is as if he infringed the law of incest" (Yeb. 39b).

70. Ibid. 54a, B.M. 74b, Taan 24a.

71. L. M. Epstein, *The Jewish Marriage Contract* (New York, 1927), pp. 92–93. See Mishnah Keth. 78a.

72. Ibid. *Pilgrims in a New Land*, 1948, p. 255. Avot De R. Nathan (ed. S. Schechter) 10a, Erub. 18b, B.B. 75a, Pirkei De R. Eliezer, ch.12. According to Maimonides the act of *Hachnasat Kalah* is enjoined by the command "Thou shalt love thy neighbor as thyself." (Lev. 19:18) Nachmanides (on Deut. 6:18) relates it to the biblical verse "And thou shalt do that which is right and good in the sight of the Lord" (Deut. 12:28).

73. Mishnah Peah 1:1; Shab. 127a; See Suk. 49b. J. D. Eisenstein, *Otzar Israel*, 1911, 6, p. 283; Grunwald, "Statuton," *MGJW*, XO, 31 no. 77.

74. Bez. 36b: Resp. of R. Moses Isserles, ed. Siev (Jerusalem, 1970), no. 125, pp. 488–495.

75. Karo, Eben haEzer Kethuboth 66: 3.

76. One who refuses to feed his wife must give her a divorce and give her a ketubbah. Keth. 63a; see Yeb. 20a, Git. 12a.

77. Kid. 2b.

78. Taan. 26b. The fifteenth of month of Ab (August) was a feast instituted by the Rabbis also to celebrate the reentry of the tribe of Benjamin into the Jewish nation through marriage (see Judg. 21:23, and Taan, 26b). Said the Yud haKadosh (The Zaddik of Pshizche): "The reason that the Talmud compares the fifteenth of Ab to Yom Kippur is as follows: The 15th day of Ab commemorates the granting of permission for marriage between the various tribes of Israel, and the sins of the young people are forgiven on a wedding day, as on Yom Kippur" (J. K. K. Rakotz, *Niflaoth haYehudi*, 1908, p. 67).

79. See Deut. 22:13–19, 22:28–29; Exod. 22:16; compare Erak. 15a; and 40b. See Maimonides, Yad, Naarah Betulah 2:5; also L. M. Epstein, *Sex Laws and*

Customs in Judaism (1948), p. 154–7, 182–7; and R. Patai, Sex and Family in the Bible and the Middle East, pp. 66–70 on virginity and the ceremony of the blood-stained garment amongst Oriental Jews and Arabs. The Moslems for this reason made their wives and daughters wear veils in public, while the Hindus celebrated the wife's purity as the main theme of their religious epic, the Ramayana.

See further Sifrei, Deut. 22:21, Rabbinic protection was extended to the girl in a case where her virginity was in doubt. The girl's testimony that the loss of her virginity was a result of an accident or heredity was accepted. Curious tests of virginity as used in antiquity is recorded in Talmudic lore, see Yeb. 60b and Keth. 10b. The Sages also claimed that the loss of virginity through sexual intercourse in a girl below the age of three is not considered a true loss since the hymen will reappear. Nid. 45a.

The following Talmudic examples illustrate the rabbinic concern to preserve the woman's honor: There was a woman whose virginity was in question. The case came before Rabbi Yehuda haNasi. He asked her: "What happened?" She said to him: "The steps of my father's house are very high and the hymen was destroyed." And Rabbi believed her, Keth. 10a, Yer. Keth. 1:1.

Someone came before Rabban Gamaliel the Elder and said to him; "My Master, I have had intercourse with my newly-wed wife and I have not found any blood." She said to me, "My Master, I am of the family of Dorkati, the women of which have neither blood of menstruation nor blood of virginity." Rabban Gamaliel investigated among her women and relatives and found the facts to be in accordance with her words. He said to him: "Go, be happy with thy treasure." Keth. 10b.

80. Sot. 22a.

81. Pes. 87a.

82. Pessikta Rabbati, Piska 20.

83. Keth. 7a, Jer. Keth. 1, Maimonides, Yad Ishut 10:12.

84. B.B. 92b; on canabis (marijuana) see Aruk haShalem, canabis. Kil. 2:5.

85. See supra 72.

86. Shab. 150a; Maimonides, Yad. Shab. 24:5.

87. Ber. 6b, Songs Rabbah 2.

88. Yoma 66b; T. Gaster, Holy and Profane, p. 82; See I. Holzer in Z.G.J.D.V, p. 176. Personal communication by my revered father-in-law, the late Grand Rabbi M. S. Friedman, the Boyanner Rebbe, z.t.l.

89. Maharil, 1556 ed., fol. 82b; Magen Abraham to Orah Hayim 551; 6, based on Git. 89a.

90. Sot. 49a, Tosef. Sot. 15, Sot. 49a; compare ibid. 12a.

91. Avot De R. Nathan 4. Once, as R. Tarfon sat teaching the disciples, a bride passed by in his presence. He ordered that she be brought into his house, and said to his mother and wife: "Wash her, annoint her, have her outfitted, and dance before her until she goes on to her husband's house" (Avot De R. Nathan, 41).

92. Keth. 17a; Karo, Eben haEzer 65:1; Yafe leLayv 9, Eben haEzer 21:8; Otzar haPoskim, Eben haEzer 21; 46;2.

93. Resp. Baeyer Moshe 4, 132; Karo, O. H. 529:4, Derushe haZelah, no. 23, fol. 35b, 19, Sefer Hasidim, no. 168.

94. See J. Kosman, Noheg Katzon Yosef, Hannau, 1718 based on B.B. 9:5.

95. See Git. 7a; Sot. 49b; Ket. 15b. Compare Baron, Social and Religious History, II, p. 14.

96. Exod. Rabbah 23 and 41, See Yoma 39b; Gen. Rabbah 8; Avot De R. Nathan 4.

97. B.B. 92b; compare Mishnah Berurah 75, 12 and Pithei Teshuvah, Eben haEzer 21:2 and Resp. Seridei Aysh 3:30. The veil is also discussed in Resp. MaHaRaM b. Barukh, Prag 1608, no 81. See S. Parhon in Mahberet heAruk, & dam, re: wearing the wig or sheitl and Resp. of Geonim, Asaf, 689, p. 160.

98. Rokeah 353, 355; Maharil, loc. cit., Resp. R. Moses Minz 99b; S. Yereim, 96; L. Ginzberg, R.E.J. LXVII (1914) 149f.

99. Sot. 49b, Yer. Sot. 9.

100. Git. 57a, Ber. 50b.

101. Git. 57a.

102. L. Ginsberg, On the Differences Between the Palestinian Jews and the Babylonian Jews, 25, and I. M. Guttman; Mafteach HaTalmud 3 (Breslau, 1930), p. 133. See Daat Zekenim to Gen. 38:18 that Judah betrothed Tamar by giving her a ring.

103. Yer. Bikkurim 3.

104. In Deut. 20:7 a man who is engaged though not married, is excused from going to war; Sefer haHinukh, Ki Tetze, 582. See further Ber. 16a; Suk. 25b, for being excused of dwelling in a small crowded sukkah during the seven days-wedding feast. Maimonides, Yad. Koriat Shema 4:1.

105. Pesikta de Rav Kahana, 1a; Lev. Rabbah 9. See Gen. 24:67, 29:15–21; 1 Sam. 18:17–19 and 18:26–27; Keth. 4a, See Rashi ad loc.

106. Yom, 78b.

107. Ber. 54b, Pirkei De R. Eliezer 16.

108. Tur Eben haEzer and Karo ad loc. 75:18.

109. "Both are pleased (to be married to each other) and that they be known as married people." Yeb. 107a. See Tosaf. ad loc.

110. "Before you marry, make sure you know whom you are going to divorce," claims a Yiddish proverb. Mishnah Keth. 77a–b and Tosaf. Rid ad loc. A study conducted in Los Angeles was concerned with the problem of choosing mates. The men were more concerned with esthetic and physical aspects, and the women more with intelligence and popularity with the opposite sex. R. C. Williamson, Marriage and Family Relations, p. 269. T. Reik quotes a patient saying: "A girl who has psoriasis cannot love." What she really meant is that a girl affected by a dermatological condition anticipates men not to be attracted to her, not daring to hope that the unimaginable will happen, Of Love and Lust (1967), p. 331.

111. "Because a woman is particular about herself." Kid. 11a; compare Aruk, erekh ha'in and Rashi to Keth. 84a.

112. R. B. Blood and D. M. Wolfe, Husbands and Wives (New York: Free Press, 1960), p. 81.

113. "It is better to sit together than to sit alone." Keth. 118b. "More than the man desires to marry does the woman desire to be taken in marriage." Yeb. 113a, compare Ben Sirah (Schechter ed.) 36:21; Zohar Exod. 12. Similarly the Hatam Sofer taught his daughters talmudic Aggadah.

114. M. Gray, The Normal Woman (New York: Scribners, 1967), p. 187.

115. Keth. 75a; See Kid. 79a; compare I. Lepp, The Psychology of Loving (New York: New American Library, 1963), p. 49.

116. Shab. 33a.

117. F. Caprio, The Sexually Adequate Female (New York: Citadel, 1953), p. 25.

118. E. Chesser, Love and the Married Woman (New York: Putnam, 1969), p. 165.

119. Sot. 10a.

120. "The wife of man is called 'Yonah' pigeon—Ber. 56a, Ibid 17a like a dove, it is not the thought of woman to attach herself to many men." M. Gaster Sefer haMasiyoth No. 112; Pes. 87a; Yebamoth 107a; Tanhuma Naso 2a. When a wife has stolen, and brings food to the thieves, she does so out of fear; this is in no way an indication of faithlessness to her husband. Keth. 51b.

121. M. Ruitenbeek, Psychoanalysis and Female Sexuality (New Haven: College and University Press, 1966), p. 53. A husband is expected to support his wife in a more expensive style as he grows more prosperous, while parental support of children does not increase with the affluence of the parents. Karo, Eben haEzer 73:6.

122. Keth. 70b.

123. Keth. 71b; compare Exod. Rabbah 35:5; N. W. Bell and E. F. Vogel, The Family (New York: Free press, 1968), p. 29. Menachem Recanate sees a wife as "a protective wall to her husband."

124. T. Lidz, The Person, p. 413; R. O. Blood, Jr., and D. M. Wolfe, op. cit., pp. 83, 101–102.

125. Ned. 73b. Rashi and Tosaf. ad loc.; Yeb. 89a, see RaN (ad loc.), Yalkut Shoftim 247:42.

126. Keth. 86b; Lederer and Jackson, The Mirages of Marriage (New York: Norton, 1968), p. 112.

127. Yer. Keth. 9. The manner to avoid arguments at home is thus: A husband should not be so particular about household expenditures as to make his wife account for each penny, instead consider woman's sensitive nature, Pele Yoetz on Ahavah.

128. Ned. 91a. See RaN ad loc., Keth. 22a and B.M. 3a.

129. Avot De R. Nathan 7.

130. Bek. 35b, see Ber. 24a; H. Jenner and M. Segal, *Men and Marriage* (New York: Putnam, 1970), pp. 145–6.

131. K. Menninger, *Love Against Hate*, p. 74.

132. See Ber. 62b.

133. B. M. 75b, Bez. 32b.

134. Erub. 41b, Yeb. 63b, San. 100b.

135. Ibid., compare Tanhuma 59b.

136. Yeb. 63a.

137. See Rashi Kid. 30b, "*reshus*", Maimonides Commentary to the Mishnah Kid. ad loc., ShakH to Yoreh Deah 240:17, Maimonides, Yad, Ishut 15, 20, Merorat haMaor 3, 6:4, 2.

138. Massekhta d'Amalek 11 to Exod. 18:7, ed. Horowitz-Rabin, p. 193. See Yalkut Shimeoni to 1 Sam. 24:11; (based on Mishnah Sot. 9:15), Keth. 61b; and Karo S. A. Yoreh Deah 240:24, BakH and ShakH ad loc., note 22.

139. M.K., 20b and 26b; Seder Eliyahu Rabbah ed. M. Friedmann, 24, p. 135, Sefer Haredim, chap. 5.

140. Cited by Nahmanides to Hullin 63a (ed. S. Reichman, p. 128), Reshit Hokhma; Hupat Elyahu 4, see Yeb. 117a.

141. Mishnah Yeb. 15:7, see Yeb. 117a–b; 118a.

142. See R. Meir of Rothenburg, Responsum 81, ed. M. Bloch quoting a gaonic responsum by R. Paltoi (9th c.) of Pumbedita based on Keth. 61a.

143. Resp. R. I. Alfasi no. 235 (ed. W. Leiter, p. 65a); Teshuvot haGeonim, Harkavy, no. 134. Karo, Eben haEzer, 74, 10. See further Maimonides. Yad. Ishut 13:14. Magid Mishneh ad loc. See also Resp. Maimonides II (ed. Blau) no. 234. For other cases in this matter see G. Blidstein, *Honor Thy Father and Mother* (New York: Ktav Publishing, 1975), pp. 102–105.

It is assumed that a father will find more security in his daughter's house than in his son's, in the belief that a son-in-law would show more hospitality than a daughter-in-law. (Erub. 86a; See also Keth. 61b, where a daughter-in-law is not obliged to serve her in-laws).

In a case where a wife fled her home blaming her mother-in-law and not her husband for having abandoned the domicile, the RaShBa granted her the right to support (Responsa IV, 168).

144. Resp. RaShBa, IV, 168 Karo, Yora Deah 240, 24 and Birkei Yosef, *loc. cit.* 22.

145. Pele Yoetz, I., letter Kaph. Exemplary filial concern and ideal solicitousness as a Jewish model is recorded in the Talmud. The mother of R. Tarfon went walking in the courtyard one Sabbath day. Her shoe tore and came off. R. Tarfon came and placed his hands under her feet, and she walked in this manner until she reached her couch. Once when he fell ill and the Sages came to visit him, his mother said to them: "Pray for my son, R. Tarfon, for he serves me with excessive honor!" They said to her: "What did he do for you?" She told them what had happened. They responded: "Were he to do that a thousand

times he has not yet bestowed even half the honor demanded by the Torah." (P. Peah 1:1, compare Midrash Aseret ha-Dibrot in Bet HaMidrash (ed. A. Yellinek), I, p. 76).

146. Yeb. 63b, B.B. 145b.

147. B.M. 59a, Yeb. 62b, Hul. 84b.

148. Yeb. 63b.

149. Saadyah Gaon The Book of Beliefs and Opinions, chap. VII, p. 377, similarly R. Yehuda ibn Tibbon, 12th century, urges man to "honor your wife to your utmost capacity."

150. See Israel Abrahams, ed., Hebrew Ethical Wills (Philadelphia: Jewish Publication Society, 1926), part 1, p. 41. See B. M. 59a.

151. Israel Al-Nakawa, Menorat haMaor, ed. H. B. Enelow (New York: Bloch, 1932), Introduction, part 4, pp. 53–55.

CHAPTER 6.

1. M. M. Brayer, "Medical Hygiene and Psychological Aspects of the Dead Sea Scroll Literature, Part II," Hebrew Medical Journal (English sec.) vol. 2, 37 (1946), pp. 261–265. Excessive cleanliness of a compulsive nature is seen as an extreme in Judaism and is, like other exaggerated or abusive manifestations of ritual, considered a deviation from the accepted norm. Over-concern with cleanliness indicates an early-childhood fear of the mother; it covers a fear, the fear of a wish to disobey the mother and be dirty. Severe, early toilet-training may cause enough emotional disturbance to foster a neurotic personality. See Susan Isaacs, Childhood and After (International Universities Press, 1949), p. 56.

2. Lev. Rabbah 34:3; see also Shab. 50b; Tosef. Ber. 4. S. R. Hirsch exhorts the Jew to respect his "own body as the receptacle, messenger and instrument of the spirit," Nineteen Letters (1836) No. 11, p. 112.

3. A.Z. 20b; We hear a later echo of early Jewish hygiene from George Washington; "A soldier must admire the singular attention that was paid in Israel to the rules of cleanliness." George Washington, "Instructions for Soldiers," 1777.

4. Maimonides, Yad., Tumeat Ohlin 15:12.

5. Lev. 18:28–29, Shav. 18b, Tanhuma Metzora 1:5; compare J. M. Epstein, Kitzur Shnei Luhot Haberit (1683), p. 61b.

6. Nid. 31b.

7. Yeb. 20a, Sifrei Reayh 14:21. The Rabbis described the symptomatology of menstrual cycle, regular or irregular, in detail. See Nid. 63a–63b, Avot De R. Nathan 1.

8. See infra chap. 19.

9. S. R. Hirsch, commentary to Lev. 20:18.

10. Rashi, for instance, would not hand the key of his house directly to his wife during her menstrual period. Tosaf. Shab. 13b, bimay; Nachmanides

prohibits a physician feeling his wife's pulse at such a period, Beth Yoseph Tur Y.D. 195. However, see lenient note of Isserles ad loc., 17, permitting service when absolutely in need.

11. Van de Velde, *Ideal Marriage* (New York: Random, 1973) pp. 315–316.

12. Nid. 65b; Karo, Y.D. 199:1–13.

13. See Norman Lamm, *A Hedge of Roses* (New York: Feldheim, 1972).

14. Karo, Y. D. 201:1. There is no need for unmarried girls (who are considered *niddot*) to perform *tvilah* in the *mikvah* (Resp. RiVaSH, 422, Isserles, Y.D. 183:1 and Baer Hetev ad loc.) lest they might be tempted to allow liberties to be taken. An unmarried girl is expected to maintain the same attitude of *tzniut* as a married woman.

15. Elie Faust-Levy, "A New Consciousness Among Jewish Woman," *American Zionist*, June 1974.

16. Nid. 30b; N. Lamm, op cit.

17. Nid. 3a, 16a, 64b.

18. Baraita Nid. 1.4.

19. Prof. Bela Shick of Vienna in *Wiener Klinishche Wochenschrift*, XIX, 395 (1920), confirmed by Drs. Zondek and Miller, *Journal of Pharmacology and Experimental Therapeutics*, vol. 22, no. 6 (Jan. 1924), p. 6, and Dr. D. Y. Macht (Baltimore, 1934).

20. Since the womb can become plugged with mucous and encrusted blood, owing to lack of drainage of the menstrual flow because of the womb's abnormally curved position, conception can be blocked at times.

21. Nid. 17b, 41b.

22. Shab. 64b, Keth. 65a. Maimonides, Yad. Issurei Beeah 11:19; Tur Yoreh Deah 195:9, compare Erub. 21b. All kinds of work which a woman performs for her husband a menstruant also may perform for her husband, with the exception of filling his cup, making ready his bed, and washing him. Keth. 61a. See also Shab. 13a.

23. Dr. H. N. Weinberg, Director, Mount Sinai Department of Women's Sexual Diseases, in *The Relative Infrequency of Cancer of the Uterus in Women of the Hebrew Race* (pamphlet).

A leading authority on obstetrics and gynecology, Dr. David M. Serr, Professor of Tel Aviv University Medical School, in *Israel Magazine*, 4 (Feb. 1972), p. 2, writes: "On the whole, it is correct to say medically, socially, and hygienic-wise that the couple practicing family purity ritual is healthier in some important aspects than the couple which does not practice this way of life. . . . Other possible medical complications of non-observance of family purity laws may involve infections of the male and female genito-urinary tracts." Moral and spiritual destruction results from lack of control of passion within hygienic limits. The Jewish people are most sensitive to hygiene. (Purification with water after menstruation and before intercourse is also decreed in the Koran).

24. Songs Rabbah 1, Zohar Exod. 173.

25. Pesikta Rabbati Parah, Lev. Rabbah 19:3.

26. Yoma 85b; see Ezek. 36:25, compare Tanhuma Metzora 9; Hermann Cohen, quoted in Q. Newman, *Living with Ourselves* (1950), p. 20.

27. A.Z. 20b.

28. Nid. 30b.

29. Yeb. 62b. See also Lev. Rabbah 15, Zohar 2:3.

30. The lighting of candles, according to the Rabbis, was imposed upon woman because she caused Adam, considered the final sanctification of Divine creation, to sin. Adam was considered the dough, the *hallah* of the world. Since Eve extinguished the soul of Adam, she was given the *mitzvah* of *hallah* to symbolize reparatory correction and spiritual elevation. Tanhuma Noah 1; Yer. Shab. 2:6. The Bible directs the *mitzvah* of *hallah* to Israel in general (Numbers 15:19–20). However, the Midrash gives another reason as to why hallah was entrusted to woman, because just as she kneads and causes to rise the dough preparing it for completion, so to the Lord with Adam (Genesis 2:6–7), Tanhuma ad loc. Ber. 31b and Gen. Rabbah 17:8, Sefer Matamim 112. Mishna Shab. 31b; Zohar Gen. 48b; Gen. Rabbah 17; ibid., 60:15.

31. Yer. Hallah 2, and Yer. Kid. 1:8; T.B. Hallah 4:8., compare Yer. Shab. 2:6, Bekh. 27b; Maimonides Yad, Terumot 1:22 and Bikurim 5:6; Sefer Yereim Hashalem 148.

32. Hallah 2:7, Erub. 83b; Maimonides, Yad. Bikurim 6:15; RoSH to Hallah 4.

33. See Pahad Yitzhak, *hallah*; *Encycl. Talmudit*, 15, *hallah*, pp. 266–276.

34. Gen. Rabbah 11; Shab. 25b; Yalkut Shimoni, Ki Tavo 938.

35. Eliahu Rabbah, Shabbat quoted by A. I. Sperling in *Taamei haMinhagim* (Jerusalem, 1957), pp. 124–125 (§244, 260).

36. Zohar Gen. 48b; Tikunei Zohar 16, 31; and *Menorat haMaor*, 4, p. 435.

37. Meg. 16a based on Prov. 6:23, Shab, 23b; see R. Behaye to Yetro from Shab. 23b; also Kol Bo 31 and Karo O.H. 261, 263. A special prayer is found in Siddur Otzar haTefilot (Vilna 1914), p. 295. Ber. 31b; Shab. 31b–32a.

38. Tur O.H. 263. See also Rashi Shab. 32a; *hareni*.

39. Shab. 23b and 25b; Yalkut Shimoni, Tavo 938.

40. Siddur Rav Saadyah Gaon, ed. Mekitzei Nirdamim (Jerusalem, 1963), p. 109, R.Ahai Gaon is first to mention the benediction on candles, see S. haManhig, Shabbat 17. See also Sidduro Shel Shabbat by R. Haym Tirer and Siddur haAri on Shabbat.

41. Esther 8:16, Ps. 97:11; Tanhuma Noah 1, See Rashi Shab. 23b and 25b, also Sepher Hasidim §1147 on the value of lighting many candles on Sabbath.

42. Yalkut Shimoni, Behaalotha 719.

CHAPTER 7.

1. While many authors, following Robertson Smith, believe that a matriarchal regime was the original form of the family among the Semites (queens, from the Queen of Sheba to Zenobia, occupy a prominent place in Near Eastern

history), there is no doubt that in historical time, the Israelite family is patriarchal. In marriage the husband is the ba'al, i.e., the master. The father had absolute authority over his children, even over his married sons if they lived with him (Gen. 38:24). A similar situation prevailed in early Babylonia (Code of Hammurabi 166). Not so the Egyptian family. The most important person in the family was not the father, as among the Semites, but the mother. She was the house-ruler, the focus of the family.

2. Lev. 19:3; Deut, 21:17, 22; 19:26; Num. 27:1–11; Compare Gen. 21:12; see B.K. 15a, Kid. 30b, Mekhilta Mishpatim.

In the Decalogue, the father is mentioned before the mother in regard to honour—kibbud (Exod. 20:12), while in Lev. 19:3 mother is mentioned first in regard to awe—yirah. The rabbinic explanation of the difference points to the father as the disciplining parent, while the mother is the exponent of affection and kindliness. Consequently, the child would "love" the mother, but "stand in awe" of the father. The Torah therefore commands the child to show love and reverence to both parents equally. In this context of filial duty as the proper policy for success in our interpersonal relations, the text employs the terms tirauh—"ye shall fear"—usually used in reference to God. "For dear to God is the honor of father and mother, for Scripture employs the same expressions about honor and revering parents as about the honor and reverence due [God] Himself" Kid. 30b; Pesikta Rabbati 24:2.

3. Mishnah. Kerit. 28a; compare Tanhuma Buber, Nasso, f. 16a; Hul. 84b; Yeb. 63a. See M. M. Brayer, "The Role of Jewish Law Pertaining to the Jewish Family, Jewish Marriage and Divorce," in Jews and Divorce (New York: Ktav, 1968), p. 4.

4. Every young woman should bear in mind that she fulfills her natural destiny completely only if she takes her part in the improvement and ennoblement of the human race, an ideal which even the enlightened nations of antiquity did not share. Tacitus deemed it a contemptible prejudice of the Jews that "it is a crime among them to kill any child." What lurid light these words throw on Graeco-Roman society! See Bauer, Woman and Love, II p. 257. "A woman after having given birth increases in esteem." B.K. 49a, Taan. 31a; Keth. 59b.

5. It is noted that the ideograph in Assyro-Babylonian for "mother," ma, is written with the sign of "divinity" within that used for "house" or "dwelling place"; that the Sumerians thought of her as "the divinity within the house." J. Hastings, Ency. of Religion and Ethics, 1928, V. p. 723. Compare Zohar, 50b. God is viewed not only as a father, but as a mother too ("You forgot God who brought you to birth," Deut. 32:18); see Sifre, ad loc., R. Meir's comment (ed. Finkelstein, p. 365) also Yer. Horayot 4.

6. V. Klein, The Feminine Character (Urbana, 1973), p. 48. Only maternity can bring the mental life of a woman to full flower. Through motherhood her character is matured and ennobled. Bauer, op. cit., II, p. 125.

7. H. Deutsch, *Psychology of Women* (1964), vol. II, p. 20, and T. Lidz, *The Person* (1976), p. 443.

8. Taan. 2b, Jer. Targum, Gen. 30:22. compare Ber. 60a, Zohar 1:102b.

9. T. Lidz, op. cit., p. 443.

Rashi, based on Gen. Rabbah 71:9, inferred from Rachel's condition that one who is childless may be regarded as dead. Compare Pseudo-Jonathan and Nachmanides ad loc., also Ned. 64a. Childlessness was considered only slightly better than death (ten years of childlessness was considered grounds for divorce). See Yeb. 64a. Childlessness often led to arguments between husband and wife. Num. Rabbah 10:14 recalls—"There was argument between Manoach and his wife. He said she was barren, and she replied: 'No, you are sterile, and therefore, I haven't given birth.' " Compare Pesikta De Rav Kahana 20. Exegetically speaking, Sarah really lived only thirty-seven years, from the birth of Isaac to her death, "for the years she spent as a barren woman cannot be regarded as life." See Or haHayim to Gen. 23:1. See also Ber. 51b, "Of both man and woman is it written, and God blessed them and God said unto them, be fruitful and multiply." Mishnah Yeb. 6:6; compare Yer. Ber. 35.

10. Gen. 30:14–16; Gen. Rabbah 72; See Aruk "dudayim", Ibn Ezra and Kimchi ad loc.; See infra chap. 14 Midrash Sekhel Tob and Nachmanides ad loc. Gen. Rabbah 45 cites the following concerning Sarah's failure to conceive: "And Sarai said unto Abram (Gen. 16:2). She said, 'It was not as they told me: 'she requires an amulet, she requires warmth,' but 'behold now the Lord hath restrained me from bearing.' "

11. R. R. Bell, *Marriage and Family Interaction* (1963), pp. 387, 390.

Yeb. 65b. If the husband pleads that his wife had miscarried within the ten years and she states, "I had no miscarriage," R. Ammi ruled she is believed in this case also, for if she had really miscarried she would not herself have sought to acquire the reputation of a barren woman. Compare Deutsch, op. cit., II, chapter V.

The psychological consequences of pregnancy on husband-wife relations are phenomenal. Some Rabbis say that when Jacob realized that he was victim of deception (Leah's substitution by Laban for his beloved Rachel), he was determined to divorce her. Because of the hatred directed toward her, God caused her to have children. This drastically altered Jacob's attitude, exclaiming; "Shall I divorce the mother of these children?" Gen. Rabbah 71:2.

12. Deutsch, op. cit., pp. 39–40. "A woman playing the harlot turns over in order to prevent conception . . . or makes use of an absorbent in order to prevent conception." Yeb. 35a and 94a, compare Git. 17b.

13. Yeb. 65b.

14. The wish for sons is expressed in the exegesis of "and glad of heart" "as because their wives conceived and each one bore a male child," Shab. 30a. Hastings, op. cit., VII, p. 450.

15. "All women are valiant. For all pregnant women we make a broth and a

bedstead to make them and their embryos well." Rashi Yoma 47a, and Keth. 60b. See also Sifra Beaalotha. "Many kinds of toast and nuts you prepared for the pregnant woman among them." Songs Rabbah 1:44.

An early rabbinic counsel makes the "woman responsible for her children. And if she cares for them quietly but firmly with proper training and nourishment, she will cause them to act properly and she, herself, will receive joy and great reward in this world and in the world to come. . . Therefore, a modest, God-fearing woman must take care during her pregnancy and time of nursing that her food be clean, and that she eats healthy foods. . . She must also be careful to dress properly so as not to be chilled and she should not go for a long length of time in the morning without eating. In the morning she should eat warm food and not drink cold liquor, nor should she go to unsanitary places or to places where water is poured in the morning or evening, which give a bad odor." S. Assaf, *Mekorot le-Toldot haHinukh*, Vol. 1.

Prenatal care was indeed a rabbinic concern. The Talmud states; "If a pregnant woman smelled [something enticing of the Day of Atonement], she must be given to eat until she feels restored, for there is nothing that can stand before (the duty) of saving life." Yoma 82a. "There was a woman with child who had smelled (a dish) on Yom Kippur. People came before Rabbi (questioning him what should be done). He said to them: 'Go and whisper to her that it is the Day of Atonement.' They whispered to her and she accepted the whispered suggestion, whereupon he (Rabbi) quoted the verse, 'Before I formed thee in the belly I knew thee.' (Jer. 1:5). She bore R. Johanan. There was a woman with child who smelled (a dish). The people came to R. Hanina who said to them: 'Whisper to her (that it is the Day of Atonement).' She did not accept the whispered suggestion. He quoted the verse: 'The wicked are estranged from the womb.' (Ps. 58). She bore Shabbatai, the hoarder of provisions." Yoma 82b–83a. Compare also Ruth Rabbah 5.

See Karo, O.H. 617:2–3; Keth, 60b–61a; Yeb. 80a and Nid. 24b.

16. Shab. 66a–66b. See Ber. 5b. B.K. 49a; Shab. 128b–129a. "If a woman is in confinement, as long as the uterus is open, whither she states, 'I need it' or 'I do not need it,' we must desecrate the Sabbath in her account." Nid. 17a, R. Simeon Bar Yohai stated: "There are five things which cause the man who does them to forfeit his life . . . removing one's nails and throwing them away in a public thoroughfare . . . (this is dangerous) because a pregnant woman passing over them would miscarry." Compare also B. K. 83a, Ber. 54b, Avot 5:7, Er. 41b, Sheiltoth De Rav Achai 167, Raba said: "A woman in confinement is forbidden to fast for the first thirty days." Yoma 53b, See Karo, O.H. 617:3.

17. Yeb. 65b. E. Parker, *The Seven Ages of Woman*, (London, 1950), p. 276; Chapman, op. cit., p. 241; Deutsch, op. cit., II, pp. 157–158.

18. Yeb. 65b.

19. People say; "A woman who is used to losing children is not shocked any more at the death of one of them." Yeb. 65b. See Rashi ad loc.

20. Mishnah Oholoth 7:6; Maimonides, Yad. Hilhot Rotzeah 2:6; Karo, Hoshen Mishpat 425:2.

21. "Most women give birth to the ninth month." Yeb. 119a, 36a, 37a; Yalkut Ruth 608.

22. "We may deliver a woman on the Sabbath, summon a midwife for her from place to place, desecrate the Sabbath on her account, and tie up the umbilical cord." Shab. 128b; Karo O.H. 330:1–10.

23. Yeb. 37a cites R. Nahman stating: "Our women bear at seven months . . . most women bear at nine months and a minority at seven." The duration of pregnancy varies in several references in the Pentateuch. The Midrash has it that at the time of Noah, the children were born after a few days' pregnancy, and immediately after birth they could walk and talk; they themselves aided the mother in severing the umbilical cord. Yeb. 80b; Gen. Rabbah 14:2; Nid. 38b, Gen. Rabbah 20, based on Gen. 3,16. "Every (fetus) that has (developed to the numerical value of) *harbeh*, I will multiply; i.e., a fetus that has developed for two hundred and twelve days is viable." Nid. 38a, Samuel stated; "A woman can conceive and bear only on the two hundred and seventy-first day or on the two hundred and seventy-second day, or on the two hundred and seventy-third day." Songs Rabbah 8:14.

24. Nid. 41a.

25. Tanhuma Buber, Ki Tetze 4. Compare *Universal Jewish Encycl.* Vol. II, p. 379.

26. Gen. Rabbah 20:6; compare F. L. Ilg and L. B. Ames, *Child Behavior* (New York: Harper, 1955), p. 191.

27. Sot. 12a; See also Erub. 100b and Avot De R. Nathan 1.

Benno Jacob (in his German commentary to Gen. 3:16) renders, "Great, great will I make thy pain and thy travail, in pain wilt thou bring forth children, and thy desire is unto thy husband and he ruleth over thee." This is no sentence upon woman, for the term "cursed" (*kll*) is not mentioned here. Moreover, God Himself considered man's multiplication as a blessing (Gen. 1:28), hence woman's pain and travail are inextricably part of it. The pronouncements to the woman, therefore, signify parenthetically: "Thee, I need not punish. A sufficiency of woe and suffering is thine because of thy physical being. Compare Nid. 31a.

28. Zohar Tazriah and Yalkut Jer. 309. "When a pregnant woman used to see one of them she would ask him: Prophesy what is in my womb, male or female? Compare Nid. 31b, Zohar 3.42b; Raziel haMalakh 13–14.

29. Based possibly on Keth. 61a and Sefer Zekhira by R. Zeharyah the Kabbalist (Lemberg, 1857), see Nezir Shimshon to Sukah and Moed Lekhol Hai by R. Hayim Fallagi, Izmir, p. 208, that Eve ate from the Tree of Knowledge which was an *ethrog*, and therefore when a woman bites up the *ethrog's* nipple, and utters a special prayer the sin is effaced. Tikunei Zohar 52:87; and 69:101.

30. Bek. 20b; See Thompson and Thompson, *Genetics in Medicine* (Philadelphia: Saunders, 1973), pp. 159–160.

31. Gen. 35:17, 38–28, and Exod. 1:15–21. Midwives nowadays have returned again as a full-fledged vocation, mainly in suburbia.

32. Although generally the baby was suckled by its mother, Gen. 21:7, 1 Sam. 1:22–23, 1 Kings 3:21. Sometimes a child would be entrusted to a nurse even in biblical times; Gen. 24: 59, 35: 8, Exod. 2:7–9; Num. 11:12; 2 Sam. 4:4 as was the custom in Mesopotamia and Egypt. See 1 Sam. 1:4–8, 22–23, 2 Kings 4:8–24 and Taan. 27b. Compare Sopherim 17;5, and Ber. 31b; Mishnah Keth. 59b, "a woman is to . . . suckle her child." A child must be breast fed twenty-four months, Ibid 60a. A woman suffers (through the accumulation of milk in her breasts) if she is not allowed to suckle her baby. Ibid. 61a. Compare Lev. Rabbah 14: B.M. 87a; Gen. Rabbah 53; Bek. 7b, and Yer. Keth, 5:6.

33. Yeb. 114a; "The ordinary child is in danger when deprived of his milk." Keth. 65b. Compare Mishnah Yoma 82a.

34. Nid. 9a; Yer. Yoma 5. "On Thursdays there is a fast-day of prayer for pregnant and nursing mothers so that they may not lose their babies," Soph. 17:5. In Taan. 27b the version reads "so that they may be able to nurse their babies." For the symbolic overtones of this issue see Karo, S.A. O.H. 494 and Magen Avraham ad loc. 6.

35. R. Meir said: "God does miracles with this baby. How? Before the mother gives birth her flow of blood continues. When she gives birth the liquid flows to the breasts where it becomes milk and the baby may nurse from them." Tanhuma, Tazria 5. See also Yer. Nid. 1:5. Because of the milk, the blood stops."

36. R. C. Williamson, *Marriage and Family Relations* (New York: John Wiley, 1966), p. 469. G. Dick, *Childbirth Without Fear* (New York: Harper, 1972), p. 245. Compare Is. 49:15; Sot. 12b, Songs Rabbah. 4;Yeb. 114a; Ber. 31b Pes. 112a;

37. H. Marlow, *Textbook of Pediatric Nursing* (Philadelphia: Saunders, 1977), p. 169.

38. Deutsch, op. cit., II, pp. 299, 414; B. Spock, *Baby and Child Care* (New York: Meredith, 1968), p. 72. See "Back to the Breast," *Newsweek*, November 6, 1978, p. 92.

39. Keth. 60a; Yer. Keth. 5:6. For specifications and regulations concerning mothers, see Keth. 60a–b and Maimonides Yad, Ishut 21:16. Ber. 40a, R. Judah said: "A baby does not know how to call father and mother until it has tasted the taste of grain." "And what (is the age of a child who may be regarded as independent of his mother)? About four or five." Erub. 82a.

40. The Rabbis set the problem as to whether a dam will give suck to a stranger or would she feel affection only for her own? Hul. 116b. They recorded the fact that if a dam did cast off her young, she was reminded in a peculiar way of her offspring by the placing of a handful of salt in her womb and the pain that would be caused thereby would remind her of her young. But not all species of mammals behave in the same manner. The unclean (forbidden by the dietary laws) animal will not (after giving birth) cast off its young, but if it does, it will not allow them to come near again. This tends to show that there are

some exceptions to the rule, the maternal instinct is sometimes absent in certain kinds of mammals, a fact attested today in hamsters and rats. Shab. 128b, B.B. 16b. It is known that some hamsters and rats will actually devour their young if starved. See Bauer, op. cit., II, p. 125.

41. See Tosaf. Riad.; Keth. 60b; Kid. 4 Deutsch, op. cit., pp. 332–334. See Threni, 4:10, Kid. 73b. Since mother's love and devotion to her daughter were virtues highly appreciated by the Rabbis, they posed the following question: Will a mother act narcissistically principle even in relation to her daughter, who is in dire straits, and will she always consider her own benefits first, or is her maternal instinct stronger than her selfishness, and will she give up her advantages in behalf of her daughter. This question remains unanswered. Keth. 43a and 79a.

42. Yoma. 38b. The Talmud records the story of Doeg ben Joseph, whose father died when he was a young child. Every day his mother would measure him by handbreaths (to know how much he had gained since yesterday), and would give his (extra) weight in gold to the Sanctuary. And when the enemy prevailed (during the final siege of Jerusalem) she slaughtered him and ate him. Concerning her, Jeremiah lamented: "Shall the women eat their fruit, their children that are dandled in the hands?" Lam. 2:12, 2:20; Lam. Rabbah 1:54; 4:13. Yeb. 42b; Compare Is. 49:15, 66:13;

A touching biblical story of a mother is Hagar's plight when lost in the desert: "And the water in the bottle was spent; and she cast the child under one of the shrubs (to protect him from the fierce sun). And she went and sat down over against him, a good way off, a bow-shot away; (i.e., within hearing), for she said: 'Let me not look upon the death of the child.' And she sat over against him, and lifted up her voice and wept.' " Gen. 21:15–16. See also Is. 66:13; and 2 Kings 4:19.

43. Lev. Rabbah 27:1.

44. Gen. Rabbah 26:5, also Ber. 20a. Classic rabbinics attributes to the eagle perfect self-sacrificing parenthood, so protective of its young that it bears them aloft on its wings ready to sacrifice its own body as a target to the hunters below. (See Rashi to Exod. 19:40). As a model of filial gratitude and help Philo points to the stork. (On the Decalogue, sec. 115–118, Loeb Classics, trans. F. Colson, p. 612).

45. E. Oppenheimer, The Articulate Woman (New York: Drake House, 1968), pp. 103–156. See Kid. 30a–b, Ber. 17a, Tosefta Erub. 2, Yer. Yeb. 1, Cant. Rabbah 1, Nazir 29a, Suk. 42a, Gen. Rabbah 20:6.

46. Oscar Wilde pointed out that "All women become like their mothers. That is their tragedy. No man does. That is his," from W.H. Auden and L. Kronenberger, The Viking Book of Aphorisms (New York, 1962) p. 175. See Keth. 102b, Yer. San. 2:6; "like the mother like the daugther" based on Ezek. 16:44. See infra 55.

47. Yer. Pes. 8. Maharal of Prague in Haggadah shel Pessach on arba kosot.

48. A mother will never forget her son, B.B. 36a, "When Joab heard King

David's words: 'Like a father pitieth his children, so the Lord pitieth them that fear Him' (Ps. 103:13), he expressed his astonishment that the comparison should be made with the love of a father for a child, and not with the love of a mother; mother love as a rule is considered the stronger and the more self-sacrificing." It is the nature of a father to have compassion and that of the mother to console. See Pesikta De Rav Kahana 19; Beth Hamidrash Jellinek, Heder 5, and Josephus' Story of Hannah and her seven martyred children. In the words of Washington Irving: "A father may turn his back on his child; brothers and sisters may become inveterate enemies; husbands may desert their wives and wives their husbands, but a mother's love endures through all."

49. J. D. Chapman, *The Feminine Mind and Body*, p. 114; Deutsch, op. cit., Vol II, pp. 307–308.

50. Gen. Rabbah 60:7, Pesikta Rabbati 23. The Bible likened fear and respect for parents to fear and respect for the Almighty. "It is known before the Creator of the world that a son honors his mother more than his father, but he fears his father more than his mother." Kid. 30b, Shab. 66b. Elyahu Rabbah 26, Zohar Exod. 17b, "A man's maternal descent is beyond any doubt." See Keth. 103b. Bauer, op. cit., Vol. I, p. 19.

51. Bell, op. cit., pp. 417–418.

52. S. Freud, *New Introductory Lectures on Psycho-Analysis* (1965), p. 118. However, the greater affection of the child for the mother than the father is not to be explained in terms of sexuality. The love of a child is composed of purely egotistical factors. The father is normally stricter, while the mother tends to be the source of only pleasurable moments. The love of a child has nothing more to do with sexuality than has the love of an irrational animal for its master, who, for the unthinking animal is the source of good. He not only imitates his mother but both boys and girls identify with the mother at this stage, picking up her ways of doing things, her intonations, and her likes and dislikes.

53. Gen. Rabbah 60:7. Boys will usually run to their father. B.M. 12a. See R. S. Cavan, *The American Family* (New York: Crowell, 1963), p. 474.

54. E. Fromm, *The Art of Loving* (New York: Harper, 1956), pp. 41, 43. On the mothers role in educating and guiding her child see Apei Zutrei to Eben haEzer 22, 32 and Zohar Hadash, Gen 7.2, and compare Sukkah 2b and Yoma 82a.

55. He who gives a loaf of bread to a child is to inform his mother. Betza 16a. A story is told of a woman who was disliked by her neighbor, who sent her [food for an] eiruv with her son. The woman took him, hugged him and kissed him. He returned to his mother and told her what happened, and his mother said to the woman: "You like me so much and I didn't know!" Because of this, they made peace. Yer. Er. 7:9. Compare Rashi Kid. 81b; see I. Lepp, *The Psychology of Loving* (New York: American Library, 1963), pp. 150–151.

56. Pes. 113a; B.B. 98b; Compare Rabbeinu Hananel's version with Rashbam. See Kid. 12b.

57. D'mai 3:6, Mak. 2:7.

58. "As the mother, so her daughter." Ezek. 16:44, Gen. Rabbah 80:1, Rashi Sanh. 82b, Compare Sanh. 52a; "The daughter of R. Akiva acted in a similar way toward Ben Azzai, as her mother had done toward R. Akiva. See supra 43.

59. Gen. Rabbah 84:19, 31; Tanhuma Buber, Vayeshev 10; Rashi Shab, 23b, s.v. *nafak*.

60. See Yeb. 117a; M. Balint, *Primary Love and Psycho-Analytic Technique* (1967), p. 98. Compare Ber. 56a. See Maharsha ad loc. Compare also Pes. 112a.

CHAPTER 8.

1. Sefer Hasidim, §123 (Jerusalem: Mossad haRav Kook, 1957), based on B.B. 165a, Zohar 1:202a, also Yoma 69b, Suk. 52b.

2. Keth. 13b, Yer. Keth. 1.

3. Kid. 81b; see Deut. 9:18, Taan. 14b and 22a. In Talmudic times after the "Eighteen Benedictions," each person prayed privately for whatever he desired. These prayers were called "supplications" (*tahanunim*) and one fell on his face when saying them. See Ismar Elbogen, *Der Juedische Gottesdienst*, pp. 73 ff.

4. Lev. 3:1–24, Deut. 22:22–29; It was the custom of the Aramaeans (Syrians) to have sexual relations with their virgin daughters. Sofrim 21:9.

5. Er. 13b, Suk. 52a, Avot 2:11, Tanhuma Beshalah 3.

6. Testament of Reuben 6:3, Testament of Judah 14:3, 16:1–5. Ben Sirah 9:2–9, 23:22–26, 25:23–26, 42:9–14.

7. Tosef. Sot. 5:9, Git. 90a, Yer. Sot. 1:7, and Kid. 4:4.

8. Gen. Rabbah, 9:9, Tanhuma 9:1, Yom. 69b.

9. Sot. 47a, A.Z. 5a. The libidinal drive is the strongest force in all living creatures. It is the foundation of the beautiful emotion of love. Upon it are built respect, self-control, sympathy, unity of purpose, many common desires blending gradually into real love. It is the libido that animates the struggle for existence; moves man to greater endeavors and achievements, and unites two human beings. It is the creative instinct which dominates all living things. J. Smithline, *Scientific Aspects of Sexual Hygiene in Torah Laws for the Woman* (New York, 1965), p. 22.

10. Yer. San. 7:4, Yeb. 20a, Sifrei Raay 14:21, I Corinthians 7:1–12, Revelations 14:4.

11. Ber. 5a, Zohar 1:212; Suk. 52b.

12. *The Book of Beliefs and Opinions*, trans. S. Rosenblatt (1948), pp. 371–373, 377. "Sexual relationships in marriage may also serve a moral function when they contribute to the emotional well-being of the spouses, and for these several reasons nearly all religions insist that marriage be solemnized in a religious ceremony." Kinsey, *Sexual Behavior in the Human Female* (Philadelphia: Saunders, 1953), p. 366.

13. Bahya Ben Joseph Ibn Pakuda, *Hovat haLevavot* I. Shaar haPerishut I (Lemberg, 1837). See also Maimonides, Shaarei haMussar, in Abrahams, Ethi-

cal Wills, I (Philadelphia: Jewish Publication Society, 1927), p. 113. Testament of R. Eliezer Rokeach of Mayence.

14. Kuzari III, 3:5.

15. Git. 70a, Rashi ad loc., compare Ber. 57b. "Three things weaken a man's strength; anxiety, traveling, and sexual intercourse." Lev. Rabbah 14. Compare also Otzar Midrashim 106.

16. Yad, De'ot 5:4–5, Issurei Beeah 21:9; Mishnah Commentary San. 7:4; see Yad., De'ot 2:1, 6 and 3:3; On Sexual Intercourse, ed. Gorlin (New York: Rambash, 1961) chap. II.

17. Ber. 22a, Yad. Issurei Beeah 21:2, Ibid. 4:19, Guide III:59.

18. Iggeret haKodesh 2, Kitvei Ramban by Chavel, Vol. 2, (Jerusalem: Mossad Rav Kook, 1953), p. 316. Hokhmah and Binah when united climax into death—the realization of the sublime expression of love. See Tikunei Zohar 69, 99.

19. Judah Alharizi (1170–1230) Rephuat haGevyiah, in haRophe haIvri I (1970), p. 77; Shem Tov ben Joseph Falaquera, Batei Hanhaget haGuf HaBaree—Batei Hanhagat haNefesh, III, see haRophe haIvri, 1938, 1, pp. 113–125.

20. Zohar 1:50 and 176; ibid. 3:43 and 49; See G. Sholem, Major Trends in Jewish Mysticism (New York: Schocken, 1967), p. 235.

21. Nachmanides, Introduction to Iggeret haKodesh. Chavel ed. (Jerusalem: Mossad Rav Kook, 1964).

22. Midrash haNeelam 112; Zohar Gen. 112a; compare Shab. 18b; Ned. 20a, Pirkei De Rabbi Eliezer 38.

23. Orot haKodesh, 6, (Jerusalem), pp. 144–146.

24. Vern L. Bulbough, The Subordinate Sex (Baltimore: Penguin Books, 1974), pp. 97–98, 174–175.

25. Throughout the Middle Ages the Christian dogma of Original Sin is accompanied by an extreme vilification of woman as the authoress of death and all our earthly woes; a view presented by the early Church Fathers. D.S. Bailey, Sexual Relations in Christian Thought (New York: Harper, 1959), pp. 10–72. "Carnal love and marriage means serving oneself and therefore are a hindrance to the service of God and man and consequently from the Christian point of view, a fall, a sin." L. Tolstoi in Kreutzer Sonata. Judaism rejects these doctrines. Instead of the fall of man (in the sense of humanity as a whole), Judaism preaches the rise of man. Instead of Original Sin, it emphasizes Original Virtue—zechut avot—the beneficent hereditary influence of righteous ancestors upon their descendants. Yer. San. 10:1; Kid.76b; Avot 2:2; Shab 55a. There is no generation without its Abraham, Jacob, Moses or Samuel, says the Midrash Gen. Rabbah 56:9. Each age is capable of realizing the highest potentialities of the moral and spiritual life. See Naz. 19a, Yer. Ned. 9, 1.

26. Yer. Ned. 9, 8.

27. R. Joshua B. Levi said: "Whoever knows his wife to be a God-fearing woman, and does not duly come unto her is called a sinner." It is forbidden for

a man to refuse his wife her conjugal rights, and if he transgressed and did so in order to cause her pain, he transgressed against a negative commandment of the Torah, for it is written, "her feed, her raiment, and her duty of marriage shall he not diminish." Yeb. 62b. Maimonides, Yad. Ishut, 14:5.

28. *Encyclopedia of Sexual Behavior*, p. 711. A. C. Kinsey, *Sexual Behavior in the Human Female* (1953), p. 346.

29. Num. Rabbah 9; Mishnah Yeb. 6:7, The school of Hillel rules that having a boy and a girl constitutes the minimal requirement of the law of procreation. See discussion in Yeb. 61b et al.

30. Rabbinic lore clearly states: "During the first three months of pregnancy, intercourse is harmful both to the woman and to the fetus; during the middle months, it is harmful for the mother but beneficial for the child; and during the last three months, it is good for both the mother and the child since on account of it, the child becomes well-formed and of strong vitality. Nid. 31a, see Rashi ad loc. and Avot De R. Nathan 1:8, Maimonides, Yad Ishut 14:1, and Levush 240:5. This fact was also discussed by Masters and Johnson who have concluded that cohabitation has no adverse effect until just before birth. In fact, it is psychologically sound to engage in sex during pregnancy, as it will afford happiness to the woman who feels herself misshapen and in need for love and acceptance. Masters and Johnson, *Human Sexual Response* (Boston: Little, Brown, 1966), pp. 158–160, 168. See Raphael Mildola, *Hupat Hatanim* (Livorno, 1796), Hilkhot Tzeniuth 1.

31. "One who vows not to have sexual intercourse with his wife: . . . (married) students may go out (of the city) for the study of Torah without permission (from their wives) for thirty days." Mishnah Keth. 5:6. See Will of R. Judah the Pious, 36; Daat haKedusha, p. 137; Maimonides, Yad Ishut, 14:5; Mishnah Keth. 5:6; Asheri Glosses to Keth. 61b–64a. A woman may keep her husband from going on a journey or a sea voyage, unless it is to an area that is near, in order that he should not fall short in his conjugal duty to her—and she has the right to restrain him from changing to an occupation which might cause a dimunition of her conjugal visits, with the exception of the study of Torah. Maimonides, Commentary to Mishnah ad loc. See RaaBaD, Baalei haNefesh. "A woman yearns for her husband when he sets out on a journey." Nid. 31a, Sanh. 70b.

32. Pes. 72a; see Sheb. 18b, Yeb. 62b. Tosaf ad loc.

33. Nachmanides, Iggeret haKodesh, sec. 2; Kid. 30b; Eccles. Rabbah 5:13; Zohar 2:93.

34. Git. 70a, Lev. Rabbah 14; compare Huppat Eliyah Rabbah.

35. San. 91b, Gen. Rabbah 34; Avot De R. Nathan 16, The Minor Tractates I, 94, 97; Zohar 1:165.

36. Regimen Sanitatis 4:8; compare also Sanh. 7:6 and Guide 3:8.

37. Maimonides, *On Sexual Intercourse*, chap. 2, ed. Gorlin, pp. 28, 69, Compare Kinsey, *Female*, p. 615.

38. B.M. 84a, "Every orgasm is of a slightly epileptical character, and although in the case of the young or healthy there is little fear of any harmful result, with old men there is danger, especially in cases of intercourse with strange women, of cerebral hemorrhage followed often enough by paralysis. Similarly, in the diseased or obese, there are often lesions of various organs. Maimonides, de Coitu 2 and 3, Gorlin, p. 70.

39. Karo, O.H. 4:8, Da'at haKedusha 7:45; see Git. 70.

40. Num. 5:18, Mishnah Sot. 1:5, Sifrei Naso 12, ed. Horowitz (Leipzig 1917), Tos. Sot. 3:3, Keth. 72a; Num. Rabbah 9, 13, 23, 42; Josephus, Antiquities III, 2:6; Rashi Naso 8:18 from Sifrei Naso 5:18 and Sot. 8a.

41. Ber. 25b; Suk. 106b; B.M. 114b; Tosef. Ber. 2:15; Yer. Ber. 13; Mishnah Hallah 2:3; Josephus, Wars II, 9:13.

42. Mordekhai in the name of R.S.B. Barukh, quoted by Isserles, Eben haEzer 21:5, Beth Shmuel ad loc. See also Tosaf. end of Kid. in the name of Derishah and Beer haGolah ad loc.

43. "It is not the nature of the daughters of Israel to walk around naked." B.B. 57b, Ber. 24a; see Sot. 8a; compare Tanhuma Noah 13; the covering of man's body is required for prayer. See Sanh. 75a, Yer. Shab. 14d, Karo, O.H. 74:75.

44. Tosef. Sot. 5:9, Git. 90a–b, Keth. 72b, Yer. Sot. 1:6, Num. Rabbah 9:8.

45. R. Hai Gaon, Ozar ha-Geonim ed. B.M. Levin, Vol. 1, sec. 2, p. 30; Orhot Hayim I, p. 13c; Adret Novellae to Ber. 24a; Resp. Moses Alshakar 35; Isserles to Orakh Hayim 75:2.

46. Mishnah B.K. 8:6; Sifrei Naso 2.

47. S. Krauss, Kadmoniot haTalmud, I, p. 189; Philo, de Special Leg. III, ed. Cohn, II p. 200.

48. Lev. Rabbah 28, Keth. 72a.

49. Ned. 20b and Erub. 100b. See R. M. haMeiri ad loc.

50. Tryon Edwards, Useful Questions (New York: Crosset & Dunlap, 1933), on modesty.

51. W. J. Fielding, Love and the Sex Emotions, pp. 111–112, compare also Hupat Hatanim, loc. cit.

52. Yeb. 61a; Sifra, ed. Weiss, p. 97c, Yeb. 61b. See Maimonides Yad, Ishut 1:7, where he considers permanent unmarried relations between a man and a woman (mistress or concubine) as prostitution, while accidental unpremeditated sexual relations are not punishable by flagellation. Yad, Naarah Betulah 2:17, see Kesef Mishnah ad loc.

53. Based on Ps. 45:14; See also B.M. 87a; Meg. 13b; Ruth Rabbah 2:23, and 4:8; Tanhuma Naso 2; See Maharal Netivot Olam, Netiv haTzneeut; Targum Kethuvim and Rashi to Songs 4:12, based on Songs Rabbati 4:24 and Lev. Rabbah 32; see also Pes. 87a.

54. Yer. Yeb. 1:2; Compare Maimonides, Yad. Ishut 24:12.

55. Songs Rabbah 4; 12; Mekhilta Bo; Yalkut Shimoni 988, See Rashi Songs

4; 12, "The daughters of Israel are known for their chastity," Er. 211b; See Meg. 10a and Keth. 3a. Philo, *de Josepho*, 43, ed. Cohn, 1, p. 167.

56. Kinsey, op. cit., pp. 322, 324, 687.

57. Yoma 19b.

58. Sanh. 21a–b; 82a. Maimonides, Yad, Isurei Beeah 22; 1–3; Otzar ha-Poskim 1; Resp. Tzitz Eliezer 6, 40. See Ginzberg, *Legends* (Philadelphia, 1938), V, p. 243, VI p. 193 "One woman may be alone with two" (well-mannered, not loose) men. But "one man should not remain alone even with two women." A.Z. 25 a–b and 36b. See Karo, E.H. 22:2.

59. A.Z. 36b; Sanh. 21b; compare Maimonides, Yad, Isurei Beeah 22:3.

60. See Tosef. Kid. 5, 10; Kid. 80b, San. 21b.

61. San. 21a; Maimonides, Yad. Isurei Beeah 22:8, 12; Karo. Eben haEzer 22:5–6; compare Esther Rabbah 3; 10; Kid. 81a and Baer Hetev to Eben haEzer 22, 5.

62. Mishnah Keth. 1:5; Tosef. Keth. 1:4, Keth. 7b and 12a. Kallah 1:1; Yer. Kid. 2.

63. Keth. 7b; Maimonides, Yad. Ishut 3:24.

64. Otzar haGeonim, ed. B.M. Levin, Keth. pp. 18–20, Ibid. to Yeb. pp. 18, 166 and note 4 thereto.

65. Ibid., pp. 17–20; Mordekhai, Keth. 132; RaBiaH, ed. Aptovitzer, I, p. 220.

66. Yad. Ishut 10; 1; Resp. Asheri 37: 1; Karo Eben haEzer, 55: 1. TaShBeZ 44: 8; Kol Bo 75 as quoted by Isserles Eben haEzer 55: 1. Mordekhai, Keth. 131 in the name of ReBaN (R. Eleazer b. Nathan).

67. J.Eisenstein, Otzar Midrashim 1, p. 166.

68. Resp. Elijah Mizrachi, 4; compare Pes. 113a; Yeb. 62b; Kid. 29a Avot 5:26.

69. *Sefer Hasidim*, pp. 175–176.

70. Resp. RaDBaZ, 3:525, R. Ovadyah Bertinoro, quoted by S. Assaf, *Jubilee Volume for S. Krauss*, pp. 169–176.

71. R. Isaiah Horowitz (1565–1630) in Shnei Luhot haBerit, Otyiot, p. 89a; see also R. J. Landsofer (1678–1712) in Resp. Meil Zedakah 19; R. Jonathan Eybeschutz (1690–1764) of Prague in Ya'arot Debash 1:3, p. 22a; R. Raphael Mildola, of Leghorn, Italy, in the 18th century, devoted an entire treatise to the pre-nuptial and the marital relations in the strict spirit of piety and modesty named Huppat Hatanim, Zeniut (Jerusalem, 1948). Compare Sdei Hemed, Hatan veKalah 12.

72. Salo Baron, *Jewish Community* Vol. II, pp. 315–316; Epstein, op. cit., p. 106.

73. Isserles to Eben haEzer, 55: 1.

74. Baron, op. cit., p. 314. Compare Ruth Rabbah 5:15, Songs Rabbah 7, Tanhuma Tazria 11, B.B. 15b. San. 39b, Ber. 23a and 32a, A. Z. 17a and 65a, Num. Rabbah 9; Maimonides, Yad. Isurei Beeah 12:2–7.

75. Yeb. 59b, 61a.

76. Maimonides, Hilkhot Ishut, 1:4; Hilkhot Isurei Beeah 18:1, See Ibn Ezra to Lev. 21:7.

77. Maimonides, Sefer haMitzvot, Lavin, 355; and Ishut 1:4; compare Keth. 51b and Ned. 90b.

78. Shab. 65a, see Rashi ad loc.; Maimonides, Yad. Isurei Beeah 17:21 and 18:2 and 13. Sot. 27a; Maimonides, loc. cit.; 2:6, 11.

79. Maimonides, Hilkhot Naarah Betulah, 2:17, and Ishut 24:16 and 19.

80. Ibid., Yad. Ishut, 3:21–22.

81. San. 21a.

82. Abraham Freiman, Sefer Kiddushin Ve-Nisuin (Jerusalem, 1964), p. 12; See Yer. Pes. 10:1.

83. B.K. 89a; Kid., 80b–81a; compare Shab. 88b; Maimonides, Yad Ishut 10:10.

84. Burgess E. and Wallin P., Engagement and Marriage (New York: Lippincott, 1953).

85. A. Tridon, Psychoanalysis and Love (New York, 1949).

86. Ibn Ezra notes that since the Hebrew Vayishak Yaakov leRachel, Gen. 29:11, is not followed by the accusative-case et, it denotes kissing the hand, shoulder, cheek, or the head, as customary in the Orient—not mouth to mouth. Ibn Ezra to Songs 1:2; compare Nachmanides Gen. 29: 11, and Kallah Rabbati 3.

87. Gen. 33:4, Exod. 4:27; compare Gen. Rabbah 7:11, Ruth 1:9, Gen. 29:11; see Wetzstein, Z.D.M.G. XXII, 93, 108.

88. 2 Sam. 14:33; Gen. 31:28, 32:1, 48:10, The children of a man's daughters are considered his own children. Pirkei De Rabbi Eliezer 36; Ruth 1:9; Gen. 27:26, 50:1; 1 Kings 19:20; Songs 8:1.

89. Gen. Rabbah 74:1, Ber. 8b, A.Z. 17a, Rashi ad loc. abei hadayrahu.

90. 2 Sam. 15:5, 10:39.

91. 1 Sam. 10:1. See also Prov. 24:26, Gen. Rabbah 70:11, Keth. 63a, 112a.

92. See infra 94–95; also Ber. 8b, Gen. Rabbah 90 ref. to Gen. 41:40, Exod. Rabbah 5:1, Isserles to O.H. 149:1.

93. 1 Sam. 20:41, Tobias 7:5, compare Gen. 29:11, 33:4, 45:15.

94. Gen. 33:4, 45:15, 2 Sam. 14:33, Prov. 27:6, Sirah 29:5.

95. Prov. 7:13. See Maimonides, Guide 3, 51.

96. Sifra, ed. Weiss, p. 85d; Avot De R. Nathan 2; Exod. Rabbah 16: 2. See also Yad, Isurei Beeah 21:1 and Maggid Mishnah ad loc.

97. Gen. Rabbah 70:11. See also Er. 53b, Torah Shleima, ed. M. M. Kasher, Gen. 29:11 fn. 33–34.

98. Exod. Rabbah 5:1; see Shab. 13a, A.Z. 17a; ShakH Yoreh Deah, 157, 10.

99. Eben haEzer 21:7 Baer Hetev 12; Aruk ha-Shulhan, Ishut 21:10; also Netiboth haShalom section Orchot Hayim 8:21–25; see Th. H. Van de Velde, Ideal Marriage (1933), p. 152.

100. Yad. Isurei Beeah 21:1, 6, 7. See Perisha to Tur 21, 7.

101. "It is related of the talmudic Amora R. Aha B. Abba, who took his

granddaughter and sat her on his lap who, although a minor, was already betrothed, in order to show his affection for her." Kid. 81b, Rashi ad loc. See Karo, Eben haEzer 6, and 21, 7 SeMaG, Lavin 126 Bet Shmuel *ad. loc.* 14-15, Be'er Hetev 16, Hokhmat Adam 125, 6, Resp. Betzel haHokhmah 3. E.H. 12, lggerot Moshe, Y.D. 2, 137 and Otzar haPoskim, E.H. 52.

102. Avot De R. Nathan 2: Exod. Rabbah 16:2, see also Karo Eben haEzer 2:16; Resp. Havot Ya'ir, 182.

103. Zohar 2:254, see Songs Rabbah 1:12, and Hor. 12a.

104. Kal. 1; Karo, Yoreh Deah 195:2; Abrahams, *Ethical Wills*, II, p. 211; Perush haTur to Gen. 24:27, 4.

105. Sdei Hemed, Hatan veKalah 14a; Yeb. 54b.

106. Resp. R. Isaac B. Sheshet 425. See Beth Shmuel, E.H. 21:9, Maggid Mishnah Yad, Ishut, 4:12; Ya'arot Debash, p. 22a; Sdei Hemed, Hatan ve Kalah 12 and 26. See Yoreh Deah 195:2. Maimomides, Yad, Isurei Beeah 418. See Iggrot Moshe, Eben haEzer 2, 14 on bodily contact in a subway or bus which is unintentional and therefore not forbidden.

107. Hos. 4:11; Kallah 3 and 5, ed. Higger, pp. 126, 129, Keth 65a: Ber. 63a. Num. Rabbah 10:42, San. 100b; compare Sirah 9:9, Yalkut Mishlei 964, (wine causes sexual frivolity).

108. Teshubot ha RMBM, ed. Freimann, 370, pp. 338–339; Yad, 1. B. 21:2; Eben haEzer 21:1; compare Resp. R. Hai Gaon's regarding permission of such music at weddings, or songs in praise of God in B. M. Levin, *Ginzei Kedem*, 5, pp. 33–35, *Otzar ha-Geonim*, Sotah pp. 272–3; Assaf, Teshubot ha-Geonim, (Jerusalem, 1928), pp. 105–106; Harkavy, Teshubot ha-Geonim, 60, pp. 27–28.

109. A. Z. 17a: Kid. 12b; Beth Yoseph and Tur Eben haEzer 21: 1; Eben haEzer 21:1.

110. Avot 1:5, Ned. 20a, Avot De R. Nathan 7, Meiri to Avot ad loc. See S. R. Hirsch commentary ad loc.

We are not advised to eliminate conversation or not to talk too much with woman, but rather not to overindulge in chatter (*sikhah*) with a woman. Man was constantly enjoined to acquire a self-disciplined attitude in relation to women so that he may control his excited passion and safeguard morality. One was discouraged from indulging in 'jesting and levity which lead a man on to lewdness' (Avot 3:17).

In order to maintain the wife's spirit it is advisable that the husband be pleasant to her and enter into pleasant conversation. It is suggested that he find place during the meal for words of the Law and ethical principles.

111. Meiri to Avot 3:17; Ned. 20b, See T. Herford, *Talmud and Apocrypha*, pp. 163; also Avot De R. Nathan 7, Ned. 20a–b; Derekh Eretz 1.

112. Rashi Kid. 70b ad loc.; see also B.M. 87a, Kid. 70b. Tosafoth ad loc. ayn. See *Hiddushei Ritva* to Kid. 81b.

113. Tur Eben haEzer 21, Bayit Hadash, cf. Baer Hetev to Eben haEzer 21:6, 11; Turei Zahab ad loc. and Bet Shmuel. See also Maggid Mishnah, Yad, Isurei Beeah 21:5, compare Pitchei Teshuva thereto.

114. Num. Rabbah 17; Ver. Ber. 1; compare Shochar Tob 14; Zohar Exod. 117, Otyiot De R. Akiva 30.

115. Job 31:1, Prov. 6:25; compare Er. 18b, Ber. 61a, Ned. 20a, Kallah 1, Derekh Eretz 1, Yer. Yeb. 3d, Sefer Hasidim 1100, Karo, Eben haEzer 21:1.

116. Sirah 9:5–8, 41: 20–21; Testament of Reuben 3:10, compare also Targum Yer., Gen. 49:22, and Gen. Rabbah 98:23 on Joseph, who did not raise his eyes at the maidens throwing jewels at him when crowned as viceroy of Egypt. Compare Num. Rabbah 9:1, Lev. Rabbah 23:12.

117. A.Z. 20a, Ber. 24a, Haye Adam 4:4, Mishnah Berurah 75:7, Resp. Iggrot Moshe, Eben haEzer 56 and 69; Yabeea Omer 4, Y.D. 15:1; BacH, O.H. 75.

118. Ta'anit 21b, Pes. 113b; compare the prohibition in Er. 18b, Ber. 61a, Ned 20a, Kallah 1, Derekh Eretz 1, Shab. 64a, Yer. Yeb. 3d.

119. B.B. 57b, Ned. 20b, Er. 18b, Ber. 24a, Shab. 64b; see A.Z. 20b; Sefer Hasidim 38:55; Karo, Eben haEzer 21:1.

120. Exod. Rabbah 41:6; Tanhuma Ki Tissa, p. 112; Yalkut Songs 4:9; Keth. 17a

121. Yad, Isurei Beeah 21:3. Eben haEzer, Ishut 21:3 based on Kid. 41a and Keth. 73a.

122. See supra 86, Keth. 17a; See Taan 28a.

123. Kid. 41a, Yad, Isurei Beeah 21:3; Eben haEzer 21:3 Sefer Hasidim 1143: see Bet Yosef, O.H. 75 and 229; Yad Malakhi 5:17a and Resp. Sridei Aysh 2, 14, and Resp. Yabeea Omer 6, O.H. 13 that one is permitted to look at a woman during their conversation but not to purposefully assess her beauty.

124. Ned. 20a; Later Responsa permit looking at a menstruating woman. See Yad, loc. cit. 21:4; Eben haEzer 21:4, compare B.B. 16a; Tanhuma Lekh Lekha 9 in regard to Abraham's reserve and saintly modesty of not looking at Sarah. Also Shab. 53b. See Karo, Y.D. 195:7 and E.H., Ishut 21:4.

125. Ber. 61a.

126. Er. 18b, Kid. 81a, Ber. 61a, Gen. Rabbah 60:13, Yad. Isurei Beeah 21:22, Eben haEzer 21:1: see also Baer Hetev ad loc. and Hupat Elyahu Rabbah 4.

127. Kid. 81b; At the end of the tenth year, the girl begins to develop physically at a much faster rate. This stage is known as adolescence; "as far as physical development is concerned, the girl begins to 'mature' at an earlier age, and reaches complete maturity before the average boy." Kinsey, *Female*, p. 122.

Let us bear in mind that physical development is not the only factor leading to sexual maturity, for, according to the general consensus of rabbinic opinion, the chronological age of twelve years and a day is a prerequisite. It is then that nature announces to the girl that she is on the way to maturity at the age of twelve.

128. Kid. 81b. Along with puberty comes the feeling of a lingering shame that mingles with coquetry and vanity. Shame in a girl may give way to pride as her breasts and body hair develop, but a strong feeling of modesty sets in, and she will refuse to expose herself naked even before her mother. S. de Beauvoir, *The Second Sex* (1968), p. 287.

129. Nid. 52a–b.

130. Yeb. 80a, Nid. 48a.

131. Mishnah Nid. 5:7, Keth. 39a, the difference separating adolescence and womanhood is six months. Nid. 65a.

132. Nid. 45a; to what may the incident be compared? To a babe whose finger was submerged in honey. The first time and the second time he cries about it, but the third time he sucks it. That is to say that she ultimately enjoys it, compare Kinsey, *Female*, p. 283. "Unreported observations suggests that infant sexual response as an undifferentiated state is not beyond possibility." William H. Masters and Virginia E. Johnson, *Human Sexual Response*, p. 140.

133. Yeb. 12b; earlier generations bore children at the age of eight years. Rashi San. 69b; *istekah*, compare Yer. Pes. 1:8.

134. Nid. 45a, 46a, 48a–b.

135. Nid. 47a–47b, compare J. F. Oliven, *Sexual Hygiene and Pathology* (1965), p. 90, and Kinsey, op. cit. p. 80.

136. "At the moment when the woman is seated on the travailing chair she says, 'I will not cohabit with my husband from this moment (on)' and God says to her, 'You will return to your desire.' " Num. Rabbah 20:7 and Nid. 31b. The woman in childbirth regards her husband as the cause of all her suffering, and forgets that she, too, longed for the child. The obstetrician always hears the stereotyped phrase, "Never again!" But we know that she will forget her resolve once the pains are over. Bauer, *Women and Love*, Vol. II, p. 124.

137. No woman agrees to stay married to her husband while being denied her sexual rights. Midrash Hanukah, Bet haMidrash, Yellinek, See Tosaf. Ned. 91a, *Kasavar*, and Gen. Rabbah 45:6.

138. See B.M. 84a. Gen. Rabbah 52:13, Yer. Keth. 5:8; see also Keth. 64b, Rashi s.v. *me*.

139. Er. 100b; J. D. Chapman, *The Feminine Mind and Body* (1968), pp. 106, 139; H. M. Ruitenbeek, *Psychoanalysis and Female Sexuality* (1966), pp. 54–55: F. S. Caprio, *The Sexually Adequate Female* (1953), p. 149, Oliven, op, cit., p. 238.

140. Keth. 61b, B.M. 84a.

141. Jules H. Masserman, *Sexuality of Women* (New York: Grune & Stratton, 1966). p. 73.

142. Whereas young men will often divorce sex from love, young women rarely consider sex except in an elaborate romantic framework. A. Ellis, *The Art and Science of Love* (1965). p. 52. Bauer, op. cit., II, pp. 177, 286. A. C. Kinsey, "Sex Behavior in the Human Male," *Annals of the New York Academy of Sciences*, 5/47, pp. 652–671.

143. It is not only the physical nature of the sex act but the attitude that accompanies it that should be the concern of morality. Just as in many other aspects of our living, it is not what we do but the way we do it that matters. Compare Kinsey, *Female* (1953), p. 644.

144. Keth. 62b, Rashi and Tosaf. ad loc: Mishnah Sot. 3:4 and 23b; Kid. 49b,

Ber. 22a, Ruth Rabbah 6:2; compare B.M. 38a, where the Germara only uses a common expression of nine *Kabin* and does not represent any definite ratio. Compare Kinsey, op. cit., p. 361. While women may be less driven to sexual behavior, they have greater capacity for orgastic response. See B.M. 84a.

145. Avot De R. Nathan 16; see M. Gaster, Sefer haMaasiyoth 34a, about R. Akiva resisting two beautiful women.

146. Yom. 29a, Rashi ad loc. *hirhurei*, Suk 52a. A woman can indulge in sexual fantasizing of her beloved which will stimulate her. Erotic chatter with her girlfriends, walking (to the *Mikvah*) is similarly exciting and sexually stimulating to the woman. The Talmud records a case of a woman who was advised by R. Yohanan not to divulge to her girlfriends the exact date of her ritual ablutions. The reason given was that her jealous friends should not cast an evil eye on her when they see her so often excited and sexually aroused because of her love for her husband. Nid. 66a.; compare Koth. 63a.

147. Keth. 59b; see Ber. 5a; Avot De R. Nathan 20; Kid. 30b and Er. 54a.

148. Keth. 72a; compare to Keth. 56a.

149. Keth. 65a; compare Caprio, op. cit., pp. 28–29.

150. Keth. 86a, Yeb. 113b; see Hor. 13a, Rashi ad loc. *amar*, Git. 13a, Avot 2:7, and Pes. 113a.

151. Ruth Rabbah 6:2, Sanh. 16a;

152. B.K. 60b.

153. Kid. 80b, see Tosaf., s.v. *Rabbi*, and Vilna Gaon's glosses.

154. Hul. 13b; Meg. 12a–b, Rashi ad loc. compare A.Z. 25b.

155. Derekh Eretz Rabbah 1:1; compare Avot 1:5 and 3:13; Letorneau quoted by H. Ellis, *Psychology of Sex.* (1937), p. 325.

156. Kinsey, op.cit., p. 676; A. C. Guyton, *Basic Human Psychology* (Philadelphia, 1971), p. 665.

157. A. Ellis and Abarbanel, eds., *Encyclopedia of Sexual Behavior*, II, p. 588.

158. Sanh. 22b, compare Yeb. 63b; Pes. 112a–b, see RaSHBaM ad loc.; compare Ber. 32b and B.M. 84b.

159. Keth. 39a–b; Nid. 31b; Shab. 8a; Sot. 4b. The pain produced from forcible intromission is composed of both somatic and psychic elements, accompanied by secondary pleasurable sensations. Fear of the event, or sex fears generally, apparently can increase the pain of first intercourse.

160. Yeb. 34b.

161. Keth. 59b.

162. B.B. 91b.

163. Karo (based on Maimonides), Eben haEzer 23:1, and Orah Hayim 240:6; see Nid. 17a, Git. 70a.

164. Yad. Deot 4:19: ibid., *On Sexual Intercourse*, ed. Gorlin, pp. 69–70; Karo, Orah Hayim 240:14, see Shab. 152a, Maimonides, *Regimen Sanitatis*, 4:8.

165. Git. 70a; see supra 172–173, Maimonides, Yad. Deot. 4:19; Karo, Orah Hayim 240:12–13, 15, see Isserles and Ateret Zekenim ad loc.

166. Compare Yer. Meg. 4:1 and B.K. 82a; Git. 70a, Ber. 44b: however, see Maimonides, infra 178, who disputes the potency of garlic or spicy foods as aphrodisiacs. Compare J. Davenport, *Aphrodisiacs and Love Stimulants* (1966), pp. 132–133.

167. Keth. 61b, 62a–b: compare Rashi and Ran *ad loc.*, Maimonides, Yad. Ishut 14:1 and Nachmanides, Iggeret haKodesh. See also Pes. 72a, Nid. 38a, and Er. 100a. Compare H.Y.D. Azulai, Mareit Ayin on Niddah 31; ibid. in Penei David on Mishpatim 8, and Shaar haKedusha p. 138:8; Zohar II:136; Tikunei Zohar 36:78.

168. The only reason sexual intercourse was prohibited during the day was for the protection of the woman. "And thou shalt love thy neighbor as thyself" (Lev. 19:18) refers to your partner, in order that no blemish of hers be seen by her husband, to prevent any distaste on his part. It is therefore that such activity is permitted in a dark room while a *talmid hakham*, being modest, will not look for blemishes; he covers up *(maafil)* with his garment and is thus permitted. Nid. 16b–17b; see Maimonides, Yad, Isurei Beeah 21:9–10; Karo, Orah Hayim 240:11 and Magen Avraham 26. "Although coition was reserved mainly for the night, if however, because of one's nature one finds himself forced to sleep at night and ought not be aroused or excited, or if the woman's nature is such that she is overtaken by sleep at night and is not sexually receptive at that time, one is permitted to have intercourse during the day, with due sexual modesty, in order that intercourse be performed with acceptance and love and not by force," M. Meiri to Nid. 17a. Compare Bek. 8a, Keth. 65b, Meg. 13a, Pes. 112b, Ruth Rabbah 2, Ber. 59b, and Shab. 86a.

169. See supra 163, Yad. loc cit.; Karo, loc cit.; see Testament of R. Eliezer the Great of Worms; based on Ned. 20b "What is the reason for selecting midnight as most adequate a time for coition?" He replied: "So that I may not think of another woman (during intercourse) lest my children be compared to bastards." Compare Hag. 5a; Maimonides, Yad. Isurei Beeah 21:12; Karo, Orah Hayim 240:9; Zohar 1:112; Midrash haNeelam.

170. Eccles. Rabbah 13:5.

171. Yad. Isurei Beeah 21:9 and SheLaH p. 100a–b; Cohabitation in a spirit of holiness and dignity receives the Divine blessings. Zohar 1:50 and 176.

172. Ber. 62a, Rashi *ad loc.* desah; see Bauer, op. cit., II, p. 242.

173. M. Meiri to Ned. 20b: see Keth. 48a not to indulge in sex while dressed as in the Persian fashion; Zohar 3:28; Tikunei Zohar 66:99; 58:92.

174. Zohar 1:49. Tikunei Zohar 56:89.

175. Tikunei Zohar 10:20, Zohar 1:49; 3:225. See Damesek Eliezer on Testament of R. Eliezer haGadol quoted in Daat haKedusha, pp. 158–159; compare Yom. 74b.

176. Er. 100b Keth. 65a, B.B. 10b, Zohar I:49, III:225. Woman's narcissism as expressed by her concern about clothes and cosmetics are expressive of her need to be loved, Kallah 32.

177. Nid. 71a, Kallah 32, Sot. 9b, Zohar 1:185. According to Kabbalah woman initiates in sexual congress. Tikunei Zohar 45:21 and 52:87.

178. Ned. 20b, Er. 100b; Maimonides, Yad. Ishut 15:17; Tur Orah Hayim 240.

179. R. Mildola, Hupat Hatanim; "Three categories of women may insert a resorbent (to prevent conception), a minor, a pregnant woman and a nursing mother." Yeb. 12b, Keth. 39a et al.

180. Zohar 3:81; Y. Azkari, Sefer Haredim, Mitzvat haTeshuvah 2; Sefer haPeliah 29b based on Ned. 20b. All such rabbinic statements relating to coital variety require mutual consent. See also Tikunei Zohar 56, 89.

181. Maimonides, Yad, Isurei Beeah 21:9; See Tosaf. Sanh. 58b s.v. mee, where occasional, incidental variation is permissible.

182. See Sanh. 100b; Zohar II, Pekudei 259; Lekah Tov 2:21, compare Bek.8a

183. R. Mildola, Hupat Hatanim 6; See Kallah Rabbati 1; Git. 70a, Tikunei Zohar 70:133.

184. Sanh. 37b; M. Aldabi, Shevilei Emunah 1889; Y. AlHarizi (1170–1230) Rephuat haGeveeah in Hebrew Medical Journal, 1 (1940), p. 77.

185. See Ber. 25b, Yeb. 90b, Keth. 60b, Maimonides, Yad, Isurei Beeah 21:14, Karo, Orah Hayim 240:6, 11, 12, 13, 16. Compare Pes. 113b; Kid. 49b; Zohar 1:111.

186. See Shab. 140b; Koran IV, Woman (New American Library, 1953), Omar Haleby (El Ktab, 1949).

187. Avot De R. Nathan 7:13 and 20; Avot 4:1; Gen. Rabbah 26; Num. Rabbah 9–10; Songs Rabbah 7; Tanhuma Balak 17; Zohar 1:11.

188. See Kallah Rabbati 52a; Maimonides, Yad, Isurei Beeah 21:18; Tur Eben haEzer 22; SeMaG, Lavin 126.

189. Yeb. 34b; Gen. 38:15, 18, 24; Gen. Rabbah 45:4.

190. Keth. 46a, Ned. 20b, Hul 37a, Ber. 13b, Pesikta Zuthati Pinhas 25, Isserles to Orah Hayim 608:4; see Baer Hetev ad loc.

191. Yeb. 76a, See Rashi ad loc. hamesolelot. Sanh. 69b, Shab. 65a, Tosef. Sot. 5:7, Yer. Git. 8; Maimonides, Yad. Isurei Beeah 21:8.

192. Maimonides, Yad. Isurei Beeah. 21:8; Tur Eben haEzer 20; SeMaG, Lavin 126, Karo, Eben haEzer 20:2 and Levush loc. cit. Also Hazon Ish to E.H. 36:2, 3. Compare also Nahmanides Hiddushim cited in Hiddushei Rashba to Niddah Ch. 2.

193. Shab. 65a–b; See Tos. ad loc. pesulot; Kid. 82a; Maimonides, Yad. Beeah 22:2; Tur Eben haEzer 24, Karo, loc. cit. 241 and Beer ha-Golah ad loc.

194. Josephus, The Jewish Wars, IV, 9, 10.

195. Maimonides, Guide 3:37; Sefer haMitzvot, Lavin 40.

196. Sifrei Deut. 22:5, Naz. 59a.

197. Ibid., the view of R. Eliezer ben Yaakov; compare Josephus, Antiquities IV, 6:3; Maimonides, Yad, Akum 12:10; Targum Onkelos and Pseudo-Jonathan to Deut. 22:5.

198. Maimonides, Yad. loc cit; ibid., Akum 12:9; Karo, Yoreh Deah 182:5.

See Naz. 59a, Shab. 94b, Targums Onkelos and Pseudo-Jonathan loc cit.

199. Midrash Tanaiim Deut. 22:5, p. 143; Sifrei and Targums loc cit. See Karo, Yoreh Deah 182:6; compare TaSHBetZ, (Warsaw 1902), 542–543. As reported of the Tzadik Rabbi A. Y. Heschel of Apt, who looked into the mirror to adjust his tefilin. Permission for bright-colored clothes nowadays is found in Darkei Theshuvah to Yoreh Deah 178:7, 16 and Resp. Az Nidberu II, 55.

200. Sefer Hasidim 206–207; See Isserles Orah Hayim 696:8.

201. Gen. 38:21–22, 23:7; Hos. 4:14, Sifrei Deut. 260; Esther Rabbah to 1:9.

202. 1 Sam. 2:22, I Kings 14:24 and 15:11, 2 Kings 22:47 and 23:7. Compare L. Epstein, Sex Laws and Customs in Judaism (New York, 1967), p. 153.

203. Num. 31:16–17; see Testament of Judah 12:2, Baruch 6:43; compare Herodotus, History (London 1875), I, 199; Justin, History, Philippicae 18:5; Westermarck, History of Human Marriage, I (London: Macmillan, 1921), pp. 208–214.

204. Keth. 3b, compare Herodotus, op. cit., IV, 168; see Ibn Ezra to Haggai 2:12.

205. Lev. 19:29; 21:7, 14. The verb hll—generally translated as "profane"—is applied to the Sabbath, priesthood, and the name of God. Exod. 31:14; Lev. 10:10, 20:3, 21:9, 22:15, and is also used in connection with a woman, thus rendering the sense obscure. It is unlikely that "profanation" is what is meant by the Bible, when applied to a girl. The literal sense of the word, "a perforated one," seems more likely. See L. Ginzberg, "Beitrage zur Lexicographie des Aramischen," in Festschrift Adolph Schwartz, p. 354, s.v. HRF. See also A. Ehrlich, Mikra KiPeshuto, Lev. 21:7, and L. Epstein, Marriage Laws (1968), p. 322.

206. See article on Jus. Primae Noctis in Jewish Encyclopedia; see also Soferim 21, 9. Pirkei De R. Eliezer 16; Yeb. 34b; Gen. Rabbah 51:11, Compare Joel Miller, Hiluf Minhagim (Vienna, 1878), p. 40.

207. Gen. 34:31, Is. 23:15 et passim; for a unique rationale against promiscuity see Maimonides, Guide III:49.

208. Git. 17b and 81a; see also Yeb. 35a and 107a; Num. Rabbah 9.

209. Philo, de Josepho, 43, ed. Cohn, I, p. 167; ibid., Spec. Leg. III:51; II, p. 198. He may have read Deut. 23:18, lo tehayeh, "there shall not live," instead of "there shall not be." So in the Samaritan Targum. Further evidence from Gen. 38:24 and Deut. 22:21. See Ritter, Philo und die Halacha, pp. 91–93.

210. Resp. R. Judah b. haRosh, 17:1, Arama, Akedat Yizhak, Vayera (Warsaw, 1904), p. 114a; S. Bernfeld, Dor Tahapukhot, p. 30.

211. Ber. 62a; Maimonides, Yad, Ishut 14:5 and 15:1, compare B.M. 84a, Sexual relations between husband and wife are considered holy and an exercise in oneness. Zohar 3:81.

212. Max Grunwald, "Biblische und Talmudische Quellen Juedischer Eugenik," in Hygiene and Judentum, ed. H. Goslar (1930), p. 60.

213. M. M. Brayer, "The Role of Jewish Law Pertaining to the Jewish Family, Jewish Marriage and Divorce," in *Jews and Divorce*, ed. J. Freid (New York: Ktav, 1968), pp. 26–27.

214. Gen. Rabbah 35.

215. Yoma 88b.

216. Yeb. 63b, Gen. Rabbah 34:10, Tosefta Yeb. 8:2, Tanhuma Noah 12, Karo, E. H. 5:12; see Beer haGolah ad loc.

217. Hiddushei haRan to Kid. 41a.

218. Yeb. 12b.

219. See infra pp. 388–392. John T. Noonan, Jr., *Contraception: A History of Its Treatment by the Catholic Theologians and Canonists* (Cambridge, Mass.: Harvard University Press, (1965), p. 130.

220. (1) Nid. 31b, Yeb. 35a; (2) Ket. 37a and 72a; (3) Yeb. 65b, Shab. 109b, 110b, Tosefta Yeb. 8:2, also see Karo, E. H. 5:12; (4) Yeb. 12b, using the absorbent *mokh*. For detailed and relevant discussion on this topic see D. Feldman, *Birth Control in Jewish Law* (New York: New York University Press, 1968), pp. 169–193, 227–248; also, *Sefer Assia, shaar 2, nashim poreeot*; Resp. Tzitz Eliezer, 9, 51; RaDBaZ 3, 596; Resp. Avnei Nezer 81, 83; Resp. Ahiezer, E.H. 23.

221. Yeb. 65a. also Shab. 109b-110b.

222. R. Shlomo Luria, Yam Shel Shlomo, Yeb. 6:44.

223. Ibid., loc. cit. Yeb. 1:8. Post-Lurian responsa agreeing with his lenient view are those of R. Shelomo Zalman of Posen in Resp. Hemdas Shelomo, E. H. 46; Rabbi S. B. Sopher in Resp. Shevet Sofer, E. H. 2; R. Haym O. Grodzensky in Resp. Ahiezer, E. H. 23; Rabbi S. M. Schvadron in Resp. MaHaRShaM, I, 58; Rabbi D. Z. Hoffmann in Resp. Melamed LeHoeil, E. H. 18, also see R. Moshe Feinstein in Resp. Iggrot Moshe, E. H. 63, on permitting the diaphragm in cases of pregnancy hazards.

224. Resp. Hatam Sopher, E. H. 20.

225. R. Moshe Feinstein, Iggrot Moshe, IV, E. H. 17:65, Resp. Tzitz Eliezer, 9:51. See S. Hubner in *haDarom*, Tishri 5725.

226. *De Fide* 27, quoted by D. Feldman, op. cit., p. 269.

227. See Resp. MaHaRaSH Engel V:89 and VI:18; also R. Yehiel Weinberg in *Noam*, IX (1966), 207, Resp. Mishptei Uziel, III, H.M. 46.

228. Hul. 58a, B.K. 78a, Yeb. 78a, Naz. 51a.

229. Resp. Tzofnas Paaneah 1, no. 49.

230. B.K. 91b; Yad, Hovel uMazik 5:1, See M. M. Brayer, "The Role of Jewish Law Pertaining to the Jewish Family," in *Jews and Divorce* (New York: Ktav, 1968), pp. 26ff. Resp. MaHaRit, 1, no. 99 by R. Yosef Trani.

231. Y. L. Unterman, Shevet MeYehuda (1955), pp. 26–30; 49–50. *Noam*, VI (1963), 1–11. See M. M. Brayer, *Psychedelic Drugs and Religious Consciousness* (New York, 1973), p. 24, note 81.

232. Yad, Rotzeah uShemirat HaNefesh 2:6; Hoshen Mishpat 423. For a detailed discussion of the Rabbinic views on this matter, see Feldman, op. cit., chap. 15.

233. Nid. 44b; Karo, Yore Deah 344:8.

234. Sanh. 72b, Rashi ad loc.

235. Sanh. 57b, based on Gen. 9:6; Yad, Melakhim 9:4, 10, 11.

236. Philo, *De Specialibus Legibus*, II, 19 (ed. Cohn 5:180 ff.). Josephus, *Antiquities of the Jews*, IV, 8:33 (ed. Niese, I, 280). V. Aptowitzer, "Observations on the Criminal Law of the Jews," *J.Q.R.* 15, (1924), p. 85.

237. Nid. 30b.

238. F. Rosner and S. Muntner, "The Oath of Asaph," *Annals Int. Med.*, 63(2):317–320 (1965).

239. H. Friedenwald, "The Oath of Amatus Luisitanus," in *The Jews and Medicine* (Baltimore: Johns Hopkins Press, 1944), pp. 368–370.

240. H. Savitz, "Jacob Zahalon and His Book 'The Treasure of Life,' " *New England J. of Med.* 213:167–176 (1935).

241. Mishnah Oholot 7:6. See also Tosefta Yeb. 9:9; Bekh. 22a and San. 72b.

242. Even haAzel to Yad., Hovel uMazik 8:15.

243. Yad, loc cit. 4.1; Karo, H. M. 423, 1 based on Exod. 21:12. Compare also Yad. Rotzeah 1:9 where the fetus is viewed as a *rodeph*, or mother's "pursuer." See Tosafat R. Akiva Eger to Oholot 7:6 and Hidushei R. Haym haLevi ad loc.

244. *De animalibus historiae* VII, 3.

245. Joseph B. DeLee, *Obstetrics*, 4th ed., p. 274.

246. San. 91b; Gen. Rabbah 34:12.

247. Yeb. 69b, Nid. 30b, Mishnah Keritot 1.

248. Resp. Havot Yair, no. 31.

249. San. 81b, Gen. Rabbah 34:10.

250. Resp. Or Gadol, no. 31, Resp. Sheelat Yaavetz, 1, no. 43; also see Resp. Mishptei Uziel, III, H.M. no. 47.

251. Resp. Tzitz Eliezer IX, no. 51:3, 9. See Nid. 23b–24a dealing with observable malformations "Monster births" of the defective births.

252. Y. L. Unterman, Beinyan Pekuah Nefesh shel Ubar, *Noam* 6 (1963)), pp. 1–11.

253. I. Jakobovitz, "Deformed Babies and Thalidomide Babies," in *Journal of a Rabbi* (New York: Living Books, 1966), pp. 262–266.

254. Resp. Mishptei Uziel, III, 46, 47.

255. Resp. Peri haAretz III; Yoreh Deah, no. 2, by Rabbi I. M. Mizrahi, also Resp. Netzer Mataai, I, no. 8, by Rabbi N. Z. Friedman.

256. Resp. Beth Yehuda, no. 14; Resp. Hayim veShalom, I, no. 40; Resp. Sheeilat Itzhak no. 69; Resp. Tzitz Eliezer, IX, no. 51:3. For an updated halakhic view on the subject see *Harefuah Leor haHalakha*, ed. R. M. Stern (Jerusalem: Institute for Research in Medicine and Halakha, 1980).

CHAPTER 9.

1. On the various responsa related to the problem, see *Otzar haPoskim* vols. 3–8 (Jerusalem, 1954–1963). Git. 26b and 33a, Yeb. 87b–88a.

2. Yad. Gerushin 13:19; Karo, E. H. 17:32–33.

3. Resp. Benjamin Zeev 64; A. C. Freimann, *Seder Kiddushin veNissuin* (Jerusalem, 1945), pp. 385–397. 1, 2, Kahana, *Sefer haAgunot* (Jerusalem, 1954).

4. Yeb. 16:7; Maimonides, Yad. end of Gerushin.

5. Resp. Asheri 51:2; Resp. Y. Kolon 30; Karo, E. H. 17:3. Git. 33a; Yad. Gerushin 13:29; Karo, E. H. 17:3, 56; Resp. Ginat Vradim, E. H. 3:11; Resp. Shevut Yaakov 100.

6. Mishnah Yeb. 15:1–2; Karo, E.H. 17:11, Resp. Hatam Sopher, E.H. 1:43.

7. Yeb. 116b; Yad. Ishut 16:31; Karo, E.H. 43–44; Yeb. 87b; Yad, Gerushin 19:5, 7; Karo, E.H. 17:56.

8. Git. 90b, compare Pes. 113b, Yeb. 37b, Kid. 13a, and Lev. Rabbah 34. The antithesis is exemplified by the attitudes of the later Romans, for whom the altar would have shed many tears. By the time of the Empire, and even towards the end of the Republic, women had legal and economic independence, and the purpose of marriage was solely political. F. Guglielmo, *The Women of the Caesars*, chap. 1. The Roman attitude was best expressed by Antonius Seneca, when he said: "Now no woman need blush to break off her marriage, since the most illustrious ladies have adopted the practice of reckoning the year not by the names of the consuls but by those of their husbands. They divorce in order to re-marry. They marry in order to divorce." J. Carcopino, *Daily Life in Ancient Rome*, New Haven: Yale, 1940), p. 100.

9. Isaiah too speaks of the bill of divorcement given by God to Zion (Isa. 50:1), and so did Jeremiah (3:8). See Yor. Kid. sub Mishnah 1:48a; Yeb. 31a and Git. 90a, Maimonides, Yad, Gerushin 1:1–5.

10. In the Jewish colony at Elephantine the husband pronounced in front of witnesses in Hebrew: "I divorce my wife." In Assyria he said: "You are no more my wife." But in Israel and Mesopotamia, and Elephantine as well, the husband had to draw up a writ of divorce (Deut. 24:1–3) which allowed the woman to remarry. The Greeks and early Romans also gave the man the right to "send away" his wife. In ancient Greece, women were legally no more than chattel. Marriage was a matter of social economics—its purpose was the production of legitimate children to whom property could eventually be handed over. Although there was a contract involved in the marriage, the husband, bearing unlimited authority over his family, could divorce his wife without even stating his reasons. W. H. Hale, *Ancient Greece*, pp. 186–188.

11. Git. 90a; Maimonides, Yad, Ishut 4:1 and 25:11–13, and Bet Yosef, Eben haEzer 134. While no legal action was necessary in order for the Greek husband to divorce his wife, the wife, in order to initiate divorce action, had to appear

before the Archon, Demosthenes, *Against Onetor*, VIII. During the first centuries of Rome, the religious marriage *cum manu* (*confarreatio* or *farreum*) was prevalent. The woman was thereby placed under the man's authority and could in no way repudiate him, while he could repudiate her for any reason; Carcopino, op. cit., p. 95. In Rome, this power was derived from the Twelve Tables of 451 B.C.E., which recognized the formula *Res tuas tibi habeto* ("take your things and go"). F. R. Cowell, *Everyday Life in Ancient Rome*, (New York: Putnam, 1961), p. 60.

12. Mishnah Git. 9, 8; Maimonides, Yad. Ishut 24; 17.

The Talmud quotes the School of Shammai saying: "A man should not divorce his wife unless he has found something very blameworthy about her." The School of Hillel says: "He may do so even if she overcooked his food." R. Akiva says: "Even if he found someone more beautiful" (*Gittin* 90a). Maimonides in his *Commentary on the Mishnah* considers R. Akiva's view very difficult. If a man finds another woman more beautiful than his wife, why should R. Akiva permit him to divorce his wife so freely? One answer is suggested by R. Aryeh Levin (see Simcha Raz, *A Tzaddik in Our time* [Jerusalem: Feldheim Publishing, 1977], p. 455).

In R. Akiva's time it was permissible to take more than one wife. The question is: Why shouldn't he marry the prettier woman in addition to his wife? The answer is found in the Talmud in the tractate *Shabbat* (26b) where R. Akiva states: "Who is wealthy? Whoever has a wife beautiful in her deeds." The Maharsha in his glosses explains it to mean a woman who makes do with little. If so, R. Akiva himself was blessed with Rachel—the daughter of Kalba Savua— a wife whose way it was to content herself with little. She lived happily with R. Akiva and was content with her poverty during the early years of their marriage. He realized that if a man has a wife who is not "beautiful" in her deeds, who cannot make do with little, he surely would want to marry "another woman, more beautiful than she," meaning, a wife who *can* make do with little. For after marrying the other woman possessing such a good quality, he will no longer be able to accept the presence of the first wife, whose shortcomings will appear more blatantly evident, overshadowed as they are by the virtues of the second wife.

13. Mishnah Git. 9; 8; Maimonides, Yad, Ishut 24:11, 12, 15–18; ibid., Gerushin 10:22. Nowadays, in most states in the United States either spouse may initiate divorce action, but only such grounds as adultery, cruel and inhuman treatment, separate living, and desertion are acceptable grounds for divorce. Thus, a couple interested in divorce must either separate for a period of time ranging from one to ten years (depending upon in which state the action is taken), or one must be accused of being guilty of something. Unsubstantiated adultery is not accepted as grounds for divorce in American courts. Substantiated adultery merely gives grounds for divorce but does not compel it. M. F. Mayer, *Divorce and Annulment in the 50 States* (New York, 1975).

Against a wife proved guilty of adultery, Greek law compelled the husband to use his right of repudiation. On the other hand, adultery of the husband gave the wife no legal right to divorce. (In contradistinction to this, Solonic law in ancient Greece, although permitting the husband to kill an adulterer, also encouraged authorized adultery.) Plutarch, *Solon*, X, iv, and *Lycurgus*, XXIV.

14. Maimonides, Yad, Gerushin 1:1, Resp. Asheri 42;1 to Mishnah Git. 1. See also Kid. 13a. The Ketubbah, or marriage contract, is essentially an instrument to safeguard the wife's rights, not the husband's. The rabbinic amendments to the talmudic law which gave the husband the right to divorce his wife were aimed basically to eliminate the unfair disadvantage to the wife. This was a positive social evil.

15. Git. 90a, Bet Hillel, defending the wife against her ever-demanding husband who mistreats her offers her, in fact, a way to freedom by allowing her husband the right of divorce for little cause. See Sot. 47a, Yer. Yoma 4;1. Compare Resp. R. Meir of Rothenburg (Prag. 1605), no. 113.

16. Mishnah Git. 2;1; Maimonides, Yad, Gerushin 6:1–4.

17. According to the Babylonian Hammurabi Code, a man might divorce his wife if he wished, but must make certain specified monetary settlements which varied according to whether the wife had or had not borne him children (#137). A woman might take the initiative in divorce but her husband could, if he wished, divorce her without alimony (#141). If the wife's complaint of ill treatment proved true, she could take her marriage portion and return to her father's house; if untrue, she was to be thrown into the river (#142). American law on the whole primarily recognizes adultery as grounds for divorce.

18. See also A. H. Cowley, *Aramaic Papyri of the Fifth Century (B.C.E.)* (London, 1923). A writ of divorce dating from the beginning of the second century C.E. has been found in the caves at Murabba'at, at the Dead Sea. J. M. Allegro, *The Dead Sea Scrolls* (Baltimore: Pelican, 1959), p. 177.

19. Yer. Kid. 1;1. This may be the first source for the contemporary new prenuptial agreement.

20. Bet Yosef to Tur Eben haEzer 134, compare Maimonides, Yad, Ishut 4:15.

21. J. Mueller, *Einleitung in die Responsen der Babylon, Otzar haGeonim*, Levin, pp. 63 and 115. See Maimonides, Yad, Ishut 13:11.

22. Rabbenu Gershom of Mayence and his Synod decreed as follows: "To assimilate the right of the woman to the right of the man, it is ordained that even as the man does not put away his wife except of his own free will, so shall the woman not be put away except by her own consent."

Resp. Asheri 42:1; R. Moses Isserles to Eben haEzer 19:6. For, as R. Nissim states in one of his responsa, "We have a tradition that there exists a communal ban or an edict of Rabbenu Gershom which has been universally accepted that no woman may be divorced without her consent." Sheeloth uTeshuvoth haRaN. The brutality of early Roman law is apparent in its laws concerning adultery. They not only permitted a husband to kill an adulterous wife, but also allowed him to torture, mutilate, and otherwise punish her. Finally, a law was passed by Augustus (18 B.C.E.) which deprived the adulterer of half of his fortune and forbade them marriage with each other forever. Furthermore, the husband was compelled to divorce a wife guilty of adultery. If he refused, he himself was to be punished as an adulterer. Balsdon, *Roman Women* (1975), pp. 216 f.

23. While in form, the husband executes the divorce, Talmudic Law recognizes the woman's right to institute divorce action and have the court compel the husband to issue the Bill of Divorce, Mishnah Ned. 90b; see Git. 88b. See G. F. Moore, *Judaism in the First Centuries* (Cambridge, Mass.: Harvard University Press, 1927), II p. 122.

24. Resp. Rashi, p. 207, ed. 1, Elfenbein (New York 1943), no. 207, p. 233.

25. The following is from the declaration of the groom to the bride at the wedding: "Be thou consecrated unto me with this wedding ring according to the Law of Moses and Israel." Tosefta Keth. 13:11; Keth. 77a based on Mekhilta Mishpatim 3, Bet Joseph to Tur E.H. 134, compare also Maimonides, Yad, Ishut 4:15 and 12:11.

26. An early Ketubbah clause from Damascus reads: "That at no time may the husband or his agent divorce her except with her consent and through a just (Jewish) court. See infra 28. Until 1967, New York State law required that a "guilty" party in a divorce wishing to remarry obtain permission from the court. Other states vary in the time period one must wait, up to year, depending at times upon whether the person was the plaintiff or the defendant in the divorce. Mayer, op. cit. The Damascus Ketubbah, 1706 and Livorno, 1787 of the Adler Collection, in the British Museum, Lunz, Jerusalem, VII.

27. Though not mentioned in the Bible, it is likely that in Israel, as in Mesopotamia, certain financial conditions were attached to divorce. In the marriage contracts of the Jewish colony of Elephantine, the husband divorcing his wife lost the claim to the *mohar*; and paid the "price of divorce." The wife, too, who separated from her husband paid the same "price of divorce," but reclaimed her personal property. Cowley, op. cit.

In Hindu culture either husband or wife could separate from the adulterous partner, though the husband might retain all the adulterous wife's possessions. See *Encyclopedia of Religion and Ethics*, I, p. 130.

28. Ned. 66b, Git. 90a–b. Compare Yalkut Tehilim 743.

29. Only three states (Alabama, Oklahoma, New Mexico) recognize incompatibility as grounds for divorce. In the rest of the United States, the only cases resembling mutual consent are when the accused party puts up no defense or presents a mere *pro forma* defense. This is often done in situations where there is mutual consent to the divorce but this consent is not recognized grounds for divorce.

30. Maimonides, Yad, Ishut 15:9; Karo, Eben haEzer, 154:10 and gloss. Impotence and not sterility are grounds recognized in some American states,

Mayer, op. cit. None of the above grounds were necessary for the dissolution of marriages in ancient Greece and Rome. Balsdon, op. cit., p. 210. Compare M. Kasher, Torah Shleima to Gen. 16:3.

31. Yeb. 14:1, 113b; compare Maimonides, Yad, Gerushin 10:23 and RaBaD ad loc. In the event of a wife's prolonged illness, it was deemed inhumane for the huband to pay her the Ketubbah and give her a divorce. Maimonides, Yad, Ishut 14, see Magid Mishneh ad loc. Twenty-one American states allow divorce on grounds of existence of a "loathsome disease," interpreted as syphilis, gonorrhea, or even tuberculosis.

32. Keth. 4:7, Maimonides, Yad, Ishut 14:18–20, Tur Eben haEzer 78:1.

33. Maimonides Yad, Gerushin 11:1–3: minor marriages with parental consent are valid in America, but without consent they can be annulled by the ineligible partner or by a parent.

34. Yeb. 65a–b, Maimonides, Yad, Ishut 14:6–7. A woman is considered a moredet only when her refusal is out of malice. See Keth. 64a, Teshuvot Geonim Kadmonim 91; Maimonides, Ishut 14:12. Compare Magid Mishnah Ishut 14:8–9, and Bet Shmuel to Eben haEzer 77:7. In American law, refusal of sexual union is sometimes categorized as desertion. New Hampshire recognizes refusal to cohabit as grounds for divorce. Male impotence (the woman remaining a virgin for three years) is grounds for divorce in all states except Louisiana.

35. Keth. 64a; Teshuvot Geonim Kadmonim 91, Maimonides, Yad, Ishut 14:12. Compare Magid Mishnah to Maimonides, Yad, Ishut 14:8–9; Bet Shmuel to Eben haEzer 77:7.

36. R. Nissim and Tossafot Riad to Keth. 64a. The New York State Divorce Law which went into effect on September 1, 1967, provides for compulsory reconciliation procedure, but this procedure is omitted in 80% of the cases—claimed to be beyond reconciliation. New York Times, January 4, 1970. Among the twenty-five states in the United States that recognize separation for a period of time as grounds for divorce, some, such as New York, allow the separation to be initiated by either spouse regardless of the feelings of the other.

37. Compare B.K. 47a. Resp. of Geonim (ed. Constantinople) No 137; Resp. of Geonim, Shaarei Tzedek 64, 1, no. 42; Resp. TaSHBeTZ II, 6; Resp. R. Meir of Rothenburg, 291. In addition, eleven states recognize "indignities over a period of time" as grounds for divorce. Cruelty is the most common stated cause of divorce in America. F. Haussanont and M. A. Guitar, The Divorce Handbook, p. 248.

38. See supra §22. The Romans allowed the man concubines and female slaves, so that Roman civilization could hardly be termed a monogomous one. Carcopino, op. cit., pp. 101–103. Serious criminal conviction and imprisonment are grounds for divorce in most states. "Seriousness" is determined on the basis of the crime (felony) or the period of the sentence (in New York, three years).

39. Maimonides, Yad, Ishut, 13:17; ibid., loc cit. 14:2. American law also recognizes the right of the man to choose a domicile. If the place is relatively comfortable and within his means, the wife is expected to follow him. Otherwise, desertion charges may be allowed. Tennessee recognizes refusal by a wife to live in the state as grounds for divorce. In most states in the United States nowadays absence of a spouse for a period of time qualifies dissolution of marriage on the grounds of desertion or presumption of death.

40. See Ab. Z. 36b Nonsupport and neglect are grounds in thirty-two states. In modern times, marital drunkenness and narcotics addiction have, perhaps, replaced leprosy as a cause of divorce. Bigamy is cause for divorce or annulment in all states. Although American law gives the husband the right to choose the domicile, due to the wife's insistence which is mentioned here, mental cruelty may be involved in the husband's refusal to heed her wishes. Therefore, American law may grant a divorce as Judaism does. An additional five cases forbidding such action were added in the Mishnah. See Karo Eben haEzer 154 passim. Compare Michael F. Mayer, *Divorce and Annulment in the Fifty States* (New York: Arco Publishing Co., 1975).

41. Eben haEzer 82:7. Isserles ad loc. See Keth. 59b–60a and 65b.

42. Mishnah Yeb. 4:7. See also Maimonides, Yad, Gerushin 11:20. The Romans remarried immediately. Remarriage regulations for widows were strict, since a widow had to wait ten to twelve months. This law was later modified by Augustus and ultimately abolished by the Christians, who regarded a second marriage as an impropriety. According to the Code of Hammurabi #137–138 the husband divorces his wife by pronouncing a special formula, but he has to pay her compensation. In Greece upon dissolution of marriage on the initiative of either party or by mutual agreement, the dowry must be refunded to the woman. Thus, the dowry follows the wife, or goes to her children. Compare E. Neufeld, *Ancient Hebrew Marriage Laws,* (1944) and E. M. McDonald. *The Position of Women as Reflected in Semitic Codes* (1931).

43. Ned. 90b, Yeb. 112a. See Nachmanides and Seforno to Deut. 24:1–50.

44. Locke, *Predicting Adjustment in Marriage: A Comparison of a Divorced and Happily Married Group,* (Westport: Greenwood, 1968), chaps. 5, 6.

45. David Levine, *How to Get a Divorce With or Without a Lawyer* (New York: Bantam, 1979), pp. 129–241.

46. *New York Times,* February 16, 1983.

47. Exod. Rabbah 30:16.

48. Maimonides, Yad; Deot 6:10; Karo, Hoshen Mishpat 107, Sefer haHinukh 65:591 and Minhat Hinukh ad loc.

49. Yeb. 59b–60a, Keth. 29a, Kid. 77b–78a, Maimonides, Yad, Isurei Beeah 17:1, Sefer haHinukh 274.

50. Maimonides, Yad, Nahalot 1:3–4, Sefer haHinukh 400.

51. B.B. 52b, Maimonides, Yad, Nahalot 9:7–8.

52. Tosef. Keth. 11:20.

53. Yer. Keth. 11:2.

54. Rashi ad loc.

55. San. 22a.

56. M. Brayer, "The Spiritual Component and the Psychological View in Understanding Bereavement and Grief," ed. N. Linzer, New York: Ktav (1977), pp. 47–52.

APPENDIX A

1. Bek. 45a

2. Gen. Rabbah 1 and 18, Er. 18b, Ber. 61a.

3. Kimber, Gray, Stackpole, Leavell & Miller, *Anatomy and Physiology* (New York: Macmillan, 1971),p. 315; L. Hellman and J. Pritchard, *Obstetrics,* 14th ed. (New York, 1971), chap. 1.

4. Lev. Rabbah 14:3, Tanhuma Tazria 3, Nid. 31a. Compare Midrash Tehilim, Ps. 103: Yalkut haMakiri 31–25.

5. Yeb. 42a. See Rashi: *behilukha;* ibid. 37a, Nid. 8b, Gen. Rabbah 81:9 and 85:10.

6. Avot De R. Nathan 1. Lev. Rabbah 14.

7. Gen. Rabbah 8:9, Tanhuma Tazria 2, Lev. Rabbah 14:6.

8. Lev. Rabbah 14:3; The Talmud discusses the fertilization of the egg by the sperm and the circumstances under which it is successful. Nid. 9a, Bek. 6b. Lev. Rabbah 14:9. Compare Hag. 14b–15a.

"The nutritional status of the mother appeared to be especially reflected in the vitamin content of her milk." This is understandable, as the blood of the mother is the source, bringing products of digestion, as well as various unwanted products, to form the milk. K. D. West and A. Kirksey "Influence of Vitamin B6 Intake on the Content of the Vitamin in Human Milk," *American Journal of Clinical Nutrition* 29 (9): 961–969, Sept. 1976.

9. See Eccles. Rabbah 2. Although early rabbinic sources point to a clearer and more naturalistic understanding of the process, popular belief concerning the enigma of conception was indeed strange. At first, it was not the father who engendered the child. Then it was claimed that the female merely carried and nourished the living seed which was the father's exclusive creation. In 1677, the "spermatic animalcules" were discovered, and it was observed that they penetrated into the uterus. The belief was that the child was perfectly preformed in them. The role of the female was to protect and nourish this "little man" or "homunculus," which was hidden in the spermatozoon. Such pictures are recorded into the 19th century. The female genitals had borne the name of "feminine testicules" and were regarded as "homologus to the male gland" until the Danish anatomist Steno (end of the 17th century) renamed them "ovaries" when he noted the small swellings on their surface that had been identified by von Graaf, in 1677, to be the eggs, and which turned out to be what we call the Graafian follicles.

Harvey's experiments at the end of the 17th century led, in 1827, to the discovery of the mammalian egg by von Baer. In 1879, the observation of the penetration of the spermatozoon into the starfish egg was observed, and the equivalence of the two nuclei of the two gametes—the sperm and the egg—was finally established and the union clarified in 1883 by van Beneden. Telegony implies that at the first conception the mother is affected by something that will be transmitted to later offspring, even though resulting from coitus with another mate. See Hellman and Pritchard, *Obstetrics*, pp. 122–123, 667.

10. Gen. Rabbah 8:9, Lev. Rabbah 14:6.

11. Kid. 30b, Eccles. Rabbah 8:13, Midrash haGadol 85b.

12. Nid. 31a–b.

13. Yer. Yeb. 4:2; Hag. 15a, see Nid. 43a, Yeb. 34a; Gen. Rabbah 51:9, Midrash haGadol Gen. 16. However, this is medically unproven, for if the time is right, if the hymen is sufficiently broken, and if the sperm is deposited in sufficient number, then pregnancy will ensue. It is therefore likely that Samuel's statement must refer to total impotence.

14. Compare Lev. Rabbah 14:6, Nid. 27a; John Archer, the first American physician, related in 1810 that a white woman who had had intercourse with both a white and a black man within a short period, was delivered of twins, one of which was white and the other mulatto. Since that time many instances of alleged superfecundation have been reported. In 1917, a most convincing case was recorded by Robertson in which a mare covered by a horse and 10 minutes later by a jackass gave birth to twins, one a horse and the other a mule. Compare Yer. Yeb. 4:2.

15. Lev. Rabbah 14:9, San. 37b; see Rashi *haoher*. The wisdom of this statement is backed up by present knowledge. The female orgasm may also serve to keep the woman in the supine position for some time after termination of coitus, thus preventing leakage of semen from the vagina. See Nid. 31b. It is of interest that the human female is the only female (other primates included) in which the vagina is vertical when she is in the locomotive posture. Compare Lev. Rabbah 14.

Nid. 27a. Yer. Yeb. 4:2. As to fear of double pregnancy, the RaBaD says not to worry, as it is rare. Today we know that only one spermatazoan actually penetrates the ovum and the vitalline membrane becomes refractory to the penetration of other spermatazoa after fertilization. Medical science recognizes two processes: superfecundation-fertilization of two ova within a short period, but not at the same coitus; and superfetation where there is an interval longer than one ovulatory cycle. Superfecundation is a recognized fact in lower animals, and although it is impossible to ascertain the frequency, it does occur in humans. Although superfetation is theoretically possible, and is known to occur in mares, it has never been demonstrated in humans. Its unlikeliness is due to the inhibition of ovulation during pregnancy. Most authorities believe that the alleged cases of human superfetation result from either abortion of one twin or marked inequality of development. Robert Street, *Modern Sex Techniques* (New York, 1959), p. 169. Compare T. C. Ruch and H. D. Patton, *Physiology and Biophysics*, 19th ed. (Philadelphia and London: Saunders, 1966), p. 1192.

16. Nid. 27a and 31b, Yer. Yeb. 4:2, Yeb. 34a, Baal Halakhot Gedolot, Bek. 21b, Yeb. 34a and 69b.

17. Mishnah Nid. 30a–b, 31b; Sanh. 37b; W. J. Hamilton et al., *Human Embryology*, (Baltimore: Williams & Hopkins, 1962), p. 284. A story is told of Cleopatra, the queen of Alexandria, that when her handmaidens were sentenced to death by royal decree, they were subjected to a test (fertilization and subsequent operation) and it was found that both (male and female embryo) were fully fashioned on the forty-first day. Nid. 30b. Compare Nid. 25b and Midrash Aggadah Toledot 26. See Nachmanides, Torat haAdam, Sha'ar haSakanah; also RoSH and RaN to Yoma, ad loc.; Ha'amek Sh'alah (loc. cit.) aligns She'iltot with BaHaG. Yeb. 69b (*maya b'alma*): e.g., Nid. 15b; Mishnah and Gemara, Nid. 30a–b; Ber. 60a (the time of *pekidat ha'tippah* is "forty days before *y'tzirat hav a lad*"). SHaKH to Hoshen Mishpat 210, I, and Mishnah l'Melekh to Yad, Tumeot Met 2:1.

The Talmud, in the name of R. Ishmael, understands the forty days and eighty days after birth as parallel to those between conception and formation of the embryo. The view of the Sages—which equalizes them at forty days—prevails. See Nid. 30b. Aristotle, in *De Animalibus Historiae* 7, 3, specified forty days in the case of a male and 80 days in the case of a female. Westermarck, in *The Origin and Development of the Moral Ideas*, 2 vols. (London: Macmillan, 1906), calls this an "absurd misinterpretation" of Lev. 12:2–5, where these time periods are for after birth.

18. Lev. Rabbah 4:9 and 14:5, Yeb. 98a, Nid. 25b, 27a, and 65a. Compare Nid. 38a.

19. Two curious examples of Talmudic thinking regarding sex determination which have no confirmation in medicine may be cited. The king of the Arabs put this question to R. Akiva: "I am a black and my wife is a black, yet she gave birth to a white son. Shall I kill her for having played the harlot while living with me?" Asked R. Akiva: "Are the figures painted in your house black or white?" "White," said the king. R. Akiva assured him: "When you had intercourse with her she fixed her eyes upon the white figures and bore a child like them." Tanhuma Naso 7, see also Gen. 30:37–38, Gen. Rabbah 73:10, Num. Rabbah 15.

The timing of intercourse is a critical factor in sex determination. Shettles' study suggests that intercourse at ovulation or very close to it, when the secretions are most alkaline, would most likely result in a male offspring, while intercourse two or three days before ovulation, when an acidity still prevails, would probably result in a female offspring. The female-producing sperm cells can survive those two or three days, while the androsperm (male-producing sperm) rarely last longer than twenty-four hours. In an experiment, nineteen out of twenty-two women who used an acidic douch before intercourse had female offspring, and twenty-two out of twenty-six women who used an alkaline douch had male offspring. See D. Rorvik and L. Shettles, *A Chance to Choose Your Baby's Sex* (Dodd, Mead, 1970), p. 15, no. 83. Compare Zohar Bereshit 30. The Talmud claims that of all births half are male and half females. Bek. 20. According to modern medical statistics the number of male conceptions is higher than that of females, but there is a higher birth rate of females, as well as a higher survival rate of premature females than males. The reason for the greater intrauterine male fetus death is still unknown. See Hellman and Pritchard, *Obstetrics*, p. 125.

20. Lev. Rabbah 14:9, Ber. 60a, Nid. 31a, Aggadah Tazriah 48; The Rabbis, in explaining the development of the fetus, say: "By the fortieth day the child is created, and from the fortieth to the sixtieth the child is recognizable between either a male or a female, from the sixtieth to the ninetieth the womb shall be closed." See also Hellman and Pritchard, *Obstetrics*, pp. 149–151. On the meaning of woman's "zera" see Nachmanides and Seforno to Lev. 12:2.

21. Ruch and Patton, op. cit. p. 1192. See J. Money and A. A. Ehrhardt, *Man and Woman, Boy and Girl* (Baltimore: J. Hopkins Univ. Press, 1972).

22. See supra, note 16, and Lev. Rabbah 23.

23. Nid. 30a. Of such a fetus there is this description in the post-Pentateuchal Scriptures: "Hast thou not poured me out as milk and curdled me like cheese? Thou has clothed me with skin and flesh and knit me together with bones and sinews. Thou has granted me life and favour, and Thy providence hath preserved my spirit" (Job 10–12). To ascertain whether the fetus was male or female, see Nid. 25a–b and 31a, Zohar I:30a. See further Nid. 30b; and Songs Rabbah 7:3. "Just as the embryo, so long as it is in its mother's womb, lives only from its navel." Compare Sot. 45b; Midrash Aggadah Tazria; Nid. 26a and Bek. 21b. Doctors today say that the fetus is alive in every sense but not self-sustaining (requires oxygen and nutrients from the mother). He is nurtured by the mother—"the umbilical cord extends from the fetal umbilicus to the fetal surface of the placenta"—the major agent of nutrition and homeostasis, vital to the survival of the infant. See Hellman and Pritchard, *Obstetrics*, pp. 143–150.

24. See Nid. 30a–b, Yeb. 69b; W. J. Hamilton, J. D. Boyd, and H. W. Mossman, *Human Embryology* (Baltimore: Williams & Wilkins, 1962), pp. 87–93. Compare Hellman and Pritchard, op. cit., p. 320.

There were various rabbinic ideas pertaining to the elements that determine the sex of the child. For example, the Talmud explains that since the sperm is a male cell and the egg cell is female, whichever one enters last into the womb overtakes the one before it and determines the sex of the child. Therefore, whichever parent experiences a delayed emission, the child will be of the same sex. Another idea was based upon the structure of the womb. Within the womb there are seven sacs. There are three sacs on each side and one sac in the middle. If the sperm cell should enter the sacs located on the right of the womb, the infant will be a boy. If it enters into the left sac, the child will be a girl, and if in the middle, the child will be hermaphroditic. It is surmised, therefore, that by lying on a certain side, the mother can determine the sex of the child. See Nid. 31a, Ber. 60a, Hadar Zekenim and Da'at Zekenim on Exod. 1:16 and Lev. 12:2; Menachem Recanati, Ta'ame haMitzvot 13b, and Commentary on the Pentateuch, beg. of Tazria; Pa'aneah Raza 87a.

25. "The Holy One, Blessed Be He, has conferred a great boon on woman in this world in that He does not commence the formation of the embryo with that of the sinews and bones, for these would break through her womb and come out." Lev. Rabbah 14:9. Compare Yoma 85a; Nid. 25a; Gen. Rabbah 22:3; Yalkut Job 905. Modern medicine substantiates this fact. Chondrification (formation of cartilage) centers first appear at six weeks of gestation, while the first indication of ossification (bone formation) appears at eight weeks of gestation. While ossification does begin in utero, major areas of bone formation remain unjoined (notably those of the skull) permitting moulding of the infant's head as it passes through the birth canal. Birth of this now semi-pliable cranium is obviously easier than if the bones were joined to form the rigid skull present throughout life.

26. Git. 23b, Hul 58a. See further Nid. 30b.

27. Nid. 30b–31a.

28. Nid. 26a, Bek. 21b.

29. Midrash Aggadah Tazria. Hellman and Pritchard, op. cit., pp. 149–151, 352.

30. Lev. Rabbah 143 and Yeb. 103a. Uterine contractions represent the greatest force in the birth of the infant. Intraabdominal pressure is a necessary auxiliary to uterine contractions, especially during the second and third stages of labor. According to Exod. 1:16, women in labor used to sit on two stones placed at a slight distance from each other; these stones would be equivalent to the chair of childbirth mentioned in rabbinical times and still used in some parts of the East. God makes the limbs of a woman as hard as stones (abanim) when she sits on the birthstool, in order that she should have strength to give birth, for otherwise she would die. When she stoops to give birth her thighs grow cold like stone. (By means of this symptom the Rabbis were able to detect a mother who tried to conceal a birth.) Sot. 11a; Exod. Rabbah 1:14; 45:1–2. See also Lev. Rabbah 27:7, Pirke De R. Eliezer 34.

31. Nid. 31a. Compare Sot. 11b. See Etz Yoseph, who cites sources that this is no longer the case (Nid. 31a). Similarly in Sot. 11b. See Exod. Rabbah 1, where symbolic reason is given: The male looks towards the ground from where he was created, while the female looks upwards towards the ribs from where she was created.

32. Hellman and Pritchard, op. cit., p. 352.

33. Taan. 8a. For more on the subject see Nid. 26a; Tosefta Nid. 4; Hul. 71a, Maimonides, Yad, Issurei Beeah 10:13.

34. "How long may protracted labor continue? R. Meir replied: 'Even forty

or fifty days.' R. Judah ruled: 'Her ninth month suffices for her.' R. Jose and R. Simeon ruled: 'Protracted labor cannot continue for more than two weeks.' "
Nid. 36b. If a woman is in hard travail, one cuts up the child in her womb and brings it forth member by member, because her life comes before that of the child. Oholoth 7:6; Shab. 129a. Compare Nid. 21a and Hellman and Pritchard, op. cit., pp. 387, 415, 956.

35. "The embryo leaves its mother's abdomen the size of a liberal cubit." Gen. Rabbah 12, Lev. Rabbah 14, Tosephta Nid. 4:4, Shab. 129b. See further Nid. 26a; compare Hellman and Pritchard, op. cit., pp. 320, 352, Midrash Aggadah, Tazria.

36. Shab. 134a.

37. Mishnah Oholoth 7:5.

38. Yoma 71a, Ber. 32a. See Tosephta Kid., ed. Zuckermandel 3:30. In the task of watering the cattle in the Near East, the division of labor was rabbinically arranged: the more strenuous part of drawing well-water was man's task, while that of pouring it was the woman's. Sot. 11b, "and Moses looked on their burdensome labors" What did Moses see? He saw the burden of man placed upon woman. Compare Exod. Rabbah 1, and Lev. Rabbah 34.

39. Yeb. 115a (Rashi—woman does not weaken in the face of robbers). See Tosaf. ad loc. *ikka,* quoting Yerushalmi as woman not being a murderer.

40. One cup of wine is becoming to a woman; two are degrading; Keth. 65a.

41. "It is written in the Hilchot Eretz Yisrael that women are not to slaughter, since they may perhaps become faint." Tosaf. Hulin 2a, s.v. *hakol.* See Drisha Tur Yoreh Deah 11 and Maadanay Yom Tov to 'RoSH' Hul. 1, quoting the Sefer Mitzvot Gadol. Also Shab. 33b and Kid. 80b.

42. Documentary proof of *reshuiot* (permits) issued to women are dated as far back as 1556, when R. Isaac B. Immanuel de Lattes of Mantua, Italy, authorized a lady to engage in this profession. In 1938, there were two women in Florence practicing Shehitah for their own households. Between these two widely-separated dates, many licenses attest to the fact that ritual slaughtering was undertaken by women in the Sephardic countries. See Charles Duschinsky, "May a Woman be a Shoheteth?", in *Gaster Memorial Volume* (London, 1936), pp. 102, 139. With the passing of the years, women began to be excluded from this work, which they had shared with the men in all Oriental lands, and it was finally entrusted to men only, with the exception of Italy. The Ashkenazic authorities were vehemently opposed to have women engage in this practice. Tosaf. Hul. 2a, *hakol* and Karo, Yoreh Deah 1:1. R. Moses Isserles (1520–1572) of Cracow, Poland, states, "There is an opinion that we do not permit women to slaughter, since they have been forbidden by long-established practice. It is the rule that women do not slaughter." Gloss on Shulhan Arukh, Yoreh Deah 1:1. For a further study on the topic, see: Jeremiah Berman, *Shehitah: A Study in Cultural and Social Life of the Jewish People* (New York: Bloch, 1941), pp. 134–136.

43. Keth. 59a, Meg 15a, Ta'an. 31a.

44. See Ber. 57b.

45. Gen. Rabbah 40:5.

46. Ta'an. 24a; Songs Rabbah 4; compare Yoma 74b.

47. San 100b, Num. Rabbah 17:6; compare San. 45a and Gen. Rabbah 17:7.

48. Ber. 24a; It is impossible for a man to live with a woman who is bald. Naz. 28a; Songs Rabbah 4:3; Ber. 61a. Compare Iggrot Moshe, Orah Hayim 4, pp. 22–24.

49. Nid. 31b, Ber. 57b, Gen. Rabbah 17:8, Ber. 24a. On the fetishistic aspects of woman's physique, see B. A. Bauer, Woman and Love I, (New York: Liveright, 1971), chap. 7. Listening to instrumental music played by a woman is permitted, Aruch haShulhan, 75, 8. See also Otzar HaPoskim, E.H. 21, 20, 2.

50. H. Ellis, Studies in the Psychology of Sex (New York: Random House, 1928), chap. 1. W. Goethe, in Iphigenia auf Tauris, Oct. 1, sc. 2, l. 162. "When men sing and women join in, it is licentiousness." Sot. 48a. See Meiri, Keth. 75a., who distinguishes between types of voices. Some theorists have held that the voice, whether of men or of women, is herald of the innermost spiritual life. "The power of song, the power of speech, are fetishistic influences; they must be numbered amongst those influences which arouse what is called love at first sight, and should here be called love at first sound." Bauer, op. cit., p. 125.

51. Songs Rabbah 4:5–1. The Talmud compares the two poles of the Holy Ark to the protrusion of two breasts of a woman. Yoma 54a. Also Zohar Genesis 45. The separation between the breasts of a woman is a handbreath. Keth. 75a; Rashi, ad. loc. Yer. Keth. 7:7. Compare Lev. Rabbah 14:3, Commentary of R. Avigdor Katz to Midrash Shir haShirim 8:8 (Jerusalem, 1982) and Ber. 10b.

52. Ned. 66b. see Ellis, Psychology of Sex, p. 15; compare Bauer, op. cit., pp. 109–112.

53. Ned. 66b, Gen. Rabbah 7:1, 2 Kings 22:14; Jud. 4:6; Meg. 14b.

54. "The daughters of Israel are beautiful, but poverty makes them homely." Mishnah Ned. 66a (other editions read "but pain disfigures them"); compare Yalkut Shimoni, Behalotha 738.

"He who wishes his daughter to have a bright complexion, let him on the approach to her maturity feed her with young fowls and give her milk to drink." Keth. 60a see Midrash haGadol Lekh Lekha, Schechter ed., Y. Yadin, Genesis Apocryphon, V, 43. R. Israel of Ruzhin (1798-1850) see Eireen Kadishin Teenyana (Jerusalem, 1970), p. 2b.

55. Mishnah Keth. 77a, see also Bauer, op. cit., p. 79.

56. Keth. 59b.

57. Shab. 64b.

"Would woman adorn herself if not for her husband . . . " See Sot. 47a, Shohar Tov 44; Midrash Hidoth, same in Bauer, op. cit., p. 48; See Ned. 81b; H. L. Mencken, In Defense of Woman (New York: Knopf, 1918), p. 76, compare Naz. 45b.

58. Ta'an. 31a, Shab. 62b.

59. "Can the Evil Desire be very good? That would be paradoxical! But if not for the Evil Desire, however, no man would build a house, take a wife, and beget children." Gen. Rabbah 9:7 See Yoma 69b.

60. Keth. 65a. See also Rashi, Ki Tisah 32:2, states, "Women and children cherish their adornments.

61. Esther Rabbah 3:10.

62. R. Hiyya (further) taught: "He who wishes his wife to look graceful should clothe her in linen garments." Keth. 59b, Yeb. 63b.

63. Ber. 57b (see Shab. 25b); M.K. 9b.

64. Shab. 62b; compare Sot. 3b.

65. "Women like to display and will untie their ornaments for their neighbors." Yer. Shab. 6:7. Exod. Rabbah 32:5. See Bauer, op. cit., p. 172. An ornament with a picture of gold engraving of Jerusalem worn by a woman of rank will not be removed for display. Shab. 59b, compare Arukh haShulhan 75.

66. J. C. Flugel, *The Psychology of Clothes*, pp. 214–215.

67. Ibn Ezra to Exod. 38:8. See Targum Onkelos, Pseudo-Jonathan, and Rashi ad loc.

68. Keth. 71a–71b, Shab. 57b.

69. W. Fielding, *Love and Sex Emotions*, (New York: Perma Books, 1961), p. 89. See Bauer, op. cit., p. 84.

70. "A wife needs to be perfumed." The bidegroom must undertake (to give his wife) ten Denarii for her (perfume) basket." Mishnah Keth. 66b; Gen. Rabbah 8:17. Compare Yoma 39b, Yer. Maaser Sheni 5:2, Shab. 62b. See Karo, Eben haEzer 73:1–6 and compare Tanhuma Vayislah. See Shaar haTakanot, p. 120, ed. Bloch, and Elyiahu Zutta 16. Women have a far greater fondness for flowers than men. The sweetness of the fragrance is more important than the beauty and color of the flower.

71. See Shab. 62b; a woman enjoys jewelry more than any other form of decoration. Midrash haGadol 309.

72. Rashi, Ki Tisa 32:2.

73. See supra 65. Shab. 59b and M. K. 8a–9b.

74. Resp. Geonim, ed. Asaf, no. 689, p. 160; Rashi, Shab. 64b; and Shiltei ha-Gibborim ad loc., also Iggrot Moshe II, Eben haEzer 12. However, not all women are tolerant of foreign hair. Many women find it undesirable, since it is displeasing to their husbands. Tosaf. Naz. 28b. The reference here is to a broad band which a woman tied very tightly about her, so as to give herself a plump appearance. Rashi, Shab 57b. See the "Rav," Bertinoro on Sot., 1:6 compare Bauer, op. cit., II, p. 226.

75. The Rabbis considered every bride to have a natural beauty. "No powder and no paint and no waving (of the hair), and still a graceful gazelle" was the customary praise bestowed upon a bride. Keth. 17a. "A poor woman who is used to not adorning herself does not suffer if she vows not to adorn herself." Keth. 71b and Yer. Keth. 7:3.

76. Zohar Gen. 231b; see Meir of Rothenburg, Responsum no. 199. Women should be careful about fixing their hair and doing their nails, her nose should not run, and if she has any blemish she should cover it up and keep it from her husband. Shevet Mussar 2.

77. Yoma 2:24. Women are required to beautify themselves for their husbands' sake (constantly), and they may use charcoal for their eyes and perfumes for their lips in order that they will always be desired by their husbands as if they were brides. Otzar haGeonim, ed. Levin.

78. ". . . a bride we adorn (with jewelry, etc.) and perfume her." Exod. Rabbah Beshalah: ibid, Ki Tisa; see also Zohar I:8a.

79. Likewise, the Law excused her from immersion the day after the wedding because of her sexual contact. "The Torah showed concern for the bride's cosmetics, so that the makeup should not come off when she immerses herself in water." Yeb. 34a, Rashi ad loc.

80. "The daughters of Israel adorn themselves on a festival." Keth. 71b. "A man is duty bound to make his children and his household rejoice on a festival. For women in Babylonia, with colored garments, in Israel, with iron linen garments." Pes. 109b, Kid. 34b, R.H. 6b. This proves that R. Hiyya edited the braitot in Israel, since he stated in Keth. 59b: "He who wishes his wife to look graceful should clothe her in linen garments" (the dress of Israel, and not of Babylonia). "These new clothes should be given to her on the occasion of a major festival so that she might derive joy from them." Keth. 65b.

81. The following rabbinic psychological discussion is of paramount interest: The Gemara asks, "But we had previously stated that one who is boastful is not even accepted by his own household. How can you, therefore, state that the daughters of Israel choose the boastful?" The Gemara answers: "At first, the woman becomes impressed with the outward impression of the man. After a while, however, she sees his true character and despises him." Yer. Shab. 6.

82. Who is regarded as "an old woman"? When one is called "mother" because of old age in her presence and she does not mind or does not blush. Nid. 9b and Gen. Rabbah 47:3. Compare Yer. Nid. 4:4. The age when her women friends speak of her as an old woman. See Yalkut Shimoni Behaalotha 738; Gen. Rabbah 48:17. Compare also Tosaf. Shab. 64b; see Keth. 48a. Where the marriage of the daughter has been accompanied by threats to the mother's conception of herself as a young, attractive woman, the threat posed by grandparenthood may be even greater.

83. "At sixty as of six. The sound of a timbrel makes her nimble." M.K. 9b (note Psalms 68:26). See Or Hachayim on the Torah, who quotes in the name of the Rabbis, "Shkem of Canaan brought the daughters of the land round the tent of Jacob to play their instruments to entice his daughter, Dinah, to come out, for it is the pleasure of women to go after song." The Bible often relates dance and music to women. "Then shall the virgin rejoice in the dance." Jer. 31:3, 12; "with timbrels and with dances," Exod. 15:20, Judg. 11:34, "and they dance in the vineyards," Ta'an. 26b.

84. M. Mead, *Male and Female*, (New York: Morrow, 1967), pp. 357–8.

85. R. Abbahu stated: "one is allowed to teach his daughter Greek, since it is an adornment for her." Yer. Shab. 6:1. Compare Rashi, Sot. 49b.

APPENDIX B

1. J. Drever, *A Dictionary of Psychology* (London: Penguin, 1972).

2. S. Freud, *The Autobiographical Study* (London: Hogarth, 1935). For a discussion of whether love or hate are instincts, see Gordon W. Allport, *Personality and Social Encounter* (Boston: Beacon Press, 1960), pp. 207–211.

3. Shab. 33b, Tanhuma Vayeshev: compare Bauer, *Women and Love*, II, p. 285, Nid. 31b. See Gen. Rabbah 17 and Etz Yosef ad loc.

4. Meg. 14b; Ber. 10a.

5. "One should always be heedful of wronging his wife, for since her tears are frequent she is easily hurt." B.M. 59a, see Rosh ad loc. The same statement is attributed to Pythagoras. "A widow converses excessively, a tear flows down her cheek, and a sigh against those who rebelled against her." Ben Sirah 35:15. An orphan's or a widow's tears are frequent. Shab. 11a; see Rashi BB. 59a and 123a; Nid. 52a; Lament. Rabbah, Petichta 2.

6. Girls are taught that is is perfectly proper for them to cry, boys, on the contrary, are taught that is is unmanly to cry. Montagu, loc. cit., p. 86.

7. "If a man forbade his wife by vow that she shall not visit a house of mourning (or a house of feasting), he must divorce her and give her the Kethubah, because thereby he has closed (people's doors) against her." Mishna Keth. 71b.

8. "The merit of a funeral oration lies in lifting one's voice in lamentation and sorrow so that the listeners should weep." Rashi. Ber. 6b.

9. Gen. Rabbah 17:8. See Sanh. 20a; "Women are always in front of the procession," Yoreh Deah 359.

10. The prophet summons the daughter of Zion to repentance and bids her "lament like a virgin girded with sackcloth for the husband of her youth," "call for the women who chant dirges, and send for wise women that they may come." Jer. 14:2, 9:71. Such mourning rituals are amply described in Jeremiah 16:6–8; and Ezekiel 24:16–17; Yer. M.K.1. "Even the poorest of Jews should not have less than two women professional mourners and one flute (at a funeral)." Keth. 46b. Compare Gen. 23:2, 24:67; Judg. 11:40, Ps. 35:14.

11. Quoted in Ellis, *Studies in the Psychology of Sex*, p. 27.

12. Montagu, op. cit., p. 96. Woman is overcome by her fears, being afraid to go alone to any distant place after dark. She insists upon having a man accompany her. Keth. 20b; see Bertinoro Oholot 42:16, Sanh. 19a, Git 45a, compare A. Scheinfeld, *Women and Men* (New York: Harcourt, Brace, 1944), p. 95.

13. Psychologists are becoming more and more aware of the immense ego-reinforcement derived from religion. Such acknowledgment began with Wil-

liam James, Leuba, E. Fromm, Gordon Allport, Carl Menninger, J. Arlow, Linn, and others.

14. "Greater is the promise made by the Holy One, Blessed be He, to the women than to the men, for it says, 'Rise up, ye women that are at ease; ye confident daughters.' " (Isa. 32:9) Ber. 17a, Pes. 113b.

15. Exod. Rabbah 28:2; Tanhuma Metzora 9, Pesikta Zut, Gen. 27:5, Pirkei De R. Eliezer 45; See Rashi Yetro 19:3 from Mekhilta. Compare Scheinfeld, *Women and Men*, p. 221.

16. Ber. 20a.

17. Yer. Pes. 4:1 and Menorat haMaor 131.

In our opinion the Aggada here engaged in a homiletic enlargement on this theme. Originally the men also observed the First of the Month, which was considered as holiday. See 2 Kings 4:23, also 1 Sam. 20:5. However, for men it was an extremely difficult task to observe eleven days of the year, and even more in case of a leap year, and thus they did do work on the first of the month. However, men who remained in the house undoubtedly observed the ancient tradition. See Tosaf. Meg. 22b and Rashi, who quotes from Pirkei De R. Eliezer, "women were given this commandment, because they did not remove their nosebands for the golden calf—thus we see that the first of the month is not a day of action." Similarly in Tur Orah Haim 670:1, see Targum Pseudo-Jonathan Exod. 32:3.

18. Quoted by Elyahu Rabbah and Darkei Moshe, see also Levush and Tur, O.H. 417.

19. A "prayerful maiden" (In Yerushalmi: "a self-afflicting maiden"). Sot. 22a. It is impossible to live with a woman that makes too many vows, Keth. 71A. "An abstinent (modest) woman sits and laughs at the statements from the Torah," Yer. Sot. 3.

20. "In order to gratify women." Hag. 16b. See Erub. 96a, Yer. Ber. 2:3; see Karo, S.A., O.H. 38:3, and Mishna Berura 640:1.

21. "Though they were Sadducee women they feared the Pharisees." Nid. 33b. Compare Tosaf. Nid. 5a and notes of the Gaon of Vilna.

22. Based on Exod. 22:18, see Yer. Kid. 4:17; Sanh. 67a; Avot 2:9, Ber. 53a, Erub. 64b, Yer. Pes. 7, Yer. Shab. 15:3, Zohar 1, 126b.

23. Gen. Rabbah 20, 45; see Rashi, Naz. 23b. Tanchuma Ki Taitzei.

24. S. Freud, *Certain Neurotic Mechanisms in Jealousy, Paranoia and Homosexuality, Collected Papers*, vol. II (London: Hogarth Press), p. 930.

25. K. Horney, *Feminine Psychology* (New York: Norton, 1967), pp. 76, 230

26. Scheinfeld, op. cit., p. 191.

27. The Rabbis observed that woman's envy is more intense than that of man. Envious wives will ruin their husbands. Lev. Rabbah 25:6, Pes. 49b. Envy is hatred without a cure says Bahya Ben Asher (14c) Kad haKemach on Kineah. Hag. 22a, Pes, 49b, Kid. 35a. Anger in a home is like rottenness in fruit. Sot. 3b.

28. A barren wife in the early Israelite family would be despised by her

companion (e.g., Hanah and Peninah, 1 Sam. 1:6), even if the latter were a slave (Sarah and Hagar, Gen. 16:4–5) and the barren wife could be jealous of one with children, as Rachel was of Leah (Gen. 30:1). The husband's preference for one of his wives could make this rivalry more bitter (Gen. 29:30–31, 1 Sam. 1:5) until the law (Deut. 21:15–17) had to intervene (W. Fielding, *Love and the Sex Emotions*, p. 60). "As for the case of a man who marries an additional wife, if the second wife is her superior, the first will not be jealous of her; if she is her inferior, the first wife will be jealous of her." A.Z. 55a. See Rashi ad loc. s.v. ein; for the opposite outcome, compare Maharsha ad loc. and Yoma 73a.

29. J. C. Rheingold, *The Fear of Being a Woman* (New York: Grune Stratton, 1967), p. 244. S. de Beauvoir, *The Second Sex* (New York: Bantam, 1968), p. 507.

30. The Rabbis sought to determine what effect this psychological principle had in the various phases of life. For instance, a woman will testify in court against her rival, in a case in which she herself is also a principal, even though it will reflect detrimentally upon her own character as well. The question arises whether she is telling the truth, or is her testimony merely spitework, to destroy her rival? Factually, this extreme jealousy is not common among the average woman. She would not be so vindictive as to damage herself, in order to ruin her rival. Yeb. 120a. See Keth. 23b, Sanh. 110a, Pes. 113b, Shab. 34a. Compare S. de Beauvoir, *The Second Sex*, p. 530.

31. "There is no jealousy but (in love for a friend)." Zohar Metzorah 54b and Zohar Gen. 245a.

32. Meg. 13a. The way to rouse a woman is to make her jealous. "Thigh" implies that a woman does not become jealous even of another woman, except for things touching upon her relationship with her husband. See also Yeb. 63b.

33. A daughter-in-law dislikes her mother-in-law because the latter talks ill about her to her son. The mother-in-law usually finds fault with her daughter-in-law, and tries to avert her son's love from his wife. Yeb. 117a. See Rashi 117b *deragish*. The psychological ground for her grudge, according to Tradition, is that she cannot bear the idea that her daughter-in-law will acquire what she considered her sole domain and possession. "A mother-in-law hates her daughter-in-law, since the former believes the latter squanders her savings." Yeb. 117a. (see Rashi). The mother-in-law expects her son's wife to treat him as she would have, were he to marry her. A daughter-in-law who becomes a mother herself seems to the jealous mother-in-law to endanger her tender possession of her son more than a daughter-in-law who does not have that hold over him. Rheingold, *Fear of Being a Woman*, p. 503, see Tzeror haMor, Haye Sarah.

Concern for mother's welfare and security is a Talmudic explanation for the jealousy aroused in the husband's sisters towards his wife who they claim "she eats up what is accumulated for our mother." Yeb. 117a. Another reason why her sisters-in-law dislike her is their identification with their mother's jealousy of her. This reaction is present only if the mother is alive, however; if she isn't, the reason for such jealousy doesn't exist, see Kid. 81b.

34. G. W. Allport, "Personality Character and Temperament," in *Pattern and Growth in Personality*, (New York: Holt, 1961).

35. English and English, *Dictionary of Psychological and Psychoanalytical Terms* (New York: Longmans, 1968).

36. A. A. Roback, *The Psychology of Character* (New York: Harcourt, 1927), p. 450.

37. Tanhuma 59.2.

38. Kid. 80b; see R. Nissim on Alfasi ad loc.

39. Sot. 47a, P. Rieff, *Freud: The Mind and the Moralist* (New York: Anchor, 1961), pp. 202–203. "The essence of love is spiritual love, and it is incumbent upon him to criticize her in a pleasant manner and to guide her in the ways of modesty." Pele Yoetz. Therefore a husband's constructive criticism of his wife is not merely a sign of his love for her but rather causes her to love him. Psychology teaches us that chastisement which comes from the heart enters the other's heart to arouse faith and friendship.

40. Shab. 33b, Avot De R. Nathan, Yoma 84b, Men. 110a.

41. Sot. 47a, Rashi *yetzer* ad loc. Kate Millet, *Sexual Politics* (Garden City: Doubleday, 1970), pp. 176–203

42. The wife of a scholar is trusted as a scholar. This is an accepted rule. The wife of a scholar who married an *am-haaretz* and similarly the daughter of a scholar who married an *am-haaretz* do not have to officially "renew" their trustworthiness. This is the opinion of R. Meir. A.Z. 39a. Despite the fact that generally where R. Meir and R. Judah disagree, the law follows to R. Judah, here we follow R. Meir. It is possible that Rebbi also regarded women to be generally worthy of trust until proven otherwise, as inferred from Yer. Kid. 4:4. "As long as woman did not make herself impure, she remains pure." "No genuine woman ever gives a hoot for law if law happens to stand in the way of her private happiness." Mencken, *In Defense of Women*, p. 51.

43. S. Freud, *New Introductory Lectures on Psycho-Analysis*, Lecture 33, Standard ed. vol. 21 (London: Hogarth Press, 1961).

44. Yer. Sot. 5:8, See P. Rieff, *Freud: The Mind of a Moralist*, pp. 20–23. It is highly likely that the reason why "a woman is not to judge" (Yer. Shav. 4:5) is because "we are not to feel mercy in judgment" (Keth. 84b) and "It is the nature of woman to have pity." See also Sefer Malki baKodesh.

45. Num. Rabbah 10:17, Yer. Pes. 1:4.

46. Yeb. 114b.

47. F. C. Redlich and D. X. Friedman, *The Theory and Practice of Psychiatry* (New York: Basic Books, 1966), pp. 357, 377.

48. "Dirty hands are unfit for the recital of Grace." Bathing is part of a woman's adornment, for she desires to make herself look beautiful. Ned. 80b.

49. Nid. 48b., A. Gesell, F. L. Ilg and L. B. Ames, *The Years from Ten to*

Sixteen (New York, 1956), p. 266. In Talmudic times due to lack of hygienic facilities and of water resources, a village or country woman could do without bathing for two weeks, but a woman of the town could not go longer than a week. However, if she was accustomed to bathing more frequently, not taking her bath for two days caused her considerable discomfort. Yer. Keth. 7:4. See also Tosaf. and Ran to Ned. 80a.

50. A. Scheinfeld, *Women and Men*, pp. 74, 155. Reported by Army Medical Research and Development Command; *see New York Times*, Feb. 27, 1971.

51. Ber. 48b, Gen. Rabbah 70:10, Deut. Rabbah 6:5. Kid. 49b, Ber. 3a. See Rabbeinu Tam—whenever "with" is mentioned, the second plays the inferior role. Thus she is the primary speaker.

52. T. Reik, *Sex in Man and Woman* (New York: Noonday Press, 1960), p. 82.

53. Ben Sirah 26:14; Deut. Rabbah 6, see Bauer, *Women and Love*, II, p. 103; Ned. 21b.

54. Sanh. 100b, Shab 33b; see John Macy, *About Woman* (New York: Morrow, 1930), p. 157,

55. Taharoth 7, Mishnah; Gen. Rabbah 45; Esther Rabbah 3:10; Targum Shayni to Esther 1:9. H. Deutsch, *Psychology of Women*, vol. I, p. 19.

56. "The strength (feeling) of women is greater than that of men. Men say 'let's choose a leader and return to Egypt,' whereas women say, 'give us property in Israel.' " See Rashi Keth. 83b, *mehira*—a woman does not want to sell the property of her father. B.B. 155b, see RoSH Kid. 2:15.

57. Yeb. 26a, N. W. Bell and E. F. Vogel, *The Family* (1968), p. 401. N. Ackerman, *The Psychodynamics of Family Life* (1958), p. 57.

58. According to Rashi, "It is better for two bodies to live together "*tan doo*" than to live alone." Kid. 41a. There is no doubt that the reason is because woman is more socially oriented. See Aruch haShalem, *tan doo*. I. Lepp, *The Psychology of Loving* (1963), p. 48. For an opposite view, see Bauer, *Woman and Love*, I, pp. 72, 98.

59. Pes. 87a; see R. Tam in Tosaf. ad loc.

60. Yer. Pes. 8:1

61. James, *Psychology*, p. 439.

62. Tanhuma 59:3; see same in Mantegazza, *Psychology of Love*. Compare Pes. 87b. Pirkei De R. Eliezer 32.

63. Mishnah Keth. 7:4, Rashi ad loc and Tosaf. Riad.

64. "Because a woman is particular about herself." Kid. 11a, See RoSH to Kid. 3a, who states that a woman not offer herself in marriage for free.

65. Kid. 49a.

66. Yer. Kid. 2:3

67. Ibid, Yerushalmi, as quoted by the RoSH in Kid. 2:2, which differs from the version in our Yerushalmi Kid. 49a, Tosafot ad loc. *mai* and Hag. 4b.

68. Keth. 27b, Sot. 7b, Rashi *sheliba*. Tosafot Kid. 49a, see Hag. 4b.

69. Gen. Rabbah 17:7, Tanhuma 59:2, Yeb. 63b; compare Ab. Z. 39a; Bech.

39b. "The wise among women builds her home but the foolish one pulls it down with her hands." Num. Rabbah 18:20. See Pirkei De R. Eliezer 41, "men follow the values (though literally) of woman." Rashi to Gen. 32:23 from Gen. Rabbah 76.

70. F. S. Caprio, *The Sexually Adequate Female*, p. 9, "On the other hand, Gold and Slater find that wives of white-collar bureaucrats concentrate on encouraging the husband's effort to get ahead." O. Blood, Jr., and D. M. Wolfe, *Husbands and Wives*, (New York: Free Press, 1960), pp. 91–92.

"The favour of a woman is in the estimation of her husband." Sot. 47a. The meaning of *hayn* could be interpreted as "influence," as found in Keth. 84a, *mishum hinah*, compare Midrash Tehilim 44. See Pele Yoetz. "How good for a man to have a devoted friend. Someone with whom to take counsel and not rely on his own understanding, but he must be a faithful friend unto him, and there is no more faithful one to a man than his wife, therefore, it is said, if your wife is short, bend down, ask her advice and allow yourself to be advised by her." B.M. 59a. "He whose wife has died . . . his wits collapse." San. 22a (see opposite in re: to Manoah, father of Samson, Ber. 61b). "He whom his wife dominates—his life is no life." Bez. 32b, Avot De R. Nathan 25:5. A Talmudic dictum states, "Among those who cry but nobody takes any notice of him is the husband who is ruled by his wife." Sot. 8b.

71. Shek. 9b; quoted by J. H. Hertz, *The Pentateuch* (London, 1958), p. 685.

72. Keth. 67b; Yer. Sotah 3.

73. Gen. Rabbah. 18:2, Tanhuma Vayeshev 6, Git. 90a.

74. Num. Rabbah 1:3. see supra 2.

75. In discussing this subject, Chapman voices the modern view, which reflects the same basic needs: Woman "wants and needs a home, a baby, and the things marriage can give her," as a rule, "she needs to get married more than a man does." He contends that a "husband is a priceless 'commodity,' " since our social structure demands that a girl should marry, D. Chapman, *The Feminine Mind and Body*, (New York: Citadel, 1968), p. 191.

76. Keth. 67b. See also Tosaf. Riad ad loc.; Kid. 22a; Mishnah Horayoth 13a (See Gemara). "In order to save a woman from degradation we dispose of a woman's lawsuit first."

77. Yeb. 100a. "It's not the nature of women to go to the courts, because no man wants his wife to suffer the indignity of appearing in court" Keth. 74a, 97b; see Git. 41a, Sot. 8b, Yeb. 42b, Rashi to Yeb. 42b.

78. Keth. 104b, see Rashi, 67a, and 84a Rashi.

79. Kid. 35a; compare Keth. 9:4, Shab. 62b, and Ruth Rabbah 4.

80. Keth. 71b.

81. Pes. 86b. Rashi and R. Hananel; Shab. 57b, *Itztamach*.

82. "A bride should not go out in a palanquin . . . for reasons of chastity" (there was a danger of her being attacked). Sot. 49b, B.K. 82a (see *Shaar haTakanoth*, Bloch, p. 121).

83. Quoted in A. Scheinfeld, *Men and Women*, p. 190. As long as a woman is involved with her domestic duties and is not a gad-about she is considered modest *(tzenuah)*. Zohar, Gen. 115.

84. See Rashi to Git. 12a, Gen. Rabbah 18:1, compare San. 105b. A similar identification of women with the tent is found in Deborah's song (Judg. 5:24), "Blessed above women shall Jael be, the wife of Heber the Kenite. Above women in the tent shall she be blessed." As known, Bedouin women even nowadays are seen as tenting-women. The Yiddish proverb also says: "There is no greater honor than to stay home." Gen. Rabbah 8:12; compare Keth. 63b, "It is not the nature of woman to roam the streets."

85. See Rashi to Kid. 70a; Sefer haHinukh 188. Hiddushei Ritva to Kid. 81b.

86. "If one sees a male chasing a female, accept it (as fact); a female chasing a male, do not accept it." Gen. Rabbah 2:21, Shab. 152a, Kid 2b.

87. "Do daughters need surveillance?" ("Daughters, even when they are small do not need to be watched over, since it is not their nature to go outside"—Rabbeinu Nissim). In Rashi we find the quoting of the passage in Psalms 45:14 "the entire glory of a princess is from within." See Num. Rabbah 11:7 "The Lord should bless you," with sons, "and he should watch over you," with daughters, who need watching over. It is possible that the Midrash was referring to grown daughters, in a similar to the statement of Ben Sirah quoted in San. 100b, "guard her in her maturity so that she should not become unchaste." See also Beth Sefer, Schechter ed., vol., VII, 24.

88. Ber. 3b, "It is more likely for an accident to occur (on a trip) to a woman than to a man." Rashi Kid. 53b; Rashi Sanh. 82b.

89. See Karo, O.H. 75:1 and Mishnah Berurah ad loc. 1 and 74:1; Resp. Iggrot Moshe, Eben haEzer, 1, 69.

90. "It is the nature of man to conduct war, but it is not the nature of a woman." Kid. 2b. "It is not the nature of woman to subdue." Yeb. 65b.

91. Rashi to Shab. 53b, B.K. 48a, B.B. 57a; see Rashi and R. Gershom ad loc.

92. "It is customary for a man to meet wayfarers and not for a woman." Yeb. 76b.

93. Semahot 9:7, ed. Higger (New York 1931), p. 171.

94. Shab. 98b.

95. Shab. 80a, Rashi explains that the type of woman the Talmud refers to is the city woman. She dresses in a more modest manner because of her knowledge of the world. See Er. 21b.

96. Yer. Keth. 7:4.

97. Sifrei Naso, 11, "It is not like the daughters of Israel to walk out with heads uncovered." Rashi to Keth. 72a. also Ned. 30a. See also supra on Beauty, footnote 48. "A man once uncovered the head of a woman in the market place. When he was brought to court before R. Akiva, he ordered him to pay four hundred zuz." Mishnah B.K. 90b. The Talmud states that from the law of *sotah* (a married woman suspected of adultery, Num. 5:18), we learn that a married

woman's hair is normatively covered. Sifrei Naso; Keth. 72a. The pious say: "cursed be the man who lets the hair of his wife be seen . . . a woman who exposes her hair for self-adornment brings poverty." Yer. Meg. 7:2; Num. Rabbah, end chap. 2,; Yoma 47a. One of the first features of feminine beauty mentioned in the Song of Songs is the hair. "Your hair is like a flock of goats trailing down from Mount Gilead" glossy in its color, (4:1) pointing out that hair is so intimate a part of a woman that it is considered "nudity." (Ber. 24a) Rabbinic law, therefore, forbids the recitation of blessings or prayers in the presence of a bareheaded married woman. (Karo, S.A. O.H. 21:1) The reason may be that the hair forms a frame for the most expressive part of the human body—the face. Hence, the Torah recognizes a woman's hair as a prime element of her femininity, since God, Himself, at Creation, braided the hair of Eve before he brought her to Adam to make him like her (Shab. 95a, Ber. 61a). It follows, therefore, that a woman's beauty is intended for her husband only. Symbolically, a woman's hair represents also her intuitive and comprehension qualities, since the hair is the coronet of the head, the seat of human intellect. (Hafetz Hayim, Geder Olam).

98. Yer. Keth. 3a, Gen. Rabbah 70:11.

99. Meg. 14b."Who is regarded as a screamer? A woman whose voice can be heard by her neighbors when she speaks inside her house." Mishnah Keth. 72a. Compare Num. Rabbah 9. The Gemara interpreted the Mishnah allegorically, not wishing to punish her that severely for speaking, so as not to receive the ascribed sum of her Ketubbah. They were forced to explain the Mishnah as referring to a wife who loudly asks her husband for conjugal rights. Perhaps when Israelites were living in their own land there was great stress placed on a woman not being excessively noisy. In the times of the Amoraim in Babylon, however, this etiquette may have been taken more in stride, and thus they interpreted the Mishnah in a broader sense. Compare the argument between Zeirah and Rav Assi in Keth. 16a in re: to medaberet. See Suk. 31a—Rashi ad loc and Keth. 72a.

100. A "tent" refers to woman, as it is stated "return to your tents." M.K. 7b and Midrash Aggada, Buber ed., Lekh lekha.

101. "His house refers to his wife." Yoma 2a based on Lev. 16:6. See supra on Modesty note 84.

102. Shab. 118b. "The house of Jacob—these are the women." Exod. Rabbah 28.

103. Philo, Questions and Answers, Genesis also B.M. 59a. "It is the nature of woman to remain within her own household." Gen. Rabbah 18, Kid. 35a. "She is the guardian of the house." Rashi to Ber. 56a. itetah, Tosaf. Keth. 59b arba: Even if a woman brought with her maids (to do the housework), she still has to perform light work in the house, including the charity to the bypassing poor. Compare B.M. 59a.

104. Yer. Keth 5:6. See Shab. 32b and Pes. 50b; Mishna Keth. 5:5. Turkish

folklore states that "the devil tempts all other men, but idle men tempt the devil," or in the words of Mme. Roland, "idleness is the sepulchre of virtue."

105. Women are diligent. Pes. 47a. "The hardest work is to go idle" claims a Yiddish proverb, or as Chesterfield has it, "idleness is only the refuge of weak minds, and the holiday of fools." In primitive cultures women have been responsible for most of the useful arts in their early stages. The making of baskets, pottery, spinning, weaving, the preparation of skins, the making of clothes from cloth and skin, and the preparation of food, including the grinding of corn, were among woman's duties. *Encyclopaedia of Religion and Ethics*, vol. 6, pp. 505–506.

106. "She plays with little cubs (dogs or lions) and in *nardshir*" (Persian word, in Arabic: *nard*), a game similar to checkers. Keth. 61b; see Mishnah Keth. 5:5.

107. Meg. 14b; Rashi Keth. 66b. Exod. Rabbah 30: See Yoreh Deah 324:2 and ShaKH ad loc.; Kid. 82a: Tem. 6a; Ber. 17a.

108. Sot. 3b in Rashi s.v. *beiteta*.

109. B.M. 59a; Tem. 16a; Keth. 65a; Pesikta d'Rav Kahana, Bahodesh Hashlishi; Songs Rabbah 1.

110. "Changing residences is harder for man than for woman." Keth. 28a, see Maharshah ad loc., compare Erub. 47b.

111. Erub. 19a.

112. Ibid. and B.K. 92b.

113. Tosafot to Keth. 65a "venotnin."

114. Sheiltoth de Rav Achai Gaon, quoted by Rashbam Pes. 108a.

115. A woman prefers to dwell in beautiful (designed) homes and to wear beautifully designed clothes than to eat stuffed calf-meat (fancy meat). Esther Rabbah 3:10, Yalkut Esther 1049.

116. Nid. 56b. See Gen. Rabbah 17:8, Tanhuma Noah 1, Takanat Ezra according to version of the Yerushalmi; see Shaar haTakanoth, Bloch; p. 120, # 217. See Mishnah Pes. 48b, where R. Akiva states that "not all women are alike." Gen. Rabbah 20, Compare Yer. Pes. 1:1, 2:4. R. Zera's statement according to Pnei Moshe and Ahavat Zion v'Yerushalayim. "They check bit by bit and do their work slowly." San 7a see Rashi; Yer. Pes. 2:4. "Thus girls are conscientious and boys are slow, which implies that *atzlut* in women is their 'laggardliness.' " The reading in Yerushalmi Keth. 5:6 tends to substantiate the opinion that "laggard" and not "lazy" is the proper definition for *atzlut*. Yer. Keth. 5:6. "Who does he praise? The women who are not accustomed to rise early (but yet did rise early)." Hag. 12b.

117. "A woman stays at home and gives bread to the poor which they can at once enjoy." Taan. 23b. See also Menorat haMaor 10, compare B.M. 87a.

118. See Karo, Y.D. 248:4 and 5, and 257:4, see Seforno to Exod. 35:22, also Resp. Noda beYehudah I, 14:72, ibid. II, 10:158 based on B.K. 118b. Shakh Hoshen Mishpat 96, 9, Resp. Beer Moshe 1, 53, Resp. Maharam Mintz 7, Yam shei Shlomo, Perek Hagozel Umaakhil [B.K., Ch. 10], 59.

119. Keth. 71b.

120. A. Montagu, *The Natural Superiority of Women* (London: George Allen & Unwin, 1945), p. 166.

121. See C. Gilman, *Women and Economics* (New York: Harper, 1970), p. 336.

APPENDIX C

1. This teaches us that the Holy One gave more understanding to woman than to man. The RoSH explains this to mean that comprehension develops earlier in women than in men. RoSH to Nid. 45b, Tossefta ad loc. and Gen. Rabbah 18:1.

2. The RaN and Madanay Yom Tov claim that woman's mental development is precocious because she also develops quicker physically. Men. 110a. A. Gesell, Frances Ilg, and Louis B. Ames, *Youth: The Years from Ten to Sixteen* (1956), pp. 27–28; and 279; T. Lidz, *The Person* (New York: Basic Books, 1968), p. 305.

3. Nid. 45b. The Rabbis considered three basic stages of development in relation to the woman's religious and legal obligations:

    1. *Ketannah*—(Lit. small)—a girl from three to the age of twelve years and a day.

    2. *Na'arah*—a girl at puberty between the age of twelve years and a day and twelve years and a half plus one day, when she becomes a *bogereth*. *Na'aruth* is considered maidenhood.

    3. Bogereth—a girl from the age of twelve years and a half plus one day and onwards, entering womanhood.

4. Aristotle, *Historia Animalium*, trans. by D. W. Thompson in *The Works of Aristotle* (Oxford: Clarendon Press, 1910), 4, 608B.

5. Yoma 66b. They said to him—the daughters of Israel have manners. The Munich Ms. (Strack ed. 1912) has a different version: "all the daughters of scholars have manners." Kalah Rabbati. There would appear to be an apparent contradiction. On the one hand woman's intellect is extolled, and on the other its existence is denied. R. M. Epstein in his Torah Temimah on Deut. 6:7 explains as follows: *daat* is the intellectual ability to perceive things at the first glance. It is the immediate grasp of a situation. In this intellectual area women may appear shallow. This primary perception which makes a first impression and many times a lasting one can be sensed in many a fashion. Women at first glance may not perceive well. The area of *binah*, however, which women have been blessed with, refers to thinking in depth. Since the intellect is composed of many differing qualities, it is possible that women could have both positive and negative traits in the intellectual make-up. Aristotle, *Nicomachean Ethics*, VIII, VII, 1; *Politics* 1, 13, 7-8; *Rhetoric*: 1, V, 6; Philo, *On the Creation*, Colson ed. pp. 69-70, 151, 162 and *Questions and Answers on Genesis*, Marcus ed. I, 40.

6. See Nid. 45b, Gen. Rabbah 18:1; compare Yoma 66b; Eccles. Rabbah 1; Shab 113b, Philo, Fugitives 34.

7. Midrash Tehilim 22, Yoma 66b.

8. J. F. Adams., Understanding Adolescence (Boston: Allyn & Bacon, 1973), p. 137; see A. Montagu, The Natural Superiority of Women, p. 117.

9. J. A. Sherman, Psychology of Women (Springfield, Ill: Charles C. Thomas, 1971), pp. 16–18; Gary M. Ingersoll, Adolescents in School and Society (Lexington: Heath, 1982), p. 118.

10. P. Rieff, Freud: The Mind of the Moralist, pp. 55, 191.

11. For every derogatory statement on woman, we find two of praise. Compare M. Gray, The Normal Woman (New York: Scribners, 1967), pp. 177–179.

12. I. Bauer, Woman and Love, p. 292.

13. Philo, Fugitives 34.

14. E. Kretschmer, The Psychology of Men of Genius (New York: Harcourt, 1931), p. 126.

15. M. F. Freehill, Gifted Children (New York: Macmillan, 1961), p. 145.

16. H. L. Mencken, In Defense of Woman (New York: A. Knopf, 1926), p. 6.

17. A woman recognizes the character of a guest better than a man. Ber. 10b.

18. H. Deutsch, The Psychology of Women, II (1967), pp. 15, 121.

19. A. Montagu, National Superiority of Women, pp, 51–52, 118–119.

20. We have previously seen that a woman's influence over others is great. Here we see that woman has greater faculties for seeing into the future than man does. Perhaps the Talmudists were hinting at this when they proclaimed that woman was bestowed with "added understanding" similar to "added love" in Ethics of the Fathers 6, where it undoubtedly is to be taken literally. See RoSH Nid. 45b. The Rabbis' regard for woman's counsel is cited in Sot. 12a: "And it was said regarding Amram that he was the greatest man of his generation and nevertheless he took advice from his daughter."

21. A. T. Schofield, Mind of a Woman, p. 80; B. Forisha-Kovach, The Experience of Adolescence (Glenview, Ill.: Scott-Foresman, 1983), p. 173.

22. Apocrypha, XII Patriarchs, Judah 15:5.

23. Tamid 32a–b.

24. Pirkei De R. Eliezer 41, Phineas; see D. Luria's comment no. 37 and Exod. Rabbah 28.

25. Similarly, Rabban Gamaliel went and consulted his wife. Ber. 27b and 61a; B. M. 59a. Similar examples in the Biblical period are: On ben Pelet, Manoach, Samson's father, Judith, the warrior, etc. Mencken believes that not even the most egoistic man would fail to sound the sentiment of his wife about taking a partner or public office, etc. (In Defense of Women, p. 20).

26. No decision was reached in the Talmud as to whether a woman who had quarreled with her husband prior to his departure would accept as final a report of his death or would question its validity and thus show her usual circumspection. Yeb. 116b.

27. A woman makes careful inquiry before she marries. Yeb. 25a; Keth. 14a, RaN Yeb. 94a. A proselyte intending to embrace the Jewish faith takes care to distinguish those children conceived before his conversion and those after. Yeb. 35a, 93b, 94a. "The House of Jacob" (Exod. 19:3) refers to women. Why did the Lord address the women first at Sinai? For they are more diligent concerning the performance of the commandments." Exod. Rabbah 28:2.

28. See Tosaf. Yeb. 93b, compare Yalkut Vaethanan 845.

29. Meg. 14b ref. I Sam. 25:31, B.K. 92b; see Mencken, op. cit., p. 31.

30. Yeb. 42a, Keth. 51b. See also Rashi and Tosaf. Riad to Keth. 51b. See B.M. 71a Rashi ad loc.

GLOSSARY

ABIZRAIHU. Legal commands and all requisites appertaining thereto.

ADMOR. Title by which Hasidic rabbis are known. Abbreviation of Hebrew words *Adonenu, Morenu, ve-Rabenu* ("our lord, teacher, and master").

AGGADAH. That portion of rabbinic teaching which is not *halakhah*. Mostly an amplification of portions of Bible which include narrative, history, ethical maxims, and reproofs and consolations of prophets.

AGUNAH. Married woman who for whatever reason is separated from her husband and cannot remarry, either because she cannot obtain a divorce from him or because it is unknown whether he is still alive. Term also applied to *yevamah* if she cannot obtain *halizah* from levir or if it is unknown whether he is still alive.

AIZER, AIZER KE-NEGDO. Biblical term connoting a helpmate; the wife is considered the equal other self and helper of man.

AKERET HA-BAYIT. Lit., biblical term for barren woman; in a later sense, matron of the house or *balabosteh*.

ALIYAH. Lit., going up; being called up to the Torah. Also, the coming of Jews to land of Israel for permanent residence; a major ideal of Zionism and primary means for its realization through immigration.

ALIYAH BET. Lit., (the second aliyah). Second migration to Israel (1904–1914); laid foundation for labor movement and consisted mainly of pioneers from East Europe. They established first Jewish labor parties, *haShomer* watchmen's association, and first *kevuzot*.

AM HA-ARETZ. In later times referred to person who is ignorant of rule of Jewish ritual and ceremonial customs. In common usage connotes an ignoramus or boor. See *talmid hakham*.

AMORAIM. Post-Mishnaic scholars who were active from completion of Mishnah until completion of Babylonian and Jerusalem Talmuds.

ARAYOT. All unions between sexes—whether temporary or permanent; primarily sexual union between blood relatives whose marriage is forbidden.

ASHKENAZ. Designation of first relatively compact area of settlement of Jews in northwest Europe, initially in Rhineland. Term became identified with Germany, German Jewry, and German Jews (*Ashkenazim*), as well as their descendants in other countries.

AYM HA-BANIM. Biblical term; lit., the mother of children.

323

BAKOSHES (Heb., *bakashah*). Prayer, petition of plea by individual or congregation.

BALABOSTEH. Housewife; matron; mistress of house.

BAR KAYYAMA. Viable child, having vitality.

BAT MITZVAH. Lit. daughter of commandment; girl attaining her majority at twelve years and a day, accepting responsibility of fulfilling religious law. Also, celebration of this event.

BE-GIRSA. For study of Oral Tradition by heart.

BET DIN. In rabbinic sources, Jewish court of law. In modern times, usually ecclesiastical court dealing with religious matters such as divorce and supervision of the dietary laws, and acting, with the consent of all concerned, as a court of arbitration.

BET HILLEL AND BET SHAMMAI. Two schools of exposition of Oral Law, named after Hillel and Shammai, their founders, who lived at end of first century B.C.E. and beginning of first century C.E. These two schools existed from time of these two Sages until second generation after the destruction of the Second Temple.

BET MIDRASH. House of study; academy where study of Torah was carried on under guidance of rabbinical authority. At later period served double function of study and prayer, used in eastern Europe interchangeably with *kloiz* (an enclosed place for service).

BILUIM. Organized group of young Russian Jewish nationalists who pioneered modern return to Eretz Israel as a reaction to 1881 pogroms in southern Russia.

BIRKHAT HA-GOMEL. Blessing of thanksgiving recited upon escape from danger, release from prison, recovery from illness, and after ocean voyage or air travel.

BIRKHAT HA-MAZON. Grace After Meals, central feature of liturgical service in Jewish home.

BIYAH. Coition.

BOGERET. Girl coming of age at twelve years and a half.

BRAKHAH LE-VATALAH. Blessing pronounced for no purpose; vain argument.

BRIT MILAH. Covenant of circumcision.

BROKHE (Heb., *brakhah*). Benediction pronounced on various occasions before performing positive commandment. Blessing given by Hasidic Rebbe to Hasid.

BUSHAH. Shame.

CHOLENT. Stew traditionally prepared on Friday and placed in oven before Sabbath begins, to cook overnight and be eaten warm at Sabbath lunch.

DEREKH ERETZ. Desirable behavior of a man toward his fellows, in keeping with natural practice and accepted social and moral standards, including rules of etiquette and polite behavior.

DINIM. Authoritative decisions or observances in Jewish Law.

EINGEMACHTS. (Yiddish) yarn made of fruit.

EREV SHABBAT. Day preceding Shabbat; Friday.

ERUSIN. Lit., betrothal; formal betrothal, which cannot be annulled without a bill of divorce.

ERVAH. Lit., nakedness; body areas which, according to *halachah*, must be covered. Also connotes a marriage contracted with a blood relation.

ERVAT DAVAR. Lit., nakedness of anything; an unseemly thing that one would be ashamed of, i.e., indecency in anything.

ESH DAT LAMO. Lit., a law of fire unto them (Israel), from Deut. 33:2; the Torah (*esh*) given to the Jewish people.

ESHET HAYIL. A woman of valor; name of traditional *Shabbat* Eve song sung in praise of women, based on Proverbs, chapter 31.

ETZEL. Acronym for Irgun Tzevai Leumi—Jewish underground in Palestine under British Mandate.

FARHAYR. To hear or to test one's ability; usually used to refer to testing of a boy's ability in Talmud.

FARSHTELEN. To put on a mask, usually on Purim.

GABBAI. Official of Jewish congregation; originally a charity collector.

GAON. Head of academy in posttalmudic period, especially in Babylonia.

GARTEL. Traditional belt worn by Hasidim at prayer.

GEHINOM. Lit., the valley of Hinnom. In Greek, Gehenna. Name of valley south of Jerusalem, where horrors of human sacrifice were practiced; used in rabbinic Hebrew as name of place where wicked expiate their misdeeds after death.

GEMARA. Traditions, discussions, and rulings of Amoraim; commentary on and supplement to Mishnah and forming part of Babylonian and Palestinian Talmuds.

GEMILAT HESSED. Deeds of kindness to one's fellowman.

GET. The Jewish Bill of Divorce.

GOYIM. Lit., nations, Gentiles, anyone except Jews.

HADLAKAT NEROT. Lighting of candles on erev *Shabbat* to welcome in Sabbath. (Usually performed by women.)

HA-KADOSH BARUKH HU. The Holy One Blessed Be He—a name for God.

HAKHEL. Gathering of whole nation to hear reading of Torah by king on seventh year of *Shemitah*.

HAKHNASAT ORHIM. Bringing guests into one's home, hospitality.

HALAKHAH - rabbinic law

HALAKHAH LE-MAASEH - Practical *halakhah*.

HALALAH. Daughter of *kohen* from invalid marriage.

HALITZAH. Biblically prescribed ceremony (Deut. 25:9–10) performed when a man refuses to marry his brother's childless widow, enabling her to remarry.

HALLAH. Portion of dough which belongs to *Kohen*. (Num. 15:20); in Diaspora it is burnt.

HAMETZ. Any product made of or containing one of five grains which are forbidden on Passover.

HASHATAT ZERA. Spilling of human seed.

HASHAVAT AVEDAH. Returning of lost article.

HASIDISM. Religious revivalist movement of popular mysticism among Jews of Germany in Middle Ages; religious movement founded by R. Israel Ben Eliezer Ba'al Shem Tov in first half of 18th century.

HASKALAH. "Enlightenment"; movement for spreading modern European culture among Jews, c. 1750–1880.

HEDER. Lit., room; school for teaching children Jewish religious observance in which traditional methods of teaching are used.

HEN. Grace, Loveliness; women's division in Israeli army.

HEVRAH KADISHA. Generally limited to associations for burial of dead.

HIYUV. One's obligation in performing mitzvot.

HOSHANA RABBA. Seventh day of *Sukkot,* on which special observances are held.

HOVEVEI ZION. Federation of Hibbat Zion, early, pre-Herzl Zionist movement in Russia.

ISSUR DE-ORAITA. Something prohibited by the Five Books of Moses.

KADESH. Homosexual, sodomite.

KEDESHAH. Prostitute.

KAPITEL TEHILIM. Chapter from Book of Psalms.

KAVANAH. Lit., intention; term denoting spiritual, mental concentration accompanying prayer and performance of ritual or commandment.

KEDOSHIM. Jewish martyrs.

KEHILAH. Congregation.

KERIAH. Act of tearing one's garment, as upon hearing of someone's death.

KERIAT SHEMA. Recitation of three paragraphs of *Shema* twice a day (morning and night).

KETANAH. Female minor; girl under twelve years of age.

KEST. European custom in which boys living away from home are given sustenance; also, support given to newlyweds by bride's father.

KETUBBAH. Marriage contract, stipulating husband's obligations to wife.

KETUBBAH DE-IRHASEI. Substitute *ketubbah* for one that has been lost.

KIDDUSH. Prayer of sanctification recited over wine or bread on eve of Sabbaths and festivals.

KIDDUSH HA-HAYIM. Sanctification of one's life for God.

KIDDUSH HA-SHEM. Term connoting martyrdom or act of strict integrity in support of Judaic principles.

KIDDUSHIN. Lit., sanctification; act of affiancing or betrothal, Talmudic tome. Also, money or article given to effect betrothal.

KIMPETUREN. Woman who has just given birth: a nursing mother.

KIYUM. Fulfillment (of a *mitzvah*).

KLAL YISRAEL. Term used to denote all Jews; the congregation of Israel.

KNIPPEL. Little bundle: sometimes, money reserved in a handkerchief or the like by a woman for "extras."

KODESH KODASHIM. Holy of Holies—a section of *Mishkan* entered only by *kohen gadol* on *Yom Kippur*.

KOHEN. Jew of priestly (Aaronide) descent.

KOHEN GADOL. *Kohen*, High Priest.

KOLEL. The community in *Eretz Yisrael* of persons from a particular country or locality, often supported by their fellow countrymen in the Diaspora. Also, institution for higher Torah study for married students.

KVITTEL. Note with special prayers, written to a Hasidic Rebbe; note placed in holy places.

KEVUTZOT. Small communes of pioneers constituting agricultural settlement in *Eretz Yisrael* (evolved later into *kibbutzim*).

LEHAYIM. Lit., to life. A toast to life.

LEHI. Acronym for *Lochamei Herut Israel*, "Fighters for the Freedom of Israel," radically anti-British armed underground organization in Palestine, founded in 1940 by dissidents from *Etzel*.

LEKET. Gathering of leftover crops by the poor.

LEVITICAL. Pertaining to tribe of Levi.

LO TAASEH. Section of negative commandments.

LULAV. Palm branch, one of four species used on *Sukkot* together with the *etrog*, *hadas*, and *aravah*.

MAASER. Lit., tenth part. Annual tithe due to the *Levi* or to be consumed by the owner in Jerusalem, or distributed to the poor every third year.

MAMME LOSHEN. Mother tongue: first language learned.

MAMZER. Bastard; according to Jewish Law, offspring of incestuous relationship.

MAZIKIN. Demons.

MEGGILAH. Lit., scroll, term commonly applied to the book of Esther.

MEHITZAH. Lit., separation; partition used to separate men and women in Orthodox synagogues.

MELAMED. Religious teacher.

MEYUHOS. Having noteworthy genealogy.

MEZUZAH. Parchment scroll with selected Torah verses placed in container and affixed to gates and doorposts of houses occupied by Jews.

MIDRASH. Method of interpreting Scripture to elucidate legal points (*Midrash Halakhah*) or to bring out lessons through stories or homiletics (*Midrash Aggadah*). Also, name of a collection of such rabbinic interpretations.

MIKDASH MEAT. Essence of tabernacle of Holy Temple; synagogue.

MIKVAH, MIKVEH. Ritual bath containing not less than forty *se'ahs* of water; ritualarium.

MINHAH. Afternoon prayer, originally, meal offering in Temple.

MINYAN. Group of ten male adult Jews, minimum required for communal prayer.

MI SHE-BEIRAKH. Prayer recited between the *Aliyot* of the reading of the Torah for one that is sick, for one that has given birth, or just to bless the one called up to the Torah.

MISHNAH. Earliest codification of Jewish Oral Law; subdivision of tractates of Mishnah as edited by R. Yehuda haNasi at beginning of 3rd century.

MITZVAH. Biblical or rabbinic injunction; applied also to good or charitable deeds.

MITZVAH TANZEL. Dance at conclusion of wedding when bride dances with members of her family.

MITZVOT ASEH: Positive commandments.

MITZVOT LO TAASEH. Negative commandments.

MI'UN. Lit., refusal. Declaration by underage, fatherless girl, who has been married off by her mother or brothers, that she does not wish to live with her husband. Such a declaration, made by her in the presence of a *Bet Din* secures her freedom without the requirement of a *get*.

MOHAR. Exchange; price paid for wife as specified in ketubbah.

MOKH. Precoital resorbent.

MORED, MOREDET. Rebel (male, female) refusing marital duties.

NAARAH. Girl between ages of twelve years and a day and twelve years and a half plus one day, when she becomes a *bogeret*.

NADAN. Dowry.

NAGID. Statesman, prince, or wealthy person.

NAHES. Gratification or fulfillment.

MOKH. Precoital resorbent.

NASI. Talmudic term for president of Sanhedrin, who was also spiritual head and, later, political representative of Jewish people; from second century, a descendant of Hillel recognized by Roman authorities as patriarch of the Jews.

NEDUNYAH. Dowry.

NEFESH. Soul of a person.

NEGI'AH. Physical contact between men and women.

NETUREI KARTA. Lit., watchers of the city. Extreme right political group of Jews who do not believe in supporting State of Israel before Messiah comes.

NIDDAH. (Menstruant woman); woman during the period of menstruation.

NIKHSEI MULUG. Denotes property which belongs to a wife and of which husband has only the rights to interest without any rights to capital, or responsibility for its loss or deterioration.

NISSU'IN. Ceremony of home-taking, which completes marriage.

NOSHING. Snacking.

OHL MALKHUT SHAMAIM. The yoke of God's sovereignty.

OLAM KATAN. Small world; microcosm.

ONAH. Season; timing for coition.

ORAL LAW. Term used for law which was originally transmitted orally and later written down—mainly Talmud, Mishnah and Gemara.

PALMACH. (Abbr. for *Peluggot mahaz*, "shock companies"), striking arm of the Haganah.

PARNASSAH. Livelihood; means of support.

PAYAH. Corner of one's field left for the poor; earlocks.

PENTATEUCH. Five Books of Moses: Genesis, Exodus, Leviticus, Numbers, and Deuteronomy.

PERITZUT. Frivolous breaking of code of law.

PERU U-REVU. Words pronounced by God to man in Genesis that man and woman must be "fruitful and multiply"; law of Torah that man must have offspring.

PERUTAH. Small coin.

PIDYON HA-BEN. Ceremony to redeem firstborn male from kohen.

PIDYIONOT. Redemptions or that which is given to redeem; gifts to a Hasidic Rebbe.

PIDYON SHEVUYIM. Redeeming of captives.

PIKUAH NEFESH. Matter where one's life is endangered.

PILPUL. In talmudic and rabbinic casuistic literature, a sharp dialectic used in Poland from the 16th century particularly by talmudists.

PIRYAH VE'RIVYAH. Producing of offspring.

PIYYUT. Hebrew liturgical poem.

RISHONIM. Early rabbinic authorities. Distinguished from later authorities.

ROSH HODESH. New moon, marking beginning of Hebrew month.

RUAH HA-KODESH. Divine inspiration—a lesser form of prophecy.

SAFEK HAI. Question whether something or someone is considered alive.

SANHEDRIN. Assembly of ordained scholars which functioned both as supreme court and as legislature before 70 C.E.

SCHNORER. Beggar

SEDER. Ceremony observed in Jewish home on first two nights of Passover, (in Israel, on first night only), when *Haggadah* is read.

SEFIRAT HA-OMER. Counting of the Omer—between *Pesach* and *Shavuot*.

SEFORIM. Holy Books.

SEGULLOT. Objects which are connected with luck, spiritual remedy, talisman.

SEHOIRA. Merchandise.

SEPHARDIC. Referring to Jews of Spain and Portugal or Orient and their descendants, wherever resident, as contrasted with Ashkenazic.

SHABBOS KOIDESH. Holy Sabbath.

SHADKHAN. Matchmaker or marriage broker.

SHAHARIT. Morning services.

SHALIAH. In Jewish Law, messenger, agent.

SHALOM BAYIT. Peace in one's house between the members of one's household; marital harmony.

SHALOSH SE'UDOT. Third and culminating meal on *Shabbat*.

SHAMES. (Hebrew, *shamash*), sexton; person who looks after the needs of synagogue.

SHAMOR. Negative commandment that one must keep or guard the *Shabbat*.

SHE-ASANI KIRTZONO. Lit., according to His will. One of the blessings of morning service recited by women.

SHE'ELAH. Halakhic question posed to a rabbinic authority.

SHEHITAH. Ritual slaughtering of animals.

SHE-HA-ZEMAN GERAMAH. Something or a commandment bound by time.

SHEITL. Wig traditionally worn by married women.

SHE-HEHEYANU. Blessing recited when performing certain *mitzvot* for the first time during the year; for example, when eating a fruit for the first time in season, and on certain other joyous occasions.

SHEKHINAH. Divine Presence. Spirit of the Omnipresent as manifested on earth.

SHEMA (Yisrael). "Hear O Israel" (Deut. 6:4). Judaism's confession of faith, proclaiming the absolute unity of God.

SHIDDUKH. Arrangement and negotiation prior to betrothal.

SHIKHAH. Forgetfulness, the forgotten sheaf left for the poor man.

SHIKSAH. Non-Jewish female.

SHIR HA-SHIRIM. Song of Songs, written by King Solomon. One of the five *Meggilot*.

SHIVAH. Seven days of mourning following burial of a relative.

SHOHET. Person qualified to perform *shehitah* or slaughtering.

SHOFAR. Ram's horn sounded for memorial blowing on *Rosh Ha-Shanah* and other occasions.

SHOLOM ZUKHOR. Greeting a male. Celebration given for newborn male child on Friday night before circumcision.

SHTETL (diminutive of *shtot*—city). Small Jewish town community in Eastern Europe.

SHUL. Synagogue.

SHULHAN ARUKH. R. Joseph Caro's Code of Jewish Law in four parts.

SIDDUR. Prayer book. Volume containing daily festivals (in distinction to the *Mahzor*, which contains those for yearly festivals).

SIMHAH. Happy occasion or feast.

SIMHAT HATAN VE-KALAH. Celebration of a bride and a groom.

SOFER. Scribe of ritual scrolls.

SOTAH. Married woman suspected of infidelity who has been formally warned by her husband; fifth tractate in Mishnaic order of *Nashim*.

SUKKAH. Booth or tabernacle in which the children of Israel lived during forty years in the desert. Today, a small structure or hut built for eight-day holiday of *Sukkot*.

TABA'AT KIDDUSHIN. Ring given as part of marriage ceremony.

TAHANUN. Prayer of penitence to God recited every morning except on *Shabbat* and holidays.

TAHARAH. Ritual purity.

TAHARAHAT HA-MISHPAHA. Set of laws of ritual purity which govern relationship between man and woman during their married life.

TAHAROT. Name of sixth order of Mishnah. Also, purity condition of cleanliness, purification.

TAKKANOT. Enactments by Rabbis.

TALIS, TALIT. Four-cornered woolen prayer shawl with fringes (tzitzit) at each corner.

TALIT KATAN. Garment with fringes (tzitzit) worn by observant male Jews under their outer garments.

TALMID HAKHAM. Lit., disciple of the wise. Scholar, student of the Torah.

TALMUD TORAH. Term generally applied to Jewish religious (and ultimately to talmudic) study; also to traditional Jewish religious public schools or supplementary schools.

TAMEH. Ritually impure.

TANAKH. Acronym for Torah, Neviim, Ketuvim. The Hebrew Bible, which contains twenty-four books.

TANNAIM. Rabbinic teachers of the Mishnaic period.

TARGUM. Aramaic translation of Bible.

TASHMISH HA-MITAH. Conjugal relations.

TEHINAH. Prayer for grace.

TEECHEL. Scarf worn by women to cover their hair after marriage.

TEFFILAH. Prayer, halakhic term for the Shemoneh Esrei, or 18 benedictions.

TEFFILAH BE-TZIBUR. Communal prayer.

TEFILLIN. Phylacteries, or small leather cases containing passages from Scripture and affixed on forehead and arm by male Jews during recital of morning prayers.

TEHILIM. Psalms.

TEHORAH. Ritually pure woman.

TESHUVAH. Rabbinical responsum. Also repentance.

TEVILAH. Ritual immersion.

TIKUN. Lit., restitution, reintegration. Order of service for certain occasions, mostly recited at night. Also, mystical term denoting restoration of right order and true unity after spiritual catastrophe which occurred in the cosmos.

TORAH LI-SHEMA. Study of Torah without ulterior motives.

TORAH SHE-BEAL PEH. Oral Law: Talmud, etc.

TORAT HAYIM. Torah of Life.

TOSAFISTS. Talmudic glossarists, mainly French (12th–14th century), who added to commentary by Rashi.

TOV ME'OD. Very good.

TREIFAH. Lit., torn by beasts. Diseased animal which, though ritually slaughtered, is forbidden to be eaten.

TZE'ENAH U-RE'ENAH. Yiddish version and commentary to the Bible.

TUM'AH. Ritual impurity.

TZADDIK. Person outstanding for his faith and piety, especially a Hasidic Rebbe or leader.

TZAHAL. Acronym for *Tzevah Haganah Le-Yisrael*: name of Israeli army.

TZEDOKA PUSHKE. Charity box.

TZENIUT. Modesty, the way one should act and dress.

TZITZIT. Biblical name of fringes attached to each of four corners of garment. (Num. 15:38)

TZORES. Troubles.

UBAR YERAH IMO. The embryo is a thigh (part) of its mother, i.e., comes under the same law.

VE-SHINANTAM LE-VANEKHA. And you shall inculcate into your sons (Deut. 6:7) what is written in the Torah.

VORSAGERIN, FIRZOGERIN. Woman in *shul* who recites prayers before other women who do not know.

WRITTEN LAW. The Five Books of Moses.

YAVAM. The brother of a married man who dies childless, levir; the widow is called *yevamah*. See *halitzah*.

YAHRZEIT. Yearly commemoration of a person's death on date the person had died.

YARMULKE. Skullcap worn by Jewish males.

YETZER HA-RA. Evil inclination in a person. Also, the tempter, Satan, and the Angel of Death.

YETZER HA-TOV. Inclination in every person which prompts one to do good.

YICHUS. Noteworthy genealogy.

YIDDISHKEIT. Jewishness; anything pertaining to Judaism.

YIDDISH NACHAS. Jewish happiness and pleasure.

YIHUD. Lit., privacy. Prohibition instituted by Rabbis against private association of sexes.

YIR'AT SHAMAYIM. Fear of Heaven.

YISHUV. Settlement; more specifically, Jewish community of *Eretz Yisrael* in pre-State period. The pre-Zionist community is generally designated the "old *yishuv*," and the community evolving from 1880 the "new *yishuv*."

YOD HEE. First two letters of the Tetragrammaton.

YOM TOV. Lit., good day. Holiday such as *Pesach*, *Shavuoth*, and *Sukkot*.

YOTZE DOFEN. Not ordinary; by Caesarean birth.

ZAFTIG. Pleasantly plump.

ZAKHOR. Remember.

ZEKHUT. Worthiness, merit.

ZIMMAH. Harlotry.

ZOHAR. Mystical commentary on Pentateuch; main textbook of Kabbalah.

ZONAH. Harlot.

ZORGEN. Worries.

Hebrew Bibliography

Bible and Commentaries

Abraham ibn Ezra (d. 1167), in *Mikrat'ot Gedolot*. Also ed. Mantua, 1559.
Mikraot G'dolot. New York: Pardes Publishing Co., 1951.
Ramban (R. Moses ben Nahman, Nahmanides, d. 1270). Also ed., in *Mikra'ot Gedolot*. C. Chavel. Jerusalem: Mosad haRav Kook, 1962.
Rashi (R. Solomon Yitzhaki, d. 1105), in *Mikrat'ot Gedolot*.
Yosef B'khor Shor (fl. 12th cent.). Jerusalem: Kiryat Sefer, 1957.

Targum-Midrashim

Mekhilta. Ed. M. Friedmann. Vienna, 1870.
Mekhilta. Ed. Lauterbach. Philadelphia: Jewish Publication Society of America, 1949.
Midrash Aggadah. Ed. S. Buber, Berlin, 1910.
Midrash Rabbah. Vilna: Romm, 1921.
Midrash Tannaim. Ed. D. Hoffmann. Berlin, 1908–9.
Ozar Midrashim. Ed. J. D. Eisenstein. New York, 1915.
Pesikhta DeR. Kahana. Ed. S. Buber. Lyck, 1868.
Pesikhta Rabbati. Ed. M. Friedmann. Vienna, 1885.
Pirkei DeRabbi Eliezer. Ed. D. Luria, Warsaw, 1852.
Seder Eliyahu Rabba. Ed. M. Friedmann. Vienna, 1904.
Sifra. Ed. I. H. Weiss. Vienna, 1862.
Sifrei Numbers. Ed. H. S. Horovitz. Leipzig, 1917.
Sifrei Deuteronomy. Ed. M. Friedmann, Vienna, 1864.
Tanhuma. Ed. S. Buber, Vienna, 1885.
Tanhuma. Ed. S. Buber. Vilna, 1913.
Tanna D'vei Eliyahu. Ed. M. Friedmann. Vienna, 1902.
Targum Onkelos, (2d cent. Aramaic translation-paraphrase of Bible), in *Mikraot G'dolot*, and ed. A. Berliner, Berlin, 1884.
Targum Pseudo-Jonathan (c. 7th cent.) in *Mikraot G'dolot*
Yalkut Shim'oni. Warsaw, 1876.

Talmud and Commentaries, including volumes of Novellae

Avot De R. Nathan. Ed. S. Schechter. London, 1887.
Babylonian Talmud. Vilna: Romm, 1895.
Beit haB'hirah. Menahem haMeiri of Perpignan. New York, 1930.
Commentary to the Mishnah. Moses ben Maimon (Maimonides). In Babylonian Talmud.
Maharsha. Samuel Edels, *Hiddushei Halakhot veAggaddot.*
Mishnah. New York: Pardes Publishing Co., 1963.
Mordekhai, abstract of talmudic law (Halakhot) by Mordekhai b. Hillel Ashkenazi. In standard edition of Babylonian Talmud.
Palestinian Talmud. Vilna: Romm, 1922.
RaN, (R. Nissim Gerondi). New York: Feldheim, 1946.
Sefer haYashar. Rabbenu Ya'akov Tam. Ed. Schlesinger. Jerusalem: Kiryat Sefer, 1959.
Tosephta. Ed. M. Z. Zuckermandel. Pasewalk, 1881.

Codes and Commentaries

Sefer Abudraham. David Abudraham. Amsterdam, 1726.
Alfasi. Isaac Al-Fasi. Vilna: Romm, 1911.
Arokh haSulhan. Yehiel Michael Epstein. Warsaw, 1900–12.
Asheri. Asher ben Yehiel. Printed with the Babylonian Talmud.
Bayit Hadash (BaH). Joel Sirkes. Printed with *Babylonian Talmud.*
Beit Yosef (and *Bedek haBayit*). Joseph Karo. Printed with Tur, N.Y., 1967.
Beur haGRA. Elijah Gaon. Printed with *Shulhan Arukh.*
Dar'khei Moshe. Moses Isserles. Printed with Tur, N.Y., 1967.
D'risha and *P'rishah (Beit Yisrael).* Joshua Falk. Printed with *Sulhan Arukh*
Elyah Rabbah. Composed primarily as a commentary on the *L'vush.* Elijah Shapiro, Sulzbach, 1757.
Halakhot G'dolot. Simon Kaira. Ed. Hildesheimer. Berlin, 1892.
Hassagot RaVaD. Abraham ben David.
Hazon Ish. Isaiah Karelitz. B'nai B'rak, 1958.
Sefer haHinukh. Attributed to R. Aaron haLevi. Vilna, 1912.
Kitzur Shulhan Arukh. Solomon Ganzfried. Leipzig, 1933.
Kol Bo. Author uncertain (14th cent.). Fiorda, 1782.
L'vush(im). Mordekhai Jaffe. Venice, 1620.
Sefer (Likkutei) Maharil. Jacob haLevi Moelin. Lvov, 1860.
Magen Avraham. Abraham Gumbiner. Printed with *Shulhan Arukh.*
Maggid Mishneh. Vidal of Tolosa.
Mappat haShulham: Glosses of RaMA. Moses Isserles. Printed with *Shulhan Arukh.*
Mishneh Torah (or *Yad haHazakah*). Maimonides. Vilna: Rosencrantz, 1900.

Or Zarua. Isaac of Vienna. Zhitomir, 1862.

Pithei T'shuvah. Abraham Zvi Eisenstadt. Shulhan Arukh. Printed with Shulhan Arukh.

Sefer Mitzvot Gadol. Moses of Coucy. Venice, 1522.

Sefer Mitzvot Katan. Isaac of Corbeil. Ladi, 1805.

Sefer haMitzvot L'Rambam. Maimonides. Lemberg, 1860.

Sefer haMitzvot L'RaSaG. Saadia Gaon. Warsaw, 1914.

ShaKH (Sif'tei Kohen). Shabb'tai haKohen. Printed with Shulhan Arukh.

Sh'iltot De Rav Ahai Gaon. with Haamek Shealah (N'tziv). Jerusalem, 1949. Vilna: Romm, 1861.

Shulhan Arukh. Joseph ben Ephraim Karo. Vilna: Romm, 1911.

Shulhan Arukh haRav. Shneur Zalman of Ladi. Zhitomir, 1848.

TaZ (Turei Zahav). David haLevi. Printed with Shulhan Arukh.

Tur (Arba'ah Turim). Jacob ben Asher. Vilna, 1900.

Yam Shel Shlomoh. Solomon Luria. To Bava Kamma, Prague, 1715; to Yevamot, Altona, 1739.

Extralegal Literature: Moralistic, Philosophic, and Mystic

'Aruk. Nathan b. Yehiel of Rome, talmudic dictionary. Josefov, 1869.

Ba'alel haNefesh ‚(RaVaD). Sha'ar haK'dushah. Jerusalem: Masorah, 1955.

Emunot VeDeot. Saadiah Gaon. Ed. Judah Ibn Tibbon. Constantinople, 1562.

Huppat Hatanim. Raphael Meldola. Lublin, 1872.

Iggeret haKodesh. Ascribed to Nahmanides. Ed. C. Chavel, Jerusalem, 1964.

Kuzari. Judah haLevi. Pressburg, 1860.

Malmad haTalmidim. Jacob Anatoli. Lyck, 1866.

Menorat haMaor. Isaac AlNakawa. Ed. H. G. Enelow. New York: Bloch, 1932.

Orhot Zaddikim. Ethical treatise, anonymous. Zalkowa, 1838.

Moreh Nevukhim. Maimonides. Warsaw, 1872.

Reshit Hokhmah. Elijah de Vidas. Vilna, 1900.

Sefer Haredim. Eliezer Azkari. Venice, 1601.

Sefer Hasidim. Judah heHasid. Ed. Reuben Margoliot. Jerusalem: Mosad haRav Kook, 1964.

Sefer Yere'im. Code, Eleazar b. Samuel of Metz. Zalkowa, 1804.

Shnei Luhot haBerit. Isaiah Hurwitz. Fuerth, 1764.

Zohar. 5 vols. Ed. Reuben Margoliot. Jerusalem: Mosad haRav Kook, 1960.

Responsa

Hai Gaon. In T'shuvot haGe'onim. Ed. Harkavy. 1887, 1949.

Hatam Sofer. Moses Schreiber (Sofer). Vienna, 1855.

Havvot Yair. Yair Bachrach. Lemberg, 1896.

Iggerot Moshe. Moshe Feinstein. E.H. II, New York, 1961; E.H. and O.H., New York, 1961; Y.D., New York, 1973.
Sifrei Maharal, Yehuda Löw b. Bezalel. Jerusalem, 1971.
Maharam Rothenburg. Meir of Rothenburg. Jerusalem, 1957.
Ozar haGe'onim. B. M. Lewin. Jerusalem, 1928–42.
T'shuvot haGe'onim. Ed. Asaf. Jerusalem, 1929.
T'shuvot haGe'onim. Ed. Harkavy. Berlin, 1887.
T'shuvot haRambam. Ed. Blau. Jerusalem, 1958.
T'shuvot haRosH. Asher ben Yehiel. Zalkowa, 1803.
T'shuvot haRaShBa. Salomon ben Adret. Jerusalem, 1903.
RiVaSH. Isaac Bar Sheshet (Barfat). Lemberg, 1805.
Sefer Tashbatz. Simon ben Tzemah Duran. Amsterdam, 1739.
Shoel UMeshiv. Joseph Saul Nathansohn, Lemberg, 1868.

Other works of Halakhah or Commentation

Mekorot leToldot haHinnukh beYisrael. Simha Asaf. 4 vols. Tel Aviv–Jerusalem: Devir, 1925–1942.
Moznaim laMishpat. Zalman Sorotzkin. Jerusalem, 1941.
S'dei Hemed. Hayyim Hizkiyah Medini. Warsaw, 1903–7.
Yosef Ometz. Joseph Hahn. Frankfurt am Main, 1723.

General Bibliography

Abrahams, Beth Zion, ed. *The Life of Glückel of Hameln.* New York: Yoseloff, 1963.

Abrahams, Israel. *Hebrew Ethical Wills.* Philadelphia: Jewish Publication Society, 1926.

———. *Jewish Life in the Middle Ages.* London. E. Goldston, 1932.

Ackerman, Nathan. *The Psychodynamics of Family Life.* New York: Basic Books, 1958.

Adams, James F. *Understanding Adolescence.* Boston: Allyn & Bacon, 1973.

Adler, Alfred. *What Life Should Mean to You.* New York: Capricorn Books, 1958.

Agus, Irving A. *Urban Civilization in Pre-Crusade Europe.* New York: Yeshiva University Press, 1965.

Allport, Gordon W. *Personality and Social Encounter.* Boston: Beacon, 1960.

Angoff, Charles. *Emma Lazarus: A Biography.* New York: Jewish Historical Society, 1979.

Arendt, Hannah. *Rahel Varnhagen: The Life of a Jewish Woman.* New York: Harcourt, Brace, 1974.

Balint, Michael. *Primary Love and Psycho-Analytic Technique.* New York: Liveright, 1967.

Balsdon, J. P. *Roman Women.* New York: John Day, 1963.

Baron, Salo. *A Social and Religious History of the Jews.* New York: Columbia University Press, 1958–1965.

———. *The Jewish Community.* Philadelphia: Jewish Publication Society, 1945.

Basok, M. *Sefer haMapilim.* Tel Aviv, 1947.

Bauer, Bernhard A. *Women and Love.* 2 vols. New York: Liveright, 1971.

Bell, Norman W., and Ezra F. Vogel. *The Family.* New York: Free Press, 1968.

Bell, Robert R. *Marriage and Family Interaction.* 3d ed. Homewood, Ill.: Dorsey Press, 1971.

Ben-Zvi, Rahel Yenait. *Coming Home.* New York: Herzl Press, 1978.

Berliner, A. *Geschichte der Juden in Rom.* Frankfurt, 1893.

Berman, Jeremiah. *Shehitah: A Study in the Cultural and Social Life of the Jewish People.* New York: Bloch, 1941.

Blidstein, Gerald. *Honor Thy Father and Mother.* New York: Ktav, 1975.

Blood, Robert O., Jr., and Donald M. Wolfe. *Husbands and Wives*. New York: Free Press, 1960.

Bowman, Henry A. *Marriage for Moderns*. 7th ed. New York: McGraw-Hill, 1974.

Brayer, Menachem M. in *Jews and Divorce*. New York: Ktav, 1968 pp. 1-43.

———. "Medical Hygiene and Psychological Aspects of Dead Sea Scrolls." *Hebrew Medical Journal*. New York, 1964 pp. 145-179.

Briffault, Robert. *The Mothers*. New York: Grosset & Dunlap, 1963.

Brod, Max. *Paganism-Christianity-Judaism*. University of Alabama, 1970.

Brody, Sylvia. *Patterns of Mothering*. New York: International Universities Press, 1956.

Buber, Martin. *I and Thou*. New York: Scribner's, 1943.

———. *Tales of the Hassidim*. New York: Schocken, 1956.

Burgess, Ernest W., and Harvey J. Locke. *The Family*. New York: Van Nostrand, 1971.

Caprio, F. S. *The Sexually Adequate Female*. New York: Citadel Press, 1953.

Carcopino, Jerome. *Daily Life in Ancient Rome*. New Haven: Yale University Press, 1940.

Cavan, Ruth. *The American Family*. New York: Thomas Y. Crowell, 1969.

Chapman, Dudley. *The Feminine Mind and Body*. New York: Citadel Press, 1968.

Chesser, Eustace. *Love and the Married Woman*. New York: Putnam, 1969.

Cook, S. A. *The Laws of Moses and the Code of Hammurabi*. London: A. & C., 1903.

Cowell, F. R.. *Everyday Life in Ancient Rome*. New York: Putnam, 1961.

Cowley, A. H. *Aramaic Papiri of the Fifth Century, B.C.*. Oxford: Clarendon Press, 1923.

Deutsch, Helene. *The Psychology of Woman*. 2 vols. New York: Grune & Stratton, 1967.

De Beauvoir, Simone. *The Second Sex*. New York: Bantam Books, 1968.

De Vaux, Ronald. *Ancient Israel*. New York: McGraw-Hill, 1961.

Dick, J. G. *Childbirth Without Fear*. New York: Harper & Row, 1972.

Drever, James. *A Dictionary of Psychology*. Rev. ed. London: Penguin, 1972.

Dubnow, Simon. *History of the Jews*. 4 vols. New York: Yoseloff, 1971.

Duvall, Evelyn. *Why Wait Until Marriage*. New York: Association Press, 1965.

Ellis, Albert. *The Art and Science of Love*. Secaucus, N.J.: Lyle Stuart, 1965.

Ellis, Havelock. *Psychology of Sex*. New York: Random House, 1937.

———. *Studies in the Psychology of Sex*. Philadelphia: Davis, 1901.

Encyclopedia of Religion and Ethics. New York: Scribner's, 1908–1927.

Encyclopedia of Zionism. New York: McGraw-Hill, 1971.

English & English. *Dictionary of Psychological and Psycho-analytical Terms*. New York: Longmans-Green, 1968.

Epstein, Louis. *Pilgrims in a New Land*. New York, 1948.

―――. Sex Laws and Customs in Judaism. New York: Bloch, 1948.

―――. The Jewish Marriage Contract. New York: Jewish Theological Seminary, 1927.

Feldman, David. Birth Control in Jewish Law. New York: New York University Press, 1968.

Fielding, William J. Love and Sex Emotions. New York: Perma Books, 1961.

―――. Strange Superstitions and Magical Practices. Philadelphia: Blakiston, 1948.

Flugel, J. C. The Psychology of Clothes. New York: International Universities Press, 1969.

Freehill, Maurice F. Gifted Children. New York: Macmillan, 1961.

Freud, Sigmund. Collected Papers. New York: Basic Books, 1959. The Autobiography. New York: Norton, 1935.

―――. New Introductory Lectures on Psycho-Analysis. New York: Norton, 1965.

Friedan, Betty. The Feminine Mystique. New York: Norton, 1963.

Friedenwald, H. The Jews and Medicine. Baltimore: Johns Hopkins University Press, 1944.

Fromme, Allan. Sex and Marriage. Englewood Cliffs, N.J.: Prentice-Hall, 1955.

Fromm, Erich. The Art of Loving. New York: Harper & Row, 1974.

―――. The Sane Society. New York: Rinehart, 1955.

Gaster, Moses. Maaseh Book. Philadelphia: Jewish Publication Society, 1934.

Gesell, Arnold, and Frances Louise Ilg. The Years from Ten to Sixteen. New York: Harper & Row, 1956.

Gilman, Charlotte. Women and Economics. New York: Harper & Row, 1970.

Ginzberg, Louis. Legends of the Jews. 7 vols. Philadelphia: Jewish Publication Society, 1938.

Goode, William J. The Family. Englewood Cliffs, N.J.: Prentice-Hall, 1964.

Gorlin, Morris. Maimonides on Sexual Intercourse. New York: Rambash, 1961.

Gray, M. The Normal Woman. New York: Scribner's, 1967.

Gurney, Oliver R. The Hittites. Baltimore: Penguin, 1969.

Halkin, Simon. Modern Hebrew Literature. New York: Schocken, 1970.

Hamilton, William J. Human Embryology. Baltimore: William & Hopkins Co., 1962.

Hellman, Louis M., and Jack A. Pritchard. Obstetrics. 14th ed. Englewood Cliffs, N.J.: Prentice-Hall, 1971.

Herodotus. History. London: Heinemann, 1921.

Hirsch, Nathaniel D. Genius and Creative Intelligence. Cambridge, Mass., 1931.

Hirsch, S. R. Horeb. London: Soncino, 1981.

―――. Judaism Eternal. London: Soncino, 1959.

Hodgson, C. Leonard. A Short Guide to Christian Sex Education. London: Mowbrou, 1949.

Horodetzky, Shmuel A. HaHasidut VehaHasidim. Tel Aviv: Dvir, 1953.

————. *Leaders of Hassidism*. London: Hasefer, 1928.

Horney, Karen. *Feminine Psychology*. New York: Norton, 1967.

————. *The Neurotic Personality of Our Times*. New York: Norton, 1937.

Hsia, L. *Human Developmental Genetics*. Chicago: Yearbook Medical Publication, 1968.

Hunt, Morton M. *Her Infinite Variety*. New York: Harper & Row, 1962.

————. *The Natural History of Love*. New York: Minerva Press, 1969.

Ilg, Frances L., and Louise B. Ames. *Child Behaviour*. New York: Harper & Row, 1955.

James, William. *Psychology*. New York: Dover, 1950.

Jersild, Arthur, T. *Child Psychology*. Englewood Cliffs, N.J.: Prentice-Hall, 1968.

Josephus, Flavius. London: Loeb ed., 1926–1937.

Kaplan, Benjamin. *The Jew and His Family*. Baton Rouge: Louisiana State University Press, 1967.

Kayserling M. *Judische Frauen*. Leipzig, 1879.

Kelly, Robert K. *Courtship, Marriage and the Family*. New York: Harcourt, Brace, & World, 1969.

Kimber, D. C., and C. E. Gray. *Anatomy and Physiology*. New York: Macmillan, 1971.

Kinsey, Alfred C. *Sexual Behavior in the Human Female*. Philadelphia: Saunders, 1953.

————. *Sexual Behavior in the Human Male*. Philadelphia: Saunders, 1948.

Kirkendall, Lester. *Sex Education as Human Relations*. New York: Alnor, 1961.

Klein, Melanie, and Joan Riviere. *Love, Hate and Reparation*. New York: Norton, 1964.

Klein, Viola. *The Feminine Character*. Urbana: University of Illinois Press, 1973.

Kretschmer, E. *The Psychology of Men of Genius*. New York: Harcourt, Brace, 1931.

Kurzweil, Z. E. *Modern Trends in Jewish Education*. New York: Yoseloff, 1968.

Lamm, Norman. *A Hedge of Roses*. New York: Feldheim, 1966.

Lazarus, Moritz. *Ethik das Judenthum*. 2 vols. Frankfurt: Kauffmann, 1898–1911.

Lederer, William J., and Don D. Jackson. *The Mirages of Marriage*. New York: Norton, 1968.

Lepp, Ignace. *The Psychology of Loving*. New York: New American Library, 1963.

Leslie, Gerald R. *The Family in Social Context*. London: Oxford University Press, 1967.

Levine, David. *How to Get a Divorce With or Without a Lawyer*. New York: Bantam, 1979.

Levy, David M. *Maternal Overprotection*. New York: Norton, 1966.

Lidz, Theodore. *The Family and Human Adaptation*. New York: International Universities Press, 1963.

————. *The Person*. New York: Basic Books, 1968.

Litvin, B. *The Sanctity of the Synagogue*. New York: B. & A. Litvin, 1962.

Locke, Harvey J. *Predicting Adjustment in Marriage: A Comparison of a Divorced and Happily Married Group*. Westport, Conn: Greenwood Press, 1968.

Loewe, L. *Diaries of Sir Moses and Lady Montefiore*. London, 1805.

Mace, David, and Vera Mace. *Marriage East and West*. New York: Doubleday, 1960.

Maimon, Ada. *Hamishim Shnot Tenuat haPoalot*. Tel Aviv, 1955.

Maspero, Gaston. *The Struggle of the Nations*. New York: Appleton, 1897.

Masserman, Jules H. *Sexuality of Women*. New York: Grune & Stratton, 1966.

Masters, William H., and Virginia E. Johnson. *Human Sexual Response*. Boston: Little, Brown, 1966.

Mayer, Michael F. *Divorce and Annulment in the Fifty States*. New York: Arco, 1975.

Mead, Margaret. *Male and Female*. New York: Morrow, 1967.

Mencken, Henry L. *In Defense of Women*. New York: Knopf, 1926.

Menninger, Karl. *Love Against Hate*. New York: Harcourt, Brace, 1959.

Meyer, Johann. *Sexual Life in Ancient India*. London: George Routledge & Sons, 1930.

Montagu, Ashley. *The Natural Superiority of Women*. New York: Macmillan, 1953.

Moore, G. Foot. *Judaism*. Cambridge, Mass.: Harvard University Press, 1927.

Neufeld, E. *Ancient Hebrew Marriage Laws*. London: Longman's, 1944.

————. *Hittite Laws*. London: Longman's, 1951.

Neuman, A. *The Jews in Spain*. Philadelphia: Jewish Publication Society, 1942.

Oliven, John F. *Sexual Hygiene and Pathology*. Philadelphia: Lippincott, 1965.

Oppenheimer, Evelyn. *The Articulate Woman*. New York: Drake House, 1968.

Parker, Elizabeth. *The Seven Ages of Woman*. Baltimore: John Hopkins Press, 1960.

Parsons, Talcott, and T. Bales, *Family: Socialization and Interaction Process*. New York: Free Press, 1955.

Patai, Raphael. *Sex and Family in the Bible and the Middle East*. Garden City, N.Y.: Doubleday, 1959.

Peck, Robert F. *The Psychology of Character Development*. New York: John Wiley, 1964.

Peretz, I. L. *Stories and Pictures*. Trans. H. Frank. Philadelphia: Jewish Publication Society, 1947.

Philo Judaeus. London: Loeb ed., 1929–1935.

Ploss, H. *Das Weib*. 2 vols. Leipzig, 1899.

Pritchard, James B. *Ancient Near Eastern Texts Relating to the Old Testament*. Princeton: Princeton University Press, 1969.

Read, Grantly Dick. *Childbirth Without Fear*. New York: Harper & Row, 1959.

Redlich, F. C., and D. X. Friedman. *The Theory and Practice of Psychiatry*. New

York: Basic Books, 1966.

Reik, Theodore. *Of Love and Lust.* New York: Bantam Books, 1967.

————. *Sex in Man and Woman.* New York: Noonday Press, 1960.

————. *The Psychology of Sex Relations.* New York, 1945.

Remy, Nahida. *The Jewish Woman.* New York: Bloch, 1916.

Rheingold, Joseph C. *The Fear of Being a Woman.* New York: Grune & Stratton, 1964.

Rieff, Phillip. *Freud: The Mind of the Moralist.* New York: Anchor Books, 1961.

Roback, A. A. *The Psychology of Character.* New York: Harcourt, Brace, 1927.

Rosenbaum, Salo, and Ian Alger. *The Marriage Relationship.* New York: Basic Books, 1968.

Rosenthal, Gilbert S. *The Jewish Family in a Changing World.* New York: Yoseloff, 1970.

Rorvik, D., and L. Shettles. *A Chance to Choose Your Baby's Sex.* New York: Dodd, Mead, 1970.

Roth, Cecil. *History of the Jews of Italy.* Philadelphia: Jewish Publication Society, 1946.

Rubin, Z. *Liking and Loving.* New York: Rinehart, 1963.

Ruch, T. C., and H. D. Patton. *Physiology and Biophysics.* 19th ed. Philadelphia: Saunders, 1973.

Ruitenbeek, Hendrik M. *Psychoanalysis and Female Sexuality.* New Haven: College and University Press, 1966.

Sachar, H. M. *The Course of Modern Jewish History.* New York: Delta, 1963.

Saul, Leon J. *Emotional Maturity.* Philadelphia: Lippincott, 1971.

Schwartz, Gwen Gibson, and Barbara Wyden. *The Jewish Wife.* New York: Wyden, 1969.

Scheinfeld, Amram. *Women and Men.* New York: Harcourt, Brace, 1944.

Scholem, Gershom G. *Major Trends in Jewish Mysticism.* New York: Schocken, 1967.

Sherman, J. A. *Psychology of Women.* Springfield, Ill.: Charles C. Thomas, 1971.

Smithline, Jacelyn. *Scientific Aspects of Sexual Hygiene in Torah Laws for the Woman.* New York: 1965.

Spock, Benjamin. *Baby and Child Care.* New York: Meredith Press, 1968.

Stekel, Wilhelm. *Patterns of Psychosexual Infantilism.* New York: Liveright, 1952.

Stern, Selma. *The Court Jew.* Philadelphia: Jewish Publication Society, 1950.

Terman, Louis M. *Psychological Factors in Marital Happiness.* New York: McGraw-Hill, 1968.

Thompson, J., and L. Thompson. *Genetics in Medicine.* Philadelphia: Saunders, 1973.

Trachtenberg, Joshua. *Jewish Magic and Superstition.* New York: Atheneum, 1970.

Tridon, A. *Psychoanalysis and Love.* New York, 1941.

Van de Velde, Theodore H. *Ideal Marriage*. New York: Random House, 1973.

Westermarck, Edward A. *The History of Human Marriage*. London: Macmillan, 1921.

Winch, Robert F., ed. *Selected Studies in Marriage and the Family*. 4th ed. New York: Holt, Rinehart & Winston, 1974.

Yadin, Yigael. *Genesis Apocryphon*. Jerusalem: Hebrew University, 1956.

Index

345

About the Author

Dr. Menahem M. Brayer has combined careers as a clinical psychologist and Biblical scholar. He joined the faculty of Yeshiva University in 1948, and was appointed chairman of the Jewish Education Department at the Ferkauf Graduate School of Humanities and Social Sciences in 1970.

He also serves as Professor of Biblical Literature and Stone-Sapirstein Professor of Jewish Education. In addition, he serves as a consulting psychologist for Yeshiva University students.

Dr. Brayer has published many studies and articles relating to Biblical and Targumic literature, psychology, Jewish education, history, music, Hasidism and on the problems facing contemporary Jewry. His paper on drug use gained national attention, and was cited by *The New York Times*.

Born in Poland, he was ordained at the Kishinev Yeshiva in Rumania, where he later received his bachelor's degree at the University of Iassy. While in Rumania he was interned in Nazi labor camps. He was an active member of the Jewish underground, and was involved in the rescue of hundreds of children.

After his arrival in the United States, he earned two doctorates, one in Hebrew Literature, and one in clinical psychology. He has lectured extensively, both here and abroad, and has been twice honored as Senior Professor by Yeshiva University. His name appears in several *Who's Whos*.

A practicing psychologist, he is a member of several professional societies.